DANTE STUDIES AND RESEARCHES

DANTE STUDIES

AND

RESEARCHES

BY

PAGET TOYNBEE, M.A., D.Litt.

Dietro alle poste delle care piante

Inf. xxiii. 148

KENNIKAT PRESS
Port Washington, N. Y./London

DANTE STUDIES AND RESEARCHES

First published in 1902
Reissued in 1971 by Kennikat Press
Library of Congress Catalog Card No: 78-118417
ISBN 0-8046-1194-7

Manufactured by Taylor Publishing Company   Dallas, Texas

PREFACE

THE articles and notes contained in this volume are for the most part the outcome of researches undertaken for the purposes of my *Dictionary of Proper Names and Notable Matters in the Works of Dante*, which was published three years ago at Oxford by the Clarendon Press. As the results of these researches are necessarily only given in brief in the *Dictionary*, and as the articles themselves are more or less inaccessible in their original form, I have, in deference to suggestions from various quarters, collected together here such of them as seemed likely to be of permanent value to the English student of Dante.

Of the more important articles and notes, eight were published originally in *Romania*, seven in the *Giornale Storico della Letteratura Italiana*, two in the *Annual Reports of the Cambridge (U.S.A.) Dante Society*, one in the *English Historical Review*, one in the *Modern Language Quarterly*, and one in *An English Miscellany*.[1] All of these, except the last three, are now for the first time published in England. The rest of the notes were published either in the *Academy* (under the editorship of Mr. J. S. Cotton), or in the *Athenæum*.

Six of the longer articles have been translated into Italian and published at Bologna, under the title of *Ricerche e Note Dantesche (Serie Prima)*, as the first volume of the *Biblioteca*

---

[1] Presented to Dr. F. J. Furnivall in honour of his seventy-fifth birthday (Oxford, 1901).

Storico-Critica della Letteratura Dantesca, edited by Count G. L. Passerini and Professor Pasquale Papa. It is proposed to issue the remainder shortly in the same form.

The selected articles here printed have been carefully revised, and, in several cases, considerably enlarged. One or two, on the other hand, have been condensed by the omission of matter which it was more convenient to introduce in another shape elsewhere.

In order to render the contents of the volume as easily accessible as possible, two full indices have been provided, *viz.*, a subject-index, and an index of the passages in Dante's works which are quoted or referred to in the course of the various articles.

It remains for me to express my acknowledgments to the editors and publishers of the several journals and reviews, French, Italian, American, and English, in which these articles and notes originally appeared, for permission to reprint them in the present volume.

PAGET TOYNBEE.

DORNEY WOOD,
    BURNHAM, BUCKS,
        May, 1901

CONTENTS

DANTE AND THE LANCELOT ROMANCE[1]

DANTE twice in the *Divina Commedia* makes allusion to the old French romance of *Lancelot du Lac*, each time to the same episode, that of the first guilty meeting between Lancelot and Queen Guenever.[2]

[1] Reprinted, with additions, from the *Fifth Annual Report* (1886) *of the Cambridge (U.S.A.) Dante Society.*

[2] Dante alludes to another incident in the Lancelot Romance, in the twenty-eighth chapter of the fourth book of the *Convivio*, where he refers to Guido da Montefeltro having, like Lancelot, ended his days in a monastery. Comparing the return of the noble soul to God after death to the return of a ship from the high seas into port, he says: "Oh miseri e vili che colle vele alte correte a questo porto: e là dove dovreste riposare, per lo impeto del vento rompete, e perdite voi medesimi là ove tanto camminato avete! Certo il cavaliere Lancilotto non volle entrare colle vele alte, nè il nobilissimo nostro Latino Guido Montefeltrano. Bene questi nobili calaron le vele delle mondane operazioni, chè nella loro lunga età a religione si rendèro, ogni mondano diletto e opera diponendo " (ll. 55-65). Malory gives the following account of how Lancelot, after King Arthur's death, and after his farewell interview with Guenever in the nunnery at Amesbury, rode away, and himself retired into a hermitage, where he was afterwards joined by Sir Bors and six other knights: "And syr Launcelot went and took his hors and rode al that day and al nyght in a forest wepyng, and atte last he was ware of an ermytage and a chappel stode betwyxte two clyffes ; and then he herde a lytel belle rynge to masse, and thyder he rode and alyght and teyed his hors to the gate and herd masse ; and he that sange masse was the bysshop of Caunterburye. Bothe the bysshop and sir Bedwer knewe syr Launcelot, and they spake to gyders after masse ; but whan syr Bedwere had tolde his tale al hole syr Launcelottes hert almost braste for sorowe, and syr Launcelot threwe hys armes abrode and sayd: alas, who may truste thys world ! And than he knelyd doun on his knee and prayed the bysshop to shryve hym and assoyle hym, and than he besought the bysshop that he myght be hys brother. Than the bysshop sayd : I will gladly ; and there he put an habyte upon syr Launcelot, and there he servyd God day and nyght with prayers and fastynges. . . . And syr Bors, syr Ector de Maris, syr Blamour, syr Bleoboris, with moo other of syr Launcelotte's kynne toke on hem to ryde al Englond overthwart and endelonge to seek syr Launcelot. So syr Bors by

The first of these allusions occurs at the close of the fifth canto of the *Inferno*, which contains the account of Dante's interview with Francesca da Rimini. The poet, deeply moved by Francesca's unhappy fate, inquires of her as to the manner in which she first became conscious of her love for Paolo. Francesca in reply describes how she and Paolo were one day reading together the story of Lancelot's love for Guenever, and how, as the tale advanced, their hearts were stirred, until at last, when they read of the kiss given by Lancelot to Guenever, they were both overcome, " and that day read no more " :—

> Noi leggevamo un giorno per diletto
> Di Lancelotto, come amor lo strinse :
> Soli eravamo e senza alcun sospetto.
> Per più fiate gli occhi ci sospinse
> Quella lettura, e scolorocci il viso :
> Ma solo un punto fu quel che ci vinse.
> Quando leggemmo il disiato riso
> Esser baciato da cotanto amante,[1]
> Questi, che mai da me non fia diviso,
> La bocca mi baciò tutto tremante ;
> Galeotto fu il libro e chi lo scrisse : [2]
> Quel giorno più non vi leggemmo avante.
>
> (ll. 127-138.)

fortune rode so longe tyl he came to the same chapel where syr Launcelot was ; and so syr Bors herde a lytel belle knylle that range to masse, and there he alyght and herde masse. And whan masse was doon the bysshop, syr Launcelot, and syr Bedwere came to syr Bors, and when syr Bors sawe syr Launcelot in that maner clothyng, than he preyed the bysshop that he myght be in the same sewte. And so there was an habyte put upon hym, and there he lyved in prayers and fastyng. And wythin halfe a yere there was come syr Galyhud, syr Galyhodyn, syr Blamour, syr Bleoboris, syr Wyllyars, syr Clarras, and syr Gohaleaniyne. So al these vij noble knyghtes there abode styll, and whan they sawe syr Launcelot had taken hym to suche perfeccion they had no lust to departe, but toke such an habyte as he had. Thus they endured in grete penaunce syx yere ; and than syr Launcelot took thabyte of preesthod of the bysshop, and a twelve monthe he sange masse. And there was none of these other knyghtes but they redde in bookes, and holpe for to synge masse, and range bellys, and dyd bodoly al maner of servyce " (*Caxton's Malory*, bk. xxi. chap. x.).

[1] As a matter of fact, in the romance it is Guenever who kisses Lancelot— " la reine le prent par le menton et le bese voiant Galehout assez longuement ".

[2] " A pandar was the book and he who wrote it." Gallehault (not by any means to be confounded with Galahad) was the knight who acted as inter-

The second allusion occurs at the beginning of the sixteenth canto of the *Paradiso*. Dante, in addressing the spirit of his ancestor Cacciaguida, whom he meets in the Heaven of Mars, makes use of the consequential *voi* (the plural of dignity), thus betraying the pride he feels in the relationship ; whereat, he says, Beatrice, smiling, appeared like her who coughed at the first fault recorded of Guenever :—

> Ridendo, parve quella, che tossío
> Al primo fallo scritto di Ginevra.

(ll. 14-15.)

This allusion has been a stumbling-block to the commentators. No mention of any such incident is made in the printed editions of the *Lancelot du Lac*,[1] and the early commentators, who might

mediary between Lancelot and Guenever, and who, having brought them together, urged the Queen to give Lancelot the kiss which was the beginning of their guilty love. From the part played by Gallehault on this occasion, his name came to be used, like that of " Sir Pandarus of Troy," as a synonym for a pandar. Hence Francesca's meaning is that the book and its author played the same part with Paolo and herself as they read the story together, that Gallehault did with Lancelot and Guenever in the romance itself.

[1] The printed editions of the romance are considerably abridged ; they no doubt reproduce some of the later compilations, in which, from various motives, many of the detailed incidents of the original are omitted. This was the case with the compilation made by Rusticiano da Pisa (who, though an Italian, wrote in French, just as did Brunetto Latino). In this version, for instance, the guilty loves of Lancelot and Guenever are merely hinted at. Paulin Paris observes (*Les MSS. François de la Bibliothèque du Roi*, iii. 56-57): "Quand Rusticien nous a conduit Lancelot à la cour d'Artus, il garde le silence sur la suite des ses aventures avec la reine, par respect pour les mœurs. ' Bien fist,' dit-il, ' entre la royne Genievre et Lancelot aucune chose de laquelle le maistre ne fera ore mention, pour garder l'onneur de l'un et de l'autre. . . . et bien sont autres livres qui le comptent en autre manière.' " This reminds one of the reticence of Froissart with regard to the passion of Edward III. for the Countess of Salisbury. Jean le Bel, Froissart's predecessor, had given a detailed account of the violence done by the king to the countess. Froissart suppresses the incident, and excuses himself as follows: "Vous avez bien chy dessus oy parler comment li roys Englès fu enamourés de la Comtesse de Sallebrin ; touteffois les cronikes Monseigneur Jehan le Bel parollent de ceste amour plus avant et moins convignablement que je ne dois faire, car se il plaist à Dieu, je ne pense jà à encoupper le roy d'Engleterre ne la comtesse de Sallebrin de nul villain reproche ". With regard to Rusticiano's tenderness for the good name of Lancelot and Guenever, Paulin Paris cynically observes: "Il est déplorable que Françoise de Rimini ne soit pas tombée sur un exemplaire de Lancelot *expurgé* par notre bon Rusticien ! "

have been expected to know the version of the romance current in Dante's time, differ considerably in their remarks upon the passage. Pietro di Dante, for instance, confining himself to the bare record of the incident, though he gives the name of the lady, says :—

Beatrix risit ut fecit illa dama de Malehault dum Gineura osculata est primo de Lancialotto.

The author of the *Ottimo Comento* says :—

Quando presente Galeotto . . . Lancelotto fu baciato dalla reina Ginevra . . . la donna di malo abito [1] tossío, in segno che avveduta s' era del fallo della reina.

Similarly Benvenuto da Imola :—

Al primo fallo scritto di Ginevra, idest, ad osculum quod fuit primum fallum amoris Ginevrae. . . . Cum enim Lancillottus pervenisset ad colloquium cum regina Genevra opera principis Galeoti, nec auderet prae nimio pudore pandere flammam amoris sui, princeps Galeotus interposuit se, et fecit eos pervenire ad osculum : tunc quaedam domina nomina Damma, socia reginae, perpendens de actu, tussivit et spuit, quasi dicens : bene te video ; ita in proposito Beatrix risit nunc, quasi dicat : bene audio te, vel tu bene audiris, cave quid dicas.[2]

The Postillator Cassinensis, in his comment on the passage in the *Inferno*, says :—

Legitur in gestis illorum *de la tabula rotunda*, quod Galeoctus amore Lanzalotti fecit quod quedam dama de Malaut proca dicti Galeocti conduxit reginam Geneveram ad quoddam viridarium, ubi breviter dictus Lanzaloctus ejus procus secrete osculatus est eam.

[1] Evidently a corruption of, or copyist's error for, *Malehault*.

[2] Identical with this is the comment, in Italian, contained in one of the manuscripts of the *Divina Commedia* in the Bibliothèque Nationale : " Beatricie parue ridendo quella che tossío al primo fallo scrito di Gieneura, cioe el bacio che fue la prima falsita damore di Gieneura el quale fu scripto al chapitolo V⁰ del Inferno, che essendo uenuto Lancilotto a parlamento chon la Regina Gieneure per lopera del Principo Galeotto, parendogli di grande sua uergogna ad appalentare e manifestare la fiama del suo amore, e 'l Principo Galeoto se interpuose e fecie che lor se peruenne a baciare luno laltro. Alora una donna, chiamata Dama, chompagna de la ditta Regina auedendossi de latto chomincio a tossire et asputare quasi dicat : Io te ho ben ueduto, chussi nel proposito Beatricie rise mo quasi dicat : Io te aldo bene o uer tu seray bene udito, guarda cio che tu dichi."

This is no doubt the Italian translation of Benvenuto's commentary which is referred to by Colomb de Batines in his *Bibliografia Dantesca* (ii. 315).

He remarks on the present passage :—

Hic comparat Beatricem dame Molaut dum nutu tuxivit videndo reginam Geneveram obsculari a Lancialocto inductu Galaocti ut scripsi in inferno capitulo quinto.

On the other hand, the Anonimo Fiorentino, with whom several others agree, annotates :—

Qui vuol mostrare come Beatrice continuo il sollecitava, ed esemplifica : Ella gli fe simile cenno ch' egli domandasse suo desiderio a quella anima beata, qual fece quella che tossío al primo fallo di Ginevra che si ha scritto. Et ad intendere ben tal novella, sì è da sapere che la reina Ginevra innamoroe di Lancialotto, per molte prodezze che gli vide fare ; et anche perchè era di sua persona piacevole, e facundo in parlatura : pensò la detta reina di palesarlo al principe Galeotto, al quale, dopo toltogli fidanza, aperse suo intendimento, et soggiunsegli : acciò che tu sia più fervente, io soe che tu ami la donna di Manoalt ; io farò sì che ella seguirà tuo intento. Ora, abbreviando la novella, lo detto prencipe seppe tanto fare dall' un lato, e la reina Ginevra dall' altro, che soli essi quattro si convennono a debita ora nella sala ; sì che dall' uno lato era Lancillotto colla Reina, dall' altro lo prencipe Galeotto e la donna di Manoalt. Or Lancialotto, costretto d' amore, stava timido appresso la reina Ginevra, nè parlava, nè s' argomentava di fare altro : la donna di Manoalt, sì come ricordata, e che conosceva lo luogo e 'l perchè dov' erano, tossío, e fece cenno a Lancialotto che dovesse prendere alcuno diletto : ond' egli, così favoreggiato, gittò lo braccio al collo alla Reina e baciolla ; e questo è quel bacio del quale è fatto menzione nel quinto capitolo dello' inferno. . . . Or fa l' Auttore sua comparazione, sì come la donne di Manoalt mostrò a Lancialotto suo dovere circa alla Reina, così Beatrice mostrò a me mio dovere circa quella anima beata.[1]

Francesco da Buti writes much in the same strain :—

Secondo che io òne udito dire, scritto è nei Romansi de la Tavola Ritonda che la reina Ginevra, donna del re Artu, s' inamorò di Lancellotto, e sì per pia-cevilezza sua e sì per la prodezza e bellezza sua ; unde ella si manifestò al prince Galeotto e disse : Io so che tu se' innamorato di Branguina[2] donna di Malaot, se tu mi vuoi promettere di tenere credenza e far quello ch' io ti dirò, farò che verrai ad effetto del tuo desiderio ; et elli liel promise. Allora li disse : Vedi, io sono innamorata di Lancellotto che è tuo compagno : se tu fai sì ch' io abbia mio intendimento, io farò, sarà che tu arai lo tuo ; e Galeotto li promise allora di farne suo potere. Et a la fine arrecate queste parti al fine desiderato, et essendo insieme la reina Ginevra e Lancellotto ; et in altro luogo presi a mano Galeotto e Branguina, sicchè si poteano vedere, accorgendosi Branguina che Lancellotto stava stupido e timoroso e niente diceva a la reina, ella inco-

---

[1] This account corresponds almost verbatim with that given by Jacopo della Lana in his commentary.

[2] Buti appears to be the only one of the commentators who gives this name to the Lady of Malehault.

minciò a tossire, quasi dicesse: Che fai tu? Sente che io sono con Galeotto : fa quello, per che tu se' co la reina; e così dice che Lancellotto, preso ardire, diede compimento a la intenzione. E così dice l'autore che lo riso di Beatrice fu cenno a lui che li dovesse addimandare di quello che dubitava e voleva esser certo, e non lassasse per riverenzia, come fu cenno lo tossire di Branguina a Lancellotto che facesse quello, per che v' era, e non lassasse per riverenzia del re.

Alessandro Vellutello takes a similar view ; he says :—

Parve ridendo, quella che tossio Al primo fallo scritto di Ginevra : il quale fu, secondo ch' è scritto ne le favole de cavalieri de la tavola rotonda, quando ella, al principio del suo amore, si lasciò baciar da Lancilotto, il qual non ardiva di cominciare, ma la compagna di Ginevra, per darli animo, tossì. Adunque così, come il tossie di costui [1] diede animo a Lancilotto di baciar Ginevra, così il rider di Beatrice diede animo a me di parlar a Cacciaguida.

Cristoforo Landino, on the other hand, who makes Guenever the wife of King Mark,[2] thus showing his ignorance of the romance (which, with the contempt of the Renaissance scholar for such literature, he characterises as prolix and inelegant), inclines to the opinion of Benvenuto :—

Et pone l' auttore similitudine, che quel riso fu così cenno a lui, come a Ginevra nel suo primo fallo il tossire, quando venne al bacio pel mezzo di Galeotto. Et la compagna sua, la qual non veduta, vide loro, tossì, a dimostrare, che se ne fosse accorta, come prolissamente è scritto nel favoloso et non molto elegante libro della tavola rotonda.

Daniello da Lucca seems to suggest that there was something of contempt implied in the comparison :—

In un libro chiamato Galeotto [3] de' cavalieri della tavola rotonda, si legge, come basciando Lancillotto Ginevra, la compagna di lei cominciò a tossire, dimostrando essersene accorta, senza però disturbare i loro piaceri : così ridendo

---

[1] *Sic :* correct *costei.*

[2] In his comment on the passage in the *Inferno :* " Era ne' tempi di Dante in prezzo un libro chiamato della tavola rotonda, nel quale è scritto, che Lancilotto era innamorata di Ginevra moglie del Re Marco, et Galeotto fu mezzano, che si potessero congiungere ".

[3] This notion that the title of the book was *Galeotto* is probably due to the fact that the section of the Romance of Lancelot which deals with the episode of Gallehault was sometimes called by his name, *e.g.*, in MS. Brit. Mus., *Harl.*, 6341, the colophon to this section runs : *Cy fine Gallehoz,* " Here ends Gallehault ". The name occurs as a sub-title of Boccaccio's *Decamerone* in the colophon of the old editions (" Il libro chiamato Decameron cognominato Principe Galeotto "), probably as an indication of the nature of the contents.

Beatrice, dimostrò a Dante che s' era accorta de' suoi ragionamenti con Caccia-guida, ma non curava di udirli, perche non era il proprio della Teologia il dare orecchi a cose di sì poca importanza, come erano quei ragionamenti.

These renderings of the occurrence differ very considerably,— according to some the cough would be a sign of warning or of disapproval ; according to others, it was meant as an encourage-ment.

Modern commentators have been equally at a loss to explain the allusion. Philalethes (King John of Saxony) remarks in a note upon this passage :—

Von einem Husten bei dieser Dame (von Mallehaut) als Zeichen der Missbilligung oder der Warnung kommt mindestens in dem Französischen Roman nichts vor, und auch in dem Italienischen Bruchstück jener Erzählung, welches in der Paduaner Ausgabe der *Divina Commedia* von 1822 abgedruckt ist, findet sich nichts davon. Gleichwohl muss man annehmen, dass in irgend einer Bearbeitung dieses Romans etwas der Art vorkomme, weil Dante Beatrice's warnendes oder missbilligendes Lächeln mit solchem Husten vergleicht.

Similarly Scartazzini, in his laborious edition of the *Paradiso* (1882), says :—

Di questo tossire non si fa menzione nel romanzo di Lancillotto del Lago quale si conosce oggi . . . ai tempi di Dante dovera esserci una versione del famoso romanzo, in cui si raccontava la circonstanza quì accennata.

It has, therefore, been concluded that Dante made use of some version of the " Arturi Regis ambages pulcherrimae " [1] which has been lost to us. Witte supposes it may have been one by the Provençal poet, Arnaut Daniel.[2]

---

[1] This term, *ambages*, which Dante applies to the Arthurian romances in the *De Vulgari Eloquentia*, i. 10, is used in the same connexion by Raymond de Béziers in his *Procœmium* to the *Liber Kalile et Dymne* (written in 1313). Addressing the courtiers of Philip the Fair, Raymond says : " Vos igitur regalem curiam frequentantes, qui tempus vestrum in narracionibus anbagicis, verbi gracia, Lanceloti, Galvani, consimilibusque consumitis, libros quibus nulla consistit sciencia, vel modica viget utilitas, crebrius instudentes, abjecta vanitatis palea, librum istum regium virtutum graniferum, non solum semel, immo pluries attentissime perlegatis . . . " (see Novati, in *Arte, Scienza e Fede ai giorni di Dante*, pp. 281-2 ; and Hervieux, *Les Fabulistes Latins*, vol. v. pp. 387-8).

[2] The opinion that Arnaut Daniel wrote a prose Romance of Lancelot seems to have been founded upon a misunderstanding of *Purgatorio*, xxvi. 118, and upon a remark of Tasso's on that passage. M. Gaston Paris has shown that this opinion is erroneous : Il n'y a aucune raison, he says, de supposer que le poète florentin ait connu d'autres œuvres d'Arnaut que celles qui nous sont par-

Recent investigation, however, has put an end to all uncertainty with regard to this question.

Dante, as may be gathered from the *De Vulgari Eloquentia*,
i. 10, read the story of Lancelot in the *Lingua Oïl;* and
by a happy chance I have been able to identify the passage
alluded to by him, in an extract from one of the old French
manuscripts in the British Museum, made for me by a friend [1]
for the purposes of a note upon *Inferno*, v. 137.

On pursuing the subject further, I found that of nineteen
manuscripts examined in the British Museum, and Bibliothèque
Nationale at Paris (ten of the thirteenth century, four of the
fourteenth, and five of the fifteenth) all save one—where the
omission is evidently owing to the carelessness of the copyist—
contain the passage in question, of which, as I have since discovered, a paraphrase in modern French is given, with a reference
to Dante, by Paulin Paris in his *Romans de la Table Ronde*

venues : dans le *De vulgari eloquentia*, Dante cite comme exemples des chan-
sons d'Arnaut Daniel, et elles font toutes partie du recueil que nous connaissons.
Dans l'éloge qu'il fait du troubadour, Dante dit : *Versi d'amore e prose di romanzi
Soverchiò tutti*, et c'est ce passage qui, mal interprété à ce que je crois, a donné
naissance à diverses erreurs. On l'a toujours entendu en ce sens qu'Arnaut
aurait composé des vers d'amour et des romans en prose qui surpassaient tous
les autres ; mais il signifie simplement : " Il a dépassé tous les vers d'amour et
toutes les proses de romans ; il est supérieur à la fois aux auteurs de vers
d'amour et de romans en prose ; " c'est-à-dire, si on tient compte de la manière
toujours très particulière dont Dante formule ses jugements, si on se reporte
à un passage bien connu du *De vulgari eloquentia*, " il a effacé tous ceux qui ont
écrit soit en provençal, soit en français ".   Dante dit en effet dans le *De vulgari
eloquentia* que la langue d'oïl allègue pour elle que tout ce qui existe en prose
vulgaire, soit traduit, soit original (*quicquid redactum sive inventum est ad vulgare
prosaicum*) lui appartient : ce *vulgare prosaicum* c'est *la prosa di romanzi*. (On
a prétendu, il est vrai, que *vulgare prosaicum* et *prose di romanzi* désignaient des
romans en vers, car les romans arthuriens qui circulaient à l'époque de Dante
étaient en vers. . . . C'est une erreur qu'il est inutile de réfuter aujourd'hui.)
S'il en était autrement, si Dante avait voulu dire dans la *Comédie*, qu'Arnaut
écrivit les plus beaux romans en prose qui existent, comment aurait-il pu
affirmer ailleurs que tout ce qui est écrit en prose vulgaire est en langue d'oïl ?
Comment surtout aurait-il pu ajouter : " comme les belles histoires du roi Arthur
(*Arturi regis ambages pulcherrimæ*)," si la plus célèbre de ces histoires, le
Lancelot, eût été en provençal ? (*Études sur les Romans de la Table Ronde.*
Romania, x. 484 ff.)

[1] Professor W. P. Ker.

(vol. iii. p. 263). He does not, however, appear to have been aware that the commentators on the *Divina Commedia* were in the dark as to the allusion.[1]

The following extract, which I have transcribed, with the usual expansions, from a thirteenth century manuscript,[2] describes how Gallehault (not *Galahad*, as many wrongly have it) contrived the meeting between Lancelot and Guenever, how they kissed, and how they were observed by the Lady of Malehaut. It thus serves to illustrate both Dante's allusions to this incident in the romance.

By way of introduction, it may be premised that Lancelot on his first appearance at the court of King Arthur, who knighted him, became deeply enamoured of Queen Guenever, "la Dame des dames," as she is styled in the old Romances.

[1] Novati points out (in *Arte, Scienza e Fede ai giorni di Dante*, pp. 280-1) that two other writers, previous to Paulin Paris (whose Lancelot volumes were published in 1872-7), had printed passages from the Lancelot romance with a view to the illustration of Dante, viz., Louis Moland in his *Origines Littéraires de la France* (Paris, 1862), and Filippo-Luigi Polidori in his edition of *La Tavola Ritonda* (Bologna, 1864-5). Prof. Novati adds that consequently I was mistaken in my supposition that I was the first to draw attention to the passages in the French romance to which Dante makes allusion. Though I was unaware that either Moland or Polidori had printed extracts from the romance, yet I can still claim to have been the discoverer, from the point of view of the Dante commentator, of the passage alluded to in the *Paradiso*. Paulin Paris, as I have already observed, was not aware that the passage was unknown to the commentators on the *Divina Commedia*; while neither Moland nor Polidori seems to have been acquainted with Dante's allusion to the incident of the cough. Otherwise Polidori (whose extract is printed on pp. 260-4 of his second volume) would certainly not have stopped short, as he does, precisely within a line of the very passage in which the mention of the cough occurs; nor would Moland, who includes this passage in his extract (pp. 373-383), and gives a reference to the *Inferno* (p. 51), have omitted the incident from his paraphrase as he does (p. 54), thus showing pretty conclusively that he did not know of the allusion in the *Paradiso*. I may add that, as I pointed out long ago in the *Academy* (27th February, 1886), the whole passage in question was also printed by W. J. A. Jonckbloet in the second volume (p. xlv) of his *Roman Van Lancelot* ('S. Gravenhage, 1846-50).

[2] Lansdowne, 757 (*fol.* 71, *verso* b.-*fol.* 76, *recto* b.) in British Museum. This version of the *Lancelot du Lac* is attributed to Maistres Gautiers Map, or Walter Map, one of the king's clerks at the court of Henry the Second of England.

Inspired by his love for her, he performed such deeds of chivalry as made him the most famous among all the knights of the Round Table. He, however, strictly concealed his name, and endeavoured by constantly changing his armour and his shield to escape recognition. It is for this reason that Guenever, during her interview with him, so closely questions him as to his identity. While in quest of adventures, Lancelot comes to a town called Le Puy de Malehaut, where he is detained a prisoner by the Lady of Malehaut. She, having fallen in love with him, offers him his liberty if he will disclose his name. This he declines to do, but the Lady of Malehaut, relenting, allows him to depart in order that he may fight against Galle-hault, "Roy d'Outre les Marches," who was in arms against King Arthur; while the lady herself repairs to the court and becomes the companion of Queen Guenever. By Lancelot's means Gallehault is induced to tender his submission, and a close friendship springs up between the two, the result of which is that Gallehault undertakes to bring about a meeting between his friend and the Queen. Guenever, who has a great admiration for the unknown knight, becomes impatient for the interview, and at last Gallehault comes to Lancelot, who is living in his camp, and tells him that it can no longer be put off, and must take place that very day. At this point our story begins[1] :—

Einsint aloit Galehout a son compaingnon au main et au soir . et a chascune foiz quil reuenoit li demandoit la roine quil auoit troue . Et la nuit reuint Galehout la ou il soloit . lende-main par matin a son compaingnon[2] et si li dist . Il ni a plus . car hui en cest ior . couient que la roine uos uoie. Sire por deu fetes issi . que nulle riens ne le sache . fors uos et li . car il a assez de tex en la meson lo roi qui me conoistroient bien sil me ueoient. Or naiez garde . fet Galehout . car ge en penserai molt bien . atant prent de lui congie . si apele son seneschal . Gardez . fet il . se ge uos enuoi querre que uos ueingniez a moi

---

[1] For translation, see below, pp. 22 ff.

[2] *Et lendemain leua bien matin . et reuint a son compaignon;* Royal 19, B. vii.   *E lendemain bien par matin reuint a son compaignon;* Royal 20, D. iii.

et amenez mon compaingnon si que nulle riens ne sache que ce soit
il. Sire . fait cil . uostre plesir. Lors reuient Galehout au tref lo
roi. Et la roine li demande quex noueles. Dame . fet il . beles
assez . uenuz est la flor des cheualiers del monde. Et dex . fet
ele . coment le uerrai gie . car ge le uoil ueoir en tel maniere
que nus ne lo sache fors lui et moi et uos . car ie ne uoil mie que
autres genz en aient aise. Et en non deu dame . fet Galehout .
einsi iert il . car il dit quil ne uoldroit mie que nules genz de la
meson lo roi artur le coneussent por nule rien. Coment . fet
ele . est il donc coneuz a rienz.[1] Dame . fet il . tex genz le
porroient ueoir qui bien le conoistroient. Dex . fet la roine .
qui puet il estre. Dame . fet Galehout . si mait dex ge ne
sai . car onques ne me dist son non ne dom il est. Non . fet
ele . si maist dex merueilles oi . et or mest assez plus tart[2] que
ge le uoie conques mes. Dame . fet il . uos le uerroiz assez (?)
encor anuit . et si uos dirai coment. Nos en irons senpres
deduire la aual . si li mostre un leu en mi la praerie tot plains
darbroisieaus . si aurons au meins de conpaingnie que nos por-
rons . et la le uerroiz . si irons un poi deuant ce que anuitier
doie. Ha . fet ele . traus doz amis com auez or bien dit. Et
pleust or au seingnor[3] del mont quil anuitast ia . lors comencent
andui a rire et la roine lacole et li fait molt grant ioie. Et la
dame de maloaut les uoit rire si pense que or est la chose plus
hastiue quel nel seut . si sen prent molt garde et ne uient cheualier en la meson cui ele nesgart en mi le uis. Molt fait la roine
grant ioie del cheualier qui uenuz est et molt li tarde que la nuit
uiengne . Si entent a parler et a ragier[4] por le ior oblier qui li
ennuie.

Einsi passa le ior tant que uint apres souper quil auespri.
Et la roine a pris Galehout par la main . et la dame de malout
auoc li . et damoisele lore de cardoil . et une soe pucele sanz

---

[1] *Des gens de caienz;* manuscript 344 in Bibliothèque Nationale.

[2] Partially erased. Royal 20, D. iii., and Royal 19, B. vii. read *tart.*

[3] *Sauueor;* manuscript 339 in Bibliothèque Nationale.

[4] So manuscripts 339 and 773 in Bibliothèque Nationale; two manuscripts
in British Museum read *a ioier.* Manuscript 96 in Bibliothèque Nationale reads
au menyer. All three words mean very much the same.

plus de conpaingnie . si sentorne tot contreual les prez . droit
la ou Galehout auoit dit.   Et quant il out un poi ale . et Galehout se regarde et uoit un escuier si lapele et li dit quil aille dire
a son seneschal quil uiegne a lui e li mostre en quel leu.   Et quant
la roine lot si se regarde et dit . coment . fet ele . est il uostre
seneschaus. Nenil dame . fet il . mes il uendra auoc lui. Atant
sen uient soz les arbres . si sasient a une part entre la roine et
Galehout bien loing des autres.   Et la dame de maloaut et les
autres autresi se merueillent molt de ce quil sont si priueement .
et li uallez uint au seneschal . si fist son message.   Et cil prist
tantost le cheualier auoc lui si passerent leue et uindrent tot
contreual les prez la ou li uallez lor mostra.[1] Quant il apro-
chierent et les dames les esgardent si connut la dame de maloaut
le buen cheualier comme cele qui maint ior lauoit eu en sa baillie
et por ce quele ne uoloit mie quil la coneust senbroncha et se
traist pres de madamoisele lore.   Et cil trespassent outre si se
traist pres li seneschaus des dames et les salue . et Galehout dit
a la roine. Dame uez ci le meillor cheualier del monde. Li
quex est ce . fet la roine. Dame li quex uos resenble ce estre.
Certes . fet ele . il sont andui molt bel cheualier . mes ge ne
uoi ci cors ou il deust auoir la moitie de proece quil auoit el
noir cheualier. Dame . fet il . bien sachiez que ce est li uns de
cez deus.

Atant uienent deuant la roine et li cheualiers tranble si
durement quil ne puet la roine saluer . et a tote la color
perdue si que la roine sen merueille molt . lors sagenoillent
ambedui . et li seneschax Galehout la salue et ausi fait li autres
cheualiers . mais ce est molt pourement ainz fiche ses euz en
terre comme honteus. Et lors sapense la roine que ce est il. Et
lors dist Galehout au seneschal . alez si fetes conpaingnie a
ces dames qui trop sont seules.   Et la roine prent le cheualier
par la main[2] la ou il est agenouz si lasiet deuant li et li fet molt

---

[1] Manuscript 1340 in Bibliothèque Nationale has here : *si furent andui si
bon cheualier et si bel que por noient queist en plus bel en nul pais.* And so
several other manuscripts.

[2] Manuscript 16,999 in Bibliothèque Nationale has here : *et le fait lever de
la ou il estoit a genouls deuant.*

bel senblant . et li dit tot en riant. Sire molt uos auons desirie
tant que deu merci et Galehout qui ci est que or uos ueons. Et
neporquant encor ne saige mie se uos estes le cheualier que ge
demant. Mes Galehout me dit que ce estes uos . et encor
uoldroie ge bien sauoir de uostre boche se uostre plesir estoit
qui uos estes. Et il li respont quil ne set . nonques nule foiz
ne la regarda en mi le uis. Et la roine meruelle molt que il
puet àuoir . et tant que ele sospiece bien une partie de ce que il
a.[1] Et Galehout qui honteus le uoit et esbahiz pense quil diroit
ancois a la roine son penser sol a sol . si se regarde et dit si haut
que les dames loent. Certes . fet il . molt sui or uilains que
totes ses dames non cun sol cheualier a conpaingnie ainz sont si
soles . lors se drece et uient a eles . et eles se uienent totes en
contre lui . et il les rasiet. Et lors commencent a parler de
maintes choses. Et la roine met le cheualier en paroles . et si
li dit . beax doz sire por quoi uos celez uos uers moi . certes
il ni a mie por quoi. Et neporquant uos me poez bien dire se
uos estes celui qui uenquie lassemblee deuantier. Dame . fet
il . nenil. Comment . fet ele nauiez uos unes armes totes
noires. Dame oil. Et dont nestes uos celui cui messire G.[2]
enuoia les trois cheuaus. Dame oil. Donc nestes uos cil qui
porta les armes Galehout le desreain ior. Dame oil. Donc
nestes uos celui[3] qui lassenblee uainquie le segont ior. Dame
non fis uoir. Lors sapercut bien la reine quil ne uoloit pas
conoistre que il leust uaincue . si lemprise mout en son cuer.
Or me dites . fait ele . qui uos fist cheualier. Dame uos .
fait il. Gie . fait ele . quant. Dame . fet il . membre uos
il que uns cheualiers uint a monseignor lo roi a camaalot qui
iert naurez parmi le cors de dous troncons de lance et dune
espee parmi la teste e que uns uallez uint autresi a lui a uendredi
a soir qui fu cheualiers au diemenche matin. De ce . fet ele .
me souient il molt bien . e se dex uos ait fustes uos ce que la
damoisele amena a cort uestuz de la robe blanche. Oil dame .

[1] Manuscript 98 in Bibliothèque Nationale has here : *et la royne qui honteux
le voit pence quil diroit plus tost son penceir cilz estoient soul a soul . si regarde
Galehos . et Galehos qui bien sen apparsoit dit si hault*, etc.

[2] *Gauuains*, Jonckbloet.   [3] From here in another hand.

fait il.   Et porcoi . fet ele . dites uos donc que ge uos fis
cheualier.   Dame porce que il est uoirs . car la costume est tels
el roiaume de logres que cheualiers ni puet estre fez sanz espee
ceindre . et cil de cui il tient lespee le fet cheualier et de uos la
tienge dame car li rois ne men dona point . et ʼporce dige que
uos me feistes cheualier.   Certes . fet la roine . de ce suige
mout liee . et ou alastes uos diluec.   Dame ge men alai a un
secors a la dame de noant . si iuint puis missire kex et nos com-
batismes moi et lui a dous cheualiers.   Et deuant ce . fet la
roine . menuoiastes uos nule riens.   Dame oil dous puceles.
Par mon chief . fet ele . il est uoirs . et quant uos fustes
repairiez de noant trouastes uos nului qui deparmoi se reclamast.
Dame certes oil un cheualier qui gardoit un gue si me dist que
ge alasse ius de mon cheual . et ge li demandai a cui il estoit .
et il me dist que il estoit a uos . alez tost ius . fist il . et ge li
demandai qui le commandoit . et il dist quil nauoit commande-
ment se le suen non . et ge remis le pie en lestrier que ge en
auoie ia oste . et li dis sanz faille que il nen auroit mes hui
point.   Si iostai a lui et si sai bien que ge fis outrage . si uos
en cri merci dame et] uos emprenez lamende tele comme il uos
plaira.   Et la reine qui bien uoit quil ne li puet guenchir que
suens ne soit li respont . certes biaus douz amis . fet ele . moi
ne mesfeistes uos rien . car il nestoit pas a moi . ainz len soi
molt malues gre quant il uint a moi et il le me dist . mes or me
dites ou alastes uos diluec.   Dame . fet il . a la dolerouse garde.
Qui la conquist . fet ele.   Dame . fet il . gi entrai.   Et ui uos
i ge onques . fet ele.   Dame oil plus dune foiz.   En quel leu .
fet ele.   Dame un ior que ge uos demande se uos uoldriez entrer
enz . et uos deistes que oil . si estiez mout esbahie par semblant .
et ce uos dis ge par dous foiz.   Quel escu . fet ele . portiez uos.
Dame . fet il . ge portoie a la premiere foiz un escu tot blanc
a une bende de bellic uermeille . et a lautre foiz un a dous
bendes dautretel color.[1]   Cet ensegnes . fet la roine . conoisge
bien et ui uos i ge plus.   Dame oil la nuit que uos cuidiez auoir
pardu monseigneur Gauuain uostre nies et ses compaignons et

---

[1] From this point in a third hand.

que les genz del chastel crioient . prenez le prenez le . et ge men uing hors un escu a mon col a trois bendes de bellic uermeilles . et missires li rois estoit deuant unes loges auec uos et quant ge uing uers [uos][1] lui si sescrierent les genz . prenez le roi prenez le roi . mes il men laissa aler soe merci. Certes . fet ele . ce poise moi . car sil uos eust retenu tuit li enchantement del chastel fussent remes. Mais or me dites fustes uos ce qui gitastes Gauuain et ses compaignons de la prison. Dame ge i aidai a mon pooir. En totes les choses . fet ele . que uos mauez dites naige encore troue se uerite non . mes por deu or me dites qui estoit une pucele qui uit[2] la nuit en une tornele qui estoit de sus lostel monseignor lo roi uestue dun chainsil blanc. Certes dame . fet il . ce fu la damoisele uers cui ge uilenai onques plus . car la dame del lac la mauoit enuoiee . et ele me troua en cele tornele si fu assez enoree por moi. Et quant ge oi les noueles de monseignor Gauuain qui pris estoit si fui mout corrociez . si me parti de la damoisele qui auec moi uoloit uenir . et ge li priai par icele foi que ele me deuoit que ele ne se meust deuant ce que ele ueist mon mesage ou moi . si fui si sorpris de si granz afaires que ge len obliai . ne a li ne retornai puis . et ele fu plus leax uers moi que ge ne fuis cortois uers lui . car onques diluec ne se mut deuant que ele oi mes enseignes . et ce fu grant piece apres. Et quant la roine loi parler de la damoisele del lac si sot bien tantost que cestoit lancelot. Si li enquist de totes iceles choses que ele auoit oies retraire de lui et de totes le troua uoir disant. Or me dites . fet ele . apres puis que uos fustes cheualiers partiz de camaalot uos i ui ge onques puis. Dame . fet il . oil tele ore que uos meustes grant mestier . car ge ieusse este noiez se uos ne fussiez qui me feistes trere hors del eue a monseignor yuain. Coment . fet ele . fustes uos ce que daguenez li coarz prist. Dame . fet il . ge ne sai qui ce fu mes pris fui ge sanz faille. Et ou aliez uos . fet ele. Dame . fet il . ge suioie un cheualier. Et quant uos fustes . fet ele . partiz de moi a la desreaine foiz ou alastes uos. Dame apres le cheualier que ge suioie.

---

[1] *Uos* underlined in the manuscript as not wanted.   [2] *Uint*, Jonckbloet.

Combatistes uos uos a lui. Dame oil. Et ou alastes uos apres.
Dame ge trouai dous granz uileins qui mocistrent mon cheual .
mes missire yuains[1] qui buene auentere ait me dona le suen.
Ha . fet la roine . donc saige bien qui uos iestes . uos auez a
non lancelot del lac. Et il se taist. Par deu . fet ele . por
naient le celez . pieca que len le set . car missire Gauuains
aporta premierement uostre non a cort. Lors li conte tot eissi
com missire Gauuains auoit dit que cestoit la tierce assemblee
quant messire yuains dist que la pucele li auoit dit cest la tierce.
Lors li redemande porcoi il auoit soffert que li pires om del
monde len auoit amene par le frein. Dame . fet il . gel pooie
bien soffrir comme cil qui nauoie pooir ne de mon cuer ne de
mon cors. Or me dites . fet ele . antan fustes uos a lassemble.
Dame oil. Queles armes . fet ele . portastes uos. Dame . fet
il . unes totes uermeilles. Par mon chief . fet ele . uos dites
uoir . et auant ier a lassemblee por cui feistes uos tant darmes.
Et il commence a sospirer mout durement. Et la reine le tient
mout cort comme cele qui bien uoit comment il est. Dites le
moi . fet ele . seurement car ge ne uos en descouerrai ia . et
ge sai bien que por dame ou por damoisele auez uos tot ce fet .
et dites moi qui ele est par la foi que uos li deuez. Ha dame .
fet il . ge uoi bien quil le me couient dire. Ce iestes uos
dame. Gie . fet ele . por moi ne portastes[2] uos mie les dous
glaiues que ma pucele uos porta . car ge mestoie bien mise
hors del mandement as autres dames. Dame . fet il . ge
fis por eles ce que ge dui et pors uos ce que ge poi. Or me
dites . fet ele . totes les choses que uos auez fetes por qui
les feistes uos. Dame . fet il . por uos. Coment . fet ele .
amez me uos donc tant. Dame . fet il . ge naim tant ne moi
ne autrui. Et desquant . fet la reine . mamez uos tant. Dame .
fet il . des le ior que ge fui apele cheualier et si ne lestoie
mie. Par la foi . fet ele . que uos me deuez dont uint cest
amor que uos auez en moi mise si grant et si enterine.[3]

---

[1] *Gauuains*, Jonckbloet.

[2] Corrected to *bruisastes: peceiastes*, Jonckbloet: *ployastes*, Paulin Paris:
pechoiastes, add. 10,293.

[3] Here follows the incident alluded to by Dante. In the printed editions
(Rouen, 1488, and Paris, 1494) it is entirely omitted. The passage there runs:

A ces paroles que la reine li disoit auint que la dame de
maloaut sestossi tot a escient et dreca la teste que ele auoit
embronchiee.   Et li cheualiers lentendi maintenant car mainte
fois lauoit oie . et il lesgarde et quant il la uit si ot tel peor et
tele angoisse que il ne pot mot respondre a ce que la reine li
demandoit[1] si commence a sospirer si durement que les lermes
li coroient des eux tot contreual les ioes si espessement que li
samiz dont il estoit uestuz en fu moilliez iusque sor les genolz
deuant . et quant il plus esgardoit la dame de maloaut et sis
cuers estoit plus a maleese.   De ceste chose se prist la reine
garde . et uit quil lesgardoit mout peoreusement la ou les
dames estoient . et ele laresna.   Dites moi . fet ele . dont ceste
amors mut que ge uos demant.   Et il sesforce de parler au plus
que il puet et dit.   Dame si mait dex des le ior que ge uos ai
dit.   Coment fu ce donques . fet ele.   Dame . fet il . uos le
me feistes fere . qui de moi feistes uostre ami se uostre boche ne
men menti.   Mon ami . fet ele . coment.   Dame . fet il . ge
uing deuant uos quant ge oi pris congie del roi monseignor toz
armez fors de mon chief et de mes mains . si uos commandai
adeu . et dit que estoie uostres cheualiers et uostre amis et uos
respondistes que uostre cheualiers et uostre amis uoliez uos bien
que ge fusse en toz les leus ou ge seroie . et ge dis . adeu dame .
et uos deistes adeu biaus dolz amis . onques puis ciz moz ne
me issi del cuer . ce fu li moz qui proudom me fera se ge ia le
sui . ne onques puis ne uing en si grant meschief que de cest

---

"*Par la foy que vous me deuez dont vindrent ces amours que vous auez en moy
mises ?*"   "*Dame,*" *fait il,* "*vous le me feistes faire qui de moy feistes vostre
amy, se vostre bouche ne me a menty.*"   Dante, as Novati observes, appears to
have retained a confused recollection of the passage in which this incident
occurs; it was not, as Dante implies in the *Paradiso*, on the occasion of the
actual kissing of Guenever and Lancelot that the Lady of Malehault coughed,
but at Guenever's inquiry of Lancelot as to what was the origin of his deep
love for her.   The old commentators, many of whom obviously had no first-
hand acquaintance with the romance, one and all give the incorrect version of
the incident of the cough.

[1] Royal 19, C. xiii. is rather fuller here : *Et quant li cheualiers a cui la roine
parloit oi la dame de malohaut tussir cui il auoit meinte foiz oie et ueue si regarde
cele part et la conoist erranment si a lors teil honte et tel angoisse quil ne set quil
doie fere.*

mot ne me membrast.   Ciz moz ma conforte en toz mes ennuiz.
Ciz moz ma de toz max este garanz . et ma garde de toz perilz.
Ciz moz ma saole en totes mes granz feins.   Ciz moz ma fet riche
en mes granz pouretez.

Parfoi . fet la reine . ci ot mot de buene ore dit . et dex en
soit aorez qui dire le me fist . mes ge nel pernoie pas si acertes
comme uos feistes . et a maint cheualier ai ge autresi dit ou ge
ne pensai onques que le dire . e uostre pensers ne fu mie uileins .
mes dolz et debueneres . si uos en est bien auenu car prodom
uos a fet. Et neporquant [1] la costume est mes tele es cheualiers
quil font semblant as dames de tex choses dont pou lor est as
cuers . et uostre semblant me mostre que uos amez ne sai la
quele de cez dames qui la sont plus que uos ne faites moi . quar
uos auez assez plore de peor ne nosez regarder uers eles de droit
esgart . si maparcoif bien que uostre pensers nest pas a moi tant
com uos me fetes entendant . et par la foi que uos deuez a la
rien que uos plus amez . la quele des trois est ce que uos amez
tant. Si mait dex . fet il . onques nule deles not mon cuer en
sa baillie. Ce na mestier . fet la reine . uos ne men poez rien
embler car iai ueues meintes choses autreteles . et ge uoi bien que
uostre cuers est la comment que li cors soit ci . et ce disoit ele
por ueior de combien ele le porroit metre a malese . car ele cuidoit
bien sauoir quil ne pensoit damors [2] se a li non . ia mar eust il
fet por li que seulement la iornee que il fist es armes noires [3] .
mes ele se delitoit mout durement en sa mesaise ueoir et
escouter. Et cil en fu si angoisseus que par un pou que il ne
pasma . mes la peor des dames qui lesgardoient le retint et la
reine meesmes sen dota porce que ele le uit palir et color
changier. Si le prist par le braz quil ne chaist et apela
Galehout et il salt sus si uient a li corant . et uoit que sis
compainz est issi conreez . si en a si grant angoisse a son cuer

---

[1] *Et neporquant la costume nest mies tele des cheualiers qui font ;* manuscript
339 in Bibliothèque Nationale.   *Et non pour tant la coustume est ore telle des
cheualiers qui font ;* Paulin Paris.

[2] *Darme ;* manuscript 751 in Bibliothèque Nationale.

[3] *Ja mar eust il plus fait pour li que la iournee des armes noires ;* manuscript
16,999 in Bibliothèque Nationale.

comme il puet greignor auoir . et dit . Ha dame por deu dites
moi que il a eu.   Et la reine li conte ce que ele li ot mis deuant.
Ha dame . fet Galehout . merci . uos le nos porriez bien tolir
par tex corroz . et ce seroit trop grant domages.   Certes . fait
ele . ce seroit mon . mes sauez uos por cui il a tant fet
darmes.   Dame . fet Galehout . naie uoir.   Se ce est uoirs .
fet ele . quil ma dit ce fu por moi.   Dame . fet Galehout
. einsi uoirement mait dex bien lempoez croire . car autresi
comme il est plus proudom que nul ome autresi est sis cuers
plus uerais que tuit li autre.   Voirement . fet la reine .
diriez uos quil est proudom se uos sauiez quil a fet darmes
puis quil fu cheualiers.   Lors li conte les cheualeries si comme
il les auoit fetes . et si li auoit coneu quil auoit portees les
armes uermeilles a lautre assemblee . et sachiez de uoir quil
a totes cez choses fetes por un sol mot.   Lors li deuise la
reine le mot si com uos auez oi quil lauoit dit.   Ha dame . fet
Galehout . aiez en merci por ses granz desertes et fetes le por
moi autresi comme ge ai fet ce que uos me proiastes.   Quel
merci . fet ele . uolez uos que ge en aie.   Dame . fet Galehout
. uos sauez bien que il uos aime sor tote rien . et plus a fet por
uos que onques nus autres cheualiers ne fist mes por dame . et
ueez le ci . si sachiez de uoir que ia la pes de monseignor lo roi
et de moi ne fùst se il sescors ne leust faite.   Certes . fet ele .
ge ne dot mie que il nait plus fet por moi que ge ne porroie
deseruir . sil nauoit plus fet que ceste pes porchaciee . ne il ne
me porroit nule riens requerre que ge li peusse belement neer .
mes il ne me requiert nule rien . ainz est si dolenz que il ne fina
de plorer onques puis que il commenca a regarder uers cez dames
la . neporquant ge nel mescroi pas damor que il ait a nule deles
. mes il dote se deuient que aucune deles le conoisse.   Dame .
fet Galehout . de ce ne couient il tenir nule parole . mes aiez
merci de lui car il uos aime assez plus que il ne fet soi meesmes
. ne mie porce que si mait dex ge ne sauoie riens de son couine
quant il iuint . fors tant quil dotoit estre coneuz . ne onques
riens plus ne men descouri.   Gen aure . fait ele . tel merci com
uos uoldroiz . car uos auez fet ce que ge uos requis . li doi bien
fere ce que uos uoldroiz . mes il ne me prie de rien.   Dame .

fait Galehout . quil nen a pooir ne len ne puet nule riens amer
que len ne dot . mais ge uos pri por lui . et se ge ne uos
emprioie sel deuriez uos porchascier . car plus riche tresor ne
porriez uos mie conquerre.   Certes . fet ele . gel sai bien et gen
ferai quanque uos commanderoiz.   Dame . fet Galehout . granz
merciz . et ge uos pri que uos li doigniez uostre amor . et que
uos le prengniez a uostre cheualier a toz iorz . et uos deuenez sa
loiaus amie a toz les iorz de uostre uie . lors si lauroiz fet plus
riche que se uos li doniez tot le monde.   Einsint . fet la reine .
lotroi gie que il miens soit et ge tote soe . et par uos soient
amende tuit li mesfait et li trespas des couenances.   Dame . fet
il . granz merciz . mais or icouient commencement de seurte.
Vos nen deuiseroiz ia nule chose . fet la roine . que ge nen face.
Dame . fet Galehout . donc le besiez par commencement damor
ueraie.   Del besier . fet ele . ne uoi ge ore ne leu ne tens . mes
ne dotez mie que ge ausi uolenteiue nen soie comme il seroit .
mes ces dames sont iluec qui mout se meruentellent que nos auons
ici tant fet . si ne porroit estre que eles nel ueissent . et neporquant sil uelt ge le besere mout uolentiers : et il en est si liez
et si esbahiz que il ne puet respondre mot fors tant solement .
dame granz merciz.   Ha dame . fet Galehout . del suen uoloir
ne dotez uos ia quil iest toz . et si sachiez bien que ia riens
nule ne sen apercuera . car nos nos trairons tuit troi ensemble
autresi comme se nos conseillions.   De coi me feroie ge prier .
fet ele . plus le uoil ge que uos ne il.   Lors se traient tuit troi
ensemble et font semblant de conseillier.   Et la reine uoit bien
qui li cheualiers nen ose plus fere . si le prent par le menton et
le bese uoiant Galehout assez longuement[1] . si que la dame de
maloaut sot de uoir que il la baisoit.   Lors commence la reine
a parler qui molt estoit uaillant dame et sage.

Biaus douz amis . fet ele . ge sui uostre tant auez fet por
moi . et mout en ai grant ioie . or si gardez que la chose soit
si celee con uos sauez quil en est mestiers . car ge sui une des

---

[1] I have already drawn attention to the fact that Dante in his reference to
this incident (*Inferno*, v. 133-4) represents Guenever as being kissed by Lancelot, whereas it was she who kissed the knight.   The old commentators, almost
without exception, make the same mistake.

dames del monde dont len a greignors biens diz . et se mis lox empiroit par uos ci auroit amor laide et uileine . et uos Galehout . fet ele . empri ge qui plus iestes sages . car se maus men uenoit ce ne seroit se par uos non . et se ge en ai bien ne ioie uos la mauroiz donee. Dame . fet Galehout . certes il ne porroit pas uers uos mesprendre . mes ge uos ai fet ce que uos me priastes . or si me seroit mestiers que uos moissiez dune proiere que ge uos fis tres ier . quant ge uos dis que uos mi porriez plus aidier par tens que ge a uos. Dites . fet ele . seuremeut . car uos ne me sauriez nule rien requerre que ge ne feisse por uos. Dame . fet il . donc mauez uos otroie que uos me donroiz sa compaigniez a toz iorz. Certes . fet ele . se il de ce uos failloit malement auriez emploie le grant meschief que uos auez fet por lui.[1] Lors prent la reine le cheualier par la main destre . et dit . Galehout . ge uos doign cest cheualier a toz iorz sauf ce [2] que ge iai auant eu . et uos le creantez . fet ele . et li cheualiers li creante . et sauez uos . fet ele a Galehout . qui ge uos ai done. Dame . fet il . nenil. Ge uos ai done . fait ele . lancelot del lac le filz au roi ban de benoic. Einsint li fet la reine le cheualier conoistre qui molt en a grant honte.[3] Lors a Galehout greignor ioie que il not onques mes . car il auoit assez oi dire einsi com paroles uont que lancelot del lac estoit li mieldres cheualiers del monde poures om . et bien sauoit que li rois bans auoit este mout gentils et mout puissanz damis et de terre. Einsi fu fez li premiers acointemenz del cheualier et de la reine par Galehout . ne Galehout ne lauoit onques coneu fors de ueoir . et porce li auoit fet lancelot creanter que il ne li demanderoit son non deuant ce que il li deist ou autres por lui. Lors se leuerent tuit troi . et il anuitoit ia mout durement . mes il faisoit cler que ia estoit la lune leuee si ueoit len mout cler tot contreual la praerie. Atant sentornent tuit troi contreual les prez droit uers la tente lo roy . et li seneschaus Gale-

---

[1] *Que vous avez souffert pour lui ;* manuscript 16,999 in Bibliothèque Nationale.

[2] For *ce* there is a marginal reading *le droit*, which is the reading of Roy. 20, D. iii. : *Sauue le droit que ieo aie auant eu.*

[3] *Honte* is a substitution for *ioie*, which has been erased.

hout uient apres entre lui et les dames tant que il uienent endroit la tente Galehout. Et lors en enuoie Galehout son compaignon . et il prent congie de la reine si empassent outre entre lui et le seneschal. Et Galehout conuoie la reine dusquau tref lo roi. Et quant li rois les uoit si demande dom il uienent. Sire . fet Galehout . nos uenons de cez prez a si petite compaignie que uos ueez. Lors sasient et parolent de maintes choses . et mout sont aese entre Galehout et la reine. A chief de piece se lieue la reine et dit que ele ueut aler cochier . et Galehout la conuoie iusque la et la commande adeu . et li dit que il ira anuit gesir auec som compaignon . si le solacera car or set il bien de coi . mes auantier ne sauoie ge de coi gel solacasse. Ha sire . fet ele . comme auez uos ore bien dit . quil en sera mout plus aese. Atant se part Galehout de li . et uient au roi si prent congie . et dit que il ne li poist mie quil ira anuit gesir en son tref entre sa gent . ou il ne uit pieca . et il me couendroit . fet il . mout fere lor uolente car il font mout uolentiers lamoie et mout maiment. Certes . fet missire Gauuains . uos auez mout bien dit . car mout doit len ses proudes genz amer et enorer quant en les a. Lors sen uet Galehout a son compaignon . et se cochierent la nuit . ambedui ensemble en un lit . et parolent de ce dont lor cuers sont aese.

TRANSLATION.

Thus went Gallehault to his comrade morning and evening ; and each time he came back the Queen asked him what he had contrived. And at night Gallehault went back where he was wont ; and on the morrow early he came to his comrade and said to him : " Now is the end, for this very day behoves it that the Queen see you ".

" Sir, for heaven's sake, contrive so that no one know it save you and she, for there are plenty of folk in the household of the king who would know me well if they saw me."

" Have no fear, quoth Gallehault, for I will see to it right well."

Thereupon he took leave of him, and called his seneschal.

"See, quoth he, if I send to fetch you, that you come to me and bring my comrade so that no one know that it is he."

"Sir, quoth he, according to your pleasure."

Then Gallehault returned to the pavilion of the King, and the Queen asked him "What news?"

"Lady, quoth he, fair enough; the flower of the knighthood of the world has come."

"Heaven, quoth she, how shall I see him? for I desire to see him in such wise that no man know it save he, and I, and you; for I desire not that other folk be gladdened thereby."

"By heaven, lady, quoth Gallehault, thus shall it be; for he said that he would not any folk of King Arthur's household should know him on any account."

"How, quoth she, is he then known to any?"

"Lady, quoth he, there are folk might see him, who would know him well."

"Heaven, quoth the Queen, who can he be?"

"Lady, quoth Gallehault, fore heaven, I know not, for never did he tell me his name, nor whence he is."

"Nay! quoth she, fore heaven, a strange thing do I hear; and now do I long to see him more than ever."

"Lady, quoth he, you shall see him this very night, and I will tell you how. We will go forthwith to take our pleasure down yonder,—and he shows her a place in the midst of the meadows all full of bushes,—and we will have the least company we may, and there you shall see him; and we will go a little before nightfall."

"Ah, quoth she, true sweet friend, how well you have spoken. And would the Lord of the world were pleased it were nightfall now."

Then they began both to laugh, and the Queen embraced him, and made him very joyful. And the Lady of Malehaut saw them laugh, and thought that now the affair was more advanced than she was aware; and she took great heed, and no knight came into the house but she looked him full in the face. And the Queen was very joyful that the knight was come, and she longed greatly for the night to fall. And she strove to talk and to frolic in order to forget the day, which was wearisome to her.

Thus passed the day till it came about, after supper, the evening fell. And the Queen took Gallehault by the hand, and the Lady of Malehaut with her, and the damsel Laura of Carduel, and one of her maidens, without more company. And she wended her way adown the meadows straight to where Gallehault had told her. And when he had gone a little way, Gallehault looked about and saw an esquire, and he called him, and told him to go and bid his seneschal come to him; and he showed him in what place. And when the Queen heard it, she looked and said : " How, quoth she, is he your seneschal ? "

" Nay, lady, quoth he, but he will come with him."

Thereupon they came beneath the trees, and the Queen and Gallehault sat down together apart some way from the others. And the Lady of Malehaut and the others likewise marvelled much that they sat so privately. And the varlet came to the seneschal, and gave his message. And the other straightway took the knight with him, and they crossed the water and came all adown the meadows to where the varlet showed them.[1] When they came near, the ladies looked at them, and the Lady of Malehaut knew the goodly knight to be him whom many days she had had her in her keeping; and inasmuch as she did not wish him to know her, she bent down and drew close to the damsel Laura. And the others passed beyond, and the seneschal drew near to the ladies and greeted them ; and Gallehault said to the Queen :—

" Lady, see here the best knight in the world."

" Which is that ? " quoth the Queen.

" Lady, which do you think it is ? "

" Indeed, quoth she, they are both right fair knights, but I do not see here any that should have the half of the valour the black knight had."

" Lady, quoth he, know that he is one of these two."

---

[1] Here in several manuscripts follows, " and both were such goodly knights and fair, that in vain would one seek fairer in any land ".

Thereupon they came before the Queen ; and the knight trembled so greatly that he could not greet the Queen ; and all his colour went from him, so that the Queen marvelled much thereat. Then they both knelt down, and Gallehault's seneschal greeted her, and the other knight did likewise, but in very poor fashion,—nay, he fixed his eyes on the ground as though ashamed. And then bethought the Queen that this was he. And then said Gallehault to the seneschal, " Go and keep company with yon ladies, who are all too lonely."

And the Queen took the knight by the hand as he was on his knees, and seated him before her, and looked very kindly upon him, and said to him laughing : " Sir, much have we desired you, so that, thanks to heaven and Gallehault who is here, we now see you. Nathless still I know not if you be the knight whom I desire. But Gallehault tells me that you are ; and yet I would fain know from your lips who you are, if such were your pleasure."

And he answered her that he knew not ; nor ever once did he look her full in the face. And the Queen marvelled much what ailed him ; yet she suspected in part how it was with him. And Gallehault, seeing him abashed and ashamed, thought he would sooner tell his thoughts to the Queen if they were alone ; so he looked, and said aloud so that the ladies heard him : " Indeed, quoth he, now am I right churlish, for all these ladies have but one sole knight to keep them company ; nay, they are quite lonely."

Then he rose up and came to them, and they all came to meet him, and he seated them again. And then they began to talk of divers matters. And the Queen spake to the knight, and said to him : " Fair sweet Sir, wherefore do you hide yourself from me ? Indeed, there is no reason. Nathless you may well tell me if you are he who conquered in the assembly [1] the day before yesterday."

---

[1] *Assemblée :* " Ce mot *assemblée* signifioit . . . la réunion de nombre de personnes en un même lieu et pour le même dessin. . . . Dans les siècles brillans de la chevalerie, les Tornois étoient des *assemblées d'honneur.*"—Ste. Palaye.

"Lady, quoth he, nay."

"How, quoth she, had you not armour all black?"

"Lady, yea."

"And then were you not he to whom Sir Gawain sent the three horses?"

"Lady, yea."

"Then are you not he who wore the armour of Gallehault on the last day?"

"Lady, yea."

"Then are you not he who conquered in the assembly on the second day?"

"Lady, I did not, of a truth."

Then the Queen perceived, indeed, that he would not confess that he had conquered; and she prized him much in her heart therefore.

"Now tell me, quoth she, who made you a knight?"

"Lady, you," quoth he.

"I! quoth she, when?"

"Lady, quoth he, do you remember how a knight came to my lord the King at Camalot, who was hurt in the body by two stumps of lances, and in the head by a sword, and how a varlet came to him on the Friday in the evening who was a knight on the Sunday morn?"

"Of this, quoth she, I mind me right well; and so help you God, were you he whom the damsel brought to court clad in a white robe?"

"Yea, lady," quoth he.

"And wherefore, quoth she, do you say, then, that I made you a knight?"

"Lady, because it is true; for the custom in the kingdom of Logres[1] is such that no one there can be made a knight without girding on the sword; and the one of whom he holds the sword makes him a knight; and I hold it of you, lady, for the king gave me not one; and therefore I say that you made me a knight."

---

[1] The Welsh name (modern *Lloegr*) for England. Geoffrey of Monmouth (ii. 1) says that Britain was divided into three parts, *viz.*: *Loegria, Kambria,* and *Albania.*

"Indeed, quoth the Queen, of this am I right glad; and whither did you go from thence?"

"Lady, I went to the aid of the Lady of Nohan; and thither came afterwards Sir Kay,[1] and we fought, he and I, against two knights."

"And before this, quoth the Queen, did you send me nought?"

"Lady, yea, two maidens."

"By my head, quoth she, it is true; and when you were come back from Nohan did you find no one who challenged you in my name?"

"Lady, indeed yea,—a knight who was guarding a ford; and he bade me get down from my horse, and I asked him whose he was; and he said he was yours. 'Get down at once,' quoth he; and I asked him who had bidden him, and he said that bidding he had none save his own; and I put back my foot which I had taken out of the stirrup, and I told him that he would not have it[2] that day of a surety. And I jousted at him; and I know well that I did wrong, and I crave your pardon for it, lady, and you will exact what amends it shall seem good to you."

And the Queen, who saw that he could not escape being hers, answered him: "Indeed, fair sweet friend, quoth she, you did me no wrong, for he was not mine; nay, I was much displeased thereat, when he came to me and told it to me. But now tell me whither did you go from thence?"

"Lady, quoth he, to the Dolorous Keep."

"Who conquered it?" quoth she.

"Lady, quoth he, I entered therein."

"And did I ever see you there?" quoth she.

"Lady, yea, more than once."

"In what place?" quoth she.

"Lady, one day that I asked you if you would enter in, and you said yea, and were much abashed in mien; and this I said to you twice."

"What shield, quoth she, did you bear?"

---

[1] The seneschal of King Arthur.   [2] That is, his horse.

"Lady, quoth he, I bare the first time a shield all white with a band of red slantwise;[1] and the other time one with two bands of like colour."

"That device, quoth the Queen, I know well; and did I see you there any more?"

"Lady, yea, the night that you thought to have lost my lord Gawain, your nephew, and his comrades, and that the people of the castle cried out, 'Take him! Take him!' And I came out with a shield on my neck, with three bands of red slantwise. And my lord the King was before a tent with you, and when I came towards him the people cried out, 'Take him, King! Take him, King!' but he let me go, thanks be to him."

"Indeed, quoth she, this grieves me, for if he had stayed you all the enchantment of the castle would have been done away. But now tell me, was it you who delivered Gawain and his comrades from the prison?"

"Lady, I helped therein to the best of my power."

"In all the matters, quoth she, whereof you have told me, have I yet found naught save the truth; but now, I pray you, tell me who was a maiden who passed the night in a tower which was above the hostel of my lord the King, clothed in white linen raiment?"

"Indeed, lady, quoth he, this was the damsel to whom I behaved all too churlishly; for the Lady of the Lake had sent her to me, and she found me in that tower and was much honoured of me; and when I heard the news of my lord Gawain, how he was taken, I was greatly moved, and I departed from the damsel who would fain have come with me. And I prayed her by the fealty she owed me that she would not remove before she should see my messenger or me; and I was so overcome by such grave matters that I forgat her, and did not return to her after. And she was more loyal towards me than

---

[1] Cotgrave, Littré and others explain *belic* (which I have rendered "slantwise") as "red," "gules"; as, however, we read of "*bandes de belic blanches,*" this cannot be correct. Paulin Paris remarks: "Ce mot répond au latin *obliquus*, et distingue les bandes transversales des horizontales, plus tard nommées *fasces*."

I was courteous towards her, for never from there did she remove before she heard news of me, and that was a long while after."

And when the Queen heard him speak of the Lady of the Lake she knew well straightway that he was Lancelot. And she asked him of all the matters which she had heard related of him, and of all she found that he spake the truth.

"Now tell me, quoth she, after that as a knight you departed from Camalot did I ever see you again?"

"Lady, quoth he,—yea, at such an hour as you did me great service; for I should have been drowned had it not been for you, who had me drawn forth from the water by my lord Yvain."

"How! quoth she, was it you whom Dagonet the coward took?"

"Lady, quoth he, I know not who it was, but taken I was of a surety."

"And whither were you going?" quoth she.

"Lady, quoth he, I was following a knight."

"And when, quoth she, you had parted from me the last time, whither did you go?"

"Lady, after the knight whom I was following."

"And did you fight with him?"

"Lady, yea."

"And whither did you go after?"

"Lady, I found two great villains who slew my horse; but my lord Yvain, whom good luck attend, gave me his."

"Ah! quoth the Queen, then know I well who you are; your name is Lancelot of the Lake."

And he held his peace.

"By heaven, quoth she, to no purpose do you conceal it; it hath long while been known, for my lord Gawain first brought your name to court."

Then she related to him all,—how Sir Gawain had said that it was the third assembly, when Sir Yvain said that the maiden had told him that it was the third. Then she asked him again wherefore he had allowed the most worthless man in the world to lead him away by the bridle.

"Lady, quoth he, I allowed it as one who had no power over his heart or his body."

"Now tell me, quoth she, were you last year at the assembly?"

"Lady, yea."

"What armour, quoth she, did you wear?"

"Lady, quoth he, a suit all red."

"By my head, quoth she, you say true; and the day before yesterday at the assembly, for whom did you perform so great feats?"

And he began to sigh very deeply. And the Queen cut him short, as knowing well how it was with him.

"Tell me, quoth she, verily, for I will never discover you; and I know well for some lady or damsel you have done all this; now tell me who she is, by the fealty you owe her?"

"Ah, lady, quoth he, I see well that it behoves me to say. It is you, lady."

"I! quoth she, for me did you in no wise shiver the two lances which my maiden brought to you, for I kept myself aloof from the other ladies in the ordering."

"Lady, quoth he, I did for them what I should, and for you what I could."

"Now tell me, quoth she,—all the deeds you have wrought, for whom did you do them?"

"Lady, quoth he, for you."

"How! quoth she, do you love me then so much?"

"Lady, quoth he, so much love I not myself nor another."

"And since when, quoth the Queen, have you loved me so much?"

"Lady, quoth he, since the day when I was called knight, and was as yet none of it."

"By the fealty, quoth she, that you owe me, whence came this so great and entire love that you have placed in me?"

At these words that the Queen spake it came to pass that the Lady of Malehaut coughed[1] all openly, and raised her head

---

[1] *Paradiso*, xvi. 14-15.

which she had before bent down.   And the knight did hear
her now, for many a time had he heard her.   And he looked at
her, and when he saw her he conceived such fear and anguish
that he could not make answer to what the Queen asked him;
and he began to sigh so deeply that the tears ran from his eyes
all adown his cheeks, so heavily that the samite wherewith he
was clad was made wet even to his knees before him.   And the
more he looked at the Lady of Malehaut the more was his heart
disquieted.   Of this matter the Queen took heed, and she saw
that he looked very fearfully to where the ladies were, and she
spake to him: " Tell me, quoth she, whence this love arose of
the which I ask you?"

And he forced himself to speak as well as he might, and
said: " Lady, so help me God, from the day that I have told
you."

" How was this, then?" quoth she.

" Lady, quoth he, you made me to do it, who made of me
your friend, if your lips lied not to me."

" My friend, quoth she, how?"

" Lady, quoth he, I came before you when I had taken leave
of the King my lord, fully armed save my head and my hands,
and I bade you farewell, and said that I was your knight and
your friend; and you answered that your knight and your
friend you were fain I should be in what place soever I was.
And I said, 'Farewell, lady'.   And you said, 'Farewell, fair
sweet friend'.   And never since has this word gone forth from
my heart.   This was the word which will make of me a brave
knight, if so be I ever am one.   Nor ever since did I come into
so great mischance but of this word I was mindful.   This word
has comforted me in all my troubles.   This word has been my
shield from all ill, and has kept me from all danger.   This word
has filled me whensoever I have been hungry.   This word has
made me rich in my great poverty."

" I'faith, quoth the Queen, this word was said in good time,[1]
and God be praised who made me to say it; but I took it not

---

[1] Add. 10,293 in British Museum reads here, *de moult boine eure*, " of great
good chance ".

in such serious sort as you have done, and to many a knight
have I said as much when I recked nought beyond the speech.
And your thought was no wise churlish, nay rather was it
sweet and of good liking.   And well has it happened to you, for
a brave knight it has made you.   And yet no wise such is the
manner of knights who make show to ladies of like matters
whereof little is in their hearts.   And your mien shows me
that you love I know not which of those ladies yonder more
than you do me, for you have wept greatly in affright, and dare
not look towards them with direct look ; and I perceive well
that your thought is no wise wholly set on me as you make
pretence.   And by the fealty you owe to that which you most
love, which of the three [1] is it that you so much love ? "

"So help me God, quoth he, not ever one of them has had
my heart in her keeping."

"Of that there is no need, quoth the Queen; you cannot
hide aught of it from me, for I have seen many such like
things ; and I see well that your heart is yonder although your
body be here."

And this she said to see how she might disquiet him, for
she knew well that he thought not of love save for her;
otherwise would he have done her further wrong beyond the
day when he fought in the black armour ; [2] but she took
delight in cruel wise in hearing and seeing his disquietude.
And he was in such sore anguish thereat that he well-nigh
swooned, but the fear of the ladies who were looking at him
kept him therefrom ; and the Queen herself was in fear thereof,
for she saw him turn pale and change colour.   And she took
him by the arm lest he should fall, and called Gallehault.   And
he leaped up and came to her running ; and when he saw that

---

[1] There were three ladies there—the Lady of Malehaut, Laura of Carduel
and one of Queen Guenever's maidens.

[2] The black armour had been supplied him by the Lady of Malehaut; in
wearing it he had, as it were, been disloyal to Guenever.   This passage is somewhat difficult.   I have adopted an interpretation suggested to me (on a hint from
the reading of manuscript 16,999, in Bib. Nat.) by M. Arsène Darmesteter, who
paraphrases : *il se serait mal conduit envers elle plus que cette seule journée qu'il
avait faite avec les armes noires.*

his comrade was in such a plight he felt so great anguish thereat in his heart that no man can feel more, and he said, " Ah, lady, I pray you tell me, what has there passed ? "

And the Queen related to him what she had put before him.

" Ah, lady, quoth Gallehault, have pity; you might well take him from us by such wrath, and that would be too great a hurt."

" Indeed, quoth she, it would indeed. But do you know for whom he has performed so great feats ? "

" Lady, quoth Gallehault, nay, verily."

" If that be true, quoth she, that he has told me, it was for me."

" Lady, quoth Gallehault, so truly help me God, you may well believe it; for even as he is braver than any man, so likewise is his heart more true than any other."

" Verily, quoth the Queen, would you say that he was brave if you knew what feats he has performed since he was made a knight."

Then she recounted to him his feats of chivalry even as he had performed them, and related how he had confessed that he had worn the red armour at the other assembly. " And know of a truth that all these things he has done for a single word." Then the Queen told him of the word, as you have heard that he told her.

" Ah, lady, quoth Gallehault, take pity on him for his great deserts, and do it for me in like manner as I have done what you prayed of me."

" What pity, quoth she, will you that I have on him ? "

" Lady, quoth Gallehault, you know well that he loves you above everything, and has done more for you than ever any other knight has done for lady; and see him here, and know of a truth that never peace between my lord the King and me had been made if he himself had not made it."

" Indeed, quoth she, I in no wise doubt but that he has done more for me than I could requite to him, even if he had done no more than procure this peace; nor could he require aught of me that I could becomingly deny him. But he requires naught of me ; nay, he is so doleful that he has never ceased to weep after that he began to look towards yonder ladies. Nathless I misdoubt him not of love that he may have for any of them, but he fears lest it chance that any of them know him."

" Lady, quoth Gallehault, of this behoves it not to speak ; but have pity on him, for he loves you more than he does himself.   And as to this, so help me God, I knew nought of his condition when he came, save only that he feared to be known ; nor ever aught more has he discovered to me."

" I will have, quoth she, such pity on him as you would, for you have done what I required of you ; and I ought indeed to do for him what you would, but he asks naught of me."

" Lady, quoth Gallehault, because he has not the power ; nor can a man love aught without he fears.   But I pray you for him, and if I did not pray it of you, yet should you procure it, for more rich treasure could you no wise win."

" Indeed, quoth she, I know it well, and I will do whatsoever you bid me."

" Lady, quoth Gallehault, much thanks ; and I pray you to give him your love, and to take him as your knight for always, and to become his loyal friend for all the days of your life ; then will you have made him more rich than if you gave him the whole world."

" Even so, quoth the Queen, I grant that he be mine, and I altogether his.   And by you be punished all misdoing or breach of the covenant."

" Lady, quoth he, much thanks ; but now behoves it to make beginning of surety."

" You will devise naught, quoth the Queen, but I will do it."

" Lady, quoth Gallehault, then kiss him, as a beginning of true love."

" For a kiss, quoth she, see I now neither place nor time, but no wise doubt but that I am as fain as he.   But these ladies are yonder who marvel much that we have so long talked here, and it could not be but they would see it.   Nathless if he desire it I will kiss him right willingly."

And he was so joyful and astonied thereat that he could not make answer, save only, " Lady, much thanks ".

" Ah, lady, quoth Gallehault, doubt not now of his desire, for he is wholly set on it.   And know well that none shall perceive it, for we will all three draw together even as if we took counsel."

" Wherefore should I make you to pray me? quoth she; more do I desire it than you or he."

Then they all three drew together and made as if they took counsel.   And the Queen saw well that the knight dared do no farther, and she took him by the chin and kissed him [1] before Gallehault no short space, so that the Lady of Malehaut knew of a truth that she kissed him.   Then the Queen, who was a right worthy and prudent lady, began to speak : " Fair sweet friend, quoth she, I am yours, seeing that you have done so much for me, and I am right well pleased thereat.   Now see that the matter be hid, even as you know it needs should ; for I am a lady of whom the greatest good in the world has been spoken, and if my praise were to be minished through you, here would be love unlovely and churlish.   And you, Gallehault, quoth she, do I beseech as being most prudent, for if evil happed to me thereby, it could not be save through you ; and if I have thereby good hap or joy, you will have given it me."

" Lady, quoth Gallehault, indeed it could not go amiss with you ; but I have done for you what you prayed of me, now needs it that you give ear to a prayer that I made to you yesterday, when I said to you that you might betimes better help me, than I you."

" Tell me verily, quoth she, for you could naught require of me but I would do it for you."

" Lady, quoth he, then did you grant that you would give me his company for always."

" Indeed, quoth she, if this were lacking to you, ill would have served you the great sacrifice [2] you made for his sake."

---

[1] *Inferno*, v. 133-4.

[2] So I render *meschief* here, taking it to refer to Gallehault's having pledged himself to Lancelot that he would submit to King Arthur on the third day of

Then the Queen took the knight by the right hand, and said : " Gallehault, I give you this knight for always, saving the right that I have had over him before ; and do you swear it," quoth she ; and the knight sware it.

" And do you know, quoth she to Gallehault, whom I have given you ? "

" Lady, quoth he, nay."

" I have given you, quoth she, Lancelot of the Lake, the son of King Ban of Benoic."

Thus did the Queen make known to him the knight, who was greatly abashed thereat. Then was Gallehault more glad than he had ever been, for oftentimes had he heard said, after the common talk, that Lancelot of the Lake was the best knight in the world, as a plain man ; and he knew well that the King Ban had been very noble, and very mighty in lands and in friends.

Thus was contrived the first acquaintance between the knight and the Queen by Gallehault ; nor had Gallehault ever known him save by sight, and therefore had Lancelot made him swear that he would not ask of him his name before that he told it to him, or another for him.

Then they all three arose ; and now had the night fallen right heavily, but it was light ; for now was the moon risen, and it was quite light all adown the meadows. Then they returned all three adown the meadows straight towards the tent of the King. And the seneschal of Gallehault came after, he and the ladies together, until they came to the tent of Gallehault. And then Gallehault sent away his comrade, and he took leave of the Queen, and he and the seneschal together passed beyond. And Gallehault escorted the Queen as far as the pavilion of the King. And when the King saw them, he asked whence they came.

" Sir, quoth Gallehault, we come from these meadows in such small company as you see."

the Assembly, when the forces of the latter should be on the point of yielding. This undertaking Gallehault loyally performed, and it was thus that Lancelot made peace between him and King Arthur.

Then they sat down and talked of divers matters, and Gallehault and the Queen were well pleased together. And after a while the Queen got up and said that she would fain go to bed, and Gallehault escorted her thither, and bade her farewell, and said that he was going that night to lie with his comrade ; and that he would comfort him, for now he knew well wherewithal he should. "But the day before yesterday I knew not, quoth he, wherewith I should comfort him."

"Ah, sir, quoth she, how well have you now spoken, for much more will he be gladdened thereby."

Then Gallehault parted from her, and came to the King and took leave, and said that the King must not take it ill that he should go to lie that night in his pavilion with his folk, where he had not been for a while.

"And it would beseem me well, quoth he, to do their pleasure, for they do mine right willingly, and love me much."

"Indeed, quoth Gawain, you have right well spoken, for much ought one to love and to honour one's brave folk when one has any such."

Then Gallehault went his way to his comrade, and they slept the night together both in one bed, and talked of that of which their hearts were fain.

SOME OBLIGATIONS OF DANTE TO ALBERTUS MAGNUS [1]

ALBERTUS MAGNUS, who was born in 1193, and died, at the age of eighty-seven, in 1280, when Dante was fifteen years old, was one of the authors of whom Dante made considerably more use than is apparent to the casual observer. The Doctor Universalis, as Albertus was styled on account of his vast learning, is only mentioned by name four times in the whole range of Dante's works, viz., Convivio, iii. 5, l. 113 (where he is called "Alberto della Magna," and his books De Natura Locorum and De Proprietatibus Elementorum [2] are referred to); Convivio, iii. 7, l. 27, and iv. 23, l. 126 (in both of which passages he is called simply "Alberto," the reference in the former being to his De Intellectu,[3] in the latter to his De Meteoris) [4]; and Paradiso, x. 98 (where he is called "Alberto di Cologna," and is placed among the great theologians in the heaven of the sun). These four references, however, by no means represent the amount of Dante's indebtedness to him, as will be apparent from the following notes. These will show that Dante availed himself of the writings of Albertus to a considerable extent, especially of the Aristotelian treatises, which he must have studied pretty closely.

[1] Reprinted, with additions, from Romania, xxiv. 400-12.

[2] Dante quotes these two works in a general way, without citing any specific passage, in support of the opinion that the equatorial circle divides the hemisphere of the land from that of the sea almost entirely at the extremity of the first climate, in the region which is inhabited by the Garamantes.

[3] See below, pp. 52-53.

[4] See below, pp. 47 ff.

I

Convivio II. 14

In a passage (ll. 170-176)[1] in this chapter of the *Convivio*, in which the properties of the planet Mars are discussed, Dante quotes Albumazar [2] to the effect that the ignition of the vapours about that planet portends the death of kings and other political changes :—

" Dice Albumassar, che l' accendimento di questi vapori significa morte di regi e trasmutamento di regni [3] ; perocchè sono effetti della signoria di Marte."

This quotation has been sought for in vain by the commentators in the two works of Albumazar which we possess, *viz.*, his *Introduction to Astronomy* and his *Book of Conjunctions* [4] ; and it has been supposed in consequence that Dante must have inadvertently attributed to the Arabian astronomer the opinion of some other writer. If, however, the quotation has been wrongly ascribed to Albumazar, the mistake was made in the first place, not by Dante, but by Albertus Magnus, who was evidently Dante's authority for this piece of information about Albumazar. In this same chapter of the *Convivio*, in the paragraph immediately preceding the passage under discussion, Dante mentions the occasional spontaneous ignition of meteoric vapours " siccome nel primo della *Meteora* è determinato ". As no author's name is here mentioned one would naturally suppose the reference to be to the *De Meteoris* of Aristotle. But on

---

[1] The line-references here and elsewhere in this book are to the text of the Oxford Dante.

[2] Jafar ibn Muhammud Al Balkhi, *Abú Mashar ;* born at Balkh in Turkestan 805, died 885.

[3] *Cf.* Brunetto Latino, who, in speaking of a comet which appeared shortly before the death of King Manfred, says : " De cele estoile dient li sage astronomien que quant ele apert el firmament, ele senefie remuemens de regne ou mort de grans seigneurs ". (*Trésor*, i. 98.)

[4] These works were translated from Arabic into Latin under the titles of *Introductorium in Astronomiam* and *Liber de magnis conjunctionibus, annorum revolutionibus ac eorum profectionibus.* They were both printed at Augsburg in 1489.

examination it appears that Dante must have had before him as
he wrote, not Aristotle's work, but the work of the same
name by Albertus Magnus [1] ; and it was from this treatise,
as will be seen, that the quotation attributed to Albumazar was
borrowed by Dante, in spite of the fact that it is introduced as
if made at first hand from Albumazar himself. And not only
this quotation, but also that from Seneca [2], which occurs in the
next sentence of the *Convivio* (" E Seneca dice però, che nella
morte d' Augusto imperadore vide in alto una palla di fuoco "),
is taken from the same source. The passage in Albertus, which
occurs at the conclusion of a discussion as to the nature and
properties of these igneous vapours, is as follows :—

> Vapor iste . . . aliquando autem vulnerat exurendo multum vel parum
> secundum fortitudinem ignis sui. Si autem secundo modo est, debilem habet
> ignem, qui parum alterat ea super quae cadit, non vulnerando, quia statim
> extinguitur. Vult tamen Albumasar quod etiam ista aliquando mortem regis
> et principum significent, propter dominium Martis, praecipuè quando fiunt in
> formâ non consuetâ et saepius solito : unde Seneca dicit, quod circa excessum
> divi Augusti vidit speciam pilae igneae quae in ipso cursu suo dissoluta est, et
> circa mortem Seiani et circa mortem Germanici simile visum est prodigium.
> (*De Meteoris*, Lib. I. tract. iv. cap. 9.)

II

INFERNO XIV. 31-36

Dante appears to have been especially familiar with this
particular book of the *De Meteoris* of Albertus Magnus ; for it
was from the chapter preceding the one from which the above
quotation is taken that he got his version of the incident which
happened to Alexander the Great and his army in India. In
his description of the flakes of fire which were rained down upon
the spirits of the Violent in the seventh circle of Hell, he

---

[1] Albertus wrote, not merely commentaries, but paraphrases and illustrative
treatises, on each of Aristotle's works, the titles of which he adopted for his own
treatises.

[2] The original statement of Seneca is to be found in the *Naturales
Quaestiones* (i. 1) : " Nos quoque vidimus non semel flammam ingentis pilae
specie, quae tamen in ipso cursu suo dissipata est. Vidimus circa divi Augusti
excessum simile prodigium : vidimus cum de Seiano actum est : nec Germanici
mors sine denunciatione tali fuit."

compares them to the flames which fell upon Alexander's host :—

> Quali Alessandro in quelle parti calde
> D' India vide sopra lo suo stuolo
> Fiamme cadere infino a terra salde ;
> Perch' ei provvide a scalpitar lo suolo
> Con le sue schiere, acciocchè il vapore
> Me' si stingeva mentre ch' era solo.
> (*Inf.* xiv. 31-36.)

This passage has long been a puzzle to the commentators, because in the apocryphal *Epistola Alexandri ad Aristotilem*, from which it was supposed that Dante took his account of the episode, Alexander is described as ordering his soldiers to trample, not the *flames*, but the *snow*, which had fallen heavily after a great storm of wind and fire.

The *Epistola* says :—

> Cadere mox in modum vellerum immensæ cœperunt nives ; quarum aggregatione metuens ne castra cumularentur, calcare militem nivem jubebam, ut quam primum injuria pedum tabesceret.[1]

It was assumed, therefore, that Dante was quoting the *Epistola* from memory, and confused the details of the account there given of the incident. But here again he evidently got his information at second hand from Albertus Magnus,[2] who,

---

[1] Ed. Kuebler (*Bibliotheca Teubneriana*, 1888), p. 208.—A similar account is given in the Latin version of Pseudo-Callisthenes, commonly known as *Historia de Praeliis :* "Ceperunt cadere nives sicut lane majores. Continuo precepit [Alexander] militibus suis ut calcarent eas pedibus, quia timebant ne cresceret ipsa nivis". (See Paul Meyer, *Alexandre le Grand dans la littérature française*, vol. ii. p. 178.)

[2] I have since found that Benvenuto da Imola had come to the same conclusion. His note on this passage, which is very interesting, shows that he was evidently much pleased with his discovery. He says : "Antequam veniam ad literam volo te hic modicum morari, lector ; nam audivi viros intelligentes, magnos Dantistas, qui hic mirantur et dicunt ; vere comparatio ista est pulcerrima, sed non video unde autor habuerit hoc ; quia Quintus Curtius, qui curiose describit gesta Alexandri Magni, nihil de hoc dicit ; et Justinus, qui breviter illa perstringit, etiam nihil dicit. Item Gallicus ille qui describit Alexandreidam metrice,* et alii multi scribentes tam in prosa quam in metro,

---

* Gautier de Lille or de Châtillon (commonly known as Gualtherus de Castellione), fl. *circ.* 1100 ; his *Alexandreis* (in Latin hexameters) is based on the history of Quintus Curtius.

in quoting Alexander's epistle in the *De Meteoris,* makes exactly
the same confusion with regard to the trampling of the flames
as Dante does in the *Inferno.* In the passage in question
Albertus cites the experience of Alexander in India as an
instance of the occurrence of the igneous vapours[1] which he
has just been discussing :—

Admirabilem autem impressionem scribit Alexander ad Aristotilem in
epistola de mirabilibus Indie dicens quemadmodum nivis nubes ignite de aëre
cadebant quas ipse militibus calcare precepit. (*De Meteoris,* Lib. I. tract. iv.
cap. 8.)

III

Convivio II. 15

In the midst of his argument in this chapter as to the points
of resemblance between the Heaven of the Fixed Stars and the
sciences of Physics and Metaphysics, Dante makes a digression
in order to discuss the origin of the Galaxy or Milky Way,
according to the various theories held by the old philosophers
on the subject. The passage is as follows :—

È da sapere che di quella Galassia (cioè quello bianco cerchio, che il volgo
chiama la Via di Santo Jacopo)[2] li filosofi hanno avuto diverse opinioni. Chè
li Pittagorici dissero che 'l sole alcuna fiata errò nella sua via, e, passando per
altre parti non convenienti al suo fervore, arse il luogo per lo quale passò ; e
rimasevi quell' apparenza dell' arsura. E credo che si mossero dalla favola di

nullam mentionem faciunt de hoc ; sed certe, ut dicit philosophus, ad pauca
respicientes facile enunciant. Nam autor noster, licet fecerit istud opus in
somnio, non tamen somniavit ; ideo debes scire quod hanc mirabilem impressionem scribit Alexander ad Aristotelem in quadam epistola, dicens quod in
India nubes ignitae cadebant de aëre ad modum nivis, quas ipse militibus calcare
praecepit ; et huius causam assignat Albertus Magnus, libro i. Metaurorum,
quia terra illa est sub Cancro, ubi calor solis exurit vaporem aquae et elevat
grossum terrestre, et statim exurit antequam elevetur ad aestum, et a frigiditate
loci expellitur et cadit ad modum nivis."

[1] It is significant that Dante uses this same term *vapore* (l. 35) in speaking
of the fiery downpour.

[2] The authority for this statement appears to have been Uguccione da Pisa,
who under the word *Gala* in his *Magnae Derivationes* says : " *Hec galaxias,* vel
-ia, -e, id est lacteus circulus qui vulgo dicitur santi Jacobi " (see below, p. 105).

Fetonte,[1] la quale narra Ovidio nel principio del secondo di *Metamorfoseos*.[2] Altri dissero (siccome fu Anassagora e Democrito) che ciò era lume di sole ripercosso in quella parte. E queste opinioni con ragioni dimostrative riprovarono. Quello che Aristotile [3] si dicesse di ciò, non si può bene sapere, perchè la sua sentenza non si trova cotale nell' una traslazione, come nell' altra.[4] E credo che fosse l' errore de' traslatori ; chè nella Nuova par dicere, che ciò sia uno ragunamento di vapori sotto le stelle di quella parte, che sempre traggono quelli ; e questa non pare avere ragione vera. Nella Vecchia dice, che la Galassia non è altro che moltitudine di stelle fisse in quella parte,[5] tanto picciole che distinguere di quaggiù non le potemo ; ma di loro apparisce quello albore il quale noi chiamiamo Galassia. E puote essere che il cielo in quella parte è più spesso, e però ritiene e ripresenta quello lume ; e questa opinione pare avere, con Aristotile, Avicenna e Tolommeo (ll. 45-77).[6]

The commentators,[7] taking it for granted that Dante derived this account of the various opinions of the old philosophers from

---

[1] *Cf. Inf.* xvii. 107 ; *Purg.* iv. 72 ; xxix. 118-120 ; *Par.* xvii. 3 ; xxxi. 125 ; *Epist.* viii. 4.

[2] *Metam.* ii. 1-324.   [3] In the *De Meteoris*.

[4] The two translations here referred to, and spoken of by Dante as "the Old" and "the New," probably correspond respectively to the Arabic-Latin version (made by Michael Scot), and the Greek-Latin version (made by Thomas Aquinas). The latter, Dante's "New translation," is the so-called *Antiqua translatio*, which is printed in the folio edition of Aquinas' works (Paris, 1649). See a letter by Dr. Moore in the *Academy* for 2nd January, 1892, on the translations of Aristotle used by Dante ; also his *Studies in Dante*, i. 305-318, where the subject is dealt with at some length.

[5] It is evident that Albertus Magnus made use of what Dante calls the "Old translation," for in his own work *De Meteoris* he says : "Nihil aliud autem est galaxia nisi multe stelle parve quasi contigue in illo loco orbis in quibus diffinitur lumen solis ". (Lib. I. tract. ii. cap. 5.)

[6] Ptolemy's opinion, as given in the *Almagest*, is as follows : "Loca vero stellarum fixarum secundum suum ordinem sunt quemadmodum posuimus. Nos autem addemus illi secundum quod sequitur ex ordinibus modum orbis lactei : qui est maiarati (*sic*) secundum plurimum quod est secundum quod consideravimus unamquamque partium ejus. Et studeamus ponere descriptiones divisionis ejus, que nobis imaginate sunt ex eo. Jam enim declarabitur considerantibus consideratione absoluta quod orbis lacteus non est unius descriptionis absolute. Verum est cingulum, cujus color est color lacteus, secundum plurimum quod assimilatur et propter hoc nominatur lacteus. Ipse vero non est equalis creationis neque ordinis, sed est diversus in latitudine, et in colore, et in spissitudine et in loco. Et ipse in quibusdam partibus videtur cingulum duplex." (*Almagesti Dictio octava, caput secundum.*)

[7] Mazzucchelli, for instance, in his *Luoghi degli Autori citati da Dante nel Convito*, after quoting Aristotle's account, says : " Sembra esservi una lacuna in

Aristotle, have been puzzled by the fact that his description of the theories of Anaxagoras and Democritus does not correspond with that given in the Aristotelian *De Meteoris*. Dante's authority, however, was not Aristotle, but Albertus Magnus, in whose treatise *De Meteoris* Anaxagoras and Democritus are credited with precisely the opinions ascribed to them by Dante.

The following is the account given by Albertus of the various theories :—

> *De Galaxia secundum opiniones eorum qui dixerunt Galaxiam esse combustionem solis.* . . . . Fuerunt autem quidam qui dixerunt quod sol aliquando movebatur in loco suo ; et suo lumine et calore combussit orbem in illo loco. . . . Fuit autem, ut puto, hec opinio Pyctagore, qui dixit esse terram stellam et moveri, et celum stare et comburi a sole.
>
> *De opinione eorum qui dixerunt Galaxiam esse reflexionem luminis solis in quibusdam stellis.* Illi autem qui imitabantur Anaxagoram et Democritum dixerunt quod Galaxia est lumen mutuatum a sole quibusdam stellis,[1] et hoc modo dicitur lumen illarum stellarum.
>
> *De Galaxia secundum veritatem.* Nihil aliud autem est Galaxia nisi multe stelle parve quasi contigue in illo loco orbis in quibus diffinitur lumen solis, et ideo videtur circulus albescens,[2] quasi fumus ignis autem qui est juxta orbem et de natura lucidi non lucet. (*De Meteoris*, Lib. I. tract ii. capp. 2, 3, 5.)

Aristotle's own account, as given in the Greek-Latin version (the so-called *Antiqua translatio*, corresponding to Dante's " New translation "), in which the alternative Aristotelian theory mentioned by Dante occurs, is as follows :—

> *De Lacteo Circulo Antiquorum opiniones.* Qualiter autem et propter quam causam sit et quid est Lac, dicamus jam. Prepercurremus autem et de hoc quae ab aliis dicta sunt primo. Vocatorum igitur Pythagoreorum quidam aiunt viam esse hanc ; hi quidem excidentium cujusdam astrorum, secundum dictam sub

questo luogo, perchè si attribuisce ad Anassagora e Democrito, per quanto sembra, la terza opinione riferita da Aristotile, quando questi loro attribuisce la seconda, ascrivendo la terza ad altri Filosofi da lui non nominati. È da osservarsi che anche questa terza opinione differisce dalla recata da Dante, ma di poco, e forse per difetto delle versioni da lui consultate, ch' ei pure sospetta diffettose."

[1] This, as we have pointed out above, is the theory attributed by Dante to Anaxagoras and Democritus.

[2] This is the opinion of Aristotle which Dante says he found in what he calls the " Old translation ". The fact that Albertus Magnus records it is a proof, as we showed above (see note 5, p. 43), that he made use of that particular translation.

Phaëtonte lationem ; hi autem Solem hoc circulo delatum esse aliquando aiunt ; velut igitur exustum esse hunc locum, aut aliquam aliam talem passionem passum esse a latione ipsorum.[1] . . . Anaxagorici autem et Democritici lumen esse Lac aiunt astrorum quorundam.   Solem nam cum sub terra fertur non respicere quaedam astrorum.   Quaecunque igitur aspiciuntur ab ipso, horum quidem non apparere lumen ; prohiberi enim a Solis radiis ; quibuscumque autem obstitit terra, ita ut non aspiciantur a Sole, horum proprium lumen aiúnt esse Lac.[2] . . . Dicunt autem quidam Lac esse refractionem nostri visus ad Solem, sicut et stellam comatam. . . .

 De Lactei Circuli essentia opinio propria.   Nos autem dicamus, cum re-assumpserimus suppositum nobis principium.   Dictum enim est prius quod extremum dicti aëris potentiam habet ignis, ita ut, motu disgregato aëre, segregetur talis consistentia, qualem et comatas stellas esse dicimus.   Tale itaque oportet intelligere fieri, quod in illis, cum non ipsa per se facta fuerit talis excretio, sed sub aliquo astrorum, aut fixorum, aut errantium.   Tunc enim tales videntur cometae, quia assequuntur ipsorum lationem, quemadmodum Solem talis concretio, a qua propter refractionem aream apparere dicimus, cum sic fuerit dispositus aer.   Quod itaque secundum unum astrorum accidit, hoc oportet accipere fieri circa totum coelum, et superiorem lationem omnem.   Rationabile enim est, siquidem unius astri motus incendit, et eum, qui omnium est facere tale aliquid et excitare aërem, et disgregare propter circuli magnitudinem ; et cum his adhuc secundum quem locum creberrima, et plurima, et maxima existunt astra.   Zodiacus igitur propter Solis lationem et planetarum dissolvit talem con-sistentiam, quapropter multi quidem cometarum extra tropicos fiunt.   Amplius autem neque circa Solem, neque circa Lunam fit coma ; citius enim disgregant,

---

[1] Manilius alludes (*Astronom.* i. 727 ff.) to the two opinions of the Pytha-goreans as to the origin of the Galaxy :—

 " An melius manet illa fides, per saecula prisca
  Illac solis equos diversis crinibus isse,
  Atque aliam trivisse viam ; longumque per aevum
  Exustas sedes, incoctaque sidera flammis
  Coeruleam verso speciem mutasse colore,
  Infusumque loco cinerem, mundumque sepultum ?
  Fama etiam antiquis ad nos descendit ab annis
  Phaethontem patrio curru per signa volantem,
  (Dum nova rimatur propius spectacula mundi,
  Et puer in coelo ludit, curruque superbus
  Luxuriat nitido, cupit et majora parente),
  Monstratas liquisse vias, aliamque recentem
  Imposuisse polo ; nec signa insueta tulisse
  Errantes meta flammas, currumque solutum."

[2] The opinion here ascribed to the followers of Anaxagoras and Democritus is quite different from that mentioned by Dante, whose account, on the other hand, agrees with that of Albertus Magnus ; this proves beyond question that Dante's authority in the matter of these different theories was Albertus, not Aristotle (see note 1, p. 44).

quam ut coacta sit talis concretio. Iste autem circulus, in quo Lac apparet aspicientibus, et maximus existens est, et positu situs sic, ut multum tropicos excedat. Adhaec autem locus plenus est astris maximis et fulgidissimis, et adhuc sparsis vocatis (hoc autem est et oculis videre manifestum) ut et propter hoc continue, et semper haec omnis aggregetur concretio. Signum autem est. Etenim ipsius circuli amplius lumen est in altero semicirculo habente duplatum ; in hoc enim plura et crebriora sunt astra, quam in altero, tanquam non propter alteram aliquam causam fiat lustratio, quam propter astrorum lationem. Si enim et in hoc circulo fit, in quo plurima ponuntur astrorum, et ipsius circuli in eo quod magis videtur spissum esse,[1] et magnitudine et multitudine astrorum, hanc parest existimare convenientissimam causam esse passionis. (*De Meteoris*, Lib. I. summa ii. capp. 5, 6.)

Averroës, in his commentary, makes an attempt to get at Aristotle's actual opinion with regard to the origin of the Galaxy ; but, as will be seen, he, like Dante, found it difficult to come to a decision, owing apparently to the same cause, *viz.*, that the accounts differed in the different versions. The following is his comment :—

Dicamus igitur quod Galasia secundum hunc modum est, quem nunc dicam. Jam igitur declaratum est quod aër propinquus corporibus coelestibus est inflammatus, ignitus, et apparent in loco, in quo videtur Galasia in coelo stellato,[2] stellae multae magnae et parvae lucidae et propinquae lapideatae. . . . Et cum hae duae propositiones verificatae sunt nobis, possumus ex eis concludere duas conclusiones. Una earum est, quod Galasia sit ex reflexione luminum harum stellarum in aëre inflammato existente in hoc loco ; et secundum hoc oportet, si ipsa sit apparentia, ut sit lumen agens apparentiam, firmum et aeternum et speculum semper permanens. . . . Conclusio autem secunda, quae apparet primo aspectu sequi ex hoc dicto, est quod Galasia est aër accensus, ignitus, sicut est dispositio in cometis ; et secundum hoc oportet si esset ita, ut sit agens firmum illic, seu permanens, huic igni proprium semper, et huic loco, hoc autem est multitudo stellarum existentium in illa parte coeli. Alexander [3] autem credidit de Galasia, et putavit quod haec est opinio Aristotelis ; sed id, quod videtur secun-

[1] It is to this passage, apparently, that Dante alludes in the concluding sentence of his account. Aristotle's argument, at any rate, in the translation, is somewhat involved, but the general idea seems to be that attributed to him by Dante (see note 2, p. 44).

[2] Cf. *Convivio*, ii. 15, *ad init.*

[3] *i.e.*, Alexander Aphrodisiensis, the most celebrated of the Greek commentators on Aristotle, commonly known as ὁ ἐξηγητής, just as Averroës himself was known *par excellence* as "Commentator" (*cf. Inf.* iv. 144 ; *Conv.* iv. 13, l. 68). Alexander of Aphrodisias flourished at the beginning of the third century A.D.

dum majorem partem verborum Aristotelis in traductione,[1] quae pervenit ad nos, est sermo primus. Ex quibusdam autem apparet primo aspectu quod est ut decit Alexander.

IV

Convivio IV. 23

In speaking of the " arch of human life," Dante says (towards the end of this chapter) that the latter is divided into four ages, to which are appropriated the various "qualities" inherent in our composition :—

Veramente questo Arco non pur per mezzo si distingue dalle scritture ; ma secondo li quattro combinatori delle contrarie qualitadi che sono nella nostra composizione[2] (alle quali pare essere appropriata, dico a ciascuna, una parte della nostra etade) in quattro parti si divide, e chiamansi quattro etadi. La prima è *Adolescenza*, che s' appropria al *caldo* e all' *umido ;* la seconda si è *Gioventute*, che s' appropria al *caldo* e al *secco ;* la terza si è *Senettute*, che s' appropria al *freddo* e al *secco ;* la quarta si è *Senio*, che s' appropria al *freddo* e all' *umido*, secondochè nel quarto della *Meteora* scrive Alberto (ll. 111-126).

[1] It is evident that from a very early date there were important variations in the text of the *De Meteoris*. In fact there seem to have been two distinct versions of the Greek text, as appears from the circumstance that several old writers (*e.g.*, Seneca in his *Quaestiones Naturales*) quote passages which do not exist in the work as we know it (see Ideler, *Aristotelis Meteorologica*, vol. i. p. 12). Jourdain, in his *Recherches critiques sur l'âge des traductions latines d'Aristote* (chap. iv. § 5 : *Livre des Météores*), says : " Je trouve . . . deux espèces de versions de cet ouvrage, l'une faite de l'arabe, l'autre du grec. La première, à laquelle ont concouru trois traducteurs, Gérard de Crémone, Henri et Aurélius, présente des particularités remarquables. Les trois premiers livres de Gérard sont traduits de l'arabe . . . Le quatrième livre, traduit par Henri . . . est évidemment traduit du grec . . . Il se termine par trois chapitres traduits par Aurélius, qui ne se trouvent pas dans le grec, sont dérivés de l'arabe et paraissent être un fragment du livre des Minéraux.* . . . La version grecque est facile à reconnaître au mode d'expression, aux termes grecs qu'elle présente. On la trouve imprimée dans l'édition de plusieurs traités d'Aristote, publiée en 1483 à Venise." What Jourdain here says as to the composite nature of the so-called Arabic-Latin translation of the *De Meteoris* is based upon the evidence of the MSS., one of which concludes with these words : " Completus est liber Metheorum, cujus tres libros transtulit magister Gerardus de arabico in latinum : quartum transtulit Henricus de greco in latinum : tria vero ultima Avicennae capitula transtulit Aurelius de arabico in latinum ".

[2] *Cf. Par.* vii. 124-5.

* According to the *Explicit* of the MS. quoted below, these three chapters were translated from Avicenna.

Here again Dante has greatly mystified the commentators [1] on account of his reference to the *De Meteoris* of Albertus Magnus as his authority, since in that work, though Albertus discourses generally about humours, there is nothing corresponding to what Dante has attributed to him. The fact is that Dante's matter is borrowed, not from the *De Meteoris* of Albertus Magnus, but from another treatise of his, *viz.*, the *De Juventute et Senectute.* The following is the passage of that work which Dante evidently made use of:—

Etas autem in omnibus etate participantibus in quatuor etates dividitur, scilicet in etatem congruentem tam substantiam quam virtutem; et in etatem standi tam in substantia quam in virtute; et in etatem diminuendi virtutem sine diminutione substantie; et in etatem minuentem tam substantiam quam virtutem.   He autem in homine magis note sunt, et ideo in homine nomina specialia receperunt.   Quarum prima vocata est puerilis; secunda autem juventus sive virilis (rectius autem vocatur virilis quam juventus, quia juventus ad pueritiam videtur pertinere); tertia vero vocata est senectus; et quarta et ultima senium sive etas decrepita. Dicit autem Ptolemæus has etatum differentias sumi ad lune circulum, eo quod luna maxime principatum habeat in corporibus terrenorum propter duas causas vel tres. Due siquidem principales cause sunt. Una quidem vicinitas; ea enim que non distant multum efficacius movent. Et alia causa est que et principalis est; quia cum sit infima congregate sunt in ea omnes virtutes moventium superiorum,[2] ideo mare et omne humidum movet ex seipsa.[3]   Ex virtute autem luminis quod mutuat

[1] Mazzucchelli (*op. cit.*), after quoting Albertus *De Meteoris*, iv. 5, 13, says: " Non si è trovato altro in tutto il citato libro d' Alberto Magno, che più si accosti a quanto dice Dante ".

[2] *Cf. Par.* ii. 112-123.

[3] Scartazzini in the German edition of his Prolegomeni, in discussing the question as to the authenticity of the *Quaestio de Aqua et Terra*, mentions among other objections to its acceptance as Dante's work, the fact that it reveals an amount of scientific knowledge incompatible with the knowledge of Dante's day. Among " the truths of cosmology hitherto undreamt of " which the author of the *Quaestio* must have been acquainted with, but which Scartazzini assumes Dante to have been ignorant of, he includes the theory that the moon is the main cause of ebb and flow. Not only, however, does Dante himself expressly refer in the *Paradiso* (xvi. 82-3) to the connection between the moon and the tides, but it is evident from the above passage of Albertus that the influence of the moon upon the sea was well-known long before the time of Dante. As a matter of fact it is discussed by Pliny (ii. 97), in a passage which is quoted by Vincent of Beauvais in the *Speculum Naturale* (v. 18) : " Aestus maris accedere et reciprocare mirum est, verum causa est in sole et luna. Bis inter duos exortus lunae affluunt, bisque remeant vicenis quatermisque semper horis."   It was

a sole efficitur quasi sol secundus breviter operationes solis explicans; et ideo movet calores inferiorum. Dico autem breviter explicans operationes solis, quia quod sol facit in anno secundum variationem luminis et caloris, luna facit in mense, ut dicit Aristoteles in libro suo de animalibus. Tertiam autem Aristoteles videtur adjungere dicens quod luna terrestris nature sit, et ideo obscuritatem, ut inquit, aliquam retinet, etiam postquam illuminatur a sole. Propter igitur connaturalitatem terrenam magis variat, ut dicit, quam aliquod corporum aliorum que sunt in celo. Differentia autem circulationis ejus est differentia etatum. Primo enim cum accenditur est *calida* et *humida* per effectum sicut *prima etas;* et currit hec usque quo efficitur dimidia, et talis est *prima etas.* Et deinde calido paulatim extrahente humidum efficitur *calida* et *sicca* sicut est *etas secunda.* Tertio autem cum humido egrediente deficit calidum, eo quod humor erat proprium subjectum caloris; et talis est *etas tertia,* scilicet *frigida* et *sicca,* et talis luna cadens a plenitudine usque ad hoc quod efficitur dimidia secundo. Et tunc frigiditate invalescente inducitur humidum extraneum non nutriens vel augens sed humectans extrinsecum quod est humidum flegmaticum; et talis est *etas ultima* . . . *Senium* sive etas decrepita est que est *frigida* et *humida.* (Tract. i. cap. 2.)

V

Convivio II. 3

In this chapter Dante discusses the number and order of the several heavens, and expounds the opinions of Aristotle and Ptolemy on the subject:—

Dico adunque, che del numero de' Cieli e del sito diversamente è sentito da molti, avvegnachè la verità all' ultimo sia trovata. Aristotile credette, seguitando solamente l' antica grossezza degli astrologi, che fossero pure otto cieli, delli quali lo estremo, e che contenesse tutto, fosse quello dove le stelle fisse sono, cioè la spera ottava[1]; e che di fuori da esso non fosse altro alcuno. Ancora credette che il cielo del Sole fosse immediato con quello della Luna, cioè secondo a noi[2] . . .

Tolommeo poi, accorgendosi che l' ottava spera si muovea per più movimenti, veggendo il cerchio suo partire dal diritto cerchio, che volge tutto da Oriente in Occidente, costretto da' principii di filosofia, che di necessità vuole

familiar, too, in later times to Macrobius (*circ.* 430), and Martianus Capella (*circ.* 470), both of whom are quoted in this connection by Bartholomaeus Anglicus (*circ.* 1260), in his *De Proprietatibus Rerum* (viii. 29).

[1] Compare what Averroës says in his comment on Aristotle's *De Coelo,* II. summa iii. cap. 2, Q. 6: "Hoc quod dixit Aristoteles, quod octavus orbis est propinquus primo orbi, ita invenimus scriptum, et opinio Antiquorum est, quod orbis octavus seu stellatus est primus orbis."

[2] *Cf.* Averroës, *Comm. in De Coelo,* II. summa iii. cap. 2, Q. 4: "Secundum opinionem Aristotelis Sol est sub Mercurio, et Venere, et non supra."

un Primo Mobile semplicissimo, pose un altro cielo essere fuori dello Stellato, il
quale facesse quella rivoluzione da Oriente in Occidente.[1] La quale dico che si
compie quasi in ventiquattro ore . . . Sicchè, secondo lui e secondo quello che
si tiene in Astrologia e in Filosofia (poichè quelli movimenti furono veduti), sono
nove li cieli mobili: lo sito de' quali è manifesto e determinato, secondo che per
arte Prospettiva, Arismetrica e Geometrica sensibilmente e ragionevolmente è
veduto, e per altre sperienze sensibili; siccome nello eclissi del Sole appare
sensibilmente la Luna essere sotto il Sole; e siccome per testimonianza d' Aristotile, che vide cogli occhi (secondochè dice nel secondo *di Cielo e Mondo*[2]) la
Luna, essendo mezza, entrare sotto a Marte dalla parte non lucente, e Marte
stare celato tanto che rapparve dall' altra lucente della Luna, ch' era verso
occidente (ll. 16-65).

It is evident that when the above was written Dante had
just been reading the *De Coelo* of Aristotle with the commentary
of Averroës,[3] and also the treatise of the same name by Albertus
Magnus, though he makes no reference either to Albertus or to
Averroës.

What Albertus says on the subject in question is as follows :—

Omnes antiqui usque ad tempora Ptolomei consentisse videntur quod spere
fuerunt octo; quarum superior sit spera stellarum fixarum; et secunda Saturni;
et tertia Jovis; et quarta Martis; quinta autem Veneris; et sexta Mercurii; et
septima Solis; et octava Lune. His autem et ipse Aristoteles videtur assentire
frequenter nominans speram stellarum fixarum speram supremam et ultimam
secundum elongationem ad nos acceptam; quos etiam sequens Alfraganus[4]
speras celorum octo esse dicit. Et forte isti visibiles tamen speras numeraverunt
eo quod spera non dinoscitur per sensum nisi per stelle motum ; motus autem
stellarum octo diversitates ostendit ad visum. Veniens autem post hos Alpetraus[5]

---

[1] *Cf.* Averroës, *Comm. in De Coelo*, II. summa iii. cap. 2, Q. 6 : " Ptholo-
maeus tamen posuit nonum ; quia dicebat quod ipse invenit in stellis fixis
motum tardum secundum ordinem signorum ".

[2] " Vidimus Lunam intrasse secundum medietatem sub stella Martis, et
eclipsare Martem ex parte nigredinis Lunae ; deinde apparuit et exivit ex parte
albedinis Lunae et luminis ejus." (Aristotle, *De Coelo*, II. summa iii. cap. 2,
Q. 5.)

[3] See notes 1 and 2, p. 49 ; and note 1 above.

[4] " Dico igitur orbes qui stellarum omnes motus complectantur, numero esse
octo ; quorum quidem septem conveniunt stellis septem errantibus ; octavus verò,
qui supremus, universis stellis fixis ; idem cum orbe signifero." (Alfraganus,
Elementa Astronomica, cap. xii. ed. Golius, 1669.)

[5] Alpetraus (or Alpetragius) is the Arabian philosopher mentioned by Dante
in the *Convivio* (iii. 2, l. 37), where Fraticelli and Giuliani, following Scolari, read
Alfarabio instead of *Alpetragio*, which is the MSS. reading. Scolari coolly says :
" L' *Alpetragio*, che si legge in tutti i testi, non può essere altro che storpiatura

Abnisac in astrologia nova quam induxit per rationes necessarias probat plures esse speras quam . viii., quarum rationum fortiores sunt iste : quia ab uno motore primo simplici in eo quod movetur ab ipso non est nisi motus unus; igitur a destructione consequentis, si in aliquo mobili non est motus tamen unus et simplex non est illud mobile primum a primo motus tamen unus et simplex non est illud mobile primum a primo motore ; sunt autem deprehensi tres motus in spera stellarum fixarum, quorum unus est motus diurnus ab Oriente in Occidentem super polos mundi completus in . xxiv. horis. Et alter est motus stellarum fixarum ab Occidente in Orientem in omnibus centum annis per unum gradum, completus in omnibus . xxxvi. milibus annis.[1] Tertius autem motus est accessionis et recessionis qui fit in omnibus octoginta annis per gradum unum secundum Albertum. . . . Ergo spera stellarum fixarum non est mobile primum. Et hec ratio est fortissima apud quemlibet bene scientem philosophiam ; addit et alias philosophicas que non sunt tante fortitudinis, sicut quod in genere corporum non ponit primum esse diversum et multiforme. Nos autem speram stellarum fixarum videmus esse diversam valde et multiformem, igitur non est prima. Adhuc autem ante illud quod participat primi motoris bonitatem multis motibus est illud quod participat motu uno in genere corporum, sicut innuit Aristoteles in secundo libro suo de celo et mundo. Jam autem ostensum est multorum motuum esse speram stellarum fixarum. Fretus igitur his rationibus Alpetraus Abnisac pronunciat . ix. esse speras ; unam quidem uniformem cujus lumen visui non subjicitur propter sui claritatem et simplicitatem quam dicit esse mobilem a primo motore secundum motum diurnum ; et alias octo que superius sunt enumerate addens ad confirmationem dicti sui simplicissimum in genere corporum debere ordinari ad movens primum eo quod causa prima movet causatum primum, et simplex movet illud quod est simplex, et unicum movens unicum primum influit motum. . . . Ptolemei sententia autem secundum quod eum possum intelligere est quod . x. sunt orbes celorum, et ratio sua philosophica et non mathematica est.[2] Supponit enim id quod probatum est in secundo philosophie prime Aristotelis, quod scilicet omne quod est in multis per rationem unam existens in illis est in aliquo uno priore illis quod est causa omnium illorum, sicut omne calidum causatur a calore ignis. Duo autem

d' amanuense ".(!) In the Oxford Dante (*Tutte le Opere di Dante Alighieri, nuovamenta rivedute nel testo dal* Dr. E. Moore, *con Indice dei Nomi Propri e delle Cose Notabili compilato da* Paget Toynbee. Oxford, 1894) Dr. Moore has rightly restored the reading *Alpetragio*. Alpetragius wrote a work on astronomy which was translated into Latin under the title *De motibus coelorum*.

[1] *Cf. Convivio*, ii. 6, ll. 140-7 : "Tutto quel cielo [di Venere] si muove, seguendo il movimento della stellata spera, da Occidente in Oriente, in cento anni uno grado. . . . Ancora si muove tutto questo cielo . . . da Oriente in Occidente, ogni dì naturale una fiata." These data are taken from the *Elementa Astronomica* of Alfraganus ; see the article on "Dante's Obligations to Alfraganus" (pp. 56 ff.).

[2] This is evidently the origin of Dante's statement that Ptolemy assumed the existence of a ninth heaven on philosophical grounds, "costretto da' principii di filosofia ".

motus simplices inveniuntur in omnibus inferioribus orbibus secundum unam
rationem existentis in omnibus eis ; quorum unus est super polos mundi et super
circulos equidistantes equinoctiali et est diurnus ; alter autem est motus obliquus
circuli signorum qui est super polos orbis signorum, quo moventur omnes octo
orbes supra enumerati. Patet igitur quod uterque eorum sit in aliquo orbe
superiori qui causet motus istos in omnibus orbibus inferioribus, et sic ante
orbem stellarum oportet esse duos orbes. (*De Celo et Mundo*, Lib. II. tract. iii.
cap. 11.)

VI

Convivio III. 7

In this passage (ll. 26-43) Dante refers to the *De Intellectu*
of Albertus Magnus for his opinion as to the distribution of the
light of the sun :—

Dice Alberto in quello libro che fa *dello Intelletto*, che certi corpi, per molta
chiarità di diafano avere in sè mista, tosto che 'l sole gli vede, diventano tanto
luminosi, che per multiplicamento di luce in quelli . . .[1] è 'l loro aspetto, e
rendono agli altri di sè grande splendore, siccome è l' oro e alcuna pietra.
Certi sono che, per essere del tutto diafani, non solamente ricevono la luce, ma
quella non impediscono, anzi rendono lei dal loro colore colorata nell' altre cose.[2]
E certi sono tanto vincenti nella purità del diafano, che diventano sì raggianti,
che vincono l' armonia dell' occhio, e non si lasciano vedere senza fatica del viso,
siccome sono gli specchi.

[1] The *editio princeps* (1490), followed by all three sixteenth century editions
(1521, 1529, 1531), the Florence edition of 1723, and the Venice edition of 1758,
marks no *lacuna* in this passage, which is manifestly corrupt as it stands. Dr.
Moore, following nine MSS. collated by him, prints the passage without a
lacuna in the Oxford Dante, and suggests as an emendation—"in quelli e lo
loro aspetto, ei rendono, etc.". The Milanese editors (1827), followed by Peder-
zini and Fraticelli, read "in quelli, appena discernibile è lo loro aspetto, e
rendono, etc.," justifying their insertion of "appena discernibile" by a reference
to the text of Albertus: "Quaedam autem sunt spargentia tantum luminis et
diaphani, quod vix discerni possunt". As an alternative they propose to read
"che par multiplicamento di luce lo loro aspetto". None of these emendations
is wholly satisfactory, and it seems best consequently to print the passage with
a *lacuna* as in the text.

[2] Albertus, as will be seen below, is more precise, specifying especially
coloured glass. It is rather curious that Dante should have omitted this
particular comparison, as he is fond of similes connected with glass (*cf. Inf.*
xxxiv. 12 ; *Par.* ii. 88-90 ; iii. 10-12 ; xx. 79-80 ; xxix. 25-26). He certainly
had some knowledge of coloured glass, for he refers in the *Paradiso* (xx. 80) to
what is known as "coated" glass (*i.e.*, glass with a film of colour applied on
one side) as distinguished from "pot-metal" (*i.e.*, glass coloured throughout).

The passage of Albertus which he had in mind here occurs in the first book of the *De Intellectu* :—

Per mixtionem perspicui clari in corporibus terminatis videmus quosdam colores in luminis adventu effici scintillantes et spargentes lumen ad illuminationem aliorum ; et aliquando si vere in toto sit perspicuum corpus coloratum, si lumen superveniat, illi colores colorant alia corpora sibi apposita, sicut videmus in vitro colorato, per quod lumen veniens secum trahit colorem vitri, et ponit eum super corpus, cui per vitrum incidit lumen. Quaedam autem sunt ita vincentia in puritate diaphani, quod adeo radiantia efficiuntur, quod vincunt harmoniam oculi,[1] et videri sine magna difficultate non possunt. Quaedam autem sunt spargentia tantum luminis et diaphani, quod vix discerni possunt visu propter parvitatem suae compositionis ex perspicuo, cujus proprius actus est lumen. (I. iii. 2.)

VII

Convivio III. 9

In this passage (ll. 52-105) Dante discusses the nature of vision or eyesight, and refers to Aristotle's *De Sensu et Sensibili* (which he quotes as " il libro di Senso e Sensato "). His actual authority, however, appears to have been the following passage from the *De Sensu et Sensato* of Albertus Magnus, in which the various theories, including that of Aristotle, are discussed :—

Quatuor fuerunt antiquorum opiniones de visu : quarum tres in libro *De Sensu et Sensato*[2] tangit Aristoteles. Quarta autem fuit sua propria opinio quam tradidit tam in libro *De Sensu et Sensato* quam etiam in libro *De Anima*.[3] Hae autem quatuor opiniones sic erant divisae : quod due asserebant quod videmus extramittentes radios et nihil omnino suscipientes : et nihil extramittentes. Sed duarum opinionum quae nos extramittentes videre voluerunt : una fuit Empedoclis antiquissima ; altera Platonis quae scribitur in *Timaeo*,[4] et explanatur a Calcidio. Et opinio quidem Empedoclis fuit haec : quod dixit visum esse ignis naturae a quo continue emittitur lumen sufficiens ad omnium visibilium discretionem. Cum autem ab omni luminoso egrediatur lumen ad modum pyramidis formatum, dicebat quod ab oculis egrediuntur tot pyramides quot visibilia videntur. . . . Plato autem secundum quod in *Timaeo* scribitur et Calcidius ex-

---

[1] It will be noted that Dante has borrowed this phrase verbatim from Albertus.

[2] Note that this is the title by which Dante also refers to Aristotle's *De Sensu et Sensibili*—the passage in question occurs in the second chapter of that treatise.

[3] Dante also refers to this treatise in the same connection.

[4] Dante, though he does not name the *Timaeus* here, gives prominence to Plato's opinion as expressed in that work.

planat, convenit cum Empedocle in hoc quod dixit igneum esse visum, et visionem fieri per emissionem radiorum ; sed dixit non esse lumen oculi sufficiens ad omnium pyramidum impletionem quae ad omnia visibilia diriguntur et producuntur. Sed emitti[1] dixit unum simplicem radium ex lumine oculi et illum conjungi lumini obvianti sibi in aëre et misceri ; et tunc auctum dixit posse disgregari in figuram pyramidalem, et tunc per adjutorium luminis exterioris ad totum hemisperium contuendum posse sufficere : et hanc causam dixit esse quare non videmus in tenebris ; quia radius egrediens ab oculo extinguitur et deficit, quoniam non invenit alium radium sui generis qui mixtus sibi adjuvet eum ad perficiendum visum . . . Hi ambo [scilicet Empedocles et Plato] dixerunt quod egreditur lumen a spiritu lucido visivo qui est in anteriori parte cerebri . . .[2] Democriti quidem opinio fuit quod forma visibilis esset decursus quidam rei visibilis ad oculum ita quod quoddam materiale resolveretur a re visa et veniret ad oculum et pingeretur in oculo. . . . Aristoteles autem omnes has opiniones destruit[3] dicens visibile scilicet esse spirituale et intentionale prius effici in aëre, post in oculo, et moveri speciem rei visae ad interius oculi ubi in humido crystallino est vis visiva[4] : et ulterius procedere per continuitatem nervi optici in spiritu deductam tandem speciem usque ad locum primi sensitivi, quod est spiritus communis sensus, sicut patet in libro De Anima." (Tract. i. cap. 5.)

[1] Compare what Dante says : " Veramente Plato e altri filosofi dissero che 'l nostro vedere non era perchè il visibile venisse all' occhio, ma perchè la virtù visiva andava fuori al visibile " (ll. 99-103). The passage in the Timaeus in the translation of Chalcidius (in which form alone it was accessible to Dante) runs as follows : " Intimum siquidem nostri corporis ignem, utpote germanum ignis pellucidi, serem, et defaecati liquoris, per oculos fluere, ac demanare, voluerunt : ut per laeves, congestosque, et tanquam firmiore soliditate pandos orbes luminum, quorum tamen esset angusta medietas subtilior, serenus ignis per eandem efflueret medietatem. Itaque cum diurnum jubar se applicat visus fusioni, tunc nimirum incurrentia semet invicem duo similia in unius corporis speciem cohaerent : quo concurrunt oculorum acies emicantes, quoque effluentis intimae fusionis acies contigüae imaginis occursu repercutitur." (See also Moore, Studies in Dante, i. 161-2.)

[2] Compare Dante : " Lo spirito visivo, che si continua dalla pupilla alla parte del cerebro dinanzi . . . " (ll. 83-5).

[3] Cf. Dante : " Questa opinione è riprovata per falsa dal Filosofo in quello di Senso e Sensato " (ll. 103-5).

[4] Cf. Dante : " Queste cose visibili, sì le proprie, come le comuni, in quanto sono visibili, vengono dentro all' occhio—non dico le cose, ma le forme loro— per lo mezzo diafano, non realmente, ma intenzionalmente. . . . E nell' acqua ch' è nella pupilla dell' occhio, questo discorso, che fa la forma visibile per lo mezzo suo, si compie . . . " (ll. 66-74).

VIII

Quaestio de Aqua et Terra,[1] § 18

Dante here quotes Averroës' *De Substantia Orbis* for the opinion that all potential forms of matter are actually existent in the mind of the Creator : " Omnes formae, quae sunt in potentia materiae idealiter, sunt in actu in motore coeli, ut dicit commentator [2] in *De Substantia Orbis* " (ll. 36-39).

In spite of the fact that Dante quotes this opinion as being that of Averroës, his actual authority for it appears to have been not the *De Substantia Orbis* of the Arabian philosopher, but the *De Natura et Origine Animae* of Albertus Magnus, who attributes it to Plato. Albertus says :—

Dixit Plato formas omnes ideales esse in mente divina antequam prodirent in corpora. Sicut formae ideales artificialium sunt in mente artificis antequam in materias artium traducantur. (ii. 7.)

[1] The genuineness of this treatise has been much disputed, most Dantists regarding it as a forgery. The arguments in favour of its authenticity are ably stated by Dr. Moore (*Studies in Dante*, ii. 303-74), whose detailed examination and impartial handling of the whole question make it difficult not to accept his conclusion that the treatise is a genuine work of Dante, though corrupt in its present form.

[2] On this title as applied to Averroës, see above, p. 46, note 3.

DANTE'S OBLIGATIONS TO THE *ELEMENTA ASTRONOMICA* OF ALFRAGANUS [1]

(CHIEFLY IN THE *VITA NUOVA* AND *CONVIVIO*) [2]

OUR information with regard to the Arabian astronomer, Alfraganus,[3] is scanty. He was born, apparently, at Fergana in Sogdiana (now Samarcand), whence he derived the name by which he is generally known ; and flourished at the beginning of the ninth century, during the Caliphate of Ma'mún, who died in 833.

His work on the elements of astronomy, which consists of thirty chapters, is based upon the principles of Ptolemy, whom he frequently quotes. It was translated from Arabic into Latin, about the year 1242 (as is supposed), by Johannes Hispalensis under the title of *Alfragani Elementa Astronomica* [4]. This

---

[1] Reprinted, with additions, from *Romania*, xxiv. 413-32.

[2] *Convivio*, not *Convito*, as most modern editors write, appears to have been the original title of Dante's treatise. According to Witte (*Dante Forschungen*, ii. 574-80), the form *Convivio* occurs in twenty-six out of about thirty known MSS. (including the six which belong to the fourteenth century) ; it also occurs in the first four printed editions (1490, 1521, 1529, 1531). The form *Convito* appeared for the first time in the Florentine edition of 1723, and has been adopted in nearly every subsequent edition.

[3] Ahmad ibn Muhammad ibn Kathir, *Al-Farghani*. Besides his work on Astronomy he appears to have written treatises on Sundials and on the Astrolabe (see the extract from the commentary of Golius below, p. 60).

[4] The popularity of this work in the Middle Ages is attested by the number of MSS. still in existence. In Oxford alone (in the Bodleian and various College Libraries) there are no less than twenty. In the British Museum, singularly enough, there is only one MS. (*Arundel* 377) ; and in the Cambridge University Library only three. On Johannes Hispalensis see A. Jourdain, *Recherches sur les traductions latines d'Aristote*, pp. 115-8. A still earlier Latin version was made in the twelfth century by Gerard of Cremona (died 1187), who also translated from Arabic into Latin the *Almagest* of Ptolemy (see Jourdain, *op. cit.*, pp. 121-3).

version is the one which was in common use during the Middle Ages.

There are five printed editions of Alfraganus' work, all of which are very rare.   As these editions are little known, and we shall have frequent occasion to refer to them in the course of this article, it will be convenient to give some account of them in the first place.

The earliest (*A*) was printed at Ferrara in 1493.   It reproduces the version of Johannes Hispalensis; but it is evident that either a faulty MS. was made use of, or the printer was unusually careless, for it abounds in errors, and there are several instances where words and even sentences have been omitted. The title of this edition is as follows :—

Brevis ac perutilis compilatio Alfra | gani astronomorum peritissimi totum id | continens quod ad rudimenta astro | nomica est opportunum.

The colophon runs :—

Explicit Alfraganus | Opus preclarissimum consumatissimumque introductorium | in astronomiam explicit quod peritissimus Astrono | morum Alfraganus edidit.   Et heremitarum hujus tem | poris decus : ac celeberrimus physicus : mathemati | cusque probatissimus mira diligentia ac magno cum la | bore emendavit.   Impressum Ferrarie arte et impensa | Andree galli viri impressorie artis peritissimi.   Anno | incarnationis verbi. 1493. die vero tercia septembris.

The second (*B*) was printed at Nuremberg in 1537.   Save for the addition of a preface by Melanchthon, it is practically a reprint of the Ferrara edition (*A*), the title of which is copied *verbatim*.   It has a brief colophon :—

Explicit Alfraganus | Norimbergae apud Ioh. Petrieum, anno sa | lutis M.D.XXXVII.

The third edition (*C*) was printed at Paris in 1546.   It is entitled :—

Alfragani | Astronomorum Pe | ritissimi̇ compendium, id omne quod ad | Astronomica rudimenta spectat comple | ctens, Ioanne Hispalensi interprete, | Nunc primùm pervetusto exemplari con | sulto, multis locis castigatus redditum | . . . Parisiis. . . . M.D.XLVI.

The volume concludes with a simple "Explicit Alfraganus".

This edition is the first in which the name of Johannes Hispalensis is explicitly mentioned as the author of the Latin version contained in it. In spite of its claim to be more correct than its predecessors, it is by no means free from inaccuracies ; but it is certainly superior to (A) and (B) (see below, note 4, p. 69).

The fourth edition (D) was printed at Frankfort in 1590. It contains an independent Latin version by J. Christmann, based upon that of Johannes Hispalensis, but corrected by means of the Hebrew version of J. Antoli, who, in his turn, corrected his translation from an Arabic MS.[1]

The title of this edition is as follows :—

> Muhamedis | Alfragani | Arabis Chronolo | gica et Astronomica | Elementa, e Palatinae | bibliothecae veteribus libris versa, | expleta, et scholiis expolita. | Additus est Commentarius, | etc. Autore M. Iacopo Christmanno . . . Francofurdi . . . MDXC.

The colophon of Christmann's edition has a special interest, for it gives an alternative title to Alfraganus' treatise, and thus affords the clue to the identification of the *Elementa Astronomica* of the Arabian astronomer with the *Libro dell' Aggregazione delle Stelle* mentioned by Dante in the *Convivio* (ii. 6, l. 134), an identification which had escaped the commentators. This colophon runs as follows :—

> Explicit Alfraganus de aggregatione scientiae | stellarum, felicibus astris.

This alternative title does not seem to have been in general use. It occurs in only three out of twenty MSS. at Oxford (*viz.*, Bibl. Bodl. *Savile* 16 ; *Digby* 214 ; *Laud* 644). There is no appearance of it in the single MS. at the British Museum, nor in the three at Cambridge.[2] Christmann mentions its occur-

---

[1] Christmann prints Antoli's preface, in which he says : " Liber iste vocatur Alfraganus de nomine authoris sui, qui eum succinctè depromsit ex Almagesto, sphaerarum motuumque coelestium doctrinam, juxta veterum traditionem explicante. Ego verò Iacobus filius Antoli transtuli ipsum [Hebraicè] è libro cujusdam Christiani, eundemque correxi e codice Arabico ". Of Antoli himself Christmann says : " Fuit Arabicae et Latinae linguae peritissimus, et rerum astronomicarum scientissimus : nam ex codice Arabico Alfragani se versionem vulgatam [*sc.* Johannis Hispalensis] correxisse testatur. . . . Debemus illi multorum numerorum emendationem ".

[2] Jourdain (*Recherches*, etc., p. 123) mentions a MS. of Alfraganus in the Bibliothèque Nationale (lat. 7,400) which has the identical title employed by Dante, *viz.*, *Liber de Aggregationibus stellarum*. For the information as regards

rence in a MS. seen by him in the Palatine Library—apparently, to judge by his title-page, the same he made use of in his edition.   If this be the case, the occurrence of this title in the colophon of the Frankfort edition is readily accounted for.   In a note on the words "Liber iste vocatur Alfraganus," Christmann says :—

Haec verba sunt interpretis Hebraei, R. Iacobi Antolii: quibus commemorat opusculi hujus autorem esse Alfraganum, qui id ex Ptolemęi Almagesto compendiose depromtum, in gratiam studiosorum astronomiae conscripserit. Verisimile mihi videtur, ipsum a patria sua Fragana cognominatum fuisse Alfraganum: siquidem in Latina versione bibliothecae Palatinae tribuitur illi nomen proprium Ametus, hoc est Ahmed sive Muhamed[1]: ubi ita scribitur, *Incipit liber de aggregationibus scientiae stellarum et principiis coelestium, quem Ametus filius Ameti dictus Alfraganus compilavit* 30 *capitulis.*[2]

In another place he adds :—

Passim citat Alfraganus μεγάλην σύνταξιν Ptolemaei, quam vocant Almagestum, hoc est μέγιστον . . . Arabicè hanc isagogen scripsit, quam Iohannes Hispalensis circa annum Christi 1142[3] in Latinam linguam convertit: quae versio vulgata quidem est, sed multis in locis corrupta et mutila. Longè melior et perfectior, incerti tamen authoris, exstat in bibliotheca Palatina, cujus paulò ante mentionem feci: quae translationi Hebraeae magna ex parte respondet. Ea descripta est a Friderico monacho Ratisponensi . . . et absoluta anno Domini 1447.

The fifth edition (*E*) was printed at Amsterdam in 1669.   It contains the Arabic text, with a Latin translation and notes by Jacobus Golius.   The commentary extends as far as the ninth chapter only, as Golius died before the completion of his work, which was published posthumously.

The title-page of this edition reads as follows :—

the Oxford and Cambridge MSS. of Alfraganus I am indebted respectively to Mr. E. W. B. Nicholson, Bodley's Librarian at Oxford, and to Mr. F. Jenkinson, Librarian of the Cambridge University Library.

[1] See the Arabic name of Alfraganus given on p. 56, note 3.

[2] This MS. evidently belongs to the same family as the three Oxford MSS. referred to above as containing the alternative title of the treatise of Alfraganus. In *Digby* 214 and *Laud* 644 the *incipit* runs : " Incipit Liber de aggregationibus sciencie stellarum et principiis celestium motuum quem Ametus filius Ameti qui dictus est Alfraganus compilavit 30ta continens capitula ". In *Savile* 16 it runs: "Incipit liber de aggregacionibus sciencie stellarum et principiis celestium motuum admeti filii admeti qui dictus est Alfraganus".

[3] Jourdain (*op. cit.*) takes this to be a mistake for 1242.

[Arabic title] . . . Muhámmedis Fil. Ketiri | Ferganensis, | Qui vulgo |
Alfraganus | dicitur, | Elementa Astronomica, | Arabicè et Latinè. | Cum Notis
ad res exoticas sive Orientales, quae | in iis occurrunt. | Opera | Jacobi Golii. |
Amstelodami . . . 1669.

At the beginning of his commentary Golius gives some interesting details about Alfraganus, gleaned from Arabic sources :—

Alferganum, ut praestantem doctrina et arte virum, celebrat Abulfergius in
Scriptorum veterum et recentiorum catalogo: atque ob perspicuam puramque
dictionem commendat Ibn Cafta [in Philosophorum Historia] . . . Praeter
Isagogen hanc edidit noster librum . . . *de Sciatericis* sive *Horologiis :* prout
ambo illi autores, et alii testantur. Alium quoque, ut Muveidînus Afer in libro
de Astronomorum erratis refert, commentarium scripsit . . . *absolutum et
apodicticum, de Astrolabii descriptione et usu.* Arithmeticae quoque, et calculi
Astronomici solertiâ adeò excelluit, ut vulgo . . . *Computator* cognominatus
fuerit.

This edition and that of Christmann (*D*) are undoubtedly
the most accurate of the five printed editions, especially in the
matter of numbers, which in the first three are often hopelessly
corrupt.

This treatise of Alfraganus appears to have been a favourite
with Dante, and it is evident that he read it carefully, for, as
will be seen, he was largely indebted to it for astronomical and
other *data* in the *Convivio* and elsewhere, though only on two
occasions does he acknowledge his obligations.[1] The passages in
the *Vita Nuova* and *Convivio* in which he made use of it are as
follows :—

I

Vita Nuova, § 2

Speaking of the age of Beatrice at the time that he first saw
her, Dante says :—

Ella era già in questa vita stata tanto, che nel suo tempo lo cielo stellato
era mosso verso la parte d' oriente delle dodici parti l' una d' un grado ; sì che
quasi dal principio del suo anno nono apparve a me (ll. 9-14).

Alfraganus states (in a passage quoted below, see § 4), as
Dante has himself recorded elsewhere (*Conv.* ii. 6, ll. 140-143),
that the Heaven of the Fixed Stars moves from west to east

[1] *Conv.* ii. 6, l. 134 ; and ii. 14, l. 95.

one degree in every hundred years.   As it had moved the twelfth part of one degree since the birth of Beatrice, she must have been at the time eight years and four months old ($\frac{100}{12} = 8\frac{1}{3}$), in other words, as Dante puts it, she was in the beginning of her ninth year.

II

Vita Nuova, § 30

In this passage, in reference to the date of the death of Beatrice, Dante says :—

Io dico che, secondo l' usanza d' Arabia (*v.l.* Italia), l' anima sua nobilissima si partì nella prima ora del nono giorno del mese ; e secondo l' usanza di Siria, ella si partì nel nono mese dell' anno ; perchè il primo mese è ivi Tisrin [1] primo,[2] il quale a noi è Ottobre (ll. 1-6).

The fact that Dante made use of Alfraganus in this passage has a very important bearing upon the settlement of the disputed reading, *Italia* or *Arabia,* in the first line.   The usual reading is *Italia,* but *Arabia* occurs in more than a dozen MSS.,[3] and being the *difficilior lectio,* is consequently almost certainly the correct one ; for, as Dr. Moore points out in a note on this question,[4] it is inconceivable that a scribe should have substituted *Arabia* for *Italia,* had the latter been the original reading, whereas, on the contrary, the substitution of *Italia* for *Arabia,* the intelligible for the unintelligible (for the point of the reading *Arabia* is at first sight by no means obvious), would be natural enough.

In order that the arguments in favour of the reading *Arabia*

---

[1] Several editors read *Tismin,* but there can be no doubt about the correct reading, *Tisrin* exactly representing the *Tixryn* of Alfraganus (see quotation below).

[2] The Oxford text, following Witte, omits *primo* after *Tisrin ;* but *Tisrin primo* is the reading of the best MSS. (see the apparatus criticus of Beck's edition, p. 86), and is obviously right, as representing the *Tixryn prior* of Alfraganus (see quotation below).   The omission of *primo* in many of the MSS. is no doubt due to the occurrence of the same word immediately before.

[3] See Beck, *loc. cit.*

[4] See *Academy,* 1st Dec., 1894 ; and *Bullettino della Soc. Dant. Ital.* N.S. ii. 57-8.

may be clearly understood, it is necessary first to quote the passage from the *Elementa Astronomica* utilised by Dante. In his opening chapter Alfraganus says :—

Dies Arabum, quibus dinumerantur menses, sunt dies septem : quorum primus est dies Solis, initium capiens ab occasu Solis die Sabbati ; finem vero ab ejusdem occasu, die Solis. Quo modo etiam reliqui sese dies habent. Auspicantur enim Arabes diem quemque cum sua nocte, id est civilem, ab eo momento, quo Sol occidit : propterea quòd dies cujusque mensis apud illos ineunt à prima Lunae visione ; ea autem contingit circa occasum Solis. Sed apud Romanos, et alios, qui non instituunt suos menses ad Lunae phasim, dies nocti praemittitur, et dies quisque civilis incipit ab exortu Solis, et ad exortum ejus sequentem finitur.

Menses verò Syrorum sunt, 1. *Tixryn prior* . . . 2. *Tixryn posterior* . . . 3. *Canon prior* . . . 4. *Canon posterior* . . . 5. *Xubât* . . . 6. *Adâr* . . . 7. *Nisân* . . . 8. *Eijâr* . . . 9. *Hazirân* . . . 10. *Tamûz* . . . 11. *Ab* . . . 12. *Eilûl* . . .

Menses Romanorum numero dierum conveniunt cum mensibus Syrorum. Et quidem primus illorum mensis *Januarius* est horum *Canon posterior;* ita conveniunt, 2. *Februarius*, et *Xubât;* 3. *Martius*, et *Adâr;* 4. *Aprilis*, et *Nisân;* 5. *Majus*, et *Eijâr;* 6. *Junius*, et *Hazirân;* 7. *Julius*, et *Tamûz ;* 8. *Augustus*, et *Ab;* 9. *September*, et *Eilûl;* 10. *October*, et *Tixryn prior;* 11. *November*, et *Tixryn posterior ;* 12. *December*, et *Canon prior.*[1]

It is obviously Dante's aim in this thirtieth chapter of the *Vita Nuova* to prove that the number *nine* is intimately connected with the day, month, and year of Beatrice's death. Of the year he says :—

Secondo l' usanza nostra, elle si partì in quello anno della nostra indizione, cioè degli anni Domini, in cui il perfetto numero [2] nove volte era compiuto in quel centinaio, nel quale in questo mondo ella fu posta : ed ella fu de' Cristiani del terzodecimo centinaio (ll. 7·13).

This is simple enough ; the perfect number ten was completed for the ninth time in the thirteenth century in the year 1290.

Next comes the question of the month. In order to bring in

---

[1] From *E.*

[2] On the "perfect number" (*i.e.*, ten), *cf. Par.* xxvii. 117 ; and *Conv.* ii. 15, ll. 30-34 : "Conciossiacosachè dal dieci in su non si vada se non esso dieci alterando cogli altri nove e con sè stesso, e la più bella alterazione che esso riceva si è la sua di sè medesimo". This notion as to ten being the perfect number appears to have been derived from Macrobius, who in his *Comm. in Somn. Scipionis* (i. 6, § 76) says : "Decas . . . perfectissimus numerus est."

the number nine in this case Dante has recourse to the Syrian calendar, in which, as he learned from the above-quoted passage of Alfraganus, the first month, called *Tixryn prior*, corresponds to our *October*. Beatrice, he says, died in the ninth month according to the Syrian usage, which, as Alfraganus tells him, corresponds to our sixth month, namely June. The difficulty, therefore, as to Beatrice having died in June, the sixth month according to our reckoning, is got over by saying that she died in the ninth month according to the Syrian reckoning.

Lastly we come to the question of the day of the month. Those who read *Italia* in the sentence : " secondo l' usanza d' Italia l' anima sua nobilissima si partì nella prima ora del nono giorno del mese," have no alternative, of course, but to accept Dante's statement literally that Beatrice died on the ninth of the month. Consequently the date of Beatrice's death has been commonly received as 9th June, 1290. Dr. Moore, however, very justly remarks that, if the reading *Italia* be accepted, there is no point in the antithesis between *l' usanza d' Italia* (with regard to the day) and *l' usanza nostra* (with regard to the year), since the Italian usage and what Dante calls " our usage " would of course be one and the same thing. He therefore maintains, and there can hardly be a doubt that he is right, that the correct reading is not *Italia*, but *Arabia*, which has the support of at least thirteen MSS., and, as the *difficilior lectio*, is, as we remarked above, in any case to be preferred. The statement, then, we have to deal with is that, " according to the Arabian usage, Beatrice died in the first hour of the ninth day of the month ". Now Alfraganus explains, in the passage we have quoted, that according to the Arabian usage the day begins, not at sunrise, as with the Romans and others, but at sunset. If, then, Dante, in order to get the required connection between the number nine and the day of the month on which Beatrice died, was obliged to have recourse to the Arabian usage, in the same way that he fell back upon the Syrian usage in the case of the month itself, we are forced to the conclusion, as Dr. Moore acutely observes, that the actual date of Beatrice's death was not, as is commonly supposed, the ninth of the month, but *the evening of the eighth*, which according to the Arabian reckoning would be the beginning of the ninth day. From this conclusion, which it is difficult not to accept, Dr. Moore ingeniously derives a new argument in favour of the reality of Beatrice and of the incidents related in connection with her. Unless, he says, her death actually occurred on 8th June, unless Dante were hampered by actual facts, why should he have chosen so awkward a date, and one which required such far-fetched ingenuity in order to yield the allegorical significance desired ?

The new light thus unexpectedly thrown on this passage of the *Vita Nuova* by the help of Alfraganus is highly interesting and important. In the first place we are enabled confidently to restore *Arabia* to the text in place of the meaningless *Italia*, whereby we get the perfectly natural sequence of antitheses between *l' usanza d' Arabia, l' usanza di Siria*, and *l' usanza nostra*. In the second place, we can, with almost equal certainty, substitute 8th June for 9th June as the actual date of the death of Beatrice.

III

Convivio II. 4

In this chapter of the *Convivio*, speaking of the " poles " and " equator " of the various heavens, Dante says :—

È da sapere che ciascuno cielo, di sotto del Cristallino, ha due poli fermi, quanto a sè . . . e ciascuno, sì lo nono come gli altri, hanno un cerchio, che si puote chiamare Equatore del suo cielo proprio ; il quale egualmente in ciascuna parte della sua revoluzione è rimoto dall' uno polo e dall' altro . . . E ciascuna parte, quant' ella è più presso ad esso [*sc.* lo cerchio equatore], tanto più rattamente si muove ; quanto più è rimota e più presso al polo, più è tarda ; perocchè la sua revoluzione è minore, e conviene essere in uno medesimo tempo di necessitade colla maggiore (ll. 48-68).

This appears to have been taken from Alfraganus, who, in his second chapter, says :—

Haud controversia inter sapientes est, quin coelum figurâ sit sphericâ, et cum omnibus stellis convertatur circulari motu, super duobus polis, fixis ac immotis : quorum alter in plaga boreali consistit, alter in australi. . . . Rotunditas quoque coeli evidens maximè indicium, firmumque argumentum praebent conversiones illorum siderum, quae in tractibus borealibus perpetuò supra terram apparent. . . . Eae namque stellae ambiunt circulis aequè ab invicem dissitis : ut quae vertuntur omnes circa idem punctum. Et quae ex iis puncto huic est vicinior, minorem conficit circulum, motusque ejus apparet lentior. Quae verò longius recedit, circulum describit, qui vicinioris circulo major est ; et in quo motus cernitur velocior, pro ipsius magnitudine, et distantia ab illo puncto.[1]

IV

Convivio II. 6

In this passage, in which he mentions the *Liber de Aggregationibus Stellarum*—another name, as I have shown above, for the *Elementa Astronomica* of Alfraganus—Dante is discussing the motions of the Heavens à propos of the Heaven of Venus. He says :—

Li quali [movimenti dei cieli], secondochè nel *Libro dell' aggregazione delle stelle* epilogato si trova, dalla migliore dimostrazione degli astrologi sono tre : uno, secondochè la stella si muove per lo suo epiciclo ; l' altro, secondochè lo epiciclo si muove con tutto il cielo ugualmente con quello del Sole ; il terzo, secondochè tutto quel cielo si muove, seguendo il movimento della Stellata Spera, da Occidente in Oriente, in cento anni uno grado [2] (ll. 133-143).

Alfraganus says :—

Moventur quoque sphaerae horum planetarum [3] per gradum unum quibuslibet centum annis, juxta motum stellarum fixarum.[4] Ex his omnibus paret, quòd motus qui apparet in zodiaco, hisce 4 planetis, excepto mercurio,[5] compositus sit ex tribus motibus tantùm, videlicet ex motu planetae in epiciclo, ex motu centri epicicli in eccentrico, et ex motu communi omnium stellarum fixarum.[6]

---

[1] From *E*.

[2] *Cf.* the passage from the *Vita Nuova*, quoted above under § 1 (p. 60).

[3] The four planets, Venus, Saturn, Jupiter and Mars.

[4] In the previous chapter (cap. 16) Alfraganus says : " Sphaera stellarum fixarum movetur ab occidente in orientem, et rapit secum septem planetarum orbes, super duobus polis zodiaci, ut annis centum gradum unum promoveatur, secundum observationem Ptolemaei " (*D*).

[5] Mercury, as had been previously explained, has four motions.

[6] From *D*, cap. 17. The same passage is rendered as follows in *E* : " Omnium verò horum siderum sphaerae centesimo quoque anno peragunt partem unam : quae est stellarum fixarum conversio. Constat igitur motum, quem siderum horum quattuor singula, Mercurio nempe excepto, in zodiaco exhibent, conflari ex motibus duntaxat tribus : motu sideris in epiciclo ; motu centri epicicli in eccentrico ; et motu sphaerae totius, stellarum fixarum motum aequante " (cap. 14).

V

Convivio II. 7

Dante here states that the planet Venus, when nearest to the Earth, is distant 167 times the half-diameter of the Earth, which he puts at 3,250 miles. The least distance of Venus from the Earth, therefore, is 3,250 × 167 = 542,750 miles. This planet, he says,

> è di tanta virtute, che nelle nostre anime e nell' altre nostre cose ha grandissima podestà, non ostante che ella ci sia lontana, qualvolta più ci è presso, cento sessanta sette volte tanto, quanto è fin al mezzo della terra, che ci ha di spazio tremila dugento cinquanta miglia [1] (ll. 100-108).

These *data* are taken direct from Alfraganus. Having given the circumference of the earth as 20,400 miles, he continues :—

> Cum divisa fuerit rotunditas terrae, per tertiam et septimam partem unius tertiae, erit quod collectum fuerit quantitas diametri terrae, quae sunt sex millia et quingenta milliaria.[2]

This gives us the half-diameter of the Earth as 3,250 miles. The least distance of Venus from the Earth, which he says is the same as the greatest distance of Mercury, he gives in another place as follows :—

> Longissima Mercurii à terra distantia, quae Veneris est proxima, complectitur partes, terrae semi-diametro aequales, centum sexaginta septem; quae sunt milliaria 542,750.[3]

VI

Convivio II. 14

In this chapter Dante has borrowed several items of information from Alfraganus.

1. In a comparison between the Heaven of Mercury and

---

[1] Dante elsewhere (*Conv.* ii. 14, ll. 97-8 ; iv. 8, ll. 59-60) states the whole diameter of the Earth to be 6,500 miles.

[2] From *C, Diff*. 8. In *A* and *B* the exact number of miles is added : " erit quod collectum fuerit quantitas dyametri terre que sunt .6. millia et quingenta milliaria fere videlicet .6,491. milliaria " (*A*). The precise number, of course, is 6,490$\frac{19}{24}$ miles. The passage in *E* runs : " Quodsi totus ille ambitus [terrae] dividatur per 3$\frac{1}{7}$, dabit quotus terrae diametrum, nempe 6 millium et fere quingentorum milliarium " (cap. 8).

[3] From *E*, cap. 21.

Dialectics he gives the dimensions of the planet, referring to Alfraganus, whom he nowhere else names, as his authority :—

> Mercurio è la più piccola stella del cielo ; chè la quantità del suo diametro non è più che di dugento trentadue miglia, secondochè pone Alfragano, che dice quello essere delle vent' otto parti l' una del diametro della terra, lo qual è sei mila cinquecento miglia (ll. 92-98).

We are here told that the diameter of the planet Mercury is not more than 232 miles, according to the calculation of Alfraganus, who puts it at a twenty-eighth part of the diameter of the Earth, the latter being 6,500 miles, as we have already seen.[1] The precise number would be $\frac{6500}{28} = 232\frac{1}{7}$.

The statement of the Arabian astronomer is as follows :—

> *De quantitabus stellarum juxta terrae dimensionem.* . . . . Quantitates verò diametrorum illarum ad diametrum terrae ita se habent: diameter corporis Mercurii est vigesima octava pars diametri terrae.[2]

2. In comparing the Heaven of Saturn with Astrology Dante says :—

> Il cielo di Saturno ha due proprietadi, per le quali si può comparare all' Astrologia : l' una si è la tardezza del suo movimento per li dodici segni ; chè ventinove anni e più, secondo le scritture degli astrologi, vuole di tempo lo suo cerchio : l' altra si è, che esso è alto sopra tutti gli altri pianeti (ll. 224-231).

Alfraganus puts the zodiacal period of Saturn at twenty-nine years, five months, and about six days :—

> Saturnus in eccentrico revolvitur 29 annis, 5 mensibus, et 15 diebus: sed in zodiaco periodus ejus minor est 9 ferè diebus.[3]

---

[1] See above, § 5, p. 66, note 2.

[2] From *D*, cap. 24 This edition alone of the five printed editions of the *Elementa Astronomica* gives the diameter of Mercury as the *twenty-eighth* part of the diameter of the Earth, in agreement with what Dante says. *A* and *B* say : "dyameter corporis Mercurii est una pars ex 20 partibus dyametri terre". *C* says : "diameter corporis Mercurii est una pars ex decem partibus diametri terrae". *E* says : "diameter corporis Mercurii habet partem unam ex diametri terrae partibus 18". Four MSS. which I examined give the number 28 in agreement with *D*. These are Brit. Mus. *Arundel* 377 ("una pars ex XXVIII partibus ") ; Bibl. Bodl. *Laud* 644 (" XXVIIIa pars ") ; Bibl. Bodl. *Savile* 16 ("una pars ex 28 partibus ") ; Bibl. Bodl. *Digby* 215 ("diametrus corporis Mercurii est XXVIII partes diametri terre!").

[3] From *D*, cap. 20. *E* says (cap. 17) : " Saturnus in eccentrico quidem [peragrando haeret] annis 29, mensibus 5, diebus 15 ; in zodiaco autem hoc tempore minùs diebus 7 ". The other editions are in agreement with *D*.

The statement as to Saturn being higher than all the other planets refers, of course, to the order assigned in the Ptolemaic system to the seven planets, in which Saturn comes seventh or highest.[1]

VII

Convivio II. 15

In this chapter also Dante has freely borrowed from Alfraganus.

1. Speaking of the Heaven of the Fixed Stars, he says it has two movements; one, easily perceptible, from east to west; another, almost imperceptible, from west to east; it has also two poles, one of which is visible, the other hidden :—

Il Cielo Stellato . . . mostraci l' uno de' poli, e l' altro ci tiene ascoso : e mostraci un solo movimento da Oriente in Occidente [nel quale ogni dì si rivolve [2]], e un altro, che fa da Occidente a Oriente [per un grado in cento anni], quasi ci tiene ascoso (ll. 10-14).

The two celestial Poles are described by Alfraganus in his second chapter :—

Coelum . . . cum omnibus stellis convertitur circulari motu, super duobus polis, fixis et immotis : quorum alter in plaga boreali consistit, alter in australi.[3]

Of the two celestial motions he says :—

Dico itaque duos in coelo observari principales motus : quorum primus totum versat coelum, facitque noctem et diem. Is namque circumagit Solem, et Lunam, omnesque stellas reliquas ab oriente in occidentem, unâ quotidie conversione. . . . Motus autem secundus is est, quo Solem et stellas versari cernimus ab occidente in orientem, in partes primo motui contrarias.[4]

The nature of this second motion he explains elsewhere in speaking of the Heaven of the Fixed Stars :—

---

[1] Cf. Alfraganus : " Orbium minima, quae terrae proxima, Lunae est ; secunda Mercurii ; tertia Veneris ; quarta Solis ; quinta Martis ; sexta Jovis ; septima Saturni " (E, cap. 12).

[2] The passages enclosed in square brackets occur later on in the chapter (ll. 97, 104), where Dante explains the nature of the two movements. They are inserted here, as it is convenient to have the whole account in one paragraph.

[3] From E. The visible Pole, of course, is the one in the northern region of the sky ; the invisible, that in the southern region.

[4] From E, cap. 5.

Stellarum fixarum sphaera . . . cujus motus . . . est universis stellis errantibus communis . . . ab occidente gyratur in orientem super zodiaci polis, centenis quibusque annis, ut Ptolemaei est sententia, per spatium unius gradus. Eodem motu unà convertuntur septem planetarum sphaerae; ita ut . . . totum zodiacum percurrant annis 36,000.[1]

2. Dante next refers to the number of the Fixed Stars :—

Dico ch' il Cielo Stellato ci mostra molte stelle ; chè, secondochè li savi d' Egitto hanno veduto, infino all' ultima stella che appare loro in meridie, mille ventidue corpora di stelle pongono (ll. 18-22).

He here in part copies Alfraganus almost *verbatim*; the latter says :—

Dicamus quod sapientes[2] probaverunt universas stellas, quarum possibilis eis fuerit probatio eis (*sic*) per instrumenta usque ad ultimum quod apparuerit eis, ex parte meridiei in climate tertio, et diviserunt quantitates eorum in magnitudine, per sex divisiones luminosas. . . . Feruntque ex eis in magnitudine prima 15 stellae, in secunda 45, et in tertia 208, et in quarta 474, et in quinta 217, et in sexta 49[3] . . . erunt quae praeceptae sunt his probationibus 1,022 stellarum, praeter planetas; ex quibus sunt in parte septentrionali a circulo signorum, stellae 360; et sunt ex eis in imaginibus signorum 346 stellae; et sunt ex eis in parte meridiei a circulo signorum 316.[4]

3. Returning to the question of the two motions of the Heaven of the Fixed Stars, Dante says of the second of them (*viz.*, the almost insensible movement that the Heaven makes of one degree from west to east in a hundred years), that from

[1] From *E*, cap. 13.

[2] For *sapientes* Dante says *savi d' Egitto*, doubtless in view of the fact that the astronomer Ptolemy was a native of Egypt.

[3] *A*, *B* and *C*, all read 49 here, while *D* and *E* read 63. That 63 is correct is proved by the addition of the six sums given, which brings the total to the required amount (15 + 45 + 208 + 474 + 217 + 63 = 1,022). The erroneous reading 49 doubtless arose from the misunderstanding of the next sentence (omitted in the above quotation), in which Alfraganus remarks : "inter eas obscurae sunt novem; et nebulosae ac tenues quinque". These 14 faint stars were evidently reckoned by mistake as a separate group ; and as their inclusion brings the total to 1,036 instead of 1,022, the supposed error was rectified by substituting 49 for 63 in the sixth group.

[4] From *C*, *Diff*. 19. Both *A* and *B* omit several lines in the last paragraph, owing to the carelessness of a copyist, who was obviously led astray by the ὁμοιοτέλευτον involved in the repetition of the phrase *a circulo signorum*. They read : ". . . praeter planetas; ex quibus sunt in parte septentrionali a circulo signorum stellae 316". *C* in this instance vindicates its claim to be more correct than its predecessors.

the beginning of the world it has only caused the Heaven to accomplish a little more than a sixth part of its complete revolution :—

> Per lo movimento quasi insensibile, che fa da Occidente in Oriente per un grado in cento anni, significa le cose incorruttibili, le quali ebbero da Dio cominciamento di creazione, e non averanno fine . . . E però dico che questo movimento significa quelle, che essa circulazione cominciò, e non avrebbe fine ; chè fine della circulazione è redire a uno medesimo punto, al quale non tornerà questo cielo, secondo questo movimento. Chè dal cominciamento del mondo poco più che la sesta parte è volto ; e noi siamo già nell' ultima etade del secolo, e attendemo veracemente la consumazione del celestiale movimento (ll. 102-118).

This information as to the movement of the Heaven from west to east, one degree in a hundred years, Dante derived, as we have shown above, [1] from the thirteenth chapter of Alfraganus, where he points out that the complete revolution, through the 360 degrees, would, of course, occupy 36,000 years. Dante's calculation, that only a little more than a sixth part of the revolution has been accomplished, is based upon the belief that the creation took place five thousand years and more before the birth of Christ [2] ; so that in the thirteenth century A.D. more than six thousand years had elapsed, and the Heaven had moved through rather more than 60 degrees, or one-sixth of the whole circuit.

4. Dante goes on to speak of the Crystalline Heaven or *Primum Mobile*, the movement of which regulates the daily revolution of all the other Heavens. He says that, supposing this movement did not exist, a third part of the Heavens would not yet have been seen in each locality on the Earth's surface, and the planets would be hidden for half their revolutions : —

---

[1] See above, § 7, 1.

[2] Orosius, with whose work Dante was intimately acquainted, puts the period from Adam to Abraham at 3,814 years, and from Abraham to the Nativity at 2,015 years, making 5,199 years from the creation to the Nativity ; this sum, with the addition of the 1,300 years of the Christian era, gives a total of 6,499 years (see *Hist. adv. Paganos*, i. §§ 5, 6). Brunetto Latino gives a somewhat different estimate of the number of years between Adam and Christ ; he says : " Nostre Sires print char en la Virge Marie à .Vm. Vc. anz dou commencement dou monde ; mais plusor dient qu'il n'i avoit que .Vm.CC.liiij. ans ". (*Trésor*, Liv. I. chap. xlii.)

Lo Cielo Cristallino . . . ordina col suo movimento la cotidiana revoluzione di tutti gli altri ; per la quale ogni dì tutti quelli ricevono quaggiù la virtù di tutte le loro parti. . . . Ponemo che possibile fosse questo nono cielo non muovere, la terza parte del cielo sarebbe ancora non veduta in ciascuno luogo della terra ; e Saturno starebbe quattordici anni e mezzo a ciascuno luogo della terra celato, e Giove sei anni si celerebbe ; e Marte un anno quasi, e'l Sole cento ottantadue dì e quattordici ore (dico *dì*, cioè tanto tempo quanto misurano cotanti dì) ; e Venere e Mercurio, quasi come il Sole, si celerebbero e mostrerebbero ; e la Luna per tempo di quattordici dì e mezzo starebbe ascosa a ogni gente (ll. 132-152).

The explanation of this statement is as follows : Dante says that if the movement of the *Primum Mobile*, on which depends the daily motion of all the other Heavens, were suspended, there would remain only the almost insensible movement of the Starry Heaven from west to east of one degree in a hundred years[1] (corresponding to what is now called the Precession of the Equinoxes). In this case the Heavens would cease to revolve, and as only 180° of the Heavens would then be visible to us, the Sun and other planets would be invisible for half their revolutions, being hidden behind our backs, as it were, during the rest of the time ; further, a third part of the Heavens would never have been seen from the Earth, since from the Creation to Dante's day, which he estimates at more than 6,000 years, the Starry Heaven would only have moved from west to east about 60°, hence 60° + 180° = 240° would be the whole amount of the Heavens which had been visible, leaving 360° – 240° = 120°, *i.e.*, one third part of the Heavens, which had never been seen (Moore).

The *data* as to the periods of the several planets Dante got from Alfraganus, who says in his chapter *De orbibus planetarum :*—

Fit orbis Lunae 29 dierum et 12 horarum et dimidiae et quartae unius horae.[2] Mercurii ac Veneris ac Solis, uniuscujusque istorum rotatus fit 365 diebus et quarta unius diei ferè. Martis autem in anno Persico et 10 mensibus

[1] See above, § 7, 3.

[2] *A* and *B* put the period of the moon at " 27 dierum et 11 horarum et dimidiae et quartae unius horae ". *D* says it is completed " 27 diebus 7¼ horis et ⅙ unius horae ferè ". *E* says " Lunae periodus erit dierum 27, horarum 7 cum ½ et ferè ¼ ". *C*, from which the above quotation is taken, puts the lunar period at rather more than 29 days, which is in accordance with the period given by Dante.

et 22 diebus ferè.   Jovis verò in circulo egressae cuspidis in 11 annis et 10 mensibus et 16 diebus.   In circulo autem signorum, minus uno die et dimidio ferè. Et Saturni in circulo egressae cuspidis in vigintinovem annis et quinque mensibus, et quindecim diebus.   In circulo signorum minus hoc per novem dies.[1]

Dante, as may be seen, has not cared to be exact in giving the figures, but has calculated the half revolutions roughly. According to his figures, the periods would be : Saturn $14\frac{1}{2}$ years × 2 = 29 years, as against 29 years, 5 months, 15 days given by Alfraganus ; Jupiter 6 years × 2 = 12 years, as against 11 years, 10 months, 16 days ; Mars 1 year nearly × 2 = 2 years nearly, as against 1 year, 10 months, 22 days ; Sun, Venus, Mercury 182 days, 14 hours × 2 = 365 days, 4 hours, as against 365 days, 6 hours ; Moon $14\frac{1}{2}$ days × 2 = 29 days, as against 29 days, $12\frac{3}{4}$ hours.

VIII

Convivio III. 5

Dante is largely indebted to Alfraganus in this chapter again.

1. The first passage has reference to the celestial Poles and Equator :—

Questa terra è fissa e non si gira, e essa col mare è centro del cielo. Questo cielo si gira intorno a questo centro continuamente, siccome noi vedemo ; nella cui girazione conviene di necessità essere due Poli fermi, e uno Cerchio ugualmente distante da quelli che massimamente giri.   Di questi due Poli, l' uno è manifesto quasi a tutta la terra discoperta, cioè questo settentrionale ; l' altro è quasi a tutta la discoperta terra celato, cioè lo meridionale.[2]   Lo Cerchio che nel mezzo di questi s' intende, si è quella parte del cielo, sotto la quale si gira il sole, quando va coll' Ariete e colla Libra (ll. 63-79).

Alfraganus in his fifth chapter says :—

Coelum volvit Solem et Lunam et universa sidera ab Oriente in Occidentem in uno quoque die ac nocte semel uno ordine, et volubilitate aequalis velocitatis super duos axes fixos, qui nominantur axes motus primi, quorum unus est septentrionalis, . . . et alter versus Meridiem.[3]   Et necesse est, ut stellae volubilitate hujus motus ferantur in circulis in directo ad invicem positis,

---

[1] From C, Diff. 17.   [2] Cf. Conv. ii. 15 ; and see above, § 7, 1.

[3] Cf. cap. 2 : " Coelum cum omnibus stellis convertitur circulari motu, super duobus polis fixis et immotis : quorum alter in plaga boreali consistit, alter in australi ".

ex quibus circulis vocatur circulus magnus, circulus aequinoctii diei, qui est cingulus primi motus, quia dividit spheram coeli per medium, et longitudo ejus ab utrisque axibus est unius quantitatis. . . . Necesse est, ut abscindat circulus signorum [1] circulum aequinoctii diei, super duos punctos sibi oppositos, et declinet ab eo versus Septentrionem vel Meridiem una quantitate, et punctus super quem transit Sol a Meridie ad Septentrionem ab aequinoctio diei, nominatur punctus aequinoctialis vernalis, quod est initium signi Arietis, et alter punctus super quem transit Sol in Meridiem à Septentrione, appellatur punctus aequinoctialis autumnalis, quod est initium signi Librae.[2]

2. In the next passage Dante enters into an elaborate explanation of the movement of the Sun round the Earth, which is too lengthy to follow in detail.   It is evident that he had been studying the sixth and seventh chapters of Alfraganus, whence, among other details, he borrowed the simile of the Sun revolving like a millstone, " coma una mola ".[3]   He got from here too the measurement of the circumference of the Earth.   He imagines a city called *Maria* at the North Pole of the Earth, and another called *Lucia* at the South Pole, and then calculates the distance between these points and the city of Rome :—

È da sapere, che se una pietra potesse cadere da questo nostro Polo, ella cadrebbe là oltre nel mare Oceano, appunto in su quel dosso del mare [4] dove se fosse un uomo, la stella [5] gli sarebbe sempre sul mezzo del capo ; e credo che da Roma a questo luogo, andando dritto per tramontana, sia spazio quasi di due mila settecento miglia, o poco dal più al meno. Immaginiamo adunque, per meglio vedere, in questo luogo ch' io dissi, sia una città, e abbia nome *Maria*. Dico ancora che se dall' altro Polo, cioè Meridionale, cadesse una pietra, ella cadrebbe in su quel dosso del mare [4] Oceano, che è appunto in questa palla opposito a *Maria ;* e credo che da Roma, là dove cadrebbe questa seconda pietra, diritto andando per mezzogiorno, sia spazio di sette mila cinquecento miglia, poco dal più al meno. E qui immaginiamo un' altra città che abbia nome *Lucia ;* e di spazio, da qualunque parte si tira la corda, dieci mila dugento miglia ; e sì, tra l' una e l' altra, mezzo lo cerchio di questa palla ; sicchè li cittadini di *Maria* tengano le piante contro le piante di que' di *Lucia* (ll. 80-107).

From this we gather that the total circumference of the Earth would measure 20,400 miles [6] ; the distance from *Maria*,

---

[1] *i.e.*, the Zodiac.   [2] From *C, Diff.* 5.

[3] " Fitque rotatus circuli ut rotatus molendini " (*C*).   " Molae trusatilis instar " (*E*).

[4] *Cf.* " dorsum maris " in the *Quaestio*, § 5, l. 13.   [5] *i.e.*, the Polar Star.

[6] Dante utilised these *data* in an interesting passage in the *Divina Commedia*.   At the beginning of Canto xxx of the *Paradiso* the dawn is

the city at the North Pole, to Rome being put at 2,700 miles more or less, and the distance from *Lucia*, the city at the South Pole, to Rome being put at 7,500 miles, making the total of 10,200 miles for the half-circumference ; we are further explicitly told that the distance between *Maria* and *Lucia*, in whatever direction the measure be taken, would be 10,200 miles.

The measurement of the circumference of the Earth is thus calculated by Alfraganus :—

> Invenimus quod portio unius gradus circuli ex rotunditate terrae sit 56 milliarium, et duarum tertiarum unius milliarii per milliarium. . . . Cum ergo multiplicaveris portionem unius gradus in rotunditate in summam circuli, quod est 360 graduum, erit quod collectum fuerit ex hoc rotunditas terrae, quae sunt 20,400 milliaria [1] ; et cum divisa fuerit rotunditas terrae per tertiam et septimam partem unius tertiae, erit quod collectum fuerit quantitas diametri terrae, quae sunt sex millia et quingenta milliaria.[2]

IX

Convivio III. 6

In this passage Dante explains the difference between " equal " and " unequal " or " temporal " hours :—

> È da sapere, che *ora* per due modi si prende dagli astrologi : l' uno si è, che del dì e della notte fanno ventiquattr' ore, cioè dodici del dì e dodici della notte, quanto che 'l dì sia grande o piccolo. E queste ore si fanno picciole e grandi nel dì e nella notte, secondo che 'l dì e la notte cresce e scema. E queste ore usa la Chiesa, quando dice *Prima, Terza, Sesta,* e *Nona* [3] ; e chiamansi così

described, by an elaborate periphrasis, as the time when it is about midday 6,000 miles away from the earth. This calculation, as Tozer explains (in an *English Commentary on the D.C.*), is arrived at as follows : Seven hours are approximately the period of time which the sun takes to pass over 6,000 miles of the earth's surface ; for, according to the computation of Alfraganus, the entire circumference of the earth is 20,400 miles and consequently the amount of that circumference corresponding to seven hours out of the complete revolution of twenty-four hours was $20{,}400 \times \frac{7}{24} = 5{,}950$ miles, or in round numbers 6,000 miles. Hence when Dante says that the sixth hour is 6,000 miles distant from us, he means that with us it is seven hours before noon, or an hour before sunrise, the sun being regarded as rising at 6 A.M.

---

[1] Thus $56\frac{2}{3} \times 360 = 20{,}400$.

[2] From *C, Diff.* 8. See above, p. 66, note 2.

[3] *Cf. Convivio*, iv. 23, ll. 142-145 : " La Chiesa usa nella distinzione dell' ore del dì *temporali*, che sono in ciascuno dì dodici, o grandi o picciole, secondo la quantità del sole ".

ore temporali. L' altro modo si è, che facendo del dì e della notte ventiquattr' ore, talvolta ha il dì le quindici ore, e la notte, le nove; e talvolta ha la notte le sedici, e 'l dì le otto, secondochè cresce e scema il dì e la notte ; e chiamansi *ore eguali.* E nello Equinozio sempre queste, e quelle che temporali si chiamano, sono una cosa ; perocchè, essendo il dì eguale della notte, conviene così avvenire.[1]

This is taken from the eleventh chapter of Alfraganus, where he says :—

Posuerunt astrologi initium uniuscujusque diei cum nocte sua, ex hora medii diei usque in horam medii sequentis. . . . Omnes vero dies cum nocte sua dividuntur per 24 horas . . . et hae vocantur aequales, quia nulla diversitas est quantitati eorum. . . . Horae verò [temporariae sive][2] inaequales, cum quibus fit unaquaeque dies ac nox tam in aestate quam in hyeme 12 horarum. Earumque quantitates fiunt diversae, secundum longitudinem diei ac noctis, sive brevitatem. Cum fuerit dies prolixior nocte, erunt horae ejus prolixiores horis noctis. Et similiter, cum fuerit brevior, erunt horae ejus breviores. . . . Et nominantur tempora horarum diei.[3]

X

Convivio IV. 8.

Dante in this chapter of the *Convivio,* the last in which he appears to have made use of Alfraganus, gives the measurement of the diameter of the Sun at 35,750 miles, as calculated from the diameter of the Earth :—

Sapemo che alla più gente il sole pare di larghezza nel diametro d' un piede : e sì è ciò falsissimo, che, secondo il cercamento e la invenzione che ha fatta la umana ragione coll' altre[4] sue arti, il diametro del corpo del sole è cinque volte

---

[1] *Cf.* Brunetto Latino : " Et ja soit ce que li contes dit que nos avons une foiz le jor plus grant que la nuit, et une autre fois la nuit plus grant que le jor, toutefoiz di je que touzjors, comment que il soit, il i a autretant d'hores en chascun jor comme en chascune nuit ; car il i en a .xij. en chascun, porce que li nombre des hores ne croissent ne apetissent ; mais quant li jors est graindres les hores sont graindres, et celes de la nuit sont plus petites ; aussi est quant la nuiz est graindres et les hores sont graindres ". (*Trésor,* Liv. I. chap. cxv.)

[2] The words in brackets are supplied from *D* and *E.* They are wanting in the other editions.

[3] From *C, Diff.* 11. In *E* the chapter ends : " Perspicuum itaque est, eas horas dici aequales, quarum quidem numerus pro diei longitudine vel brevitate major vel minor est ; tempora verò manent aequalia. Horas autem temporarias vel inaequales dici, quarum tempora sunt inaequalia ; at numerus semper aequalis est."

[4] The editions read *altre,* but it seems probable that the correct reading is *alte.*

quanto quello della terra, e anche una mezza volta. Conciossiacosachè la terra
per lo diametro suo sia seimila cinquecento miglia, lo diametro del sole, che alla
sensuale apparenza appare di quantità di uno piede, è trentacinque mila settecento cinquanta miglia (ll. 51-64).

In his twenty-second chapter Alfraganus says :—

Diameter Solis aequabit totos terrae diametros 5½.

The diameter of the Earth Dante got, as we have seen,[1] from
the seventh chapter of Alfraganus.

XI

PARADISO IX. 118-119

To the above passages in the *Vita Nuova* and *Convivio* may
be added an interesting one in the ninth can 'o of the *Paradiso*.
Dante there speaks of the shadow of the Earth as extending as
far as the sphere of Venus, where it comes to a point :—

> Questo cielo, in cui l' ombra s' appunta
> Che il vostro mondo face.

This theory as to the projection of the shadow of the Earth is
based upon what Alfraganus says in his chapter on the eclipse of
the Moon. The Arabian astronomer there states that this
shadow (which, as he explains, owing to the fact that the Sun is
larger than the Earth, must be conical, thus terminating in a
point) is projected to a distance equal to 268 half-diameters of
the Earth, *i.e.*, 3,250 × 268 = 871,000 miles :—

Hic vero addo, solem illustrare quoque dimidium globum terrae: adeo
ut lumen in terrae superficie circumagatur circumactu solis ab ortu in occasum;
pariterque eandem superficiem ambiat caligo. Et quia sol terrâ est major,
necesse est terrae umbram per aëra protendi coni effigie; et in rotunditate
attenuari, donec deficiat: lineam vero, quae coni umbrosi axis est, in eclipticae
jacere plano, semperque dirigi in punctum gradui solis obversum. Umbrae
quidem a terrae superficie ad finem usque longitudo, juxta Ptolemaei dimen-
sionem, aequat dimidiam diametrum terrae ducenties sexagies octies.[2]

The least distance of Venus herself from the Earth, Alfraganus puts at 542,750 miles (this being also Mercury's greatest
distance); her greatest distance (equal to the Sun's least distance)

---

[1] See above, § 5, p. 66.   [2] From *E*, cap. 28.

he puts at 3,640,000, giving a mean of 2,091,375 miles (cap. 21). According to these *data* the Earth's shadow would project $871,000 - 542,750 = 328,250$ miles beyond Venus, when she was nearest to the Earth ; and would fall short of her by $3,640,000 - 871,000 = 2,769,000$ miles when she was furthest off. The calculation as to the least distance of Venus from the Earth was certainly known to Dante, for, as we have seen, he refers to it in the *Convivio* (ii. 7, ll. 100-108).[1]

[1] See above, § 5, p. 66.

DANTE'S THEORIES AS TO THE SPOTS ON THE MOON [1]

In the fourteenth chapter of the second book of the *Convivio* Dante ascribes the phenomenon, which he calls "the shadow in the Moon,"[2] to the rarity of the substance of the Moon in certain parts of its sphere, which allows the light of the Sun to pass through, instead of being reflected, as it is by the denser parts. "Se la luna si guarda bene," he says, "due cose si veggono in essa proprie, che non si veggono nell' altre stelle: l' una si è l' ombra ch' è in essa, la quale non è altro che rarità del suo corpo, alla quale non possono terminare i raggi del sole a ripercuotersi così come nell' altre parti . . . " (ll. 69-76).

This theory, for which Dante gives no authority, seems to have been derived from the *De Substantia Orbis* [3] of Averroës. The Arabian philosopher says :—

> Luna videtur esse densa et obscura, et recipiens lumen ab alio, scilicet a sole. Et in libro de Animalibus dixit Aristoteles quod natura ejus est unigenea naturâ terrae plusquam caeterarum stellarum. Et forte corpora coelestia diversantur in raritate et densitate, quae sunt causae illuminationis et obscuritatis, licet haec non inveniantur nisi in luna tantum (cap. 2.).

[1] Translated, with additions, from an article in Italian ("Le Teorie Dantesche sulle Macchie della Luna"), printed in the *Giornale Storico della Letteratura Italiana* (xxvi. 156-61).

[2] *Cf. Paradiso*, xxii. 140. The term "ombra" for the spots on the Moon is used also by Ristoro d' Arezzo in his *Composizione del Mondo* (i. 18); and by Jacopo Alighieri in his *Dottrinale* (xxv. 5; xxvi. 25); and also by Cecco d'Ascoli in his *Acerba* (Lib. I.).

[3] This work is quoted in the *Quaestio de Aqua et Terra* (§ 18); see above, p. 55.

With this may be compared what Albertus Magnus says in his treatise *De Juventute et Senectute* :—

Aristoteles dicit quod luna terrestris naturae sit et ideo obscuritatem, ut inquit, aliquam retinet, etiam postquam illuminatur a sole ; propter igitur connaturalitatem terrenam magis variat, ut dicit, quam aliquod corporum aliorum quae sunt in coelo. (Tract. i. cap. 2.)[1]

In the second canto of the *Paradiso* Dante decisively rejects this theory,[2] and attributes the phenomenon to the diverse effects of the divers "intelligences" which preside over the celestial bodies.

When the poet arrives, in company with Beatrice, in the Heaven of the Moon, he takes the opportunity to inquire as to the nature of the dark marks, which are seen by the inhabitants of the Earth on the face of the lunar sphere :—

> Ma ditemi, che son li segni bui
> Di questo corpo, che laggiuso in terra
> Fan di Cain[3] favoleggiare altrui ?
>
> (ll. 49-51.)

[1] Dr. Moore thinks that Dante may have got his theory from *La Composizione del Mondo* (written in 1282) of Ristoro d' Arezzo. He says: " There is a very singular explanation of the lunar spots in Ristoro corresponding exactly with that adopted by Dante in the *Convivio*. . . . Ristoro (in a somewhat obscure passage in bk. iii. chap. 8) explains that some parts of the moon are ' hard,' ' opaque ' (*ottuoso*), ' bright '. These parts, like a mirror, are ' receptive ' of the light, so that it can be passed, drawn or thrown on to other objects (*passare, trarre, gittare*, are all used). This is the case with the stars. Other parts of the moon are ' soft,' ' transparent,' ' dark '. These cannot ' receive ' the light and pass it on, but they, as it were, ' retain ' it themselves, so that it is not reflected to other objects. Such is the case with the earth. . . . The *rarità* in Dante corresponds with the ' soft,' ' transparent,' or ' dark ' parts of the moon in Ristoro, in both cases the characteristic feature being the incapacity to reflect the light ". (*Studies in Dante*, ii. 362.)

[2] This is one of the points which prove that the *Convivio*, or at any rate this part of it, was composed before the *Paradiso*.

[3] The old popular belief that the " man in the moon " was Cain with a bundle of thorns (probably with reference to his unacceptable offering), is alluded to again by Dante in the *Inferno* (xx. 126), where he mentions *Caino e le spine* to indicate the moon. The following passage from the Tuscan version of the story gives the Italian form of the tradition—Cain attempts to excuse himself for the murder of Abel: " Caino cercò di scusarsi, ma allora Iddio li rispose : Abele sarà con me in Paradiso, e tu in pena della tu' colpa sarai confinato nella luna,

Beatrice, instead of giving a direct answer, asks Dante for his opinion on the subject. He, in reply, repeats the theory which he had already propounded in the *Convivio*, namely that he supposed the spots to be caused by the difference between the rare and dense portions of the substance of the Moon :—

> Ciò che n' appar quassù diverso
> Credo che il fanno i corpi rari e densi.
> (ll. 59-60.)

Beatrice, however, demonstrates to him that this theory is untenable, because, in the first place, the various degrees of brightness in the fixed stars are known to be due, not to variations of density or rarity in their substance, but to the variety of the formal principles by which they are governed (ll. 61-72);

e condannato a portare eternamente addosso un fascio di spine. Appena dette queste parole da Dio, si levò un fortissimo vento e trasportò Caino in corpo e anima nella luna, e d' allora in poi si vede sempre la su' faccia maledetta, e il fardello di spine che è obbligato a reggere insino alla fin del mondo, indizio della vita disperata che li tocca trascinare." (See St. Prato, *Caino e le spine secondo Dante e la tradizione popolare*.) Dante's son, Jacopo Alighieri, has a reference to the same tradition in his poem *Il Dottrinale* where he speaks of :—

> " Quell' ombra della luna
> Che con Cain s' impruna " (xxv. 5-6).

A similar belief was current in England, as appears from the description of Lady Cynthia (the moon), in Henryson's *Testament of Cresseid* (formerly attributed to Chaucer) :—

> Hir gyte was gray, and full of spottis blak ;
> And on hir breist ane churl paintit ful evin,
> Beirand ane bunch of thornis on his bak,
> Quhilk for his thift micht clim na nar the hevin.
> (ll. 260-3.)

There are several references to this belief in Shakespeare (*Tempest*, Act ii. sc. 2; *Midsummer Night's Dream*, Act iii. sc. 1; Act v. sc. 1. For a list of references in other writers to the same subject, see Skeat's *Chaucer*, ii. 466-7).

Ristoro d' Arezzo, in his *Composizione del Mondo* (iii. 8), mentions a belief that not only Cain, but Abel also, is to be seen in the moon : " Tal dice che vi [nella luna] vede uomo impiccato, e tal dice che vi vede due che si tegnono per li capelli, e tal dice che vi vede un' uomo c' hae la scure in mano, e tai dicono che vi vedieno Caino e Abel ; e fu tale che disse che vi vedeva uno toro, e tale uno cavallo, e tale una cosa e tale un altra ".

in the second place, if the body of the Moon consisted of rare
and dense strata, the rare strata must either extend right through
the thickness of the lunar sphere (in which case they would let
the light of the Sun pass through in an eclipse), or they must be
arranged with the denser parts in layers, lying over them in
some parts (like the alternations of fat and lean in a body, or
like the arrangement of leaves in a book), so that the light in
the darker parts must be reflected with varying intensity according to the varying depth of the depression below the general
level of the exterior surface of the Moon (ll. 73-93); but,
Beatrice points out, an experiment with mirrors would show that
the intrinsic brightness of light is not affected by distance—let
two mirrors be placed at an equal distance from you, and a
third between them, but further off; then let a light be placed
behind you as you face the mirrors, and you will find that
though the reflection from the third is smaller in size, it will be
as bright as the others, thus demonstrating that the distance of
the reflecting medium does not affect the brightness of the
reflected light (ll. 94-105).   Having thus disposed of Dante's
theory, Beatrice proceeds to explain to him that the real cause
of these dark spots is to be sought in the "virtue" which
originates in the *Primum Mobile*, and is distributed by the
Heaven of the Fixed Stars in divers influences throughout the
universe.   After instructing him as to the operation of the
stellar influences which affect the various heavens, and as to the
functions of the "Intelligences" or Angelic Orders by whom
these influences are dispensed (ll. 106-138), she goes on to show
that the stars are bright or dim according as the influence which
proceeds from God, and is communicated to them by the "Intelligences," is pure or alloyed; and that the brightness and
dimness of the surface of the Moon are to be accounted for in
the same way:—

> Virtù diversa fa diversa lega
>   Col prezioso corpo ch' ell' avviva,
>   Nel qual, sì come vita in voi, si lega.
> Per la natura lieta, onde deriva,
>   La virtù mista per lo corpo luce,
>   Come letizia per pupilla viva.

Da essa vièn ciò che da luce a luce
Par differente, non da denso e raro:
Essa è formal principio che produce,
Conforme a sua bontà, lo turbo e il chiaro.
(ll. 139-148.) [1]

The arguments here put by Dante into the mouth of Beatrice are, as Philalethes points out, to a large extent based on the *De Coelo et Mundo* of Albertus Magnus (Lib. ii. tract. 2-3). I have shown elsewhere [2] that Dante was largely indebted to the writings of Albertus, though he very seldom makes any acknowledgment of his obligations.

In the twenty-second of the *Paradiso*, Dante once again makes a formal retractation of his earlier theory as to the cause of the spots on the Moon. On this occasion he describes the appearance of the Moon as seen from above, he being at this time in the Heaven of the Fixed Stars. From this elevation he looks down and descries at a great distance off the seven planets revolving round the Earth ; of the Moon he says :—

Vidi la figlia di Latona incensa
Senza quell' ombra, che mi fu cagione
Perchè già la credetti rara e densa.
(ll. 139-141.)

It is somewhat curious that Dante should imagine the side of the Moon which is turned away from the Earth to be free from spots. What led him to form this conclusion does not appear. It might be conjectured that the fact of no spots being visible to him was due to the immense distance which separated him from the Moon. But this hypothesis is untenable, for though he remarks upon the contemptible proportions of the Earth as seen from where he was—

[1] Dante's son, Pietro, who wrote a commentary on the *Divina Commedia*, concludes his remarks on this canto with a confession that he could make neither head nor tail of Dante's " explanation " ; addressing the reader he says: " Alia per te vide, imo omnia, quia nil vidi, nec intellexi ". The editor of the *Comentum*, however, notes that this naïve confession is not to be found in all the MSS., so that it may possibly be the interpolation of some bewildered copyist.

[2] See the article on " Some Obligations of Dante to Albertus Magnus," pp. 38-55.

. . . Vidi questo globo
Tal, ch' io sorrisi del suo vil sembiante.
(ll. 134-135)—

yet a few lines further on he asserts that he could distinguish the mountains and the river mouths on the terrestrial globe : " Tutta m' apparve dai colli alle foci " (l. 153). If the familiar features of the " aiuola che ci fa tanto feroci " were distinguishable at such a distance, *a fortiori* the markings on the surface of the Moon, had there been any, must have been visible to him. Philalethes suggests the explanation that Dante was aware that the same face of the Moon was always turned towards the east, and that consequently the " shadow in the Moon " which we see would not be seen on the further side.

A very interesting discussion of the various theories as to the origin of the spots on the Moon, which forms an instructive commentary on Dante's own theories, is to be found in the *Quaestiones super quatuor libros Aristotelis de Coelo et Mundo* attributed to Albert of Saxony.[1] The passage which chiefly interests us occurs in *Quaestio* xxiv. of the second book, dealing with Lib. II. summa iii. cap. 2, of Aristotle's *De Coelo et Mundo* :—

Quartum propositorum erat, utrum macula illa que apparet in luna causetur ex diversitate partium lune, vel ex aliquo extrinseco. Et arguitur primo, quod non ex diversitate partium lune, ex eo quod ipsa luna est corpus simplex. Corporis autem simplicis partes sunt similes ejusdem rationis, sicut patet de aqua et similiter de aëre, et sic de aliis corporibus simplicibus. Secundo, solis et aliarum stellarum partes sunt similes et uniformes in raritate et densitate, ergo similiter partes ipsius lune ; et per consequens non ex diversitate partium lune videtur pervenire apparitio macule in luna. Tertio, nam si sic hoc esset quod alique partes lune essent magis rare et alique minus. Sed probatur quod non ; nam tunc in eclipsi solis radius luminis a sole transiret ad nos per partes lune magis raras ; quod tamen apparet falsum. Deinde probatur quod talis macule fantasia perveniat ab aliquo extrinseco. Nam ex quo corpus ipsius lune est corpus tersum et bene politum et speculare, videtur quod terra obversa lune causet suam similitudinem et imaginem in ipsa luna tanquam in speculo ; et per

[1] *Quaestiones Subtilissime Alberti de Saxonia in libros de celo et mundo.* Venetiis, 1492.

consequens nobis inspicientibus lunam et videntibus terram in luna reflexe appareat nobis talis macula.

In ista questione primo videndum est de quesito, ponendo opiniones de hoc, et improbationes earum. Secundo ponam de hoc opinionem quam reputo esse veram. Tertio videbitur de figura talis macule.

De primo erat una opinio quod causa macule apparentis in luna est vapor elevatus ab ipsa luna interpositus inter nos et lunam, per quem nobis obumbratur aliqua pars lune. Et dicit commentator[1] quod aliqui dixerunt ipsam lunam attrahere ad se talem vaporem ad sui nutritionem. Aliqui dixerunt quod quia luna habet magnam proprietatem super aquas et humiditatem, ideo sue nature est attrahere sub se talem vaporem. Et isti haberent concedere dictam maculam in luna apparentem non ex diversitate partium lune sed ab extrinseco pervenire. Sed ista opinio non valet. Primo, quia exalationes et vapores non uniformiter attrahuntur omni tempore et in consimili figura, sed valde difformiter, et tamen illa macula apparet semper uniformis et ejusdem figure, et per consequens non causatur ex tali exalatione et vapore interposito inter nos et lunam. Secundo, si semper esset talis vapor sub luna, tamen non propter diversitatem aspectus, non appareret in eadem parte lune quia secundum quod luna esset propinquior vel remotior a nobis talis macula deberet apparere in alia et in alia parte lune. Nec valet precipue illud quod dixerunt primi, scilicet quod luna attrahit ad se vaporem ad sui nutritionem, postquam corpora celestia non sunt nutribilia, cum nec sint generabilia nec corruptibilia nec alterabilia.

Secunda opinio erat quod illa macula non est aliud quam imago representativa aliquorum corporum hic inferius, sicut terre, vel montium, vel aliquorum hujusmodi; quae quidem corpora videntur in luna ad modum ad quem possumus videre corpora in speculo reflexe. Et hoc ideo quia sicut dixit illa opinio luna est corpus politum tersum et speculare. Sed illud non valet nam oporteret quod ad motum lune talis imago appareret in alia et in alia parte lune, recte sicut speculo moto imagines apparent in alia et in alia parte ejus. Sed consequens est falsum. Secundo, si luna haberet sic virtutem reflectendi imagines corporum tunc imago totalis terre deberet nobis apparere simul in ipsa luna. Sed hoc est falsum, quia non est talis figure sicut est illa macula.

De secundo est tertia opinio, scilicet commentatoris[2]; quam reputo esse veram, quod illa macula pervenit ex diversitate partium lune secundum raritatem et dempsitatem majorem et minorem. Nam partes in quibus apparet macula sunt rariores, et ideo minus bene possunt lucere. Partes autem juxta illas sunt dempsiores, et ideo magis possunt lucere.[3] Patet hoc in simili de alabastro, unde illa pars que est bene dempsa vel non transparens est valde alba, et illa que est transparens ad modum vitri est obscura, et tendens ad nigritu-

---

[1] That is, Averroës' "che il gran comento feo" (*Inf.* iv. 144). He was universally in the Middle Ages known as the commentator *par excellence*, on account of his great commentary on the works of Aristotle. (*Cf.* p. 46, note 3.)

[2] That is, Averroës; see the preceding note.

[3] This, as we have seen, is the opinion at first adopted by Dante, but afterwards rejected by him.

dinem. Et si queratur quare luna est taliter difformis in suis partibus dicatur quod hoc est de ejus natura.

Quantum ad tertium, scilicet de figura talis macule, dicit Albertus[1] quod

[1] That is, Albertus Magnus, who describes the figure in his treatise *De Coelo et Mundo*. It is interesting to find the description of Albertus copied almost verbatim (allowance being made for the exigencies of the rhyme) by Jean de Meun in the *Roman de la Rose*. After a discussion as to the cause of the dark spots on the surface of the Moon (ll. 18,373-87)* which is evidently taken directly or indirectly from the opinion of Averroës † on the subject, Jean proceeds to give a detailed description of the form of the object which the dark patch most nearly resembles :—

> ". . . La part de la lune oscure
> Nous represente la figure
> D'une trop merveilleuse beste :
> C'est d'un serpent qui tient sa teste
> Vers occident adès encline,
> Vers orient sa queue afine ;
> Sor son dos porte un arbre estant,
> Ses rains vers orient estant ;
> Mès en estendant les bestorne.
> Sor ce bestorneïs sejorne
> Uns hons sor ses bras apuiés,
> Qui vers occident a ruiés
> Ses piez et ses cuisses andeus,
> Si com il pert au semblant d'eus."

(ll. 18,418-32.)

A comparison of this passage (the source of which M. Langlois in his exhaustive *Origines et Sources du Roman de la Rose* failed to identify) with the passage in the treatise of Albertus Magnus will show how closely Jean de Meun followed his authority.

Albertus, after dealing with various theories as to the cause of the image in the Moon, "causa ydoli quod apparet in luna," concludes his chapter with a minute description of the figure in question as it appeared to him after repeated and careful observation :—

" In quantum nos considerare potuimus ad visum diligenti et frequenti consideratione videtur nobis umbra hec esse ex parte orientis versus inferiorem arcum lune, et habere figuram draconis convertentis caput ad occidentem et caudam ad orientem revolventis ex parte inferioris arcus ; cuius cauda in fine non est acuta, sed lata per modum folii habentis tres portiones circuli ad se invice[m] conterminatas ; in cuius draconis dorso erigitur figura arboris, cuius

* Ll. 17,773-87 in the edition of Francisque-Michel (vol. ii. p. 199). Michel made an error of 600 lines in his numbering owing to his having jumped from 3,407 to 4,008 in his first volume (p. 112).

† In the *De Substantia Orbis*, cap. 2.

ibi est quasi figura leonis [1] cujus caput est versus orientem et super dorsum ejus est quasi arbor transversaliter sita et similiter imago hominis lateraliter appodiati, cujus pedes sunt versus posteriora leonis. Et dicit quod talis figura melius potest videri aliquəntulum post plenilunium, et circa ortum solis, quia tunc aer est purus et serenus.

Ad rationes—Ad primam dico quod corpus lunae bene est simplex substantialiter, cum hoc tamen stet quod potest habere aliquam diversitatem in suis partibus quantum ad raritatem et dempsitatem in suis partibus. Ad secundam dico quod non est simile de sole et aliis stellis ex una parte, et luna ex altera ; nec oportet assignare causam dissimilitudinis nisi quia de natura istorum corporum sit. Ad tertiam dico quod licet una pars lune sit aliquantulum rarior alia, tamen non est ita rara quod lumen solis possit transire totam profunditatem lune. Ad ultimam patet ex improbatione secunde opinionis.

This problem seems to have had a special fascination for the philosophical minds of the Middle Ages,[2] so that it is not to be wondered at that Dante too, who was of an eminently speculative cast of mind, should have felt the attraction for it.

rami a medio stipite obliquantur inferiori parte lune versus orientem ; et super obliquum stipitis eius per ulnas et caput appodiatum (sic) est homo, cuius crura descendunt a superiori parte lune versus partem occidentalem (Lib. II. tract. iii. cap. 8).''

M. Langlois does not mention Albertus Magnus among the authors whose works were utilised by Jean de Meun in his continuation of the Roman de la Rose. It is evident, however, that the name of Albertus must be added to the list. A careful study of the two would in all probability reveal other passages in which Jean Clopinel was indebted to the Doctor Universalis. (Cf. Romania, xxiv. 277-278.)

[1] Albertus Magnus, as a matter of fact, says the figure is not that of a lion, but of a dragon. (See quotation in note 1 on previous page.)

[2] Cf. Ristoro d' Arezzo, La Composizione del Mondo, iii. 8 ; and Jacopo di Dante, Il Dottrinale, xxvi.

DANTE'S REFERENCES TO PYTHAGORAS[1]

DANTE makes mention of Pythagoras eight times in his works,[2] seven times in the *Convivio*, once in the *De Monarchia*. Once also, in the *Convivio*, he mentions his followers, the Pythagoreans.[3] In only three instances does he indicate the source of his information with regard to the opinions or facts quoted in connection with the Samian philosopher.[4]

The object of the present article is, where possible, to identify the authorities made use of by Dante in this particular connection, and to point out the various passages in the works of the several writers to whom he was indebted.

I

CONVIVIO II. 14

In this passage, which is one of those where his authority is indicated, Dante refers to the Pythagorean doctrine as to the numerical origin of all things :—

Pittagora, secondochè dice Aristotile nel primo della *Metafisica*,[5] poneva i principii delle cose naturali lo pari e lo dispari, considerando tutte le cose essere numero (ll. 144-147).

---

[1] Reprinted, with additions, from *Romania*, xxiv. 376-384.

[2] *Convivio*, ii. 14, l. 144; ii. 16, l. 102; iii. 5, l. 29; iii. 11, ll. 30, 41; iv. 1, l. 5 ; iv. 21, l. 20; *De Monarchia*, i. 15, l. 16.

[3] *Convivio*, ii. 15, l. 48.

[4] *Convivio*, ii. 14, l. 144 ; iii. 11, l. 30 ; *De Monarchia*, i. 15, l. 16.

[5] Fraticelli and others read *Fisica*, but there is no doubt that *Metafisica* ought to be read, as the passage referred to comes from the *Metaphysica*, not the *Physica* (see below, § 8).

The statement of Aristotle[1] here alluded to is as follows[2]:—

Apparent etenim etiam isti [*sc.* Pythagorici] numerum existimare principium esse, ut materiam entibus, et ut passiones, ac habitus; numeri autem elementa, par et impar; quorum alterum finitum, alterum infinitum: unum vero ex ambobus his esse, par etenim et impar esse, numerum autem ex uno; numeros vero, ut dictum est, totum coelum.   Horum autem alii decem aiunt inter se coordinata esse principia : finitum, infinitum; impar, par; unum, plure . . . ; bonum, malum.   (*Metaphys.* Lib. I. summa ii. cap. 3.)

II

Convivio II. 15

Dante here alludes to the theory of the Pythagoreans as to the origin of the Galaxy or Milky Way:—

È da sapere che di quella Galassia li filosofi hanno avuto diverse opinioni. . . . Li Pittagorici dissero che 'l sole alcuna fiata errò nella sua via, e passando per altre parti non convenienti al suo fervore, arse il luogo, per lo quale passò; e rimasevi quell' apparenza dell' arsura.   E credo che si mossero dalla favola di Fetonte, la quale narra Ovidio nel principio del secondo di *Metamorfoseos* (ll. 45-55).[3]

His authority here may have been Aristotle, who in his *De Meteoris* says :—

De Lacteo Circulo Antiquorum opiniones.   Qualiter autem et propter quam causam sit et quid est Lac, dicamus jam.   Prepercurremus autem et de hoc quae ab aliis dicta sunt primo.   Vocatorum igitur Pythagoreorum quidam aiunt viam esse hanc; hi quidem excidentium cujusdam astrorum, secundum dictam sub Phaëtonte lationem; hi autem Solem hoc circulo delatum esse aliquando aiunt; velut igitur exustum esse hunc locum, aut aliquam aliam talem passionem passum esse a latione ipsorum.   (Lib. I. summa ii. cap. 5.)

There are good reasons, however, as I have pointed out elsewhere,[4] for believing that the source of Dante's information in this passage of the *Convivio* was not Aristotle, but Albertus Magnus.   The latter, in his treatise *De Meteoris*, deals at some length with the various opinions as to the origin of the Galaxy. His account of the Pythagorean theory is as follows :—

---

[1] *Cf.* Cicero, *Acad. Quaest.* iv. 37 : St. Augustine, *De Civitate Dei*, vi. 5.

[2] All quotations from Aristotle are of course given in Latin, Dante not having been acquainted with the original Greek texts.   The references are to the Giunta edition, *Aristotelis opera omnia Latine*, Venice, 1552 (11 vols., folio).

[3] *Metam.* ii. 1-324.   [4] See above, pp. 42-47.

De Galaxia secuǹdum opiniones eorum qui dixerunt Galaxiam esse conbustionem solis. . . . Fuerunt autem quidam qui dixerunt quod sol aliquando movebatur in loco suo; et suo lumine et calore conbussit orbem in illo loco. . . . Fuit autem, ut puto, hec opinio Pyctagore, qui dixit esse terram stellam et moveri, et celum stare et comburi a sole.   (Lib. I. tract. ii. cap. 2.)[1]

III

Convivio II. 16

Dante, at the end of this chapter, refers to the accepted belief that Pythagoras was the inventor of the term "philosophy" :—

Dico e affermo che la Donna, di cui io innamorai appresso lo primo amore, fu la bellissima e onestissima figlia dello Imperadore dell' universo, alla quale Pittagora pose nome *Filosofia* (ll. 99-103).

His authority for this statement, which he repeats in a different connection in another chapter of the *Convivio*,[2] was perhaps St. Augustine, who in the *De Civitate Dei*,[3] speaking

---

[1] Albertus Magnus discusses this question again in the *De Proprietatibus Elementorum*, where he attributes the above theory to Plato : "Dicit Plato quod exorbitatio solis et planetarum fuit causa diluvii ignis; et inducit fabulam de Phetonte quam Ovidius a Grecis sumptam latinam fecit ; et dicit quod licet videatur esse fabula, tamen est res vera.   Et sunt haec ejus verba: Denique enim illa etiam fama quae nobis quoque comparata (*sic*) est Phetontem quondam, Solis filium, affectantem officium patris currus ascendisse luciferos; nec servatis solennibus irrigationis (*sic*) orbis (*sic*) exurisse (*sic*) terram, et ipsam (*sic*) flammis celestibus conflagrasse, fabulosa quidem putatur, sed res vera est."   (II. xii.)

The opinion of Plato here quoted occurs in the *Timaeus*.   It is interesting to note that Albertus made use of the translation of Chalcidius, whose rendering of the passage (very corruptly given in the above version) is as follows: "Denique illa etiam fama, quae vobis quoque conperta est, Phaëthontem quondam, Solis filium, adfectantem officium patris currus ascendisse luciferos, nec servatis sollennibus aurigationis orbitis exussisse terrena ipsumque flammis caelestibus conflagrasse, fabulosa quidem putatur, sed res est vera." (*Tim.*, 22. c.)

[2] *Convivio*, iii. 11.   See below, p. 92, § 5.

[3] Dante was certainly acquainted with the *De Civitate Dei*, for he quotes it in the *De Monarchia* (iii. 4, ll. 51-59).   It may be stated that this quotation, which Witte was unable to identify, comes from *De Civ. Dei*, Lib. xvi. cap. 2 (*ad fin.*).   The same passage is quoted both by the Anonimo Fiorentino (on *Inf.* viii. *ad init.*), and by Boccaccio (at the end of *Lezione* vi, where, either by an oversight, or through a misreading of the MSS., Milanesi reads *vere* instead of *vomere*, thus entirely losing the point of the quotation).

of the two schools of philosophy, the Italian and the Ionic, says :—

> Quantum adtinet ad litteras Graecas, . . . duo philosophorum genera tradun-tur : unum Italicum . . . alterum Ionicum . . . Italicum genus auctorem habuit Pythagoram Samium, a quo etiam ferunt ipsum philosophiae nomen exortum. (Lib. viii. cap. 2.)

And again :—

> Multo magis post eos [sc. prophetas] fuerunt philosophi gentium, qui hoc etiam nomine vocarentur, quod coepit a Samio Pythagora. (Lib. xviii. cap. 37.) — Tunc et Pythagoras, ex quo coeperunt appellari philosophi. (Lib. xviii. cap. 25.)

It is not impossible, however, that Dante was thinking of a passage in the *Tusculanae Quaestiones*[1] of Cicero, in which the origin of the name "philosopher" is mentioned in connection with Pythagoras. Dante appears to have made use of this same passage in *Convivio*, iii. 11, which is discussed below (see § 5).

IV

Convivio III. 5

The reference here is to the Pythagorean theory that the Earth was a star and that there was a "counter-Earth" ($\dot{\alpha}\nu\tau\acute{\iota}\chi\theta\omega\nu$), and that both of them revolved ; also that the central place in the universe was occupied, not by the Earth, but by fire :—

> Questo mondo volle Pittagora e li suoi seguaci dicere che fosse una delle stelle, e che un' altra a lei fosse opposita così fatta : e chiamava quella *Antictona*. E dicea ch' erano ambedue in una spera che si volgea da Oriente in Occidente, e per questa revoluzione si girava il sole intorno a noi, e ora si vedea e ora non si vedea. E dicea che 'l fuoco era nel mezzo di queste, ponendo quello essere più nobile corpo che l' acqua e che la terra, e ponendo il mezzo nobilissimo intra li luoghi delli quattro corpi semplici (ll. 29-41).

This account is taken from the *De Coelo*[2] of Aristotle, where the Pythagorean doctrine is thus expounded :—

---

[1] *Tuscul. Quaest.* Lib. v. § 3.   The passage is quoted in full under § 5, below.

[2] Dante gives a reference to this treatise later on, where he says that this and other theories have been confuted by Aristotle : " Queste opinioni sono riprovate per false nel secondo *di Cielo e Mondo* da quello glorioso Filosofo, al quale la Natura più aperse li suoi segreti " (ll. 53-56).

Reliquum autem est de Terra dicere, et ubi posita sit, et utrum de iis sit, quae quiescunt, an ex iis, quae moventur ; et de figura ipsius. De positione igitur non eandem omnes habent opinionem ; sed cum plurimi, qui totum coelum finitum esse aiunt, in medio jacere dicant ; contra qui circa Italiam incolunt, vocanturque Pythagorei, dicunt. In medio enim ignem esse inquiunt ; terram autem astrorum unum existentem, circulariter latam circa medium, noctem et diem facere. Amplius autem oppositam aliam huic conficiunt terram, quam *antichthona* nomine vocant. . . . Multis autem et aliis videbitur non oportere terrae medii regionem assignare, fidem non ex iis, quae apparent, consyderantibus, sel potius ex rationibus. Honorabilissimo enim putant convenire honorabilissimam competere regionem. Esse autem ignem quidem terra honorabiliorem. . . . Quicunque quidem non in medio jacere aiunt ipsam [terram], moveri circulariter circa medium, non solum autem hanc, sed et *antichthona*. Quidam autem et jacentem in centro dicunt ipsam volvi, et moveri circa semper statum polum, quemadmodum in *Timaeo*[1] scriptum est. (Lib. II. summa iv. cap i.)[2]

[1] Plato says : τὴν γῆν, τροφὸν ἡμετέραν εἰλουμένην περὶ τὸν διὰ παντὸς πολὺν τεταμένον ("altricem nostram verti circa axem, qui per totam terram extenditur ") ; *cf.* Cicero, *Acad. Quaest.* iv. § 39. Dante also refers to the Platonic theory further on in this same chapter : " Platone fu poi d' altra opinione, e scrisse in un suo libro, che si chiama *Timeo*, che la terra col mare era bene il mezzo di tutto " (ll. 45-48).

[2] This passage is from the Greek-Latin translation of Aristotle, the so-called *Antiqua translatio*, which corresponds to what Dante speaks of (*Convivio*, ii. 15, l. 64) as " la nuova traslazione ". This version was made either by, or at the instigation of, Thomas Aquinas (see the article on " Dante's Obligations to Albertus Magnus," p. 43, n. 4). In the Arabic-Latin version (Dante's " vecchia traslazione ") the above passage runs as follows :—

" Volumus modo dicere de dispositione Terrae et perscrutari de ea, et de loco ejus, et utrum sit quiescens, aut mota. Dicamus ergo quod Antiqui diversi sunt in loco ejus ; et omnes dicentes quod coelum est finitum dicunt terram esse positam in medio. Pythagorici autem habitantes Italiam contradicunt illis, et dicunt quod ignis est positus in medio et quod terra est stellarum una, et revolvit circulariter, et ex motu ejus circulari fit nox et dies, et faciunt aliam terram, quam vocant *antugamonani*."

In the version of Joannes Argiropilus of Byzantium the last sentence is rendered as follows, the Greek word ἀντίχθων being translated, instead of being retained, as in the Greek-Latin version : " Aliam autem huic contrariam terram conficiunt, quam *terram adversam* vocant ". It is evident that Dante made use of the Greek-Latin version, whence he got the term *Antictona*. The term *Antugamonani*, which occurs in the Arabic-Latin version, is doubtless the transliteration of the Arabic equivalent for ἀντίχθων. It may be noted that the Greek word is mentioned by Cicero in the *Tusculanae Quaestiones* (i. § 28).

V

Convivio III. 11

In this passage Dante refers, as he had already done on a previous occasion,[1] to the invention of the terms " philosopher," and " philosophy " by Pythagoras. His statement is as follows:—

Dico adunque che anticamente in Italia, . . . nel tempo quasi che Numa Pompilio secondo re de' Romani, viveva uno Filosofo nobilissimo, che si chiamò Pittagora. E che egli fosse in quel tempo, par che ne tocchi alcuna cosa Tito Livio nella prima parte del suo volume incidentemente.[2] E dinanzi da costui erano chiamati i seguitatori di Scienza, non *filosofi*, ma *sapienti*, siccome furono quelli sette Savi antichissimi, che la gente ancora nomina per fama : lo primo delli quali ebbe nome Solon, lo secondo Chilon, il terzo Periandro, il quarto Talete, il quinto Cleobulo, il sesto Biante, il settimo Pittaco.[3] Questo Pittagora, domandato se egli si riputava sapiente, negò a sè questo vocabolo, e disse sè essere non *sapiente*, ma *amatore di sapienza*. E quinci nacque poi che ciascuno studioso in sapienza fosse *amatore di sapienza* chiamato, cioè *filosofo ;* chè tanto vale come in Greco *filos* dire *amatore* in Latino, e quindi dicemo noi *filos* quasi *amatore*, e *sofia* quasi *sapienza*[4] . . . per che notare si puote che non d' arroganza, ma d' umiltade è vocabolo. Da questo nasce il vocabolo del suo proprio atto, *Filosofia* (ll. 22-54).

Dante's authority here apparently was Cicero, who in the *Tusculanae Quaestiones* says :—

[1] *Convivio*, ii. 16, ll. 99-103. See above, p. 89, § 3.

[2] Livy's statement, which Dante does not seem to have read at all carefully, is as follows : " Inclita justitia religioque ea tempestate Numae Pompilii erat. . . . Auctorem doctrinae ejus, quia non exstat alius, falso Samium Pythagoran edunt, quem Servio Tullio regnante Romae, centum amplius post annos, in ultima Italiae ora, . . . juvenum aemulantium studia coetus habuisse constat." (i. § 18.)   Cicero, in the *Tusculanae Quaestiones* (i. § 16 ; iv. § 1), states that Pythagoras came into Italy in the reign of Tarquinius Superbus.

[3] Dante apparently got the names of the seven Sages from the *De Civitate Dei* of St. Augustine: " Eo tempore Pittacus Mitylenaeus, alius e septem sapientibus, fuisse perhibetur.   Et quinque ceteros, qui, ut septem numerentur, Thaleti, quem supra commemoravimus, et huic Pittaco adduntur, eo tempore fuisse scribit Eusebius, quo captivus Dei populus in Babylonia tenebatur.   Hi sunt autem : Solon Atheniensis, Chilon Lacedaemonius, Periandrus Corinthius, Cleobulus Lindius, Bias Prienaeus.   Omnes hi, septem appellati sapientes. . . . Tunc et Pythagoras, ex quo coeperunt appellari philosophi." (Lib. xviii. cap. 25.)

[4] This derivation of *filosofo* Dante doubtless found in the *De Derivationibus Verborum* of Uguccione, a work which he quotes elsewhere (*Convivio*, iv. 6, l. 39) as his authority for the derivation of the word *Autore* (see the article on " Dante's Latin Dictionary," pp. 106-107).

Illi septem, qui a Graecis σοφοὶ, sapientes a nostris et habebantur et nominabantur.

. . . A quibus ducti deinceps omnes, qui in rerum contemplatione studia ponebant, sapientes et habebantur, et nominabantur : idque eorum nomen usque ad Pythagorae manavit aetatem : quem . . . Phliuntem ferunt venisse, eumque cum Leonte, principe Phliasiorum, docte et copiose disseruisse quaedam. Cujus ingenium, et eloquentiam cum admiratus esset Leon, quaesivisse ex eo, qua maxime arte confideret. At illum artem quidem se scire nullam, sed esse philosophum. Admiratum Leontem novitatem nominis, quaesisse, Quinam essent philosophi . . .? Pythagoram autem respondisse . . . raros esse quosdam, qui, ceteris omnibus pro nihilo habitis, rerum naturam studiose intuerentur : hos se appellare sapientiae studiosos, id est enim philosophos. (v. § 3.)

There appears, however, also to be a reminiscence of a passage[1] in the *De Civitate Dei* :—

Italicum genus [philosophorum] auctorem habuit Pythagoram Samium a quo etiam ferunt ipsum philosophiae nomen exortum. Nam cum antea sapientes appellarentur, qui modo quodam laudabilis vitae aliis praestare videbantur, iste interrogatus, quid profiteretur, philosophum se esse respondit, id est studiosum vel amatorem sapientiae ; quoniam sapientem profiteri arrogantissimum videbatur.[2] (Lib. viii., cap. 2.)

[1] This passage is quoted verbatim by Vincent of Beauvais in his *Speculum Doctrinale* (i. 10).

[2] Dante's words "notare si puote che non d' arroganza, ma d' umiltade è vocabolo" seem to be an echo of this sentence of St. Augustine. This same phrase, however, occurs in Uguccione's article on the word *Philosophus*, which appears to have been in part compiled from the above passages in Cicero and St. Augustine, and may have been Dante's actual authority here (see below, pp. 106-107). It occurs also in the account of Pythagoras given in the *Fiore di Filosofi* (attributed to Brunetto Latino), which is worth quoting in this connection :—

"Pittagora fue uno filosafo, e fue d' uno paese, ch' avea nome Samo : nel quale paese regnava uno prencipe che, siccome tiranno, struggea la terra, la cui iniquitade e la cui superbia offendea tanto l' animo di questo filosofo, ch' elli lasciò lo suo paese e venne in Italia, ch' era chiamata in quello temporale la grande Grecia, e fecelo per non vedere così mala signoria. In questo Pittagora si cominciò lo nome della filosofia, chè in prima erano appellati Savi quelli ch' erano innanzi agli altri per costumi e per nobile vita. Pittagora fue domandato quello che si tenesse, ed e' rispuose, ch' era filosafo, cioè studioso ed amatore di sapienzia ; chè 'l nominarsi l' uomo savio è vizio di grande arroganza. Pittagora fue di tanta antoritade che gli uditori, ciò che gli udieno dicere, sì scriveano per sentenzia ; e quando disputavano insieme, non rendeano altra ragione ne' loro argomenti, se non che Pittagora l' avea detto."

VI

Convivio IV. 1

Dante here quotes a saying of Pythagoras :—

Pittagora dice, Nell' amistà si fa uno di più (ll. 5-6).

This is taken from the *De Officiis*[1] of Cicero :—

Pythagoras ultimum in amicitia putavit, ut unus fiat ex pluribus.   (i. § 17.)

There cannot be the least doubt as to this being the source of Dante's quotation, since a few lines further on he quotes a Greek proverb—

In greco proverbio è detto: Degli amici esser deono tutte le cose comuni (ll. 16-18)—

which comes from the previous chapter of the same book of the *De Officiis* :—

In Grecorum proverbio est: Amicorum esse omnia communia.   (i. § 16.)

VII

Convivio IV. 21

This passage (ll. 20-25), in which Dante states the Pythagorean theory as to the equal nobility of all souls, whether of men, animals, plants or minerals, seems to be rather a general statement of the Pythagorean doctrine on the subject than a direct quotation from any particular work. In illustration of it Mazzucchelli quotes the following passages from the *Vitae Philosophorum* of Diogenes Laertius :—

---

[1] This work of Cicero was an especial favourite with Dante. He directly quotes it at least ten times (*Conv.* iv. 8, 15, 24, 25, 27[2]; *Mon.* ii. 5[2], 8, 10); and several other instances besides those indicated above might be pointed out where he has made use of it without acknowledgment. A striking example is his quotation of a passage of Ennius in the *De Monarchia* (ii. 10), which comes from this same book of the *De Officiis* (i. § 12). And, as Dr. Moore has pointed out (*Academy*, 4th June, 1892), the fundamental distinction of sins of violence and sins of fraud in the *Inferno* (xi. 23-26) is adopted almost verbatim from the same source (i. § 13), a further quotation from this passage being introduced later on in the *Inferno* (xxvii. 75). See the article *Officiis, De*, in my *Dante Dictionary*.

Alii vero Pythagoram alium quendam aliptem athletas ita solitum enutrire (carnibus) dicunt, non hunc (Samium). Quo enim pacto cum hic et necare vetuerit, sustineat gustare animalia, quae commune nobiscum jus habeant animae. (viii. § 13.) Primum hunc (Pythagoram) sensisse aiunt, animam circulum necessitatis immutantem aliis alias illigari animantibus. (§ 14.) . . . Mitem stirpem non excidendam, nec laedandam : ne animal quidem laedendum quod hominibus non noceat. (§ 23.) . . . Porro fabarum interdicebat usum, quod cum spiritibus sint plenae, animati maxime sint participes. (§ 24). Ex planis autem solidas figuras ; ex quibus item solida consistere corpora, quorum et quatuor elementa esse, ignem, aquam, terram, aërem, quae per omnia transeant ac vertantur, ex quibus fieri mundum animatum, intelligibilem, rotundum, mediam terram continentem, etc. (§ 25). . . . Vivere item omnia, quae caloris participent, atque ideo et plantas esse animantes ; animam tamen non habere omnes. Animam vero avulsionem aetheris esse, et calidi, et frigidi, eo quod sit particeps frigidi aetheris. Differre autem a vita animam, esseque illam immortalem, quandoquidem et id, a quo avulsa est, immortale sit. Porro animalia ex se invicem nasci seminali ratione ; eam vero quae e terra fiat generationem, non posse subsistere. Semen autem esse cerebri stillam, quae in se calidum contineat vaporem. Haec vero dum infunditur vulvae, ex cerebro saniem et humorem, sanguinemque profluere. Ex quibus caro, nervi, ossa, pili, totumque consistat corpus : e vapore autem animam ae sensum constare. (§ 28.)

VIII

DE MONARCHIA I. 15

In this passage Dante alludes once more [1] to the Pythagorean doctrine that number and the elements of number were the elements of all things ; and he refers particularly to the " parallel tables " [2] of Pythagoras, which exhibit his ten universal principles.

---

[1] See above, § 1.

[2] The arrangement of these principles in the Pythagorean συστοιχία is as follows :—

πέρας	ἄπειρον
περιττόν	ἄρτιον
ἕν	πλῆθος
δεξιόν	ἀριστερόν
ἄρρεν	θῆλυ
ἠρεμοῦν	κινούμενον
εὐθύ	καμπύλον
φῶς	σκότος
ἀγαθόν	κακόν
τετράγωνον	ἑτερόμηκες.

Dante states that the Samian philosopher placed Unity in the same column as Good, and Plurality in the same as Evil[1] :—

In omni genere rerum illud est optimum, quod est maxime unum, ut Philosopho placet in iis quae de simpliciter Ente. Unde fit quod unum esse videtur esse radix ejus quod est esse bonum ; et multa esse, ejus quod est esse malum. Quare Pythagoras in correlationibus suis, ex parte boni ponebat unum, ex parte vero mali plura, ut patet in primo eorum quae de simpliciter Ente (ll. 10-19).[2]

Dante's authority here, as he tells us, was the *Metaphysica* of Aristotle. As the passage to which he refers has already been quoted in illustration of *Convivio*, ii. 14 (ll. 144-147),[3] it is unnecessary to give it here.

---

[1] As will be seen from the table given in the previous note, ἕν and ἀγαθόν are placed in one column, πλῆθος and κακόν in the other.

[2] *Ea De Simpliciter Ente* is one of the names given by Dante to Aristotle's *Metaphysica* (*cf. Mon.* i. 12, l. 51 ; i. 13, l. 15 ; i. 15, ll. 12, 19 ; iii. 14, l. 48) ; elsewhere he speaks of it as *Prima Philosophia* (*cf. Mon.* iii. 12, l. 3 ; *Conv.* i. 1, l. 2) ; and *Metaphysica* (*cf. Epist.* x. 5, 16, 20 ; *V. N.* § 42, l. 30 ; *Conv.* ii. 3, l. 32 ; ii. 5, ll. 13, 118 ; ii. 14, l. 145 ; ii. 16, l. 90 ; iii. 11, l. 12 ; iii. 14, l. 98 ; iv. 10, l. 83).

[3] See above, p. 87, § 1, and note 5.

DANTE'S LATIN DICTIONARY

(THE *MAGNÆ DERIVATIONES* OF UGUCCIONE DA PISA)[1]

Huguitio Pisanus, or, to give him the Italian name by which Dante refers to him in the *Convivio* (iv. 6, l. 39), Uguccione, was, as his title implies, a native of Pisa.[2] But little is known of his life beyond that he was born about the middle of the twelfth century, that he was professor of ecclesiastical jurisprudence at Bologna *circa* 1178, and that he was bishop of Ferrara from 1190 till his death in 1210, fifty-five years before the birth of Dante.[3] Besides his dictionary, the *Magnæ De-*

---

[1] Reprinted, with additions, from *Romania*, xxvi. 537-54.

[2] Uguccione himself informs us that Pisa was his native place, in a naïve autobiographical note introduced in the article on the word *Pis* in the *Magnæ Derivationes;* this article, which is reproduced as affording a typical specimen of his method, runs as follows :—

"*Pis* grece latine dicitur aurum, unde *hec pisa, -e,* quoddam genus leguminis, quia ea pensabantur ad auri minutum ; et peccant illi qui dicunt quod *pisa* est pluralis numeri et neutri generis, scilicet *hec pisa, -orum ;* peccavit ergo ille qui dixit :—

"'Hec pisa sunt bona, sunt quoque pinguia, sunt sine lardo.'

"Et a *pis* vel *pisa* dicta est *Pisa, -e,* quedam civitas Grecie ab abundantia auri, vel illius leguminis ; unde *piseus, -a, -um ;* et pluraliter *hec Pise, -arum,* quedam civitas Tuscie, quia illi qui hanc civitatem edificaverunt ab illa Pisa civitate Grecie venerunt. Vel *Pisa* quasi pensa a pensando, id est deliberando, cum enim propolleat sapientia cum pensacione, id est deliberatione et consilio, agit. Vel *Pise* dicuntur a *pis* quod est aurum, quasi auree ; sicut enim aurum prefulget aliis metallis, sic hec inter alias prefulget civitates. De hac civitate oriundus extitit qui hoc opus multis vigiliis, laboribus, et anxietatibus, quadam tamen delectatione tolerans composuit."

[3] The following brief notice of him is given in the *Fragmenta* appended to the *Chronica Fr. Salimbene Parmensis* (Parmae, MDCCCLVII), p. 414: "Huguitio natione tuscus, civis pisanus, episcopus ferrariensis fuit. Librum *Derivationum* composuit : viriliter et digne et honeste episcopatum rexit, et

rivationes (or *De Derivationibus Verborum*, as it is sometimes
called), which is his chief title to fame, he was the author of a
Summa Decretorum, a work on the canon law, written probably
during his tenure of the chair at Bologna.[1] He has also been
credited with the authorship of a treatise on the Latin accent,
De dubio accentu.[2]

The *Magnæ Derivationes*, of which a goodly number of
manuscripts are in existence,[3] has never been printed. It is one
of the authorities quoted by Du Cange in his *Glossarium Mediæ
et Infimæ Latinitatis*,[4] in which occasional extracts from it are
given ; and it was very largely utilised by Giovanni da Genova
(Joannes de Balbis) in the compilation of his *Catholicon* (completed in the year 1286),[5] which was among the earliest of printed
books.[6]   Uguccione's work is based to a considerable extent upon
the *Origines* of Isidore of Seville (his obligations to which he

laudabiliter vitam suam finivit, et alia quaedam opuscula quae sunt utilia et
habentur a pluribus, quae etiam vidi et legi non semel, neque bis. Anno
Domini MCCX, ultimo die aprilis, migravit ad Christum ; et stetit episcopatu
XX annis, minus uno die ".

[1] See Tiraboschi, *Storia della Letteratura Italiana*, iv. 441 ff., 685 ff.
(Milano, 1823).

[2] See Thurot, *Notices et Extraits de divers manuscrits latins pour servir à
l'histoire des doctrines grammaticales au moyen âge*, p. 509 (in *Notices et Extraits*,
etc., tom. xxii. part 2).

[3] There are four or five at Oxford, one at Cambridge, six in the British
Museum, and several in the Bibliothèque Nationale at Paris, and in the Biblioteca
Laurenziana at Florence.

[4] See his *Præfatio*, p. xxxiv.

[5] The MSS. of the *Catholicon* conclude with the following thanksgiving :—

"Immensas omnipotenti deo patri et filio et spiritui sancto graciarum referimus
acciones qui nostrum Catholicon ex multis et diversis doctorum texturis elabor-
atum atque contextum licet per multa annorum curricula in MCCLXXXVI
anno domini nonis marcii ad finem usque perduxit."

[6] The colophon of the Mainz edition of 1460 runs :—

"Altissimi presidio cujus nutu infantium lingue fiunt diserte, quique sepe
parvulis revelat quod sapientibus celat, hic liber egregius catholicon dominice
incarnacionis annis MCCCCLX alma in urbe maguntina nacionis inclite ger-
manice, quam dei clemencia tam alto ingenii lumine donoque gratuito ceteris
terrarum nacionibus preferre illustrareque dignatus est, non calami stili aut penne
suffragio, sed mira patronarum formarumque concordia proporcione et modulo
impressus et confectus est."

occasionally, but by no means adequately, acknowledges), and upon the *Elementarium Doctrinæ Rudimentum* (written *circa* 1060) of his fellow-countryman the Lombard Papia (more commonly known by the Latin form of his name, Papias).[1] It enjoyed a great reputation in the Middle Ages,[2] as is attested by the relatively large number of manuscripts (considering the nature and bulk of the work) still in existence ; and it continued to be quoted as an authority even as late as the sixteenth century.[3] That it was never printed was doubtless owing to the fact that it had been to a certain extent superseded by the more comprehensive and conveniently arranged *Catholicon*, which was consequently regarded as more worthy of the honour of being reproduced by the newly invented typographical process.[4]

The aim and object of his work are set forth by Uguccione in a somewhat highflown *Prologus*, which runs as follows[5] :—

Incipit Prologus super Derivationes Majores. Cum nostri prothoplasti suggestiva prevaricatione humanum genus a sue dignitatis culmine quam longe deciderit,[6] ac triplicis incommodi, scilicet indigentie, vicii, et ignorantie non modicam coartationem sumpserit, triplex huic triplici incommodo nobis a Deo suggeritur remedium, scilicet commoditas, virtus, et scientia. Nam indigentie molestiam commoditas, vicii corruptionem virtus, ignorantie cecitatem expellit scientia. Ad quam quidem a longe accedentes panniculum ab ea diripiendo sibi totam nupsisse[7] credentes, et si quandoque eam in quadam parte possideant, more tamen bestiarum degentes non modo predictam triplicem miseriam aliqua virtute

---

[1] See Du Cange, *Præfatio*, p. xxxiii. and Thurot, *op. cit.* p. 76.

[2] It is frequently quoted, for instance, in the *De Proprietatibus Rerum* of Bartholomaeus Anglicus (thirteenth century), and by Pietro di Dante, and Jacopo della Lana, and other of the early commentators on the *Divina Commedia*. " Ugutio vocabulista " is among the authorities quoted by Boccaccio in his *De Genealogia Deorum*, as well as in his *Comento*.

[3] It is mentioned, for instance, by Erasmus in one of his *Colloquia* ("Conflictus Thaliae et Barbariei ").

[4] See below, p. 101, note 6.

[5] From MS. *Misc.* 626 *Laud* (A), collated with MSS. 96 *e Musaeo* (B), and 376 *Bodl.* (C), in the Bodleian Library at Oxford, and with Codd. *Laur. Plut.* xxvii. *sin.* 1 (D), 5 (E), 6 (F), in the Biblioteca Laurenziana at Florence ; for a transcript of the passage from the last of these, together with the most important variants supplied by the other two Laurentian MSS., I am indebted to the kindness of Prof. Pio Rajna.

[6] A. *prevaricatione diabolus h. g. a s. d. c. q. l. dejecerit.*   [7] B. *implevisse.*

non redimere,[1] ut sit honestarum artium exercicio ad[2] pristine decusacionis relictum honorem aliquantulum valeant promoveri, sed etiam singulis diebus cumulare conantur.[3] Nam nec dentium exstancias[4] elimare, nec balbutientium linguarum vituligines[5] abradere, nec ingenii tarditatem excitare, nec madide oblivia memorie corripere, vel negligentiam redarguere nec maledicta[6] punire, nec sordes ac[7] vicia repellere, sed potius[8] in viciorum volutabro[9] provoluti, pecuniam congerere ac congeste inservire, vel etiam honestis officiis[10] obmissis lasciviam[11] corporis ingurgitare nituntur, quorum doctrinam, vitam, mortemque nichili[12] estimandum est.   Nos vero altius procedentes, ne si talentum a Deo nobis concessum[13] infoderemus in terra et patenter[14] furti argui[15] possemus, quod nature beneficio nobis denegabatur per famam extendere laboravimus, ut universe carnis generalitas illam licet tenuem una cum corpore neu unquam dissolveret. Opus igitur divina favente gratia componere statuimus, in quo, pre aliis, vocabulorum significationes, significationum distinctiones,[16] derivationum origines, ethimologiarum assignationes, interpretationum reperientur[17] expositiones; quarum[18] ignorantia latinitas naturaliter indiga quadam doctorum pigritia non modicum coartatur.   Nec hoc tantum,[19] ut cenodoxie vitream[20] fragilitatem lucrifaciamus, adimplere conabimur, quantum ut omnium scientie litterarum invigilantium communis inde utilitas efflorescat.   Nec cuivis[21] descendat in mentem nos in hoc opere perfectionem insinuatim polliceri,[22] cum nichil in humanis inventis ad unguem inveniatur expolitum, licet aliis de hac eadem re[23] tractantibus quadam singulari perfectione haut injuria videri possimus excellere. Nam hic parvulus suavius lactabitur, hic adultus uberius cibabitur, hic perfectus affluentius delectabitur, hic gignosophiste triviales, hic didascali quadriviales, hic legum professores, hic et theologie perscrutatores, hic ecclesiarum proficient gubernatores; hic supplebitur quicquid hactenus ex scientie defectu pretermissum est, hic eliminabitur[24] quicquid a longo tempore male usurpatum est.[25]   Si quis querat hujus operis quis sit auctor,[26] est dicendum quod Deus;[27] si quis querat hujus operis sit[28] instrumentum, dicendum[29] est quod patria pysanus, nomine Uguicio,[30] quasi Eugecio, id est bona terra, non tantum presentibus sed et

---

[1] B. *non habent redimere.*   [2] B. *aut ad.*   [3] B. *convalere nituntur.*

[4] B. *hesitancias.*   [5] B. *l. impedimenta v.*   [6] B. *male facta.*

[7] D. *nec.*   [8] A. *potius.*

[9] A. *voluptatibus,* C. *volutatibus,* B. *voluptatibus ve voluntatibus.*

[10] A. *serviciis.*

[11] E. *lacuciam;* the reading of F. is doubtful; it appears to be *lacunam.*

[12] A., *vix;* D. E., *juxta;* F. omits.   [13] B. *c. vel commissum,* D. *commissum.*

[14] F. *infoderemus, patuntur.*   [15] B. *redargui.*

[16] So the MS. quoted by Du Cange; A. reads *vocabulorum et significationum d.;* F. *v. significationum d.*

[17] B. *experientur vel r.*   [18] F. *quorum.*   [19] A. D. F. *tamen.*

[20] F. *vite eam.*   [21] Du Cange *minus.*   [22] Du Cange *adhibere.*

[23] B. *materia.*   [24] F. *elimabitur.*   [25] E. omits the rest of the *Prologus.*

[26] F. *quis auctor.*   [27] F. *Dominus.*   [28] F. *quis fuit i.*

[29] F. *respondendum.*

[30] B. *Huicio;* D. *Ugutio;* F. *Uguicio;* Du Cange *Hugutio.*

futuris[1] ; vel Uguicio, quasi Vigetio, id est virens terra non solum sibi sed etiam aliis.[2] Igitur Spiritus Sancti assistente gratia, ut qui omnium bonorum est distributor, nobis verborum copiam auctim suppeditare dignetur, et[3] a verbo augmenti nostre assertionis auspicium[4] sortiamur. *Explicit Prologus.*

Dante, who, as we shall show, was undoubtedly familiar with the *Magnæ Derivationes*, and availed himself of it pretty freely, only once mentions Uguccione by name or refers to his work. This mention occurs in the *Convivio* in connection with the etymology of the word *autore*, which Dante connects, on Uguccione's authority, with the Greek word *autentin* (*i.e.*, αὐθέντην)[5] ; he says :—

È da sapere che *autorità* non è altro che atto d' *autore*. Questo vocabolo, cioè *auctore*, senza questa terza lettera *c*, può discendere da due principii : l' uno si è d' un verbo, molto lasciato dall' uso in grammatica, che significa tanto quanto legare parole, cioè *auieo* (*i.e., avieo*). . . . Ed in quanto *autore* viene e discende di questo verbo, si prende solo per li poeti, che coll' arte musaica le loro parole hanno legate : e di questa significazione al presente non s' intende. L' altro principio, onde *autore* discende, siccome testimonia Uguccione nel principio delle sue *Derivazioni*, è uno vocabolo greco che dice *autentin*, che tanto vale in latino, quanto degno di fede e d' obbedienza. E così *autore*, quinci derivato, si prende per ogni persona digna d' essere creduta e obbedita. E da questo viene quello vocabolo, del quale al presente si tratta, cioè *autoritade ;* per che si può vedere che *autoritade* val tanto, quanto atto degno di fede e d' obbedienza. (*Conv.* iv. 6, ll. 14-49.)

The passage in Uguccione to which Dante refers comes immediately after the *Prologus*, and in fact constitutes the first article of the *Derivationes*[6] ; it runs as follows :—

[1] B. omits *id est bona t . . . futuris.*   [2] A. omits *id est virens . . . aliis.* [3] F. omits *et.*   [4] A. *affectionis auspicari.*

[5] This word, curiously enough, is in current use at the present day as a title of respect in Turkey and Egypt, in the corrupted form *Effendi.* Selden long ago noted the origin of this title in his *Titles of Honour* (1614) : " Their *aphendis,* written also by the later Greeks ἀφένδης is corrupted from Αὐθέντης, *i.e.*, Lord ".

[6] Uguccione, unfortunately, did not adopt the alphabetical order, except to a very limited extent, in the arrangement of his work ; consequently it often requires the expenditure of a good deal of time and trouble in order to find any given word. This inconvenience is to a certain extent obviated by the addition in some MSS., by way of appendix, of a list of words arranged roughly in alphabetical order, with cross references. In the *Catholicon* of Giovanni da Genova, on the other hand, a strictly alphabetical arrangement is followed. The great superiority of the latter work in this respect was doubtless one of the reasons why the *Catholicon* was printed at an early date, while Uguccione's *Derivationes* remains to this day hidden away and neglected.

Augeo, -ges, -xi, -ctum, amplificare, augmentum dare. Inde *hic auctor*, idest augmentator ; et debet scribi cum *u* et *c*. Quando vero significat *autentim*, idest autoritatem, est comunis generis, et debet scribi sine *c*, ut *hic* et *hec autor*, et derivatur ab *autentim*. Item invenitur quoddam verbum defectivum, scilicet *avieo, -es*, idest ligo, -as, et inde *autor*, idest ligator, similiter comunis generis et sine *c*. Secundum primam significationem imperatores proprie debent dici *auctores*, ab augendo rempublicam. Secundum secundam significationem phylosophi et inventores artium, ut Plato, Aristotiles, Priscianus et quelibet magne persone, debent dici *autores*. Secundum tertiam, Virgilius, Lucanus et ceteri poete debent dici *autores*, qui ligaverunt carmina sua pedibus et metris. Et ab *autor* quod significat *autentim* derivatur *hec autoritas*, id est sententia imitatione digna, et *autenticus, -ca, -cum*.

Uguccione does not state, as Dante implies, that *autentin* [1] is a Greek word ; but this fact is distinctly stated in the *Catholicon* [2] in two lines which are borrowed from the *Graecismus* [3] of Évrard de Béthune :—

> *Auctor* ab *augendo* nomen trahit ; ast ab *agendo*
> *Actor ;* ab *autentin*, quod grecum est, nascitur *autor*.

Though Dante only mentions Uguccione this once, it is evident that he made constant use of the *Magnæ Derivationes ;* and it is certain that this work was one, if not the chief, source of his knowledge (such as it was) of Greek words. We may give a few instances. In the well-known letter to Can Grande (*Epist.* x.) Dante explains the reason why he gave the title of *Commedia* [4] to his poem :—

---

[1] On this word see Thurot, *op. cit.* p. 103, n. 2.

[2] Giovanni da Genova reproduces the above passage from Uguccione almost verbatim ; under the first sense he adds : " Sepe etiam Deus dicitur noster *auctor*, id est noster dux, noster augmentator " ; and under the third sense he adds the name of Ovid to those of Virgil and Lucan.

[3] ix. 107-8. See EBERHARDI BETHUNIENSIS *Graecismus*, in Wrobel's *Corpus grammaticorum medii aevi*, Wratislaviae, 1887, vol. i. See also Thurot, *op. cit.*, pp. 100-1.

[4] *Inf.* xvi. 128 ; xxi. 2. Dante accents this word on the penultimate (*commedía*), as he does also *tragedía* (*Inf.* xx. 113), *salmodía* (*Purg.* xxxiii. 2), *teodía* (*Par.* xxv. 73), *melodía* (*Purg.* xxix. 22 ; *Par.* xiv. 32 ; xxiii. 97, 109), *armonía* (*Par.* i. 78 ; vi. 126 ; xvii. 44), *sinfonía* (*Par.* xxi. 59), *letaníe* (*Inf.* xx. 9), *gerarchía* (*Par.* xxviii. 121), *filosofía* (*Inf.* xi. 97), *fantasía* (*Purg.* xvii. 25 ; *Par.* x. 46 ; xix. 9 ; xxiv. 24 ; xxxiii. 142), etc. This accentuation was in conformity with the mediæval accentuation of the corresponding Latin words, which, with the exception of *tragedia* and *comedia*, were always accented on the

Libri titulus : *Incipit Comœdia Dantis Aligherii*. . . . Ad cujus notitiam sciendum est, quod *ccmœdia* dicitur a *comus*, villa, et *oda*, quod est cantus unde *comœdia* quasi villanus cantus. Et est comœdia genus quoddam poeticæ narrationis ab omnibus aliis differens. Differt ergo a tragœdia in materia per hoc quod tragœdia in principio est admirabilis et quieta, in fine sive exitu est fœtida et horribilis ; et dicitur propter hoc a *tragus*, quod est hircus, et *oda*, quasi cantus hircinus, id est fœtidus ad modum hirci, ut patet per Senecam in suis tragœdiis.[1] Comœdia vero inchoat asperitatem alicujus rei, sed ejus materia prospere terminatur, ut patet per Terentium in suis comœdiis. Et hinc consueverunt dictatores quidam in suis salutationibus dicere loco salutis, " tragicum principium, et comicum finem ". Similiter differunt in modo loquendi : elate et sublime tragœdia, comœdia vero remisse et humiliter (§ 10).

The derivation and definition of *comœdia* and *tragœdia* given by Dante in this passage are taken directly from Uguccione, who under the word *oda* says :—

Oda, quod est cantus vel laus, componitur cum *comos*, quod est villa, et dicitur *hec comedia*, -*e*, idest villanus cantus, vel villana laus, quia tractat de rebus villanis rusticanis, et affinis est cotidiane locutioni, vel quia circa villas fiebat et recitabatur, vel *comedia* a commensatione, solebant enim post cibum homines ad audiendum eam venire. . . . Item *oda* in eodem sensu componitur cum *tragos* quod est hircus, et dicitur *hec tragedia*, -*e*, idest hircina laus, vel hircinus cantus, idest fetidus ; est enim de crudelissimis rebus, sicut qui patrem vel matrem interficit, et commedit filium, vel e contrario et hujusmodi. Unde et tragedo dabatur hircus, idest animal fetidum, non quod non haberet aliud dignum premium, sed ad fetorem materie designandum. . . . Et differunt *tragedia* et *comedia*, quia *comedia* privatorum hominum continet acta, *tragedia* regum et magnatum. Item *comedia* humili stilo scribitur, *tragedia* alto. Item

penultimate ; in the cases of these two, however, the accentuation was unsettled, it being sometimes on the penultimate (*tragedia*, *comedia*), sometimes on the antepenultimate (*tragédia*, *comédia*), an uncertainty which was doubtless due to a hesitation between the classical pronunciation (as familiarised by the well-known lines in the *Ars Poëtica*, 93, 231), and the analogy of the large number of other words in -*ia*, which according to the mediæval usage were paroxytone. Thurot (*op. cit.*, p. 406) gives a long list of these words, with the accents marked, from twelfth century MSS. ; among them are *monarchía*, *theología*, *philosophía*, *astrología*, *armonía*, *symphonía*, *melodía*, *psalmodía*, *gerarchía*, but *comédia*, *tragédia* (with the alternative *tragedía* also registered).

[1] Scherillo (*Alcuni Capitoli della Biografia di Dante*, p. 513) regards this reference to the tragedies of Seneca as a ground, among others, for suspecting the authenticity of this letter, which, of course, is not unquestioned by Dante critics. The references, however, to both Seneca and Terence look very much like glosses interpolated in the text. But in any case it is not easy to see why they should be regarded as suspicious in themselves.

comedia a tristibus incipit, sed in letis definit, *tragedia* e contrario ; unde in salutacionibus solemus mittere et optare amicis tragicum principium et comicum finem, idest principium bonum et letum, et bonum et letum finem.

Among other Greek words or derivatives, for the meaning or etymology of which Dante was indebted to Uguccione, the following may be mentioned as examples :—

Protonoe ("la prima mente, la quale i greci dicono *Protonoe*". *Conv.* ii. 4, ll. 38-39) :—

> *Nois* idest mens, et componitur cum *prothos* quod est primum, et dicitur *hec protonoe*, id est prima nois, id est divina mens.

Peripatetici (" Perocchè Aristotile cominciò a disputare andando qua e là, chiamati furono, lui, dico, e li suoi compagni, *Peripatetici*, che tanto vale quanto *deambulatori*". *Conv.* iv. 6, ll. 138-142) :—

> *Peri*, idest circum vel de . . . item *peri* componitur, et dicitur *peripateticus*, *-a*, *-um*, quasi circumcalcans vel ambulans, unde *peripatetici* dicti sunt quidam philosophi a deambulatione, quasi circumcalcantes vel ambulantes, quia Aristotiles, autor eorum, deambulans disputare solitus erat : vel quia perambulabant de scola ad scolam disputantes et inquirentes quid melius sue scientie possent adjungere.[1]

Perizoma[2] (*Inf.* xxxi. 61) :—

> *Perizoma*, *-atis*, quaedam vestis antiquissima, idest succinctorium femorale quo genitalia tantum teguntur ; alii dicunt quod sit tunica foliis consuta quale dominus fecit Ade post lapsum (*s. v. Peri*).

Flegetonta[3] (*Inf.* xiv. 131, 134-135) :—

> *Flegeton*, *-ontis*, quidam fluvius infernalis totus ardens, a *fos* quod est ignis, vel *flegi* quod est inflammans, et totus.

---

[1] *Cf.* Isidore, *Origines*, viii. 6.

[2] This word was doubtless familiar to Dante from its use in the Vulgate : "consuerunt folia ficus, et fecerunt sibi perizomata" (*Gen.* iii. 7),—a passage to which a reference is given in the *Catholicon*. *Cf.* Isidore of Seville :—

"Vestis antiquissima hominum fuit perizomatum, id est succinctorium : quo tantum genitalia conteguntur. Hoc primum primi mortales e foliis arborum sibi fecerunt, quando post praevaricationem erubescentes pudenda velabant. Cujus usum quaedam barbarae gentes dum sint nudae usque hodie tenent" (*Orig.* xix. 22).

[3] Dante's acquaintance with the meaning of Phlegethon has been specially pointed to as implying a knowledge of Greek on his part. But even if he had not had access to Uguccione he might have gathered the meaning of the word from Virgil's description :—

Stige ("Una palude . . . che ha nome Stige, . . . tristo ruscel". *Inf.* vii. 106-107):—

A *sto* hic *stix, stigis*, palus infernalis, quia semper stet ad penam, vel a *statim*, quia potata statim interficit, vel a greco *stigestos*, quod est tristitia, quia tristes faciat, vel quia tristitiam gignat.[1]

Ermafrodito (Purg. xxvi. 82):—

Hermes componitur cum *Affrodita*, quod est Venus, et dicitur *Hermofroditus*, id est filius Veneris et Mercurii, qui quia commixtus Salmaci utrumque sexum habuit.[2]   Ideo ab illo dicitur *hermofroditus, -a, -um*, in quo uterque sexus apparet . . . hii dextram mamillam virilem sinistram muliebrem habentes, vicissim coeundo gignunt et pariunt; et quia talis homo nec vir nec femina videtur, ideo quadam similitudine *hermofroditus* dicitur castratus, qui nec vir nec mulier videtur.

Galassia ("la Galassia, cioè quello bianco cerchio, che il vulgo chiama la Via di santo Jacopo". *Conv.* ii. 15, ll. 8-10):—

Gala grece, latine dicitur lac . . . et per compositionem a *gala* et *xios*, quod est circulus, dicitur *hec galaxias*, vel *-ia, -e*, id est lacteus circulus qui vulgo dicitur via santi Jacobi.

Hagiographi (Mon. iii. 16, l. 68):—

Agyos grece, sanctum latine, ab *a*, quod est *sine*, et *ge*, quod est terra, quia sine terra, id est celeste; inde *agraphia* scriptura, quod et *agyographia* dicitur, id est sancta scriptura.   Unde hic *agyographus, -phi* substantivum, et adjectivum *agyographus*, sancta scribens.

Archimandrita (Par. xi. 99; *Mon.* iii. 9, l. 123; *Epist.* viii. 6):—

Hec mandra, -dre, id est bubulcus, a bobus sibi commendatis, vel quia boum nomina mandat memorie: Juv. "instantis convicia mandre"[3]; vel mandros

> Quae rapidus flammis ambit torrentibus amnis,
> Tartareus Phlegethon.
> > (*Aen.* vi. 550-1);

or from the comment of Servius on *Aen.* vi. 265 :—

"Per *Phlegethonta*, inferum fluvium, ignem significat; nam φλὸξ Graece, Latine, *ignis* est".

[1] *Cf.* Isidore: "Styx ἀπὸ τῆς στυγνότητος, id est a tristitia dicta, eo quod tristes faciat, vel quod tristitiam gignat" (*Orig.* xiv. 9); and Servius on *Aen.* vi. 134: "Styx, palus quaedam apud Inferos . . . *Styx* moerorem significat, unde ἀπὸ τοῦ στυγερoῦ, id est, a tristitia *Styx* dicta est".

[2] *Cf.* Ovid, *Metam.* iv. 288 ff.

[3] Redarum transitus arto
Vicorum inflexu et stantis convicia mandrae
Eripient somnum Druso vitulisque marinis.
> (*Sat.* iii. 236-238.)

dicitur ovis, unde *hic* et *hec mandra,* pastor ovium, et per compositionem *hic* et *hec archimandrita, -te,* quasi princeps vel pastor ovium, unde et quadam trans- lacione episcopi et archiepiscopi et etiam sacerdotes dicuntur *archimandrite,* quasi pastores ovium (*s. v. mando*).

Polysemus ("polysemus, hoc est plurium sensuum". *Epist.* x. 7):—

Polis, quod est pluralitas, componitur cum *senos,* quod est sensus, et dicitur *polysenus, -a, -um,* vel a *xenos* quod idem est, et dicitur *polixenus, -a, -um,* id est plurium sensuum vel significationum.   Invenitur quandoque et *polixemus* in eodem sensu, sed littera corrupta est.[1]

Allegoria ("allegoria dicitur ab *alleon* graece, quod in lati- num dicitur alienum sive diversum". *Epist.* x. 7):—

Ab *allon* et *logos* quod est sermo, vel *gore* quod est dicere, *hec allegoria,* id est aliena locutio, cum aliud sonat et aliud intelligitur.[2]

Prosopopea ("è una figura questa, quando alle cose inanimate si parla, che si chiama dalli rettorici *Prosopopea*". *Conv.* iii. 9, ll. 17-19):—

Item *poio* componitur cum *prosopa,* quod est persona, et dicitur *hec prosopo- peia, -e,* idest persone confictio vel conformatio, ut cum res non loquens intro- ducitur loquens.[3]

Filosofo, filosofia ("Dinanzi da Pittagora erano chiamati i seguitatori di scienza, non *filosofi,* ma *sapienti.* . . . Questo Pitta-

[1] The correct form of this word, of course, is *polysemus,* Gk., πολύσημος ; it is used by Servius in his comment on *Aen.* i. 1: "*Cano* polysemus sermo est, aliquando laudo, aliquando divino, aliquando canto ".

[2] *Cf.* Isidore, *Origines,* i. 364.   The *Catholicon* says: "*Allegoria* dicitur ab *alleon,* quod est alienum, et *logos,* quod est sermo". What follows in the *Catholicon* bears directly on what Dante says as to the interpretation of the *Divina Commedia* in *Epist.* x. 7 :—
    "Scias quod sacra scriptura quatuor modis potest exponi, scilicet historice, tropologice, allegorice, anagogice.   Historia docet factum, tropologica faciendum, allegoria credendum, anagogia appetendum.
        Littera gesta docet, quid credas *allegoria,*
        Moralis quid agas, quo tendas *anagogia.*
    Hec patent in hac dictione Iherusalem ; historice enim est quedam civitas, tropologice est typus anime fidelis, allegorice figura ecclesie militantis, anagogice tipum gerit ecclesie triumphantis."

[3] The *Catholicon* says: "*Prosopopeya* fit quando inanimatum loquitur ad animatum, vel quando animatum ad inanimatum " (*Cf.* Isidore, *Origines,* ii. 11).

gora, domandato se egli si riputava sapiente, negò a sè questo vocabolo, e disse sè essere non *sapiente*, ma *amatore di sapienza*. E quinci nacque poi che ciascuno studioso in sapienza fosse *amatore di sapienza* chiamato, cioè *filosofo*; chè tanto vale come in greco *filos* dire *amatore* in latino, e quindi dicemo noi *filos* quasi *amatore*, e *sofia* quasi *sapienza*; onde *filos* e *sofia* tanto vale quanto *amatore di sapienza*; per che notare si puote che non d' arroganza, ma d' umiltade è vocabolo. Da questo nasce il vocabolo del suo proprio atto, *filosofia*." *Conv.* iii. 11, ll. 33-54):—

> *Filos* grece, latine dicitur amor . . . et componitur cum *sophos* vel *sophia*, quod est sapientia, et dicitur *hic philosophus*, *-phi*, idest amator sapientie, unde *hec philosophia*, id est amor sapientie, et hinc *philosophicus*, *-a*, *-um*, et *philosophor*, *-aris*, id est studere in philosophia vel docere philosophiam. Et nota quod philosophus dicitur proprie qui divinarum et humanarum rerum habet scientiam, et omnem bene vivendi tramitem tenet. Et fertur hoc nomen primum esse exortum a Pictagora. Nam Greci veteres cum ante *sophos* vel *sophistas*, id est sapientes vel doctores sapientie, semetipsos jactancius nominarent, iste interrogatus quod profiteretur, verecundo nomine *philosophum*, idest amatorem sapientie, se esse respondit, quia sapientem profiteri arrogantissimum videbatur. Ita deinceps posteris placuit ut quisque qui de talibus rebus ad sapientiam pertinentibus doctrina vel sibi vel aliis videretur excellere non nisi *philosophus* vocaretur.[1]

Dante apparently also adopted the (to us) extraordinarily fanciful etymology of *hypocrita* given by Uguccione, an etymology which was commonly accepted in the Middle Ages, and which is repeated and approved by several of the old Dante commentators.[2] Uguccione says:—

[1] *Cf.* Isidore, *Origines*, viii. 6, whom Uguccione has closely followed; *cf.* also Cicero, *Tusc. Quaest.* v. 3, and St. Augustine, *Civ. Dei*, viii. 2; and see above, pp. 92-93. Uguccione says elsewhere:—

" A *sophos hec sophia*, idest sapientia, et componitur *sophos* et dicitur *hic philosophus* vel amator sapientie, unde *hec philosophia*, idest amor sapientie . . . et nota quod *philosophus* idem est quod sapiens, et *philosophia* idem quod *sophia* vel sapientia."

[2] Lana, for instance, says:—

" È da sapere che, siccome dice Brittone* nella esposizione de' vocaboli, *ipocrita* è a dire fittore, cioè fingitore, cioè ingannatore, simulatore, cioè uno coverto d' inganno e rappresentatore d' altra persona ch' elli non è. Distingue la sua

* On Brito see Du Cange, *Præfatio*, p. 35; and *Hist. littér.* xxix. 584.

Crisis grece, latine dicitur secretum, et judicium, et aurum . . . Item a *crisis* per compositionem *hic* et *hec ypocrita, -te,* fictor, simulator, representator alterius persone; et dicitur *ypocrita* ab *yper,* quod est super, et *crisis* quod est aurum, quasi superauratus, quia in superficie et extrinsecus videtur esse bonus, cum interius sit malus; vel dicitur sic quasi *ypocrita* ab *ypos,* quod est sub, et *crisis,* quod est aurum, quasi habens aliquid sub auro; vel componitur ab *ypo,* quod est falsum, et *crisis,* quod est judicium, quia, cum interius malus sit, bonum se palam ostendit, et ita de eo falsum habetur judicium; et inde *hec ypocrisis,* id est simulatio.

We have little doubt that Dante had in mind the first or second of the above etymologies, the fancifulness of which would especially appeal to his imagination, when he represented the hypocrites [1] in Bolgia 6 of Circle viii. of Hell (Malebolge) as wearing mantles brilliantly gilded on the outside, but of lead within (*Inf.* xxiii. 61-65):—

> Egli avean cappe con cappucci bassi
> Dinanzi agli occhi . . .
> Di fuor dorate son, sì ch' egli abbaglia;
> Ma dentro tutte piombo.

Before taking leave of the subject of the Greek words employed by Dante we may refer to his use of the term *entomata,* meaning

etimologìa in questo modo, che *ipocrita* è componuto di due parti, l' uno si è a dire *ipo,* che vuol dir *sopra,* e *crisis* in greco che è a dire in latino *auro,* si che ipocrita è a dire sovra dorato: e questo hae a significare che li ipocriti in la apparenza e in la superficie appaiono d' oro, cioè boni e santi, e dentro sono altro. Ed altri tolleno la etimologìa per altro modo, e diceno che *ipo* si è a dire *sotto,* e *crisi, crita,* si è a dire, com' è detto, *auro,* e soggiungeno: *ipocrita* è a dire altro *sotto oro.* E perciò è scritto nell' Aurora delli ipocriti: *habet aurum in superficie, latet lutum.*"

Pietro di Dante says: "*Hypocrisia,* dicta ab *epi,* quod est *supra* et *crisis,* aurum"; and both the Anonimo Fiorentino and the Postillator Cassinensis say the same.

[1] Similarly, the punishment of the Envious in Circle ii. of Purgatory, who are represented as blinded, their eyes being sewn up with wire (*Purg.* xiii. 47-72), was doubtless, as Dr. Moore points out, suggested to Dante by the current etymology of the word *invidia* (as it were *invidentia,* "non-sight"). Giovanni da Genova says in the *Catholicon:* "Invideo ab *in* et *video,* ut invideo tibi, idest non video tibi, idest non fero videre te bene agentem". In the same way, the livid rock (l. 9) and the livid mantles worn by the Envious (ll. 47-48) were doubtless suggested by the word *livor,* the synonym of *invidia* (Cf. *Purg.* xiv. 82-4).

" insects," in the *Purgatorio* (x. 128). There has been a good deal of discussion as to how Dante formed this word. Blanc in his *Erklärungen* (Halle, 1865) suggested that he found ἔντομα, τά, in Uguccione, and mistook the article for part of the word :—

> Er braucht hier das angebliche Wort *entomata*, offenbar, weil er in einem ungedruckt gebliebenen Werke *Ugutionis de derivationibus verborum* ἔντομα, τά (der Artikel als Bezeichnung des Geschlechts), gefunden und aus Unkunde des Griechischen diesen Ártikel als letzte Sylbe des Worts betrachtet hat (p. 38).

It is evident from this statement that Blanc had himself no acquaintance with the *Derivationes* of Uguccione, otherwise he would have been aware, firstly, that no Greek words as such (*i.e.*, in Greek characters) are given in that work ; and secondly, that the genders are indicated, even in the case of Latinised Greek words by the addition not of the Greek, but of the Latin, article. This theory, therefore, that the word *entomata* is formed by the agglutination of the article owing to a mistaken reading by Dante of an entry in Uguccione, falls to the ground. We have very little doubt ourselves that Dante came across the word *entoma* [1] in the Greek-Latin translation of Aristotle's *De Historia Animalium*,[2] in which transliterated Greek words are of frequent occurrence,[3] and formed the plural

[1] Representing, of course, the Greek τὰ ἔντομα (*sc.* ζῷα), of which the Lat. *insecta* is the exact equivalent. The word *entoma*, so far as we are aware, is not given in the *Derivationes ;* one would naturally expect to find it under *thomos*, but the only compound there mentioned is *athomos*. Du Cange records one instance of its use, in which it is treated as neuter singular.

[2] A work with which Dante was certainly acquainted, for he quotes it at least twice by name (*Conv.* ii. 3, l. 15 ; ii. 9, l. 79). Benvenuto refers to the *De Generatione Animalium ;* he says : " Nota quod enthomata, secundum quod scribit philosophus in tertio de generatione animalium, sunt animalia generata per putrefactionem et a casu, et sine coïtu, sicut aliqui vermes et apes et vespae ; et dicitur proprie enthomatum, id est, mirabile ". It will be noted that Benvenuto goes a step farther than Dante, and forms a singular *enthomatum* from Dante's plural *enthomata !* The *De Generatione Animalium*, as is well known, was reckoned in the Middle Ages as forming part of the *De Historia Animalium*, which in those days comprised altogether nineteen books (see Jourdain, *Recherches sur les anciennes traductions latines d'Aristote*, pp. 172-173, 327).

[3] See the specimens given by Jourdain, *op. cit.*, pp. 426-427, 429.

entomata on the analogy of *poëma*, *poëmata*,[1] and similar words.[2]

Dante's indebtedness to the *Magnæ Derivationes* was not confined to words of Greek origin ; many of his etymologies of Latin words (or Italian, which so far as we are concerned amounts to the same thing) were undoubtedly also borrowed from Uguccione, as may be seen from the following examples :—

Soave ("soave è tanto, quanto suaso". *Conv.* ii. 8, l. 36) :—

> *Sueo, sues*, non est in usu in praesenti, sed in preterito *suevi*, et supino *suetum*, et inde *suetus, -a, -um*, et *suavis, -e*, quia que *sueta* sunt *suavia* solent esse . . . , et a *suavis, suadeo, -es, suasi, suasum*, hortari, consulere, monere, quod autem dicitur *suadere* quasi *suavia dare*.

Facundo (" dicemo l' uomo facundo, per l' abito della facundia, cioè del bene parlare". *Conv.* iii. 13, ll. 83-85) :—

> A *for, facundus, -a, -um*, disertus, qui facile potest fari quod intelligitur ; inde *hec facundia, -e*, et *facunditas ;* et, ut dixit quidam sapiens, *facundia* est magnum Dei donum, cum quo comode potest loqui que comode intelliguntur.

Adolescenza (" adolescenza, cioè accrescimento di vita ". *Conv.* iv. 24, ll. 3-4) :—

> *Oleo* componitur cum *ad*, et dicitur *adoleo, -les, -levi*, vel *-lui, -letum*, vel *-litum*, pro quo utimur *adultum*, id est cremare, comburere, incendere, unde et *adolere*, id est crescere.[3]

Gioventute (" gioventute, cioè età che può giovare". *Conv.* iv. 24, ll. 5-6) :—

---

[1] With which of course he would be familiar, if only from the well-known line in the *Ars Poëtica* (l. 99) :—
" Non satis est pulchra esse poëmata, dulcia sunto ".
He himself uses the word frequently in the *De Vulgari Eloquentia*.

[2] In the *Catholicon* the rule for the declension of nouns of this kind is given as follows : " Scias quod hujusmodi (id est desinentia in *-a*) nomina greca vel hebrea, ut *manna, pascha*, declinantur ut frequentius secundum tertiam declinationem, ut *hoc pascha, -chatis*, et *hoc manna, -natis* ". Numerous other instances of similar words occur throughout the work, *e.g.*, *anathema, -atis, axioma, -atis, dogma, -atis, enigma, -atis, epigramma, -atis, epilema, -atis, epitoma, -atis, problema, -atis, sinthoma, -atis, smigma, -atis, sophisma, -atis*.

[3] Isidore (*Origines*, xi. 2) says: "Adolescens dictus, eo quod sit ad gignendum adultus, sive a crescere et augeri ".

A *juvo*, *hic* et *hec juvenis*, quia adjuvare posse incipit, et est juvenis in ipso etatis incremento positus, et ad auxilium preparatus ; nam adjuvare hominis est aliquid opus conferentis.[1]

Sometimes Dante emphatically declares himself for or against a particular etymology ; thus in discussing the derivation of the word *nobile* in the *Convivio* he says :—

Ben sono alquanti folli che credono che per questo vocabolo *nobile* s' intenda essere da molti nominato e conosciuto ; e dicono che vien da un verbo che sta per conoscere, cioè *nosco :* e questo è falsissimo. . . . È falsissimo che *nobile* vegna da *conoscere*, ma vien da *non vile ;* onde *nobile* è quasi *non vile* (*Conv*. iv. 16, ll. 59-77).

Uguccione (*s. v. conosco*) says :—

A *noto*, *notabilis*, *-le*, *-liter* adverbium, et a *notabilis* per sincopam *hic* et *hec nobilis*, et *hoc nobile*, quasi notabilis, qui facile notatur, sive cujus nomen et genus agnoscitur ; secundum quosdam autem dicitur *nobilis* quasi *non vilis*.[2]

Several of Dante's interpretations of proper names appear to have been borrowed from Uguccione ; thus :—

Babel (" Babel, hoc est confusio ". *V. E.* i. 7, l. 30 ; *cf. Epist.* vii. 8) :—

Babel interpretatur confusio, unde Babilon vel Babilonia civitas a confusione linguarum.[3]

Hebraei (" filii Heber ab eo dicti sunt Hebraei ". *V. E.* i. 6, ll. 54-55) :—

Heber fuit filius Jecte, pronepos Sem . . . ex ipso sunt orti *Hebrei*, et dicitur ab Heber *hebreus*, *-a*, *-um ;* et hoc nomine Judei vocati sunt ex quo Mare Rubrum transierint.[4]

Giovanna (*Par.* xii. 80-81) :—

Johannes interpretatur gratia Domini, *ja* idest dominus, *anna* idest gratia, unde Johannes quasi Johanna.[5]

Galilea (" *Galilea* è tanto a dire quanto *bianchezza* ". *Conv.* iv. 22, ll. 186-187) :—

---

[1] *Cf*. Isidore, *Origines*, xi. 2.

[2] Isidore (*Origines*, x. N) says : " Nobilis non vilis, cujus et nomen et genus scitur ".

[3] *Cf*. St. Augustine, *Civ. Dei*, xvi. 4.

[4] *Cf*. St. Augustine, *Civ. Dei*, xvi. 3 ; and Isidore, *Origines*, vii. 6 ; ix. 2.

[5] *Cf*. Isidore, *Origines*, vii. 9.

Gala grece, latine dicitur lac . . . item a *gala, hec Galilea, -e,* id est regio Palestine sic dicta quia gignat candidiores homines quam alia regio Palestine.[1]

The following passages afford instructive commentary upon several points in Dante's works :—

Elios (Par. xiv. 96) :—

Ab *ely,* quod est deus, dictus est sol *elyos,* quod pro deo olim reputabatur.

Heliotropium (Epist. v. 1) :—

Et componitur *elyos* cum *tropos,* quod est conversio, et dicitur *hoc elyotropium,* quedam herba que solis motibus folia circumacta convertat et estivo solstitio floreat, unde et latine solsequium dicitur, nam in sole nascente flores suos aperit, et in sero claudit cum sol occumbit[2] . . . Et ex eisdem componitur *hec elyotropia, -e,* quedam gemma valde dura et perspicua, que colores mutat secundum variationem colorum in sole, unde rubea apparet in mane et in vespere ; vel sic dicitur quia posita in labris eneis radios solis mutat sanguineo colore, si extra aquam in modum speculi solem accipit ; invenitur pro eodem lapide *hic elyotropius, -ii.*[3]

Pape (Inf. vii. 1) :—

Pape, interjectio admirantis.[4]

Racha (V. E. i. 12, l. 35) :—

Racha, id est inanis vel vacuus ; *racha* interjectio affectum indignantis ostendens ; sicut cum [dolemus] dicimus *heu,* et cum delectamur dicimus *vach ;* similiter cum indignamur dicimus *racha.*

Bos ephippiatus (V. E. ii. 1, l. 80) :—

Epiphia, -orum, ornamenta equorum. Oratius: *Optat epiphia bos piger optat arare caballus ;* unde *epiphiare* equum, idest ornare.[5]

Dante's selection of the word *onorificabilitudinitate* as an instance of "sesquipedalia verba" ("illud *onorificabilitudinitate,* quod duodena perficitur syllaba in vulgari, et in grammatica

---

[1] *Cf.* Isidore, *Origines,* xiv. 3.   [2] *Cf.* Isidore, *Origines,* xvii. 9.

[3] *Cf.* Isidore, *Origines,* xvi. 7 ; and the *Lapidaire de Berne* (ll. 941 ff.) in Pannier's *Lapid. français du moyen âge* (p. 137) ; see also *Academy,* 2nd April, 1892 (p. 321).

[4] Uguccione adds : " unde *papa,* id est admirabilis " (!)

[5] *Epist.,* I. xiv. 43. Dante's use of this phrase " bos ephippiatus " has been quoted as a proof of his acquaintance with the *Epistles* of Horace (see Moore, *Studies in Dante,* i. 198) ; but it is evident that in this case, as in so many others, Dante borrowed the phrase at secondhand.

tredena perficitur in duobus obliquis," *V. E.* ii. 7, ll. 69-72) was no doubt suggested by Uguccione, who says :—

Ab *honorifico, hic* et *hec honorificabilis, -le,* et *hec honorificabilitas, -tis* et *hec honorificabilitudinitas,* et est longissima dictio, que illo versu continetur : *Fulget honorificabilitudinitatibus* [1] *iste.*

To Uguccione also Dante was indebted, we have very little doubt, for his version of the incident to which he refers in the *Purgatorio* in connection with the charge of sodomy insinuated against Julius Caesar :—

> La gente che non vien con noi, offese
> Di ciò per che già Cesar trionfando,
> *Regina,* contra sè chiamar s' intese ;
> Però si parton *Soddoma* gridando.
>
> (*Purg.* xxvi. 76-79.)

Uguccione (*s. v. triumphus*) says :—

In illa die licebat cuilibet dicere in personam triumphantis quicquid vellet, unde Cesari triumphanti fertur quidam dixisse, cum deberet induci in civitatem : *Aperite portas regi calvo et regine Bitinie,* volens significare quod calvus erat, et quod succuba extiterat regis Bitinie ; et alius de eodem vitio : *Ave rex et regina !*

The source of Dante's version of the story has been a puzzle to the commentators, who were driven to the conclusion that he had mixed up the accounts of two separate incidents recorded by Suetonius ; the latter relates that on one occasion in the midst of a great assembly a certain Octavius hailed Pompey as king and Caesar as queen [2]; and that on another, during one of his triumphs, his soldiers greeted him with doggerel lines referring to his supposed criminal intercourse with Nicomedes, the

---

[1] It will be remembered that Shakespeare introduces this word into his *Love's Labour Lost* (v. 1). It has been argued by supporters of the "Baconian theory" that the word conceals an avowal of the authorship of the plays by Bacon. It might be argued with equal plausibility, as I pointed out in *Literature* (9th April, 1898), that the word contains a glorification of Dante by himself in the phrase *Ubi Italicus ibi Danti honor fit,* which may be formed from the same letters !

[2] "Octavius quidam . . . conventu maximo cum Pompeium regem appellasset, ipsum (Caesarem) reginam salutavit " (*Jul. Caes.* § 49).

king of Bithynia.[1] The story, however, referred to by Dante tallies exactly with that given by Uguccione, who was pretty certainly his authority for it.

We do not suppose that we have by any means exhausted the list of Dante's obligations to the *Magnæ Derivationes,* but we have said enough, at any rate, to prove what we claimed at the outset, *viz.,* that it was a work with which he was familiar, and that he was indebted to it for a variety of information, including his smattering—for it was certainly nothing more— of Greek.[2]

---

[1] " Gallico triumpho milites ejus inter caetera carmina illud pronuntiaverunt :—

> ' Gallias Caesar subegit, Nicomedes Caesarem :
> Ecce Caesar nunc triumphat, qui subegit Gallias :
> Nicomedes non triumphat, qui subegit Caesarem '."
>
> (*Id. Ibid.*)

[2] Of the Greek words mentioned by Dante, *protonoë* (*Conv.* ii. 4, l. 39), *prosopopea* (*Conv.* iii. 9, l. 19) and *autentin* (*Conv.* iv. 6, l. 41) are, as we have shown, to be found in Uguccione; *antictona* (*Conv.* iii. 5, l. 32) and ἐπιείκεια (*Mon.* i. 14, l. 38) come from Aristotle (*De Coelo* ii. 13, and *Eth.* v. 10); while *hormen* (*Conv.* iv. 21, l. 122; iv. 22, l. 35) comes from Cicero (*Acad.* iv. 8; *Fin.* iii. 7; *Off.* ii. 5). Virgil's warning to Dante not to address Ulysses and Diomed (*Inf.* xxvi. 73-5) :—

> Lascia parlare a me . . .
>   ch' ei sarebbero schivi,
>   Perch' ei fur Greci, forse del tuo detto,

would acquire a new significance if we could suppose that Dante were here hinting at his own deficiencies in the matter of Greek.

DANTE'S REFERENCE TO TARTAR CLOTHS

(*INFERNO* XVII. 14-17)[1]

In his description of the monster Geryon, in the seventeenth canto of the *Inferno*, Dante says:—

> Lo dosso e il petto ed ambo e due le coste
> Dipinte avea di nodi e di rotelle.
> Con più color, sommesse e soprapposte,
> Non fer mai drappo Tartari nè Turchi.

"His back and breast and both his flanks were painted with knots and little rings. With more colours, groundwork and design, did never Tartars nor Turks make cloth."

The Tartar cloths here referred to by Dante were so called, according to Colonel Yule, the editor of Marco Polo, "not because they were made in Tartary, but because they were brought from China and its borders through the Tartar dominions". The term in the Middle Ages appears to have been used generically of all rich stuffs of Oriental origin. Besides being of very fine material, these cloths were conspicuous for the brilliancy of their colouring and design. Their brilliant effect was produced in three different ways apparently: either by weaving designs of various colours in the material on the loom; or by making what is known as a "shot" surface; or lastly by means of embroidery or appliqué on a plain ground, enrichment with gold thread and spangles being largely used in this process.

Dante, in the passage quoted above, seems to have had in his mind material of the first sort, with the design woven in, the "sommessa" being the groundwork, and the "soprapposta" the

---

[1] Reprinted, with additions, from *Romania*, xxix. 560-4.

design—at least that seems to be the general opinion of the commentators, where they express an opinion. Boccaccio, whose comment on this passage has a certain pathetic interest, as being the last words he ever wrote, does not enter into details; he says :—

> Con più color sommesse e soprapposte, a variazione dell' ornamento, Non fer mai drappi Tartari nè Turchi, i quali di ciò sono ottimi maestri, siccome noi possiamo manifestamente vedere ne' drappi tartareschi, i quali veramente sono sì artificiosamente tessuti, che non è alcun dipintore che col pennello gli sapesse fare simiglianti, non che più belli.

It is evident, however, I think, that he is referring to stuffs woven throughout. Jacopo della Lana describes the materials as being made of silk, and mentions several of them by specific names, which are familiar to readers of Marco Polo; he says :—

> Qui fa comparazione di quello ch' era più variato che non sono li panni che vegnon di Tartaria e di Turchia di seta, li quali in ammirabil modo sono lavorati sì di colore come eziandìo di diverse e stranie ovre, come sono camuffa, taffetà, nachi e simili.

Modern commentators seem agreed in regarding the materials referred to by Dante as being ornamented with a woven design. Thus Casini, whose opinion may be accepted as representative, says :—

> La sommessa è la parte del drappo sulla quale spiccano i disegni, cioè quella che dicesi comunemente il fondo, e che può essere di vari colori; la soprapposta invece è la parte rilevata, a varî colori e figure.

There seems, however, no particular reason why soprapposta, of which no other example in the above sense is given in the Vocabolario of Tramater, should not quite as well be taken in the sense of an embroidered or appliqué design, such as are common enough in Oriental fabrics of the present day, and were evidently much in vogue in the Middle Ages. Boccaccio in his Fiammetta (Lib. iv. p. 93, ed. 1723), in an account of the costumes of certain gorgeously apparelled princes, unquestionably uses the participle soprapposto in the sense of embroidered :—

> Essi di porpora, e di drappi dalle indiane mani tessuti, con lavori di vari colori, e d' oro intermisti, e oltre a ciò soprapposti di perle, e di care pietre, vestiti.

The most usual form of embroidery on these cloths appears to have been with gold thread or with spangles, of which Dante's "nodi e rotelle" may perhaps be a recollection. Du Cange quotes a visitation of the treasury of St. Paul's in London, under date 1295, in which mention is made of " tunica et dalmatica de panno indico tarsico besantato de auro " ; and of another " tunica et dalmatica de quodam panno tarsici coloris, regulata cum besantiis et arboribus de aureo filo contextis." In another document, dated 1336, we read of " une selle de la taille d'Alemaigne, devant et derriere de veluel vermeil et asuré partiz . . . le siege de tartaire vert dyappré a oisiaus d'or " ; and in another (undated) of " unam cappam de diaspro auri samito vel tartarisco aureo de sindone foderatam " ; and again, under date 1380, of " ung petit pavillon blanc, qui est de fil, a rozes d'or, pourfillé par dessoubz de tartaille vermeille royé d'or."

What makes it probable that not woven designs, but embroidered or appliqué patterns, were what Dante was thinking of, is the fact that the Tartar cloths as such seem, as a rule, to have been " self-coloured ". Thus, in a will quoted by Godefroy, dated 1311, occur the items " ma robe de blanc tartare," and " mon gardecors de tartaire jaune ". Elsewhere we read of " une chapelle de tartaire vermeill " (1313), " un chaperon fourré de tartaire vert " (1347), " une chasuble d'un tharthaire vert " (1379), " unam capellam de tartarico rubeo " (1320), " unum coopertorium cum tribus curtinis de rubeo tartarino " (1388). In addition to this list, which includes white, yellow, scarlet, crimson and green, there are frequent mentions of " lead-coloured " or sad-coloured Tartar cloth, which was in special request for the ecclesiastical vestments used during Lent. Thus we find in church inventories (quoted by Du Cange) such items as " una tunica de panno de tartaire plumbeo pro officio quadragesimali " (1376); " un chasuble, dalmatique et tunique de tartaire plumbee pour Caresme " (1376) ; " una tunica, una casula et una dalmatica de tartara plonquata " (1335); " una casula, dalmatica et tunica de panno de tartaire, pluncata " (1340). Besides these " self-coloured " Tartar cloths, there were similar fabrics made with a " shot " surface. Of these I have only succeeded in finding two mentions[1]: one is of "troys courtines de tartare vermeil changeant" (1380); the other occurs in a curious passage of the work on surgery written between 1306 and 1320 by Henri de Mondeville, who was principal surgeon to Philip the Fair of France, "il mal di Francia" (*Purg.* vii. 109). Mondeville compares the iridescence of newly-let blood to the changing colours on the neck of a pigeon, or on the Tartar cloths, or on the material which, as he puts it, "in French is commonly called velvet":—

> Cognoscitur sanguis, quando noviter est extractus, antequam coaguletur in vase, sic ut si diversis sitibus situetur vas et inclinetur hinc et inde versus quodlibet latus, et diversi colores appareant in ipso sanguine secundum diversitatem situum, sicut videmus in collo columbae secundum diversos motus sui capitis atque colli, et sicut apparet in quibusdam pannis nobilibus delicatis qui a Tartaris apportantur, et in panno qui vulgari gallico vocatur *veluet*.[2]

References to these so-called Tartar cloths, as indications of wealth or rank, are not uncommon in mediæval literature. In an old French poem, *La Panthere d'Amors*, written towards the end of the thirteenth century, persons of consequence are recognised as such from their being clothed in fabrics of this kind:—

> Bien avisai
> Qu'il estoient de grant afaire,
> Car de samit ou de tartaire
> Ou de drap d'or de grant value
> Avoit chascuns robe vestue.
> (ll. 208-12.)

[1] Since this was written I have found another instance in the *Inventaire du Mobilier de Charles V.* (1380), from which (No. 3,534) the former of the two instances given above was taken, *viz.* (No. 3,851) "ung paveillon ront, à fers, de tartaire changeant de rouge et vert ". In this same inventory mention is made of a number of other articles made of "tartaire" of various colours; *e.g.*, (No. 3,536) "courtines de tartaire vert royé d'or "; (No. 3,539) "trois custodes de tartaire vert royé d'or "; (No. 3,544) " courtines de tartaire vermeil royé d'or "; (No. 3,552) "courtines de tartaire azurées et royées"; (No. 3,553) "courtines de tartaire violet royées d'or"; (No. 3,556) "courtines de tartaire azurée rosée " (this would appear to indicate a shot surface); (No. 3,569) "courtines bleues de tartaire plain "; (No. 3,585) "courtines de tartaire blance doubles "; (No. 3,589) "courtines doubles de tartaire blanche "; (No. 3,827) "un paveillon vert de tartaire tont plain ".

[2] *La Chirurgie de Maître Henry de Mondeville*, ed. A. Bos (Paris, 1898), vol. ii. p. 333. Glossaire, *s. v.* VELUET.

Similarly, Nerio Moscoli, a poet of the thirteenth century, speaks of cloth so rich that " niun tartaresco Paregiar lo porria "; and Boccaccio in the *Decamerone* (vi. 10) speaks of "un farsetto . . . con più macchie e di più colori che mai drappi fossero tartareschi e indiani." Mandeville, in his book of travels, says that no foreign envoy was ever admitted to the presence of the Sultan of Babylon, except his dress were of cloth of gold, or of Tartar cloth, or of some such fabric : " Devant le Soudan nul estrange message ne vient, qui ne soit vestu de drap d'or, ou de camocas, ou de tartaire en la guise que les Sarrazins sont vestus ". (cap. v.)

In England too these fabrics were well known, as appears from their mention in *Piers the Plowman*, where Charity is described as being

> As proud of a peny as of a pounde of gold,
> And is as gladde of a gowne of a graye russet
> As of a tunicle of Tarse or of a trye scarlet.
> (*B* text ; *Passus* xv. 161-3.)

And again as

> Clenlich y clothed in Cipres and in Tartaryne.
> (*B* text ; *Passus* xv. 224.)

Chaucer, in a well-known passage in the *Knightes Tale*, speaks of "clooth of Tars" embroidered with pearls, after the fashion mentioned by Boccaccio in the passage from the *Fiammetta* already quoted. Chaucer's mention occurs in his description of " the grete Emetrëus, the kyng of Inde," who

> Upon a steede bay, trapped in steel,
> Covered in clooth of gold, dyapred weel,
> Cam ridynge, lyk the god of armes, Mars.
> His cote armure was of clooth of Tars,
> Couched with perles, white and rounde and grete.
> (ll. 2156-61.)

Another reference is in the pseudo-Chaucerian *Flower and Leaf*:—

> On every trumpe hanging a brood banere
> Of fyn tartarium, were ful richly bete.
> (ll. 211-12.)

According to Skeat, this means banners of Tartar cloth, spangled with beaten gold, a mode of enrichment of which mention has already been made.

It is abundantly evident from the foregoing examples, all of which, except the last, belong to the thirteenth or fourteenth centuries, that Dante was referring to objects perfectly familiar to his contemporaries, when he compared the painted skin of " la sozza imagine di froda " to the brilliant colouring of the " drappi tartareschi."

DANTE'S OBLIGATIONS TO THE *ORMISTA*

(THE *HISTORIAE ADVERSUM PAGANOS* OF OROSIUS)[1]

DANTE, as is well known to every student of his works, was largely indebted for his knowledge of ancient history to the *Ormista*,[2] as the *Historiarum adversum Paganos Libri VII*[3] of Paulus Orosius was commonly called by mediæval writers. It is by no means so generally known that some of his favourite theories and arguments as to the divine institution of the Roman Empire were borrowed from the same source. The object of the present article is to indicate the extent of these obligations, which are more numerous than has hitherto been suspected, and to identify the passages utilised by Dante.

Though not strictly within the scope of this article, we may, in the first place, point out that, notwithstanding the divergence of opinion among the commentators, there cannot be the least doubt that Orosius is the person intended by Dante in the passage in the tenth canto of the *Paradiso* :—

> Nell' altra piccioletta luce ride
> Quell' avvocato dei tempi cristiani,
> Del cui latino Augustin si provvide.
> (ll. 118-20.)

---

[1] Reprinted, with additions, from *Romania*, xxiv. 385-98.

[2] Commonly supposed to stand for *Or[osii] m[undi] ist[ori]a*. The word is sometimes spelt *Ormesta* or *Hormesta*. Other explanations have been proposed, for which see Fabricius, *Bibl. Med. et Infim. Aetatis, s. v.* Orosius. Benvenuto da Imola three times (i. 82, 392 ; v. 43) quotes the work under the title *Ormesta mundi*.

[3] Ex recognitione Caroli Zangemeister (Lipsiae, 1889).

The title "avvocato dei tempi cristiani" points unquestionably to the author of the *Historiae adversum Paganos,* in whose
book, which was written to prove by the evidence of history that
the condition of the world had not grown worse since the introduction of Christianity, the phrase " Christiana tempora " occurs
so frequently as to make the point of Dante's allusion obvious
to any one who has read the work.[1]

We may add that the *Ormista* was undertaken, as Orosius
himself states in his Prologue and again in his concluding
chapter,[2] at the instance of St. Augustine, to whose *De Civitate
Dei* it was intended to be subsidiary.[3]

---

[1] See *Hist. adv. Pag.* i. 20, § 6; ii. 3, § 5; iii. 4, § 4; 8, § 3; iv. 6, § 35;
23, § 10; v. 11, § 6; vi. 22, § 10; vii. 5, § 3; 8, § 4; 26, § 2; 43, §§ 16, 19.—
The last instance occurs in the concluding lines of the book: " Explicui adju-
vante Christo secundum praeceptum tuum, beatissime pater Augustine, ab initio
mundi usque in praesentem diem . . . cupiditates et punitiones hominum pecca-
torum, conflictationes saeculi et judicia Dei quam brevissime et quam simpli-
cissime potui, Christianis tamen temporibus propter praesentem magis Christi
gratiam ab illa in incredulitatis confusione discretis ".

Singularly enough Benvenuto da Imola, in his commentary on *Par.* x.
118-20, although he speaks of Orosius as " defensor temporum Christianorum,"
and refers to his book, yet inclines to think that the allusion is to St. Ambrose ;
he says :—

" Ad evidentiam istius literae est notandum quod litera ista potest verificari
tam de Ambrosio quam de Orosio. De Ambrosio quidem quia fuit magnus
advocatus temporum Christianorum, quia tempore suo pullulaverunt multi et
magni haeretici ; contra quos Ambrosius defensavit ecclesiam Dei, immo et
contra Theodosium imperatorem fuit audacissimus ; et ad ejus praedicationem
Augustinus conversus fuit ad fidem, qui fuit validissimus malleus haereticorum.
Potest etiam intelligi de Paulo Orosio, qui fuit defensor temporum Christianorum
reprobando tempora pagana, sicut evidenter apparet ex ejus opere quod intitulatur
Ormesta mundi, quem librum fecit ad petitionem beati Augustini, sicut ipse
Orosius testatur in prohemio dicti libri. . . . Et hic nota quod quamvis istud
possit intelligi tam de Orosio quam de Ambrosio, et licet forte autor intellexerit
de Orosio, cui fuit satis familiaris, ut perpendi ex multis dictis ejus, tamen melius
est quod intelligatur de Ambrosio, quia licet Orosius fuerit vir valens et utilis,
non tamen bene cadit in ista corona inter tam egregios doctores."

[2] See above, note 1.

[3] Orosius is very modest in referring to his own work; in addressing St.
Augustine, he humbly likens himself to a dog: " Ego solius oboedientiae . . .
testimonio contentus sum ; nam et in magna magni patrisfamilias domo cum sint
multa diversi generis animalia adjumento rei familiaris commoda, non est tamen

Dante mentions Orosius by name seven times, once in the *Convivio*, once in the *De Vulgari Eloquentia*, four times in the *De Monarchia*, and once in the *Quaestio de Aqua et Terra* [1] ; but these references, as will be seen, by no means represent the whole amount of Dante's indebtedness.

In the *De Vulgari Eloquentia* [2] Orosius is not quoted, but is merely named, along with Frontinus, Pliny and Livy, as a master of lofty prose—a selection which does not say much for Dante's discrimination in the matter of literary style.

In the *Convivio* the period between the reign of Numa Pompilius, the second king of Rome, and the birth of Christ is computed, on the authority of Orosius, at about 650 years.[3] This computation appears to be based on a passage in the fourth book (cap. 12), where Orosius puts the interval between the reigns of Tullus Hostilius and Caesar Augustus at 700 years nearly.[4]

There is another passage in the *Convivio* (iv. 5) where Dante is evidently indebted to Orosius, although he gives Livy in a general way as the authority for his statements in the chapter. Referring to the panic of the Romans after their defeat at Cannae, and to the heap of gold rings taken from the bodies of the fallen Romans, and produced in the senate-house at Carthage

---

canum cura postrema. . . . Beatus etiam Tobias, ducem angelum sequens, canem comitem habere non sprevit. Igitur generali amori tuo speciali amore conexus voluntati tuae volens parui. (*Prol.*) "

[1] I include this treatise among Dante's works, though many Dantists regard it as a forgery. See above, p. 55, note 1.

[2] " Fortassis utilissimum foret ad illam [supremam constructionem] habituandam regulatos vidisse poetas . . . nec non alios qui usi sunt altissimas prosas, ut Titum Livium, Plinium, Frontinum, Paulum Orosium, et multos alios, quos amica solitudo nos visitare invitat " (ii. 6, ll. 78-85). Previous to the publication of Prof. Rajna's valuable critical edition of the *De Vulgari Eloquentia* it was supposed that Cicero was also included in this list ; but Prof. Rajna has shown that the reading of the MSS. is not " Tullium, Livium," but " Titum Livium," the alteration having been made by Trissino, and copied from him by all subsequent editors.

[3] *Conv.* iii. 11, ll. 22-30. The reading is not certain, for *seicento* Dr. Moore conjectures *settecento*.

[4] " Per annos prope septingentos, id est ab Hostilio Tullo usque ad Caesarem Augustum, una tantummodo aestate Romana sanguinem viscera non sudarunt " (iv. 12, § 9).

by Hannibal's envoy as proof of his victory, he says : " Non pose Iddio le mani, quando per la guerra d' Annibale, avendo perduti tanti cittadini che tre moggia d' anella in Affrica erano portate, li Romani vollero abbandonare la terra, se quello benedetto Scipione giovane non avesse impresa l' andata in Affrica per la sua franchezza ? " (ll. 164-71).

In Livy's account, to which, it may be remarked, Dante expressly refers when mentioning the same incident in the *Inferno*,[1] the circumstances of the conspiracy to abandon Italy, which was frustrated by Scipio, and of the sending of the gold rings to Carthage, are widely separated, the former being related in Lib. xxii. cap. 53, and the latter some twenty chapters further on, in Lib. xxiii. cap. 12.   In Orosius, on the other hand, the two are mentioned in close connection, as they are in Dante's own account.   Orosius says: " Hannibal in testimonium victoriae suae [apud Cannas] tres modios anulorum aureorum Carthaginem misit, quos ex manibus interfectorum equitum Romanorum senatorumque detraxerat.   Usque adeo autem ultima desperatio reipublicae apud residuos Romanos fuit, ut senatores de relinquenda Italia sedibusque quaerendis consilium ineundum putarint. Quod auctore Caecilio Metello confirmatum fuisset, nisi Cornelius Scipio tribunus tunc militum, idem qui post Africanus, districto gladio deterruisset ac potius pro patriae defensione in sua verba jurare coegisset " (iv. 16, §§ 5, 6).   There seems little doubt, therefore, that in this instance Dante was indebted to Orosius and not to Livy.

In the *Quaestio de Aqua et Terra* the reference is to the geographical section of Orosius' work, in which he gives the boundaries of the various continents and countries.[2]

---

[1] xxviii. 10-12 :—

> . . . per la lunga guerra
> Che dell' anella fe sì alte spoglie,
> Come Livïo scrive.

[2] *A. T.* § 19: " Haec habitabilis extenditur per lineam longitudinis a Gadibus, quae supra terminos occidentales ab Hercule ponitur, usque ad ostia fluminis Ganges, ut scribit Orosius " (ll. 39-43).   This is based upon what Orosius says as to the boundaries of Europe and Asia, west and east: " Europae in Hispania occidentalis oceanus termino est, maxime ubi apud Gades insulas Herculis

The four references in the *De Monarchia* are easily identified. The first (*Mon.* ii. 3, ll. 85-91) is a direct quotation (*Oros.* i. 2, § 11), introduced to prove that Mt. Atlas is in Africa. The next reference (*Mon.* ii. 9, ll. 22-29) is to Orosius' account of the reigns of Ninus and Semiramis in Assyria (i. 4, §§ 1-8).[1]

columnae visuntur . . . Asia ad mediam frontem orientis habet in oceano Eoo ostia fluminis Gangis . . . " (i. 2, §§ 7, 13). Dante was also apparently indebted to Orosius for several geographical details in the *Divina Commedia*. Tozer points out (in an *English Commentary on the Divina Commedia*) that in *Inf.* xx. 66, where the reading is disputed, Dante probably wrote not *Apennino*, but *Pennino;* for though the Pennine Alps in the ordinary acceptation of the name would be out of place in this passage, yet Orosius assigns to them just the required position, *viz.,* to the south-west of Rhaetia, as the Tyrol was anciently called : " Pannonia Noricus et Raetia habent . . . ab Africo (*i.e.,* to the south-west) Alpes Poeninas " (i. 2, § 60). Again, Tozer shows (*op. cit.*) that by "Libia con sua rena " (*Inf.* xxiv. 85) Dante meant the Roman Province of Africa, which lay to the west of Egypt, this name being assigned to that district by Orosius (" Aegyptus inferior ab orienti habet Syriam Palaestinam, ab occasu Libyam," i. 2, § 27) and other early geographers. Dante's knowledge of the Rhipaean mountains (*Purg.* xxvi. 43)—an imaginary chain in Northern Europe—was probably derived from Orosius : " Europa incipit sub plaga septentrionis, a flumine Tanai, qua Riphaei montes Sarmatico aversi oceano Tanaim fluvium fundunt " (i., 2, § 4). Other passages in which Dante may have been indebted to the geographical section of Orosius' work are *Inf.* xxviii. 82 (*cf. Oros.* i. 2, §§ 96, 104) ; *Purg.* xviii. 79-81 (*cf. Oros.* i. 2, §§ 101-3) ; and *V. E.* i. 8, l. 26 (" Maeotidae paludes," *i.e.,* the Sea of Azov ; *cf. Oros.* i. 2, §§ 5, 49, 52). In the second of these passages Dante describes the season when the sun sets west by south (*i.e.,* about the end of November) as the time when to the inhabitants of Rome it appears to set between Corsica and Sardinia. This seems to have been suggested by what Orosius says in his description of these two islands : " Sardinia habet ab oriente e borea Tyrrhenium mare quod spectat ab portum urbis Romae . . . Corsica habet ab oriente Tyrrhenium mare et Portum Urbis ". Dr. Moore proposes an emendation in the text of *Epist.* viii. § 11 (*circumsaepta* for *circumspecta*) on the ground that Dante appears to have been thinking of Orosius' phrase, " orbem totius terrae oceani limbo circumsaeptum (i. 2, § 1), of which Dante's words certainly seem to be an echo.

[1] Dante says that though Ninus and Semiramis in their attempt to attain universal empire waged war for more than ninety years, as Orosius records, yet in the end they failed of their object. This sum total of ninety years and upwards is not given in so many words by Orosius ; in the passage referred to above he merely states that Ninus carried on his conquests during a period of fifty years, without mentioning the duration of Semiramis' wars : Non contenta terminis mulier, quos a viro suo tunc solo bellatore in quinquaginta annis adquisitos susceperat, Aethiopiam . . . imperio adjecit. Indis quoque

The third, which occurs in the same chapter of the *De Monarchia* (ll. 35-42), refers to the conquests of Vesoges, king of Egypt, and to his repulse by the Scythians.[1]   The fourth reference (*Mon.* ii. 11, ll. 36-38) is to the combat between the Roman Horatii and the Alban Curiatii, whereby the struggle for supremacy between Rome and Alba was finally decided.   Dante here quotes Livy as his authority, remarking that Orosius is in agreement with him.[2]

There is also a passage in the *De Monarchia* where Dante apparently has Orosius in mind, though he actually refers to Livy.   Speaking of Cincinnatus, he says : " assumptus ab aratro, dictator factus est, ut Livius refert.   Et post victoriam, post triumphum, sceptro imperatorio restituto consulibus, sudaturus post boves ad stivam libere reversus est " (ii. 5, ll. 78-83).   There is nothing of this in Livy ; but in Orosius' account there is a passage, which Dante was probably thinking of, though his recollection of it was confused : " Quintius Cincinnatus, prae-cipuus ille dictator . . . repertus in rure, ab aratro arcessitus ad fasces, sumpto honore instructoque exercitu mox victor effectus jugum boum Aequis[3] imposuit victoriamque quasi stivam tenens subjugatos hostes prae se primus egit" (ii. 12, §§ 7, 8).

---

bellum intulit . . . " (i. 4, § 5).   In the next book, however, he states (ii. 3, § 1) that Ninus reigned for fifty-two years, and Semiramis for forty-two ; and it is evidently from this passage that Dante got his " per nonaginta et plures annos (ut Orosius refert) ".

[1] *Oros.* i. 14, §§ 1-4.   Dante says : " Vesoges . . . a Scythis, inter quasi athlothetas et terminum, ab incoepto suo temerario est aversus ".   Giuliani, not understanding the word *athlothetas* (" judges " in a contest), which Dante (as Witte points out) probably got from the *Ethics* of Aristotle, unwarrantably sub-stitutes *athletas*.

[2] Orosius does not mention the names of the combatants ; he merely says : " Tullum Hostilium militaris rei institutorem fiducia bene exercitae juventutis Albanis intulisse bellum et diu altrinsecus spe incerta, certa clade, tandem pessi-mos exitus et dubios eventus compendiosa tergiminorum congressione finisse ". (ii. 4, § 9.)

[3] Witte, who quotes this passage, oddly enough reads *equis !*   If there were the least doubt about the correct reading a reference to Livy would settle the question ; he says : " Tribus hastis jugum fit, humi fixis duabus, superque eas transversa una deligata.   Sub hoc jugo dictator Aequos misit." (iii. 28.)

Another similar case occurs in the previous chapter of the same book (ii. 4, ll. 65-70) where Cloelia's feat of swimming across the Tiber is mentioned. It is evident from Dante's phraseology that he had Orosius', not Livy's,[1] account before him at the time.

Witte, in his notes to the *De Monarchia*, draws attention to another passage in which he thinks Dante, while referring to Livy, was actually quoting Orosius. Dante describes how the Carthaginians under Hannibal were only prevented from taking Rome by a sudden storm of hail which drove them back to their camp : " At quum Romana nobilitas, premente Hannibale, sic caderet, ut ad finalem Romanae rei deletionem non restaret nisi Poenorum insultus ad urbem, subita et intolerabili grandine proturbante, victores victoriam sequi non potuisse, Livius in bello Punico inter alia gesta conscribit ". (ii. 4, ll. 58-64.) Livy's account is as follows: " Instructis utrinque exercitibus in ejus pugnae casum in qua urbs Roma victori praemium esset, imber ingens grandine mixtus ita utramque aciem turbavit, ut vix armis retentis in castra sese receperint, nullius rei minore quam hostium metu ". (xxvi. 11.) Orosius' description of the incident is evidently borrowed from that of Livy, and does not seem to justify Witte's supposition that Dante was indebted to it rather than to the authority he names : " ubi expositae utrimque acies constiterunt, in conspectu Romae praemium victoris futurae tantus se subito imber e nubibus grandine mixtus effudit, ut turbata agmina vix armis retentis in sua se castra colligerent ". (iv. 17, § 5.)

In the *Divina Commedia*, in which, as we have seen, Orosius himself is referred to, though not by name,[2] there is no direct reference to his work, but Dante's obligations to it may be traced with certainty in more than one passage.

Speaking of Semiramis in the fifth canto of the *Inferno* Dante says :—

---

[1] ii. 13. Dante asks : " Nonne transitus Cloeliae mirabilis fuit ? " Orosius speaks of Cloelia's " admirabilis transmeati fluminis audacia " (ii. 5, § 3).

[2] *Par.* x. 118-120. See above, pp. 121-122.

> Fu imperatrice di molte favelle.
> A vizio di lussuria fu sì rotta,
>   Che libito fe' licito in sua legge,
>   Per torre il biasmo in che era condotta.
> Ell' è Semiramis, di cui si legge
>   Che succedette a Nino, e fu sua sposa :
>   Tenne la terra, che il Soldan corregge'.[1]
>
>   (ll. 54-60.)

Orosius says :—

Huic [Nino] mortuo Samiramis uxor successit . . . , haec, libidine ardens, sanguinem sitiens, inter incessabilia et stupra et homicidia, cum omnes quos regie arcessitos, meretricie habitos concubitu oblectasset occideret, tandem filio flagitiose concepto, impie exposito, inceste cognito privatam ignominiam publico scelere obtexit.   Praecepit enim, ut inter parentes ac filios nulla delata reverentia naturae de conjugiis adpetendis ut cuique libitum esset liberum fieret.   (i. 4, §§ 4, 7, 8.)

There cannot be the least doubt that Dante had in mind the above passage with which we know he was acquainted [2] when he was writing his own description of Semiramis.   This phrase, *libito fe' licito* (l. 56), is an exact translation of that of Orosius, " ut cuique libitum esset liberum fieret " [3] ; and again *si legge [di Semiramis] Che succedette a Nino, e fu sua sposa* (ll. 58-9), points directly to what Orosius says : " Nino mortuo Samiramis uxor successit ".   This last identification is particularly interesting as it enables us to reject without hesitation the variant

---

[1] Dante has apparently confused the ancient kingdom of Babylonia (or Assyria) with Babylonia or Babylon (Old Cairo) in Egypt, which was the territory of the Sultan.   *Cf.* Mandeville: " The Lond of Babyloyne, where the Sowdan dwellethe comonly . . . is not that gret Babyloyne, where the Dyversitee of Langages was first made . . . when the grete Tour of Babel was begonnen to ben made " (cap. v. ed. Halliwell, 1839).   Benvenuto da Imola notices the confusion, but suggests that Dante meant to imply that Semiramis extended her empire so as to include Egypt as well as Assyria ; he says : " Istud non videtur aliquo modo posse stare quia de rei veritate Semiramis nunquam tenuit illam Babiloniam quam modo Soldanus corrigit . . . ad defencionem autoris dico, quod autor noster vult dicere quod Semiramis in tantum ampliavit regnum, quod non solum tenuit Babiloniam antiquam, sed etiam Egiptum, ubi est modo alia Babilonia."

[2] See above (p. 125) on *Mon.* ii. 9, ll. 22-29.

[3] This phrase occurs again, i. 16, § 3.   Chaucer borrowed it and applied it to Nero : " His lustes were al lawe in his decree ".   (*Monkes Tale*, l. 3,667.)

reading *sugger dette* for *succedette* in l. 59, a reading which has some slight MS. authority, and has found supporters among recent commentators.[1] Quite apart, however, from the fact that Dante's *succedette* evidently represents Orosius' *successit*, the absence of any mention by the latter of what is implied in the reading *sugger dette* is sufficient to condemn it, since Dante has followed his authority so closely as to make it in the highest degree improbable that he would have omitted such a striking detail had it been supplied by Orosius.

From Orosius Dante evidently got his estimate of Alexander the Great, whom he places along with Dionysius among the tyrants in the seventh circle of Hell.[2] It has been objected that inasmuch as Dante speaks of "Alessandro" simply, without any further qualification, it is not justifiable to assume that Alexander the Great is meant, especially as Dante introduces the latter into the *Convivio* (iv. 11, ll. 123-5)[3] as an example of munificence.

But it is quite possible that Dante should commend Alexander for his liberality, which had become proverbial in the Middle Ages,[4] and yet condemn him for the bloodshed and misery occasioned by his wars of conquest.

A glance at Orosius' description of the "felix praedo," as Lucan calls Alexander, will suffice to explain Dante's attitude towards him. On recording his birth Orosius brands him as "gurges miseriarium atque atrocissimus turbo totius orientis" (iii. 7, § 5); and later on says of him, "humani sanguinis inexsaturabilis sive hostium sive etiam sociorum, recentem tamen

---

[1] According to Dr. Moore, who discusses this reading in his *Textual Criticism of the Divina Commedia* (pp. 285-6), it occurs as an original reading in two MSS. only; in two or three it has been substituted for *succedette*; and in one it occurs as a marginal reading.

[2] *Inf.* xii. 107: "Quivi è Alessandro, e Dionisio fero".

[3] "Chi non ha ancora nel cuore Alessandro, per li suoi reali beneficii?"

[4] See Paul Meyer, *Alexandre le Grand dans la littérature française du moyen âge*: "A partir de la seconde moitié du xiie siècle, et jusqu'à la fin du moyen âge, le mérite pour lequel Alexandre est universellement célébré . . . est surtout et par dessus tout sa largesse" (vol. ii. pp. 372-3). See the article on "Dante's Seven Examples of Munificence in the *Convivio*," pp. 142-149.

semper sitiebat cruorem" (iii. 18, § 10); and again "per duodecim annos trementem sub se orbem ferro pressit" (iii. 23, § 6). Then, after stating that Alexander died at Babylon "adhuc sanguinem sitiens" (iii. 20, § 4), Orosius ends up with a long apostrophe on the ruin and misery brought by him upon the whole world (iii. 20, §§ 5 ff.).[1]

In the *Purgatorio* Dante is indebted to Orosius for the episode of Cyrus and Tomyris, Queen of the Scythians[2]:—

> Mostrava la ruina e il crudo scempio
> Che fe' Tamiri, quando disse a Ciro :
> Sangue sitisti, ed io di sangue t' empio.
> (xii. 55-7.)

Orosius, after relating how Cyrus treacherously slew the son of Tomyris, and how he himself was slain in ambush by the Queen, describes her revenge : "Regina caput Cyri amputari atque in utrem humano sanguine oppletum coici jubet non muliebriter increpitans : Satia te, inquit, sanguine quem sitisti, cujus per annos triginta insatiabilis perseverasti". (ii. 7, § 6.)

The cruel persecution of the Christians by Domitian, alluded to by Statius, *Purg.* xxii. 83-4, is recorded by Orosius, who was no doubt Dante's authority here also. Orosius says : "Domitianus per annos XV ad hoc paulatim per omnes scelerum gradus crevit, ut confirmatissimam toto orbe Christi Ecclesiam datis ubique crudelissimae persecutionis edictis convellere auderet" (vii. 10, § 1.)

---

[1] It is worthy of note that Benvenuto da Imola, one of the shrewdest of the old commentators on the *Divina Commedia*, emphatically asserts that Alexander the Great is the person intended : "Ad sciendum quis fuerit iste Alexander est notandum, quod aliqui sequentes opinionem vulgi dixerunt quod autor non loquitur hic de Alexandro Macedone, sed de quodam alio, sed certe istud est omnino falsum, quod potest patere dupliciter : primo, quia cum dicimus Alexander, debet intelligi per excellentiam de Alexandro Magno ; secundo, quia iste fuit violentissimus hominum". He then proceeds to justify his last statement from Orosius, and concludes by declaring Alexander to have been "maximus autor violentiarum in terris".

[2] Strictly speaking Tomyris was Queen of the Massagetae ; but Orosius calls her Queen of the Scythians, and Dante, who alludes to this incident again in the *De Monarchia* (ii. 9, ll. 43-8), gives her the same title

In the *Paradiso* the account of Caesar's movements during the civil wars appears to be summarised from that of Orosius :—

. . . uscì di Ravenna, E saltò Rubicon. . . . In ver la Spagna rivolse lo stuolo ; Poi ver Durazzo, e Farsalia percosse Sì ch' al Nil caldo si sentì del duolo. . . . Da indi scese folgorando a Juba[1] ; Poscia si volse nel . . . occidente, Dove sentia la Pompeiana tuba[2] (*Par.* vi. 61-72).

Orosius says :—

Caesar Ravennam sese contulit. . . . Rubicone flumine transmeato. . . . Ariminum venit . . . mox Alpes transvectus . . . ad Hispanias contendit. . . . Interea apud Dyracchium multi orientis reges ad Pompeium cum auxiliis convenerunt : quo cum Caesar venisset, Pompeium obsidione cinxit . . . inde per Epirum in Thessaliam perrexit . . . in campis Pharsalicis . . . inde . . . in Aegyptum venit. . . . Alexandriam venit . . . postea . . . in Africam transiit et apud Thapsum cum Juba et Scipione pugnavit . . . continuo in Hispanias contra Pompeios Pompei filios profectus . . . ultimum bellum apud Mundam gestum est (vi. 15, 16).

Dante's information about the effeminacy of Sardanapalus (*Par.* xv. 107-8) was perhaps also derived from Orosius (i. 19, § 1).[3]

---

[1] The allusion is to the defeat of Juba at Thapsus.

[2] The defeat of Pompey's sons at Munda.

[3] Benvenuto da Imola refers to Justinus, whose account of Sardanapalus was borrowed by Orosius. Dante may have got his information directly from the former, but it is more probable that he took it from Orosius with the rest of his ancient history. Pietro di Dante refers to Juvenal (x. 362) : "Et Venere et caenis et plumis Sardanapali "; but he also, without mentioning his authority, quotes the account given by Justinus and Orosius. It is not unlikely, however, that Dante had in mind a passage from the *De Regimine Principum* of Aegidius Romanus, a work with which he was certainly acquainted (*cf. Conv.* iv. 24, ll. 97-9). Aegidius, it will be noted, makes use of the same phrase (" in cameris ") that Dante does : " Si decet personam regiam ostendere se reverendam et honore dignam, maxime indecens est eam esse intemperatam. Exemplum autem hujus habemus in rege Sardanapallo, qui cum esset totus muliebris et deditus intemperantiae, ut recitatur in antiquis historiis, non exibat extra castrum suum ut haberet colloquia cum baronibus regni sui, sed omnes collocutiones ejus erant in cameris ad mulieres, et per litteras mittebat baronibus et ducibus quod vellet eos facere ". In the old Italian translation (*circ.* 1288) the use of the phrase " nella camera " to represent the " chambering " of Sardanapalus, is still more striking : " Quello re Sardanapalo era sì nontemperato ched elli s' era tutto dato ai diletti de le femmine e de la lussuria, e non usciva fuore de la sua camera. . . . Tutte le sue parole, e tutto il suo intendimento era ne la camera in seguire le sue malvagie volontà di lussuria ". (i. 16.)

Doubtless he was also indebted to Orosius for his estimate of Jugurtha, whom he introduces into one of his canzoni (*Canz.* " O patria, degna di trionfal fama ") as a type of corruption (or, as some think, of perfidy).   Orosius' account is as follows :—

> Jugurtha, Micipsae Numidarum regis adoptivus heresque inter naturales ejus filios factus, primum coheredes suos, id est Hiempsalem occidit, Adherbalem bello victum Africa expulit.   Calpurnium deinde consulem adversum se missum pecunia corrupit atque ad turpissimas condiciones pacis adducit.   Praeterea cum Romam ipse venisset, omnibus pecunia aut corruptis aut adtemptatis seditiones dissensionesque permiscuit ; quam cum egrederetur infami satis notavit elogio dicens : O urbem venalem et mature perituram, si emptorem invenerit !
> (v. 15, §§ 3-5.)

It was not, however, merely for information upon matters of ancient history or geography that Dante was indebted to Orosius.   It will be seen that he borrowed from the latter not only material for his historical illustrations, but also several of the principal theories and arguments which are utilised in the *De Monarchia* and elsewhere.

In the first book of the *De Monarchia* Dante, after discussing the question as to whether Monarchy is necessary for the welfare of mankind, decides in the affirmative, and points in confirmation of his previous arguments to the condition of mankind at Christ's birth, when for the first time in the world's history there was universal peace under one sole ruler (*viz.*, Augustus) :—

> Rationibus omnibus supra positis, experientia memorabilis attestatur ; status videlicet illius mortalium, quem Dei Filius, in salutem hominis hominem adsumpturus, vel expectavit, vel quum voluit ipse disposuit.   Nam si a lapsu primorum parentum . . . dispositiones hominum et tempora recolamus, non inveniemus, nisi sub divo Augusto Monarcha, existente Monarchia perfecta, mundum undique fuisse quietum. (*Mon.* i. 16, ll. 1-12.)

This point, upon which Dante insists again elsewhere,[1] is dwelt upon repeatedly by Orosius :—

---

[1] *Conv.* iv. 5, ll. 57-67 : " Allora quando di lassù discese Colui . . . nè 'l mondo non fu mai nè sarà sì perfettamente disposto, come allora che alla voce d' un solo principe del Roman Popolo e comandatore fu ordinato. . . . E però pace universale era per tutto, che mai più non fu nè fia." *Cf. Par.* vi. 80-81 :—

> Con costui [Augusto] pose il mondo in tanta pace,
> Che fu serrato a Jano il suo delubro.

Anno ab urbe condita DCCXXV. . . . Caesar victor ab oriente rediens, VII idus Januarias urbem triplici triumpho ingressus est ac tunc primum ipse Jani portas sopitis finitisque omnibus bellis civilibus clausit. . . . Et eodem die summa rerum ac potestatum penes unum esse coepit et mansit, quod Graeci monarchiam vocant. (vi. 20, §§ 1, 2.)—Ab Abraham usque ad Caesarem Augustum id est usque ad nativitatem Christi, quae fuit anno imperii Caesaris quadragesimo secundo, cum facta pace cum Parthis Jani portae clausae sunt et bella toto orbe cessarunt, colliguntur anni ii.-xv. (i. 1, § 6).—Utrum aliquando bella, caedes, ruinae atque omnia infandarum mortium genera nisi Caesare Augusto imperante cessaverint, inquirat quisquis infamanda Christiana tempora putat. . . . Indubitatissime constat sub Augusto primum Caesare post Parthicam pacem universum terrarum orbem positis armis abolitisque discordiis generali pace et nova quiete compositum Romanis paruisse legibus. . . . In ipso imperio Caesaris inluxisse ortum in hoc mundo Domini nostri Jesu Christi . . . mani-festum est . . . pacem istam totius mundi et tranquillissimam serenitatem non magnitudine Caesaris sed potestate filii Dei, qui in diebus Caesaris apparuit, exstitisse. (iii, 8, §§ 3, 5, 7, 8.)—Opportune compositis rebus Augusti Caesaris natus est Dominus Christus. (vi. 17, § 10.)—Anno ab urbe condita DCCLII Caesar Augustus ab oriente in occidentem, a septentrione in meridiem ac per totum Oceani circulum cunctis gentibus una pace compositis, Jani portas tertio ipse tunc clausit. . . . Eo tempore, id est eo anno quo firmissimam verissi-mamque pacem ordinatione Dei Caesar composuit, natus est Christus. (vi. 22, §§ 1, 5.)—Incessabilibus cladibus nullus finis ac nulla requies fuit, nisi cum salvator mundi Christus inluxit: cujus adventui praedestinatam fuisse imperii Romani pacem . . . sufficienter ostendisse me arbitror. (vii. 1, § 11.)

See also vii. 2, §§ 15, 16; vii. 3, § 4.

Orosius lays stress on the fact that Christ chose to be in-cluded in the census under Augustus, whereby he became a Roman citizen, in order to assert his human nature :—

Eodem quoque anno [quo natus est Christus] tunc primum Caesar . . . cen-sum agi singularum ubique provinciarum et censeri omnes homines jussit, quando et Deus homo videri et esse dignatus est. Haec est prima illa clarissimaque professio, quae Caesarem omnium principem Romanosque rerum dominos singillatim cunctorum hominum edita adscriptione signavit, in qua se et ipse, qui cunctos homines fecit, inveniri hominem adscribique inter homines voluit. (vi. 22, §§ 6, 7.)

And he uses this as an argument to prove the divine institu-tion of the Roman Empire :—

Nec dubium, quin omnium cognitioni fidei inspectionique pateat, quia Dominus noster Jesus Christus hanc urbem nutu suo auctam defensamque in hunc rerum apicem provexerit, cujus potissime voluit esse cum venit, dicendus utique civis Romanus census professione Romani. (vi. 22, § 8.) [1]

---

[1] *Cf.* vii. 3, § 4 : " Redemptor mundi, Dominus Jesus Christus, venit in terras et Caesaris censu civis Romanus adscriptus est ".

Dante follows exactly the same line of argument :—

Exivit edictum a Caesare Augusto, ut describeretur universus orbis. In quibus verbis universalem mundi jurisdictionem tunc Romanorum fuisse aperte intelligere possumus. (*Mon.* ii. 9. ll. 101-105.)—Si Romanum imperium de jure non fuit, Christus nascendo praesumpsit injustum. . . . Sed Christus sub edicto Romanae auctoritatis nasci voluit de Virgine Matre, ut in illa singulari generis humani descriptione Filius Dei, homo factus, homo conscriberetur ; quod fuit illud prosequi. . . . Ergo Christus Augusti Romanorum auctoritate fungentis edictum fore justum, opere persuasit. (*Mon.* ii. 12, ll. 24-54.)[1]—Quum universaliter orbem describi edixisset Augustus . . . si non de justissimi principatus aula prodiisset edictum, Unigenitus Dei Filius, homo factus ad profitendum secundum naturam assumptam edicto se subditum, nunquam tunc nasci de Virgine voluisset. (*Epist.* vii. 3.)

Again, Orosius points to Titus, who destroyed Jerusalem, as the avenger of the death of Christ :—

Capta eversaque urbe Hierosolymorum . . . extinctisque Judaeis Titus, qui ad vindicandum Domini Jesu Christi sanguinem judicio Dei fuerat ordinatus, victor triumphans cum Vespasiano patre Janum clausit. (vii. 3, § 8.)

And in another passage, after describing how Titus triumphed after his victory over the Jews and closed the temple of Janus, he says :—

Jure enim idem honos ultione passionis Domini inpensus est, qui etiam nativitati fuerat adtributus. (vii. 9, § 9.)

Here once more Dante follows Orosius. In the *Purgatorio* he says of Titus :—

> Il buon Tito con l' aiuto
> Del sommo Rege vendicò le fora,
> Ond' uscì il sangue per Giuda venduto.
> (xxi. 82-84.)

And in the *Paradiso* :—

> Poscia con Tito a far vendetta corse[2]
> Della vendetta del peccato antico.
> (vi. 92-93.)

---

[1] *Cf. Epist.* viii. 2 : " Roma, cui post tot triumphorum pompas, et verbo et opere Christus orbis confirmavit imperium ".

[2] That is " l' aquila romana ". The destruction of Jerusalem by Titus was the vengeance upon the Jews for the crucifixion of Christ, whereby Adam's sin was avenged.

The striking correspondence in so many passages between the two writers, to which we have drawn attention, shows that Dante had gained an intimate acquaintance with the book of Orosius during the lonely years of his exile—the *amica solitudo* to which he somewhat pathetically refers in his *De Vulgari Eloquentia*.[1]

The following comparative table will show at a glance the passages in which Dante was either certainly or presumably indebted to the *Ormista* :—

Orosius.	Dante.
i. 1, § 6 ; iii. 8, §§ 3, 5, 7, 8 ; vi. 17, § 10 ; 20, §§ 1, 2 ; 22, §§ 1, 5 ; vii. 1, § 11 ; 2, §§ 15, 16 ; 3, § 4.	*Par.* vi. 80-1 ; *Conv.* iv. 5, ll. 57-67 ; *Mon.* i. 16, ll. 1-12.
i. 2, § 1.	*Epist.* viii. § 11.
i. 2, § 4.	*Purg.* xxvi. 43.
i. 2, §§ 5, 49, 52.	*V. E.* i. 8, l. 26.
i. 2, §§ 7, 13.	*A. T.* § 19, ll. 39-43.
i. 2, § 11.	*Mon.* ii. 3, ll. 85-91.
i. 2, § 27.	*Inf.* xxiv. 85.
i. 2, § 60.	*Inf.* xx. 65.
i. 2, §§ 96, 104.	*Inf.* xxviii. 82.
i. 2, §§ 101-3.	*Purg.* xviii. 79-81.
i. 4, §§ 1-8 ; ii. 3, § 1.	*Mon.* ii. 9, ll. 22-9.
i. 4, §§ 4, 7, 8.	*Inf.* v. 54-60.
i. 14, §§ 1-4.	*Mon.* ii. 9, ll. 35-42.
i. 19, § 1.	*Par.* xv. 107-8.
(i. 20, § 6 ; ii. 3, § 5 ; iii. 4, § 4 ; 8, § 3 ; iv. 6, § 35 ; 23, § 10 ; v. 11, § 6 ; vi. 22, § 10 ; vii. 5, § 3 ; 8, § 4 ; 26, § 2 ; 43, §§ 16, 19.	*Par.* x. 119.)
ii. 2, § 4 ; 3, § 5 ; iv. 17, § 11 ; vi. 20, § 4.	*Mon.* ii. 9, ll. 1-3.
ii. 3, § 1 ; see i. 4, §§ 1-8.	
ii. 4, § 9.	*Mon.* ii. 11, ll. 22-38.
ii. 5, § 3.	*Mon.* ii. 4, ll. 65-70.
ii. 7, § 6.	*Purg.* xii. 55-7 ; *Mon.* ii. 9, ll. 43-8.
ii. 12, §§ 7, 8.	*Mon.* ii. 5, ll. 76-83.
(iii. 7, § 5 ; 18, § 10 ; 20, §§ 5 ff. ; 23, § 6.	*Inf.* xii. 107.)
iii. 8, §§ 3, 5, 7, 8 ; see i. 1, § 6.	
iv. 16, §§ 5, 6.	*Conv.* iv. 5, ll. 164-71 ; (*cf. Inf.* xxviii. 10-12.)
iv. 17, § 11 ; see ii. 2, § 4.	

[1] See above, p. 123, note 2.

OROSIUS.	DANTE.
v. 15, §§ 3-5.	*Canz.* xviii. 73.
vi. 1, § 16.	*Mon.* ii. 12, ll. 41-7.
vi. 15, §§ 2, 3, 6, 18, 22, 25, 28, 29 ; 16, §§ 3, 6, 7.	*Par.* vi. 61-72.
vi. 17, § 10 ; 20, §§ 1, 2 ; 22, §§ 1, 5 ; see i. 1, § 6.	
vi. 20, § 4 ; see ii. 2, § 4.	
vi. 22, §§ 6, 7, 8 ; vii. 3, § 4.	*Mon.* ii. 9, ll. 99-105 ; ii. 12, ll. 41-7 ; *Epist.* vii. 3.
vii. 1, § 11 ; 2, §§ 15, 16 ; 3, § 4 ; see i. 1, § 6.	
vii. 3, § 4 ; see vi. 22, §§ 6, 7, 8.	
vii. 3, § 8 ; 9, § 9.	*Purg.* xxi. 82-4 ; *Par.* vi. 92-3.
vii. 10, § 1.	*Purg.* xxii. 83-4.

Orosius is mentioned by name seven times by Dante, *viz.*, as " Paolo Orosio," *Conv.* iii. 11, l. 27 ; " Paulus Orosius," *V. E.* ii. 6, l. 84 ; " Orosius," *Mon.* ii. 3, l. 87 ; ii. 9, ll. 26, 38 ; ii. 11, l. 37 ; *A. T.* § 19, l. 43 ; he is alluded to, *Inf.* v. 58 ; *Par.* x. 119.

DANTE'S REFERENCE TO THE SPEAR OF PELEUS

(*INFERNO*, XXXI. 4-6)[1]

At the beginning of the thirty-first canto of the *Inferno* Dante, in speaking of the healing properties of the spear of Achilles, refers to the latter as having formerly belonged to Peleus, the father of Achilles :—

> Od' io che soleva la lancia
> D' Achille e del suo padre esser cagione
> Prima di trista e poi di buona mancia.

This is, of course, the Homeric tradition,[2] but as Dr. Moore points out in his *Studies in Dante* (i. 302), there does not appear to be any Latin authority from which Dante could have derived his knowledge of it. There can be little doubt, however, that Dante's statement is based upon a misunderstanding of Ovid's couplet in the *Remedia Amoris* :—

> Vulnus in Herculeo quae quondam fecerat hoste,
> Vulneris auxilium Pelias hasta tulit.
>
> (ll. 47-8.)

Dante, it is evident, took *Pelias hasta* to mean " the spear of Peleus," instead of " the spear from Mt. Pelion " (the abode of the Centaur Chiron, who gave the spear to Peleus).

To this same misunderstanding of the Ovidian phrase was doubtless due the not infrequent association, by other mediæval writers, of Peleus with the spear which possessed the marvellous healing power referred to by Dante. The reference to Peleus

---

[1] Reprinted, with additions, from the *Modern Language Quarterly*, i. 58-9.

[2] Πηλιάδα μελίην, τὴν πατρὶ φίλῳ πόρε Χείρων
Πηλίου ἐκ κορυφῆς, φόνον ἔμμεναι ἡρώεσσιν.
(*Iliad*, xvi. 143-4.)

and his lance had, in fact, come to be regarded almost as a poetical commonplace, especially by writers of amatory poems, as is evident from the following instances from writers of the twelfth and thirteenth centuries. The earliest is from the troubadour, Bernart de Ventadour [1] :—

> Ja sa bella boca rizens
> No cugei baizan me trays,
> Mas ab un dous baizar m' aucis ;
> E s' ab autre no m' es guirens,
>   Atressi m' es per semblansa
>   Cum fo de Peleus la lanza,
> Que de son colp non podi' hom guerir
> Si per eys loc no s' en fezes ferir.[2]

The remaining instances are from Italian poets—Messer Tommaso da Faenza [3] :—

---

[1] Twelfth century.   See Raynouard, *Choix des Poésies originales des Troubadours*, iii. 43.   This passage is printed also by Dr. Moore (to whom it was supplied by Professor W. P. Ker) in his *Studies in Dante* (i. 303).   A reference to it is given by Cary, who was apparently indebted for it to Thomas Warton. The latter says (*Hist. Eng. Poetry*, iii. 50, ed. 1824): " A passage in Ovid's *Remedium Amoris* concerning Achilles' spear is supposed to be alluded to by a troubadour, Bernard Ventadour, who lived about the year 1150.   This Mons. Millot (*Hist. Litt. des Troubadours*) calls ' Un trait d'érudition singulier dans un troubadour '.   It is not, however, impossible that he might get this fiction from some of the early romances about Troy."   Cary quotes Chaucer's reference to the spear of Achilles in the *Squieres Tale* :—

> " And othere folk han wondred on the swerd
> That wolde percen thurgh-out every-thing ;
> And fille in speche of Thelophus the king,
> And of Achilles with his queynte spere,
> For he coude with it bothe hele and dere."
>   (ll. 236-40.)

and Shakespeare's in 2 *Henry* VI. Act v. sc. 1, ll. 100-1 :—

> " Whose smile and frown like to Achilles' spear
> Is able with the change to kill and cure."

[2] " I did not think her smiling mouth would betray me in a kiss, but with a sweet kiss she slew me ; and if with another (kiss) she be not my surety, it is with me after the likeness of the spear of Peleus ; for of its stroke might no man recover, unless he made himself to be struck by it in the same place."

[3] Thirteenth century.   See D'Ancona e Comparetti, *Le Antiche Rime Volgari secondo la lezione del Codice Vaticano* 3,793, ii. 45-6.   This poem is printed

Sperando Morte, ond 'eo porìa gioire
La mia crudel feruta,
Sì ch' io nom fosse in tutto a morte dato :
Chè ricieputo l' ò per folle ardire,
Laudando mia veduta,
E credendom aver gioioso stato.
Penzo ch' ancor porìa en zo' tornare,
Sol per una semblanza,
Che d' amoroso core,
Perseverando da lei mi venisse,
C'a Pelleus la posso asimilgliare ;
Feruto di sua lanza,
Non guerìa mai s' altrove
Con ella forte no' lo riferisse.

Giovanni dall' Orto [1] :—

Pelao con la lancia attossicata
    Ferendo, l' uomo non potea guarire
    Se non londe ferisse altra fìata :
    Sì mi veggio di voi, bella, venire,
Che la feruta, che m' avete data,
    Farami d' esto secolo partire ;
    Convene per voi essere sanata,
    Che la pena facetemi sentire.

" Il Mare Amoroso " [2] :—

La boccha piccioletta et cholorita,
Vermiglia come rosa di giardino,
Piagente et amorosa per basciare ;
E be llo saccio, ch' i' l' agio provato
Una fiata, vostra gran merzede.
Ma quella mi fu la lancia di Pelus,
Ch' avea tal vertude nel suo ferire
Ch' al primo cholpo dava pene e morte,
E al sechondo vita et allegrezza.
Chosì mi diede quel bascio mal di morte
Ma sse n' avesse un altro, ben guerira.
                    (ll. 99-109.)

also by Valeriani in his *Poeti del Primo Secolo*, ii. 83 ; and by Nannucci, *Lett. Ital.* i. 358. The author is mentioned by Dante in *De Vulgari Eloquentia*, i. 14, ll. 19-20.

[1] Thirteenth century.   See Nannucci, *Manuale della Letteratura del primo secolo della Lingua Italiana*, i. 227-8. This poem is printed also by Valeriani, *Poeti del Primo Secolo*, ii. 101.

[2] Thirteenth century.   Printed by Monaci in his *Crestomazia Italiana dei primi Secoli*, p. 321.

Chiaro Davanzati[1] :—

> Così m' aven com Pallaus sua lanza,
>   Ca del suo colpo non potea om guerire,
>   Mentre ch' un altro a simile sembianza
>   Altra fiata nom si faciea ferire.
> Così dich' io di voi, donna, i' leanza,
>   Che ciò ch' io presi mi torna i' languire :
>   Se sumilgliante non agio l' usanza,
>   Di presente vedretemi morire.

This comparison, to the frequent use of which Professor Renier draws attention in his *Tipo estetico della Donna nel Medioevo*,[2] was commonly employed, as appears from the foregoing examples, with reference to the "wounds" received by the lover from the lips or eyes of his mistress. Dante borrows the hackneyed simile, but very characteristically endows it with fresh life by giving it an application quite different from the commonplace one which previous writers had made familiar. His was no case of a lover stricken down beneath the amorous glances or fond kisses of an idealised mistress—the "wound" from which Dante smarted was inflicted by the tongue of his

---

[1] Thirteenth century.   See D' Ancona e Comparetti, *op. cit.* iv. 289.

[2] Professor Renier gives a reference (p. 18) to four of the five passages quoted above, as well as to two others in which the name of Peleus is not mentioned, *viz.* : Fazio degli Uberti (in R. Renier, *Liriche di Fazio degli Uberti*, p. 54) :—

> " E la mia crudel piaga
> Mi par che ogniora, ardendo, mi consumi ;
> E farà sempre, fin che 'l dolce sguardo
> Non la risanerà d' un altro dardo."

Guittone d' Arezzo (in Valeriani, *Le Poesie di Guittone d' Arezzo*, i. 206) :—

> " Ch' uomo di pregio non poria guarire
> Quell' uom che di sua lancia l' ha piagato,
> S' ello non fina soi di referire.
> Così, madonna mia, similemente
> Mi conven brevemente
>
> Accostarme di vostra vicinanza
> Che la gioia lande volse la mia lanza
> Con quella credo tosto e brevemente
> Vincere pena, e stutar disianza."

guide and mentor, "il più che padre," Virgil,[1] in sharp rebuke,[2] and it was this self-same tongue which administered the healing words of comfort [3] :—

> Una medesima lingua pria mi morse,
>   Sì che mi tinse l' una e l' altra guancia,
>   E poi la medicina mi riporse.
> Così od' io che soleva la lancia
>   D' Achille e del suo padre esser cagione
>   Prima di trista e poi di buona mancia."
>   (*Inf.* xxxi. 1-6.)

[1] *Purg.* xxiii. 4.

[2] "il Maestro mi disse: 'Or pur mira,
  Che per poco è che teco non mi risso'.
  Quand' io 'l senti' a me parlar con ira,
    Volsimi verso lui con tal vergogna,
    Ch' ancor per la memoria mi si gira."
                      (*Inf.* xxx. 131-135.)

[3] "'Maggior difetto men vergogna lava,'
    Disse il Maestro, 'che il tuo non è stato;
    Però d' ogni tristizia ti disgrava.'"
                      (*Inf.* xxx. 142-144.)

DANTE'S SEVEN EXAMPLES OF MUNIFICENCE IN THE *CONVIVIO* (iv. 11.)[1]

Dos e servirs e guarnirs e larguesa
Noiris amors, com fai l' aiga los peis.[2]

AFTER dwelling in this chapter of the *Convivio* on the emptiness of mere riches, and upon the noble exchange made by those who part with these most imperfect things in order to gain the hearts of worthy men, Dante asks:—

Chi non ha ancora nel cuore Alessandro, per li suoi reali beneficii? Chi non ha ancora il buon re di Castella, o il Saladino, o il buono marchese di Monferrato, o il buono conte di Tolosa, o Beltramo dal Bornio, o Galasso da Montefeltro, quando delle loro messioni si fa menzione? (ll. 123-130.)

There is no question as to the identity of four out of the seven persons here mentioned, *viz.*, Alexander the Great, Saladin, Bertran de Born and Galasso da Montefeltro, though in the case of the last two it is not altogether easy to say on what grounds they were included by Dante.

Galasso da Montefeltro, who was a cousin of "il nobilissimo nostro Latino Guido Montefeltrano,"[3] according to Litta was Podestà and Capitano of Cesena in 1289, and of Pisa in 1294, Podestà of Arezzo in 1290 and 1297, and of Cesena for the second time in 1299. It is recorded of him in this last year (which was the year before his death) that he seized a castle near San Leo and impaled its two lords, one of whose relatives he also cut in pieces. He was, however, in other circumstances, eminent as a peace-maker, for we find him reconciling the rival

---

[1] Reprinted, with additions, from *Romania*, xxvi. 453-60.
[2] Bertrand de Born: "Ai! Lemozis," No. 29, ed. Stimming (Halle, 1892).
[3] *Convivio*, iv. 28, ll. 61-62.

(142)

factions in Arezzo in 1290, and, again, acting as a successful mediator in 1299 in composing the quarrels between the university town of Bologna and the rest of the Emilia. But there appears to be no record of the *messioni*[1] for which Dante selects him for praise.

As regards Bertran de Born, the famous figure of the twenty-eighth canto of the *Inferno*, we know from the cartularies of the abbey of Dalon,[2] which was in the neighbourhood of the castle of Hautefort, that he was a generous benefactor of that institution, to which in his declining years he himself retired; but there is no mention in the old Provençal biography (which was Dante's source of information concerning him) of any very striking act of munificence on his part. He appears, on the other hand, often enough as the recipient of the bounty of others. Possibly Dante had in mind the incident which is related by the Provençal biographer as having taken place during the siege of

---

[1] This word *messioni* is said by the Italian commentators to be borrowed from the Provençal. Dante uses it twice elsewhere (*Conv.* iv. 27, ll. 127-8): "Non altrimenti si dee ridere, tiranni, delle vostre messioni, che del ladro, etc."; and *Canz.* xix. 26: "Lor messione a buon non può piacere". The Provençal *messio* was the regular term for the bounty bestowed by a generous patron on the troubadour; *e.g.*, Bertrand de Born: "On solh cortes . . . que solon donar rics dos E far las autras messios A soudadier et a joglar?" (No. 23, ed. Stimming); Life of Peire Rogier: "Lo Dalfins fon larcs e de gran mession" (p. 11, ed. Mahn); Raimbaut de Vacqueiras: "Tant a d' onor, e vol onratz estar, Qu' el onra deu e pretz e messio" (Bartsch, *Chrest.* 126). It occurs also in a characteristic passage in the *Ensenhamen* of Sordello (C. de Lollis, *Vita e Poesie di Sordello di Goito*, pp. 226-7):—

> Pero el metre a obs mesura;
> Quar totz oms, pos se desmesura,
> Pert soven de metre lo grat,
> E lo li ten om a foldat.
> Quar en onrada messio
> An obs tres causas per razo:
> Que om o sapcha be aver,
> E be metre, e bo retener.
>
> (ll. 701-8.)

For other meanings of the word see Raynouard, *Lexique Roman, s. v. metre*.

[2] Copies of these have been preserved. Such as concern Bertran de Born are printed by A. Thomas in the appendix (pp. 151-160) to his edition of Bertran de Born (Toulouse, 1888).

Hautefort by Henry II.,[1] when the King of Aragon arrived on the scene, and sent his messenger to Bertran to ask for provisions, of which the latter sent a liberal supply into the camp of his false friend:—

El reis d' Arago venc en l' ost del rei Henric denan Autafort. E quan Bertrans o saup, si fo mout alegres quel reis d' Arago era en l' ost, per so qu' el era sos amics especials. El reis d' Arago si mandet sos messatges dintz lo chastel, qu' en Bertrans li mandes pa e vi e charn, et el si l' en mandet assatz. E per lo messatge per cui el mandet los presens el li mandet pregan qu' el fezes si qu' el fezes mudar los edifizis e far traire en autra part, quel murs on ilh ferian era tot rotz. Et el, per gran aver del rei Henric, el li dis tot so qu' en Bertrans l' avia mandat a dir.[2]

Instead of the name of Bertran de Born we should have expected rather to find on Dante's list that of Bertran's special patron, the Young King, Henry of England, compared with whom, says the troubadour in his celebrated *planh*, even the most bountiful appeared niggardly,

lo jove rei Engles
Ves cui eran li plus larc cobeitos,

and of whose *largesse* we hear so much in the old French poem on William the Marshal.[3]

Of the generosity and liberality of Alexander the Great and Saladin, which were a poetical commonplace in the Middle Ages, there is no need to say anything here.[4]   I may, however,

---

[1] As a matter of fact Henry II. was not present in person during the siege, as the biographer erroneously states.

[2] Stimming, p. 79.

[3] *L'Histoire de Guillaume le Maréchal*, publiée par Paul Meyer (Paris, 1891). The Young King is described as " larges sor toz crestiens " (l. 3,645); at his death " En orfenté chaï largesce " (l. 6,876), and again :—

" Ou mest largesse ? dites mei.
Ou ? enz el cuer al gienble rei,
La mest ele tot son aage,
Mais el perdi son heritage
Quant il morut, ç' oï retraire,
E remest veve sanz doaire.
(ll. 5,067-72.)

[4] On Alexander the Great see Paul Meyer, *Alexandre le Grand dans la littérature française du moyen âge*, vol. ii. pp. 372-6; to the list of examples there given, which does not pretend to be exhaustive, may be added Rustebuef :

take this opportunity of pointing out that the charge of inconsistency, which is not infrequently brought against Dante with regard to his treatment of these two personages, whom, as well as Bertran de Born, he has consigned to his *Inferno*,[1] is a wholly gratuitous one. To praise a man for his munificence surely need not imply a condonation of his crimes or shortcomings, any more than a condemnation of his misdeeds necessarily forbids an appreciation or admiration of any noble qualities he may possess. Dante's treatment of historical and fictitious personages is full of these so-called inconsistencies, the fact being that he deals with them, not as individuals endowed with complex personalities, but simply as *types,* regarding them from this point of view or from that, according as it suits his purpose at the moment to dwell upon this or that distinguishing feature in their character or career.[2]

" L'en nos a parlé d'Alixandre, De sa largesce, de son senz " (*Complainte dou Conte de Poitiers*, ll. 80-81, ed. Kressner, p. 94) ; Rostaing Berenguier : " Alexandre retrays per ardimen, E per franc cor am liberalitat" (in P. Meyer, *Derniers troubadours de la Provence*, p. 87) ; Brunetto Latino : " Tutta la sembianza D' Alessandro tenete, Che per neente avete Terra, oro, e argento " (*Tesoretto*, ll. 28-31) ; and Boccaccio, who in the *Proemio* to his *Ameto*, speaks of " le inestimabili imprese di Serse, le ricchezze di Dario, le liberalità d' Alessandro, e di Cesare gli prosperi avvenimenti."

Instances of Saladin's generosity are given in the *Speculum Historiale* of Vincent of Beauvais (xxix. 43), in the *Cento Novelle Antiche* (Nov. xxv and Nov. cxiv, ed. Biagi) and in the *Decamerone* (i. 3 ; x. 9) ; and by Benvenuto da Imola in his comment on *Inf.* iv. 129 ; see also Gaston Paris, *La Légende de Saladin* (in *Journal des Savants*, 1893).

[1] Alexander, *Inf.* xii. 107 ; Saladin, *Inf.* iv. 129 ; Bertran de Born, *Inf.* xxviii. 134.

[2] The following may be taken as instances : Julius Caesar (contrast *Inf.* iv. 123 ; *Purg.* xxvi. 77 ; and *Par.* vi. 57) ; Cato (who was a suicide and opponent of Caesar, yet is placed as a guardian of the entrance to Purgatory, while Brutus writhes in the pit of Hell) ; Guido da Montefeltro (contrast *Inf.* xxvii. 29 ; and *Conv.* iv. 28, ll. 61-62) ; Priscian (who apparently owes his place in Hell simply to the fact that he was a typical example of a class that had opportunities for the crime in question—there is not a particle of evidence to support Dante's condemnation of him) ; and, again, Aeneas (who, as Dante must have known, was equally a traitor with Antenor, yet holds a place of honour throughout Dante's works, while Antenor gives his name to one of the divisions of the pit of Hell) ; Rhipeus (a pagan in Paradise) ; and so on.

As regards the remaining three persons, *viz.*, the King of Castile, the Marquis of Montferrat and the Count of Toulouse, no serious attempt, so far as I am aware, has hitherto been made to identify them.   The earlier editors of the *Convivio*, including Fraticelli, pass them over in silence.   Giuliani, relying upon his favourite method of "spiegare Dante con Dante," and remembering that a King of Spain is referred to in the *Divina Commedia* ("quel di Spagna," *Par.* xix. 125), jumps to the conclusion that the latter is identical with the King of Castile here mentioned, and decides off-hand that the individual in question is Alphonso X., El Sabio, King of Castile and Leon, 1252-1284. As far as the reference in the *Divina Commedia* is concerned, this identification is impossible, since in the passage in which it occurs the allusions are all to princes actually reigning at the date of the Vision, that is to say, in the year 1300.   The Spanish prince there referred to is Fernando IV., King of Castile and Leon, 1295-1312.   Again, a Marquis of Montferrat (*viz.*, William Longsword, Marquis of Montferrat and Canavese, 1254-1292) is mentioned in the *Divina Commedia* (*Purg.* vii. 134), consequently, argues Giuliani, he is the same as the Marquis referred to here.   As to the Count of Toulouse, he contents himself with observing "del conte di Tolosa non trovo cenno negli altri scritti del nostro Autore," as if he were thereby absolved from taking any further trouble in the matter.   Scartazzini, in his *Enciclopedia Dantesca*, ventures the opinion that the King of Castile mentioned in the *Convivio* is Alphonso X., but he does not attempt to identify him with "quel di Spagna" of *Par.* xix. 125.   He, however, like Giuliani, and equally without hesitation, in his *Enciclopedia*, as well as in his commentary on the *Divina Commedia* (in all three editions), identifies the Marquis of Montferrat referred to in the *Convivio* with the "Guglielmo Marchese" of *Purg.* vii. 134.   On the question as to the identity of the Count of Toulouse he has nothing to say beyond the brief entry in his *Enciclopedia*, "Conte Raimondo di Tolosa, nominato e lodato di liberalità".[1]

---

[1] Art. *Tolosa.*

So far, then, the Count of Toulouse remains an unknown quantity, while the consensus of opinion, such as it is, identifies the Marquis of Montferrat with William Longsword, and the King of Castile with Alphonso X. It may be observed that no arguments are adduced in support of these identifications, which are made on the ground merely, in the one case, that Dante happens to mention a Marquis of Montferrat elsewhere, in the other, that the best known of the possible Kings of Castile happens to be Alphonso X.—" dev' essere," confidently asserts Giuliani, " sembra doversi intendere," hazards the more cautious Scartazzini.

The clue to the rightful identification of these three personages is to be found, I have little doubt, in the epithet *buono* applied to each of them by Dante. "Chi non ha ancora nel cuore il buon re di Castella, o il buono marchese di Monferrato, o il buono conte di Tolosa?"

This is precisely the characteristic epithet, the stock epithet, by which the patrons of the troubadours are constantly distinguished in the old Provençal biographies, with which, as we have already stated, Dante (as well as certain of the old commentators) was undoubtedly acquainted. Now among these we find "lo bos reis Anfos de Castela,"[1] *i.e.*, Alphonso VIII., King of Castile, 1158-1214; "lo bos coms Raimons de Toloza,"[2] *i.e.*, Raymond V., Count of Toulouse, 1148-1194; and (though without the characteristic epithet) "lo marques Bonifacis de Monferrat,"[3] *i.e.*, Boniface II., Marquis of Montferrat, 1192-1207, and first Latin King of Salonica; all of whom were

---

[1] In life of Folquet of Marseilles, repeatedly (Mahn, pp. 29-30).

[2] In lives of Bernart of Ventadour (Mahn, pp. 1-2), Peire Rogier (p. 10), Peire Raimon (p. 12), Peire Vidal (p. 15) and Folquet of Marseilles (pp. 29-30).

[3] In lives of Raimbaut de Vacqueiras (p. 32), Gaucelm Faidit (pp. 37-8), and Aimeric de Pegulhan (p. 48). We find in the same way "lo bon rei Amfos d'Aragon" in lives of Peire Rogier (p. 10) and Hugh of Saint Circq (p. 47); "lo bon vescomte de Lemogas" in life of Bertran de Born (p. 21); "lo bon rey Richart" in life of Folquet of Marseilles (p. 30); "lo bon dalfin d'Alvernhe" in life of Hugh de Saint Circq (p. 47); and "lo bon rei Jacme d'Aragon" in life of Peire Cardinal (p. 49).

well known as munificent patrons and protectors of the troubadours.[1]

Among the *protégés* of Alphonso VIII. of Castile, whom Bertran de Born refers to[2] as "il valen rei de Castela n'Anfos," were Peire Rogier, Guiraut de Borneil, Folquet of Marseilles, and Aimeric de Pegulhan, three of whom are mentioned by Dante in the *De Vulgari Eloquentia* and elsewhere.[3]

The court of Raymond V. of Toulouse was frequented by Bernart of Ventadour, Peire Rogier, Peire Raimon, Peire Vidal, and Folquet of Marseilles. Raymond had political relations also with Bertran de Born, who frequently makes mention of him in his poems.

Boniface II. of Montferrat, who was one of the leaders in the fourth Crusade, and is described by Villehardouin (in whose *Conquête de Constantinople* he occupies a prominent position) as "un des meillors barons et des plus larges, et des meillors chevaliers qui fust el remanant dou monde,"[4] numbered among his *protégés* Peire Vidal, Raimbaut de Vacqueiras and Gaucelm Faidit. Boniface was second son of William III. (who accompanied the Emperor Conrad III. on the second Crusade in 1147), his elder brother being the famous Crusader Conrad, Marquis of Montferrat (1188-92), Prince of Tyre and King of Jerusalem, whom he succeeded in the marquisate.

I have little hesitation in identifying the King of Castile, the Marquis of Montferrat, and the Count of Toulouse, referred to by Dante in this passage of the *Convivio*, with these three well-known princes[5]; and I think there can be hardly a doubt that

---

[1] See the lists given by Paul Meyer in the article *Provençal Literature* in the ninth edition of the *Encyclopædia Britannica* (vol. xix. pp. 874-875).

[2] No. 26, ed. Stimming.

[3] Guiraut de Borneil, *Purg.* xxvi. 120; *V. E.* i. 9, l. 23; ii. 2, ll. 81, 88; 5, l. 25; 6, l. 54; Folquet of Marseilles, *Par.* ix. 94; *V. E.* ii. 6, l. 58; Aimeric de Pegulhan, *V. E.* ii. 6, l. 64.

[4] § 500, ed. N. de Wailly. I may also mention here *Le dit du marquis de Montferrat*, by Le Camus d'Arras, printed in Paul Meyer's *Recueil d'anciens textes*, p. 353.

[5] Since writing this I find that Sig. Scherillo in his valuable *Alcuni capitoli della Biografia di Dante* (Torino, 1896) suggests (p. 277) that the Marquis of

they owe their honourable position among Dante's examples of munificence to the fact that they figure prominently in the Provençal biographies of the troubadours as having made the noble exchange—"il bel cambio"—which he so highly commends, of empty riches against the hearts of men, that rare exchange whereby he who thinks to gain one man by his generosity gains not one, but thousands : " E quanto fa bel cambio chi di queste imperfettissime cose dà, per avere e per acquistare cose perfette, siccome li cuori de' valenti uomini !¹ Lo cambio ogni dì si può fare. Certo nuova mercatanzia è questa dell' altre, che credendo comperare un uomo per lo beneficio, mille e mille ne sono comperati" (*Conv.* iv. 11, ll. 115-123).² " Ab larguetat," sings Bertran de Born,

Ab larguetat
Conquier reis pretz el guazanha.³

Montferrat mentioned in the *Convivio* is the Boniface eulogised by Villehardouin. Sig. Scherillo makes no suggestion with regard to the other two princes. Miss Hillard in the notes to her English translation of the *Convivio* (unfortunately a very inadequate performance) follows Giuliani in his identification of the King of Castile and the Marquis of Montferrat. As regards the Count of Toulose, she suggests Raymond VI. (1194-1222) ; this, of course, may be the person intended, but the reference is much more likely to his father.

¹ *Cf.* Sordello, *Ensenhamen* :—

" Nulz om rics be rics non sera
Si de sa gen lo cor non a ".
(ll. 839-840.)

² *Cf.* Sordello, *Ensenhamen*, ll. 759 foll.

³ No. 7, ed. Stimming.

DANTE AND "SENECA MORALE"[1]

(*INFERNO*, IV. 141)

AMONG the great men of antiquity whom Dante places in his Limbo he includes Seneca the moralist, "Seneca Morale". The qualification *morale* here applied to Seneca must not be regarded as a mere *epitheton ornans*. The term was no doubt employed by Dante in order to distinguish the philosopher Seneca, not from Seneca the rhetorician, of whom probably Dante had never heard, but from the Seneca who wrote tragedies. The latter, it may be remembered, is mentioned by Dante in his letter to Can Grande, "ut patet per Senecam in suis tragoediis" (*Epist.* x. 10).

It was a common opinion in the Middle Ages, which was held even by such a comparatively enlightened scholar as Coluccio Salutati,[2] while even Petrarch[3] had his doubts, that Seneca the philosopher and Seneca the tragedian were two distinct persons. Vincent of Beauvais, for instance, who died probably within a year or two of Dante's birth, in his *Speculum Naturale* commonly quotes the author of the *Quaestiones Naturales* as "Seneca moralis,"[4] evidently by way of distinguishing him from "Seneca tragicus". Boccaccio, in his comment on this passage of the *Inferno*, expressly states that there were two Senecas, one the philosopher, the other the tragedian; and he makes out that the latter was called Marcus Annaeus Seneca, thus confusing Seneca the philosopher with his own father, though he supposes Marcus Annaeus to have lived later than Lucius Annaeus :—

---

[1] Reprinted, with additions, from the *Giornale Storico della Letteratura Italiana* (xxxv. 334-338).

[2] See below, pp. 152 ff.   [3] See Nolhac, *Pétrarque et l'humanisme*, p. 310.

[4] For instance, see Lib. iv. cap. 70 ; and Lib. vi. cap. 38.

È cognominato questo Seneca, morale a differenza d' altro Seneca, il quale della sua famiglia medesima fu, poco tempo appresso di lui, il quale, essendo il nome di questo morale, Lucio Anneo Seneca, fu chiamato Marco Anneo Seneca, e fu poeta tragédo ; perciocchè egli scrisse quelle tragedie le quali molti credono che Seneca morale scrivesse.[1]

Guiniforte delli Bargigi goes one step further and says boldly that Seneca the tragic writer was the son of the moralist.

Boccaccio was otherwise better informed about Seneca, for he had access to the *Annals* of Tacitus, whence his details of Seneca's life were taken. In this respect he had the advantage of his friend Petrarch, who curiously enough not only never quotes, but never even mentions the name of Tacitus, thus proving pretty conclusively that he had no acquaintance with him.[2]

Boccaccio insists once more on the distinction between Seneca the philosopher and Seneca the poet in a later passage of his *Comento*,[3] where he comments on *Inferno*, ix. 97. Here, in a discussion as to the three fates, he gives first the opinion of Seneca " in una epistola a Lucillo," and then that of " Seneca tragédo in quella tragedia la quale è intitolata Edipo ". This passage, it may be observed, like most of the mythological discussions in the *Comento*, is derived from an earlier work of Boccaccio, his *De Genealogia Deorum*,[4] the mediæval classical dictionary, in which also the distinction between " Seneca philosophus " and " Seneca poeta tragicus " is consistently preserved.

Benvenuto da Imola, like his " revered master " Boccaccio, also insists on the distinction between the two Senecas. In his *Comentum* he says :—

---

[1] Vol. i. pp. 396-397 (ed. Milanesi).

[2] See Nolhac, *Pétrarque et l'humanisme*, pp. 266-267.

[3] Vol. ii. pp. 177-178 (ed. Milanesi).

[4] " Clotho, Lachesis et Atropos filiae fuere Demogorgonis. . . . Seneca has in epistolis ad Lucilium fata vocat, dato Cleantis dictum dicens : ' Ducunt volentem fata, volentem trahunt '. Circa quod non solum eorum describit officium, eas scilicet sorores omnia ducere, sed etiam trahere, non aliter quam si de necessitate contingant omnia, quod longe apertius sentire videtur in tragoediis Seneca poeta tragicus et in ea potissime cui titulus est Oedipus, ubi dicit : ' Fatis agimur, credite fatis '." (Lib. i. cap. 5.)

Autor dicit signanter *Seneca morale*, ad differentiam Senecae poetae, qui scripsit tragedias. Seneca enim tragediarum autor, fuit alius de stirpe ejus, sicut potest probari ratione et autoritate. Ratione, quia Seneca in ea tragedia, quae intiulatur *Octavia*, predicit mortem Neronis, quod facere non potuit, nisi fuisset propheta. Autoritate, quia Sidonius in quodam libro suo metrico dicit expresse quod duo fuerunt Senecae, quorum alter morum censor, alter tragediarum autor.[1]

These arguments Benvenuto derived from a letter of his friend Coluccio Salutati,[2] which he borrowed for the purpose of utilising it in his commentary on the *Divina Commedia*. Coluccio's letter[3] has a special interest as showing that the question as to the identity or not of the two Senecas was one of the debated points among literary men of that day. Coluccio himself decides against the identity of the philosopher and the poet (who he thinks may have been the philosopher's brother, Lucius Annaeus Mela), and he expresses surprise that Petrarch[4] should have inclined to the opposite opinion :—

Eliconio viro Tancredo de Vergiolensibus judici gabellarum Pisarum civi-
tatis, fratri karissimo et optimo.

Frater karissime, saepenumero mecum reputans quod et tibimet memini me verbotenus communicasse, admiratus sum vulgarem illam opinionem Senecam ethicum, Neronis praeceptorem, collocutoremque Pauli, Tragoediarum auctorem fuisse ; nec temere assentiendum vulgo arbitror, apud quod didicit saepius fama mentiri. . . . Eapropter plus apud me valebit ratio quam vulgare proloquium.

Postquam enim Tragoediarum michi lepor innotuit, admodum stili dulcedine delectatus de sententiarum pondere praesumebam, et illum Annaeum Senecam illarum auctorem fuisse michimet facile persuadebam. Habet enim hoc proprium communis opinio, ut ea mentes hominum celeriter imbuantur, maxime si traxerit ex vetustate principium. In hoc tamen re veterum quidem videntur monimenta

----

[1] Vol. i. p. 179.

[2] See letter of Coluccio to Benvenuto, printed by F. Novati in the *Epistolario di Coluccio Salutati*, i. 167-172. In the course of this letter Coluccio says : " Deinde me tanti facis ut auctoritate mea utaris ad probandum verum Tragoe-diarum auctorem, et incultam illam epistolam meam, qua id declaro et affirmo, avidissime postulasti, quasi mea sint vel digna prudentum volitare per ora vel quae possint veteres errores excutere. Id tamen utcunque sit, tuae morigerabimus voluntati."

[3] To Tancredo Vergiolesi ; *Epistolario*, i. 150-155.

[4] Petrarch in his Epistle to Seneca assumes him at the outset to have been the author of the tragedies, but subsequently confesses to a doubt as to whether the contrary may not have been the case, " nisi illa forsitan opinio vera est quae tragaediarum non te illarum, sed tui nominis alterum vult auctorem." (See Nolhac, *op. cit.* pp. 310-311.)

deficere, quippe cum meminerim apud Quintilianum, ubi in libro *De Institutione Oratoria* facit Senecae mentionem, me legisse: "extant de illo poemata"; cum nulla carmina, praeter Tragoedias et ludum *De Morte Claudii*, quae illo ferantur, in meis manibus pervenisse certus sim. Adest et Boetius *De Scholastica Disciplina*,[1] qui eo loco, in quo poetarum libros commemorat, inquit: "Virgilii prolixitas, Statii urbanitas, Senecae tragoedia"; non enim recolo textum in forma; quibus testibus cum se fama tueatur, jam memini paene venit in dubium praefatum Senecam fuisse Tragoediarum auctorem; quod adeo inolevit, ut non solum ignari, sed etiam prudentes et harum rerum studiosissimi hoc tenaciter affirment; quod etiam in *Epistola ad Senecam* ille saeculi nostri decus, Franciscus Petrarca, sentire videtur, et, quod magis admiror, eundem Senecam auctorem tragoediae *Octaviae* profitetur. Ego vero, cum diu de caeteris dubitarim eo quod longe a stilo Senecae viderentur extraneae, *Octaviam* post ejus fata compositam certissime conjectabam. Quis enim, alicujus tragoediae auctor, quae aliorum gesta commemorat, in eadem loquentem magnifice se introducat? Revolve, precor, *Octaviam;* ubi tam moralia tamque audacia verba reperies, quam ea quae Senecam irato etiam principi fabula retulisse commemorat? Quid plura? Nonne Neronis exitus in *Octavia*, ubi Agrippina ab inferis accersitur, plane, prout accidit, recitatur? Quae praemoriens Seneca nec vidit nec, si humanam prudentiam contemplemur, potuit divinare. Legimus siquidem, teste Suetonio, propraetore Julio Vindice conspirante, a Nerone primum Gallias defecisse; deinde caeteros idem secutos exercitus; mox amicos omnes eundem reliquisse; post quae a Senatu hostis judicatus, ad mortem damnatus est, ut inserta furca cervici ad necem virgis caederetur utque aliqui volunt et demum de saxo palatii praecipitaretur; quae fere omnia in *Octavia* sunt descripta et tamen ea nemo negat post Senecae obitum accidisse. Quae ipsum tamen expresse praececinisse, saltem:—

"Verbera et turpem fugam,"

monstrum est et veri non simile, ut jam eum non moralem, non poetam, sed divinum prophetamque appellare possimus; caetera namque dimittamus, ubi inquit:—

"Desertus ac destructus et cunctis egens";

quae et eundem Neronem mathematicorum praedictionibus didicisse comperimus.

Denique mirum est, cum vero propius sit Senecam adhuc juvenem Tragoedias debuisse conscribere, in tot librorum suorum voluminibus, quos provectiori aetate composuit, ex hoc divino opere nullum usquam versiculum recitasse. Nec praetereundum censeo quod, cum Senecam ad eligendam mortem Nero compulerit, si inter libellos ejusdem *Octavia* fuisset reperta, metu Caesaris atque jubente Senatu prorsus fuisset deleta. Quae cum ita conveniant et idem *Octaviae* et ceterarum auctor esse putetur, michi facile persuasi illum Senecam Tragoedias non scripsisse.[2]

[1] This work, as Novati points out, is erroneously attributed to Boëtius. It was, as a matter of fact, written in the thirteenth century by Thomas of Cantimpré.

[2] The *Octavia* is not included by modern critics among the tragedies of Seneca, chiefly on the grounds mentioned by Coluccio.

Inveni siquidem in glosula, quam in Annaeo Floro perlegi, fuisse Lucium Annaeum Senecam et Lucium Annaeum Melam germanum suum ac Marcum Annaeum Lucanum poetam, dicti Melae filium; quibus forte propter senatorii candidatus honorem, quo Lucius Seneca suis proluxisse refertur, et Senecae fuit exhibitum cognomentum, aut ex Lucii Annaeique nominibus, quibus Seneca et Mela communiter notabantur, non duo, sed unus apud posteros reputati.

Quicquid fuerit, id enim michi certum non est, habeo testem assiduum atque opulentum, Sidonium scilicet, qui in versibus suis, in capitulo quod incipit :—

> " Dic, dic quod peto, Magne, dic amabo
> Felix nomine," etc. ;

manifeste testatur alium fuisse Tragoediarum scriptorem quam monitorem Neronis.   Dum enim quodam discursu poetico in libello suo multa legenda negaret, post plura sic inquit :—

> " Non quod Corduba praepotens alumnis
> Facundum ciet, hic putes legendum,
> Quorum unus colit hispidum Platona
> Incassumque suum monet Neronem ;
> Orchestram quatit alter Euripidis,
> Pictum faecibus Aeschylon secutus,
> Aut plaustris solitum sonare Thespin,
> Qui post pulpita trita sub cothurno
> Ducebant olidae marem capellae,
> Pugnam tertius ille gallicani
> Dixit Caesaris, ut socer generque
> Cognata impulerint in arma Romam," etc.,

quos versiculos, nuper a me lectos, apposui, quia communiter ille liber non habetur, et ut tute ipse consideres si negari potest illum de alio quam de monitore Neronis Seneca cogitasse.   Frangit me tamen multum Petrarcae nostri sententia.   Ea propter te rogatum velim quatenus, si quid habeas aliud quo certius auctor tanti operis designetur, tuo michi suavissimo stilo promas. . . .[1]

The verses of Sidonius Apollinaris to which Benvenuto refers are, as we have seen, quoted *in extenso* by Coluccio Salutati, who appears to have been the first to introduce Sidonius into the discussion—at any rate, the lines in question were evidently unknown to Petrarch and Boccaccio.

The statement of Sidonius—to which Coluccio attaches undue importance, for he admits that there is the weight of Quintilian's authority[2] on the other side—was probably, as Novati points out,[3] due to a misunderstanding of Martial's reference to the

---

[1] Dated from Lucca, 15th October, 1371.   [2] *Instit. Orat.* x. 1.
[3] *Epistolario di Coluccio Salutati*, i. 155, note 3.

"duos Senecas facundos,"[1] meaning the rhetorician and the philosopher.

In the list of Seneca's works which he gives in his *Comento*[2] Boccaccio introduces yet another element of confusion. For while he deprives Seneca of his tragedies, he on the other hand wrongly credits him with the *Declamationes* of his father, a mistake which he shared with Petrarch,[3] and which was at any rate as old as John of Salisbury.

Boccaccio, like Brunetto Latino, Dante, and other mediæval writers, includes the *De Remediis Fortuitorum* and the *De Quatuor Virtutibus Cardinalibus* among the genuine works of Seneca. It is one of Petrarch's claims to scholarship that he did not accept this attribution, at least in so far as the *De Quatuor Virtutibus* is concerned. In one of his *Epistolae Rerum Senilium* he writes :—

> Senecae libellus nolenti, non dubitem, datus est, cujus titulus est *De Quatuor Virtutibus*. Omne vulgus opusculum illud avidissime legit, ac Senecae libris interserit, inque eo quod Seneca nunquam vidit Senecam praedicant miranturque. Sunt qui inter ipsius Senecae libros omnes, hunc maxime diligant, quippe illorum maxime ingeniis conforme.[4]

He then goes on to point out that the real author of the work was one Martin of Dumio in Portugal, who was Archbishop of Braga in the sixth century.

In spite of Petrarch's protest, however, the treatise, which was otherwise known as *Formula Honestae Vitae*, continued to be ascribed to Seneca, even as late as the sixteenth century. It has recently been shown by Hauréau[5] that, as a matter of fact, Martin of Braga was not the actual author of the treatise. The archbishop, it appears, with what would be regarded nowadays as somewhat doubtful morality, simply stole it from an earlier apocryphal work of Seneca, entitled *De Copia Verborum*, and wrote a preface to it, on the strength of which he has been credited with the dubious distinction of being the author.

---

[1] *Epigram.* i. 61, 7.   [2] Vol. i. pp. 397-398 (ed. Milanesi).
[3] See Nolhac, *op. cit.* pp. 132, 282, 310, 319.   [4] Lib. II. Epist. iv.
[5] *Notices et Extraits des MSS.*, XXXIII. i. 208 ff.

From what has been said above it may be pretty certainly inferred that to Dante "Seneca morale" meant the author of the works commonly attributed to Lucius Annaeus Seneca, with the exception of the tragedies, and with the addition of the apocryphal *De Remediis Fortuitorum* and *De Quatuor Virtutibus*.

The best known of the genuine works in the Middle Ages and the most highly esteemed were undoubtedly the *Quaestiones Naturales*, the *De Beneficiis*, and above all the *Epistolae ad Lucilium*. From all three of these Dante quotes in the *Convivio*, the last two directly,[1] the *Quaestiones* at second hand from the *De Meteoris* of Albertus Magnus.[2]   He also quotes from both of the apocryphal works.[3]

[1] *Conv*. i. 8, ll. 121-123 ; iv. 12, ll. 82-83.
[2] *Conv*. ii. 14, ll. 174-176 (see above, p. 40).
[3] *Conv*. iii. 8, ll. 107-110 ; *Mon*. ii. 8, ll. 24-26 ; *Epist*. iv. 5.

PROFESSOR RAJNA'S CRITICAL TEXT OF THE *DE VULGARI ELOQUENTIA* [1]

THE history of this publication [2] is furnished by Professor Pio Rajna in his preface. Soon after the foundation of the Italian Dante Society in 1888, it was resolved that the resources of the society should be devoted in the first place to the preparation of critical editions of the several works of Dante. Professor Rajna undertook to be responsible for one of the works, and to him, at his own request, was assigned the *De Vulgari Eloquentia*, an edition of which he had projected on his own account some years before. The present volume, therefore, appears under the auspices of the Italian Dante Society, of which it is " la prima mancia".

It is a remarkable proof of the enduring interest in everything relating to Dante, that Professor Rajna should have been content to expend the labour of years, represented here by more than 400 closely printed pages, upon one of the least known, and the shortest (excepting always the dubious *Quaestio de Aqua et Terra*), of the great Florentine's writings.

Professor Rajna's book is divided into two parts : the first consists of an introduction, comprising the description of the MSS. and of the various printed editions, translations, etc., together with an essay on the orthography of the mediæval Latin of Dante's day ; the second part comprises the text, accompanied by an *apparatus criticus* and notes. The notes are purely

---

[1] Reprinted, with modifications, from *Romania*, xxvi. 116-126 ; and the *Sixteenth Annual Report of the Cambridge (U.S.A.) Dante Society* (1897).

[2] Il trattato *De Vulgari Eloquentia*, per cura di Pio Rajna. Firenze, Successori Le Monnier, 1896.

critical. In his preface Professor Rajna promises another volume, an *edizione illustrativa*, which is to supply explanatory notes and commentary, and a new Italian version, besides full indices. It is to be hoped that this supplementary volume will follow at no distant date, and that the project of including a translation will be carried out ; a faithful rendering of the treatise has long been needed, and the many changes introduced into the text by Professor Rajna, the majority of which, there is little doubt, will be accepted as final, render the necessity for a new one more imperative than ever.

Only three MSS. of the *De Vulgari Eloquentia* are known to be in existence ; there was at one time supposed to be a fourth in the Ashburnham collection, but this fiction was disposed of some years ago by Professor Paul Meyer, the error having arisen apparently through a confusion of this with another of Dante's Latin works, *viz.*, the *De Monarchia*. Of these three MSS., one (indicated by Professor Rajna as *G*) is in the town-library at Grenoble; the second (*T*) is at Milan in the library of the Marchese Trivulzio ; the third (*V*) is in the Vatican library at Rome. *V*, which was executed, probably at Rome, in the early years of the sixteenth century, for Cardinal Bembo, in whose handwriting are many of the marginal notes, is practically of no independent value, being, if not an actual copy of *T*, at any rate derived from it. Professor Rajna, therefore, while giving in an appendix a comparative table of the divergences of *V* from *T*, has made no special use of the former for the purposes of his text.[1]

G, which has been reproduced in phototype by MM. Maignien and Prompt, was executed probably in the north of Italy at the end of the fourteenth or beginning of the fifteenth century. This MS. formed the base of Corbinelli's edition of 1577, the *editio princeps* of the Latin text, and many of the illustrative and critical glosses on the margins of it are undoubtedly due to Corbinelli, as Professor Rajna has satisfactorily proved.

---

[1] The chief value of *V* consists in the fact that it occasionally gives the clue to the primitive reading of *T*, where this has been subsequently obscured or altered.

T appears to have been executed in Italy in the same district as *G* (the valley of the Po), and is a little earlier than it in date, belonging almost certainly to the latter half of the fourteenth century. A special interest attaches to this MS. also, for it was at one time in the possession of Giovan Giorgio Trissino, and was the original from which he made his Italian version of Dante's treatise, the form in which the latter was printed for the first time in 1529. A large number of the corrections in this MS., both on the margins and in the text itself, are in the handwriting of Trissino, who evidently studied it with the greatest care.

Upon his collations of these two MSS., *G* and *T*, Professor Rajna has based his text, availing himself at the same time of such assistance as was to be derived from Trissino's translation and from the various printed editions. Of the latter there have been about a dozen, the best known being those of Torri, Fraticelli, and Giuliani; the most recent is that included in the Oxford edition of the complete works of Dante, published some seven years ago, under the editorship of Dr. Moore. Of each of these editions Professor Rajna gives a more or less detailed account, and he has recorded in his notes the principal differences of reading which occur in them; so that now we are in possession of a fairly complete history of the text of the *De Vulgari Eloquentia* for the last 500 years, that is to say, from the end of the fourteenth century down to the present day.

In the course of his examination of Trissino's Italian version, Professor Rajna has brought to light a curious bibliographical fact in connection with the date of its publication. The book, which was printed at Vicenza, is dated, in the colophon, January, 1529 (" MDXXIX. *Del Mese di Genaro*"), and it is dedicated to the Cardinal Ippolito de' Medici. Now the elevation of Ippolito to the cardinalate, which was somewhat sudden, took place on the tenth of that same month of that same year. How then, if the date be correct, could the book, which was printed at a place several days' journey from Rome, contain a dedication to a cardinal, who had only been created such a short time before—the dedication being printed, not on a separate leaflet, which

might have been inserted at any time, but on the first leaf of
the first *quaderno*, thus forming an integral part of the book?
At first Professor Rajna thought the explanation might be that
the book was dated according to the Venetian style, which would
correspond to January, 1530.   But on a close inspection of the
book itself, he found, from certain differences of type and paper,
which were unmistakable in each of the copies he examined, that
the leaves at the beginning of the book, where the dedication
occurs, were printed later than the rest, the originals having
apparently been cancelled in order to admit of the substitution of
others containing the dedication to the cardinal in due form.[1]

As regards his constitution of the text, Professor Rajna has
had at his disposal no materials which were not equally at the
disposal of his predecessors, from Torri downwards, no fresh
MSS. having been brought to light since the publication of
Torri's edition in 1850, he having been the first to avail himself
of *V*.   But Professor Rajna has used these materials with far

---

[1] Through the kindness of Dr. Richard Garnett and Mr. A. W. Pollard of
the British Museum I am able to state that in each of the three copies of
Trissino's version in the Museum library a peculiarity exists similar to that
mentioned above.   Mr. Pollard says: " In all three copies the first and eighth
leaf of the first gathering are printed on different paper from the other six leaves.
The water-lines on ff. 1 and 8 run horizontally, those on ff. 2-7 perpendicularly,
and the difference of folding, in the case of an uncut copy, would very likely
produce a difference of size in the leaves.   All our copies are cut."   He adds :
" It is important to note that it is not ff. 1 and 8 which are exceptional, but
ff. 2-7.   The paper for the whole of the book, with the exception of ff. 2-7, is
folded as for quarto, with the water-lines horizontal."   His own opinion is that
ff. 2-7 were printed first on small folio paper, and f. 8 was set up, but left standing,
to be printed off with the title-page and dedication.   Then the rest of the book
was printed on quarto paper, and finished in January ; and naturally quarto
paper was used again when 1 and 8 came to be printed off after the rest of the
book, which may have been in February or March.

It may not be out of place here to draw attention to the fact that variations
in the direction of the water-lines, as well as inconsistencies in the use of *lj* for
gli, occur also in other works of Trissino (at any rate in the copies in the
Bodleian library at Oxford) printed by Tolomeo Janiculo about this time, *viz.*, in
the *Castellano* (assigned by Professor Rajna to 1528, but dated 1529 by Trissino's
biographer, Pier Filippo Castelli, who wrote in 1753), in the *Epistola* and *Dubii
Grammaticali* (both dated February, 1529), and in the *Poetica* (dated April,
1529).   In the *Grammatichetta* (which is later than the others, being dated June,
1529) the water-lines are all horizontal, and *lj* is consistently used throughout.

greater skill and critical ability than his predecessors, the result being a text which is an immense advance upon any of the previous ones, even the latest.

Before proceeding to an examination of the text, a few remarks may be made upon Professor Rajna's orthographical system. Professor Rajna's aim, he explains, was to reproduce as far as possible the orthography which Dante himself presumably made use of; and he has been at great pains to fulfil this aim of preserving the mediæval character of the text. Failing Dante's autograph (which in the case of the *De Vulgari Eloquentia*, as in that of all his other works, has totally disappeared, not a trace, so far as is known, of his handwriting having been preserved),[1] he had to fall back upon such contemporary Latin documents and grammatical treatises as were available, in order to establish what was the system of spelling in vogue during the period of Dante's lifetime. For this purpose he has chiefly made use of autograph documents of two Florentines of note with whom Dante had more or less intimate relations, *viz.*, Brunetto Latino, whose "cara e buona imagine paterna" he so affectionately recalls in the *Divina Commedia*,[2] and the notary-poet Lapo Gianni,[3] the familiar friend both of Dante and of Guido Cavalcanti. The grammatical works he has consulted are those of Papias, Uguccione (an authority who is quoted and largely utilised by Dante himself),[4] and Giovanni da Genova, the *Catholicon* of the last having especially been laid under contribution. By means of these Professor Rajna has produced a text of the *De Vulgari Eloquentia*, which is probably as near to what Dante might have written as it is possible to get.

Professor Rajna's chapter on the orthography of mediæval Latin, which embodies the results of his researches, is most

---

[1] Signor Salvadori, it is true, is of opinion that a number of the poems of Guido Cavalcanti in one of the Vatican MSS. are in Dante's handwriting—"la lettera magra, e lunga, e molto corretta," as Leonardo Aretino describes it. But this opinion is not generally accepted.

[2] *Inf.* xv. 83.

[3] The "Lapo" of *Sonetto*, xxxii. 1: "Guido, vorrei chu tu e Lapo ed io"; the "Lapus Florentinus" of *De Vulg. Eloq.* i. 13, ll. 36-37.

[4] See the article on *Dante's Latin Dictionary*, pp. 97 ff.

interesting and instructive, though perhaps not altogether in its right place in a work of this kind.

We may now turn our attention to the text itself. To discuss every one of the passages, which number some hundreds, in which Professor Rajna has introduced emendations, would be beyond the scope of the present article. We must content ourselves, therefore, with an examination of some of the most important. The rest will be found indicated in detail in the subjoined collation of Professor Rajna's text with that of the Oxford edition of the complete works of Dante,[1] edited by Dr. Moore, which represents the latest critical text previous to that of Professor Rajna.

To begin with the title of the work, Professor Rajna is undoubtedly right in deciding for *De Vulgari Eloquentia* against *De Vulgari Eloquio*, which was adopted by Fraticelli and others, and, though abandoned by Giuliani, has lately reappeared in the Oxford Dante. That the former was the original title is evident from what Dante himself says. Not only does he refer to the projected work in the *Convivio* (i. 5) as " un libro ch' io intendo di fare, Dio concedente, di *volgare eloquenza*," but in the work itself he twice (i. 1, § 1 ; i. 11, § 2)[2] uses the term *vulgaris eloquentia* in speaking of the subject of which he is treating. This evidence is corroborated by that of Villani and Boccaccio, both of whom (the former in a passage which is omitted from some MSS. of the *Cronica*) in their lists of Dante's works speak of his having written a treatise " de vulgari eloquentia ". The other form of the title appears to have been due to the MSS. heading of the first chapter of the work, which runs " Incipit liber de vulgari eloquio, sive idiomate, editus per Dantem," and was reproduced, with a slight modification, by Corbinelli ; he, however, adopted the correct form for the general

---

[1] *Tutte le Opere di Dante Alighieri, nuovamente rivedute nel testo dal* Dr. E. Moore. *Con Indice dei Nomi Propri e delle Cose Notabili, compilato da* Paget Toynbee, M.A., Oxford, 1894.

[2] The breaking up of the chapters into numbered paragraphs is an excellent innovation in this edition.

title of his edition.[1]   The title of Trissino's version, before it
had been "dalle lettere al nostro idioma strane purgato," was
"de la Vωlgare Elωquenzia".[2]

In one of the rubrics or headings to the various chapters
(which, as they stand in the MSS., were assuredly not written
by Dante, for in many cases they very inadequately, if not
wholly inaccurately, describe the contents of the chapters to
which they are affixed) we have an amusing instance of the
unscrupulousness with which copyists took liberties with their
text, when the sentiments of the original did not happen to be
altogether to their liking.   In chapter xiii. of Book I. Dante
indulges in some very plain speaking concerning the Tuscans,
and their infatuation for their own particular dialect, which he
rather savagely characterises as a degraded form of speech (" tur-
piloquium").   By way of taking down their pride (" depompare ")
he gives specimens of the several local varieties of their dialect,
and in conclusion scornfully dismisses it as altogether unworthy
of the title of *vulgare illustre*, which the Tuscans " in the frenzy
of their intoxication" claimed for it.   In the face of this invec-
tive on the part of Dante, against what after all was his own
mother-tongue, it is somewhat disconcerting to find this chapter
headed in the MSS. : "Quod in quolibet idiomate sunt aliqua
turpia, sed pre ceteris tuscum est *excelens* (!)".   The substitution
of this complimentary term for whatever opprobrious epithet

---

[1] The full title of this rare book, of which there is but one copy in the Bodleian library at Oxford, and of which the British Museum has only recently
acquired a copy, is as follows:—

Dantis Aligerii | Praecellentiss.   Poetae | De Vulgari Eloquentia | libri duo
| Nunc primum ad Vetusti et unici scripti | Codicis exemplar editi | Ex libris
Corbinelli | eiusdemque adnotationibus illustrati | Ad Henricum | Franciae
Poloniaeque | Regem Christianiss. | Parisiis | Apud Io. Corbon, via Carmeli-
tarum | ex adverso coll. Longobard. | 1577.   Cum privilegio.

[2] This fancy of Trissino's for printing certain of the vowels in Greek characters, which he had already indulged in several works before the publication of
his version of Dante's treatise, gave rise to a somewhat lively literary warfare,
in which Firenzuola among others took part, and in which Trissino finally was
worsted.   Some of his proposed orthographical reforms, however, met with
approval, among them the adoption of j and v to mark the consonantal, as distinguished from the vocalic, use of i and u.

was originally in its place was of course the doing of some officious Tuscan scribe, whose patriotic feelings were outraged by the abuse showered on his *parlar materno*. Modern editors, following Trissino, in order to avoid the contradiction involved in the MSS. rubric, substitute the simple heading: "De Idio-mate Tuscorum et Januensium". Professor Rajna gets over the difficulty by reading "turpissimum" instead of "excelens".

One of the most brilliant among the many happy emenda-tions introduced into the text by Professor Rajna occurs in the well-known passage in chapter x. of Book I., where Dante, for the purpose of grouping the various dialects, takes the Apennine range as the dividing line of Italy. According to the text hitherto accepted this passage runs as follows :—

> Dicimus ergo primo, Latium bipartitum esse in dextrum et sinistrum. Si quis autem quaerat de linea dividente, breviter respondemus esse jugum Apen-nini, quod, ceu fistulae culmen, hinc inde ad diversa stillicidia grundant et aquae ad alterna hinc inde litora per umbricia longa distillant (ll. 39-46).

The general sense of the passage is clear enough : the ridge of the Apennines forms the water-shed, from which the waters are discharged through the channels of the various rivers, on one side into the Mediterranean, on the other into the Adriatic. But the words "ceu fistulae culmen" present a difficulty, which is none the less a difficulty that it has not been recognised as such by any previous editor. What is the point of the com-parison between the ridge of the Apennines and "the top of a water-pipe"?[1] This very inappropriate illustration, especially in the mouth of Dante, whose wealth of similes is one of the most striking features of his writings, led Professor Rajna to suspect some corruption of the text. After he had puzzled in vain over the passage, the solution of the difficulty was supplied to him by Professor Vitelli, who suggested that the true reading was not *fistule culmen*, as the MSS. read, but *fictile culmen*, i.e., the ridge of a tiled roof. This happy conjecture at once supplies the very

---

[1] *Fistula* is used in this sense by Pliny, *Hist. Nat.* ii. 106; as well as by Cicero, *Pro Rabirio*, § 11 (where Ernesti reads *Sistula*). Uguccione says : "*Fistula* dicitur aqueductus et meatus aquarum, quia aquas fundat et emittat sicut fistula instrumentum voces".

image required for Dante's purpose. A more apt illustration could not be selected than the comparison of the mountain ridge, with the streams flowing down on either side, to the ridge of a roof, with the runnels of rain-water coursing down its slopes. The passage, as emended by Professor Rajna, now runs: "Respondemus esse jugum Apennini, quod, ceu fictile culmen hinc inde ad diversa stillicidia grundat, aquas ad alterna hinc inde litora per imbricia longa distillat ".[1]

One important correction suggested itself to Professor Rajna too late, as he explains in a prefatory note (p. cciii), to be inserted in his text. In this case the MSS. reading had been altogether abandoned by previous editors, as being unintelligible. At the end of chapter v. of Book II. Dante says (according to all the printed editions): " Demum, fustibus torquibusque paratis, promissum fascem, hoc est cantionem, quomodo ligare quis debeat instruemus". The word *ligare* in this passage is simply a gloss on the margin of *G* opposite what appears in the MSS. to be *inere* or *mere*. Professor Rajna's first conjecture was that this was an irregular contraction of *innectere*, which accordingly he prints in his text. The right solution, however, was suggested to him later on by a passage in Uguccione (quoted on p. clxxv), in which the derivation of *auctor*, *autor* is discussed—the same passage of which Dante makes use in the *Convivio* (iv. 6).[2] Uguccione says: " Invenitur quoddam verbum defectivum, scilicet *avieo, -es*, id est *ligo, -as* ". The simple verb *viere* (in MSS. *uiere*) at once occurred to Professor Rajna as being, without doubt, what Dante originally wrote in the passage in question, the distorted form in which it appears in the MSS. being due to the fact that the word, being somewhat un-

---

[1] It will be seen that the substitution of *fictile* for *fistule* involves the further slight alteration of the MSS. *grundant, distillant*, into *grundat, distillat*. As to *grundare* Uguccione says: " *Grunda, -e*, inferior pars tecti (vel. capane), a qua distillat aqua, unde *hec grundula, -e*, et *grundo, -das*, facere grundam vel a grunda guttas aque fundere . . . et inde *hoc grundatorium*, idem quod grunda ". *Imbricia* for the MSS. *umbriria*, edd. *umbricia*, is an obvious correction; neither *umbricium* nor *umbrex* is recognised by Du Cange. Uguccione gives " *hoc ymbricium* per quod aqua elicitur, seu guttarium vel lavarium canale, quod aliter dicitur *hic* et *hec imbrex, -icis* ".

[2] See above, p. 101.

common, was unfamiliar to the copyists. *Viere* occurs, as Professor Rajna points out, in the *Etymologiae* of Isidore of Seville, who gives it as the equivalent of *vincire* in his discussion of the derivation of *vates*.[1] It is also given, we may add, in the *Liber Derivationum* of Uguccione, who says, " *Vieo, -es, vievi, vietum,* idest vincire, ligare ".

It appears that the supposed inclusion of Cicero in Dante's list of those "qui usi sunt altissimas prosas " (II. vi. § 6) is simply due to a piece of officiousness on the part of Trissino, who for *Titum Livium* arbitrarily substituted *Tullium, Livium*.

It is satisfactory at last to get in a correct form Dante's graphic description (I. vii. § 6) of the scene of the builders of the Tower of Babel, " l' opra inconsumabile," suddenly interrupted in their work by the confusion of tongues.[2]

The passage, being full of technical and unfamiliar terms, naturally suffered severely at the hands of the copyists. Several important conjectural emendations of Witte's are confirmed by Professor Rajna, who now completes the restoration of the passage by substituting *regulabant* (after *T*) for the *tegulabant* of the previous editions.

Professor Rajna draws attention to several unwarrantable alterations of proper names in the printed text. Thus for *Pergameos* (I. xi. § 4) Fraticella reads *Bergomates*, presumably as being nearer to the Italian *Bergamo*; yet, as Fraticelli ought to have remembered, Dante uses *Pergamum* as the Latin form of *Bergamo* in his letter to the Emperor Henry VII. (*Epist.* vii. 6). Again, the name of the Bolognese poet *Fabruzzo* (a diminutive of *Fabbro*), in Latin *Fabrutius*, has been systematically altered into *Fabritius* (I. xv. § 5; II. xii. § 5), representing the more familiar *Fabrizio*, and this error has been perpetuated by more than one writer on Italian literary history.[3]

---

[1] *Vates* a vi mentis appellatos, Varro auctor est ; vel a viendis carminibus, id est flectendis, hoc est modulandis. (VIII. vii. 3.)

[2] With Dante's account it is interesting to compare the scene as given in the *Mystère du Viel Testament* (vol. i. ll. 6,584 ff., in the edition published by the Société des anciens textes français).

[3] See, for instance, Bartoli, *Storia della Lett. Ital.* ii. p. 289.

Similarly, the *Namericus* of the MSS. (representing the Provençal *Naimerics*) wherever it occurs has been perversely changed by the editors into *Hamericus* (II. vi. § 5; xii. § 3); and this unauthorised initial *H* has even infected other names, Fraticelli (followed by Giuliani and the Oxford text) prefixing it to *Arnaldus* (II. vi. § 5).

In the course of Professor Rajna's remarks upon the labours of his predecessors in the same field, we get some striking instances of the extraordinary carelessness and want of critical judgment which Giuliani displayed in his capacity as editor of the *De Vulgari Eloquentia*. His lapses are such, indeed, as to make it necessary to use his edition with extreme caution. Few, save those who have made systematic use of Giuliani's editions of Dante's works, have any idea of the license he allowed himself in dealing with his texts, or of his total inability to realise his responsibilities as editor. Professor Rajna's own estimate of Giuliani's qualifications for his task, as regards this particular treatise, may be quoted here as a warning to those who may be disposed to accept the authority of the latter without question :—

Dire che col lavoro suo proprio il Giuliani facesse progredire notevolmente la critica del testo, potrebb' essere pietà verso un uomo quanto mai rispettabile, ma sarebbe in pari tempo cecità, o menzogna. Metodo, all' infuori del principio, non sempre opportuno, dello spiegar Dante con Dante, il Giuliani non ne aveva; acume, non molto ; cognizione di latinità medievale, nessuna.

Perhaps the most flagrant example of his irresponsibility is furnished by his note on a passage in chap. iv. (§ 4) of Book II., in which he justifies his emendation *intelligimus*, for the *induimus* of preceding editors, on the ground that that is the reading both of *V* and of Trissino in his version : " Il Cod. Vaticano ha per l' appunto *intelligimus*, siccome nel Volgarizzamento v' è *intendemo*". Yet, in spite of these explicit statements, it is certain that Giuliani found neither *intelligimus* in *V*, nor *intendemo* in Trissino, and this for the best of all possible reasons, *viz.*, that the passage in question happens to be *omitted* both in *V* and by Trissino (as well as in *T*)!

An example of Giuliani's ineptitude is to be found in his proposed reconstruction of the disputed passage in chapter xvi.

(§ 4) of Book I., *viz.*, "in coelo, quam in elementis, *in igne*, *quam in terra, in hac, quam in igne;*" and of his carelessness, in the omission of a whole sentence from the text in chapter xix. (§ 1) of the same Book.

What adds to the seriousness of Giuliani's tampering with the text, repeated instances of which are noted by Professor Rajna, is the fact that in nine cases out of ten he makes his so-called "emendations" quite arbitrarily, and without a word of warning to put the reader on his guard. To "emend" a text according to fancy, without regard to the MSS., is bad enough, but to do so tacitly, without drawing attention to the fact, is little short of falsification.

Enough has been said to show that Professor Rajna's text of the *De Vulgari Eloquentia* is a very great improvement upon that of any of his predecessors; and every serious student of Dante will be grateful to him for the valuable result of his prolonged labours.

In the subjoined collation [1] mere variations of spelling have been for the most part disregarded, as have differences of punctuation, except where these happen to be of real importance. The passages given in the left-hand column are from the Oxford text (O), references being to book, chapter and line (*e.g.*, I. ii. 3); those in the right-hand column are from Professor Rajna's text (R), references in this case being to book, chapter and paragraph (*e.g.*, II. iii. § 4):—

O.	R.
General title. De Vulgari Eloquio.	Incipit liber de Vulgari Eloquio, sive idiomate, editus per Dantem.
I. i. *title.* Quid sit vulgaris locutio, et quo differat a grammatica.	Omitted.
I. i. 14. Sed accipiendo vel compilando ab aliis, potiora miscentes,	I. i. § 1. sed, accipiendo vel compilando ab aliis, potiora miscentes,
22. eam qua infantes	§ 2. eam quam infantes
34. Harum quoque duarum	§ 4. Harum duarum
I. ii. 7. necessarium fuit :	I. ii. § 1. necessarium fuit loqui :
22. si obiciatur de iis qui corruere	§ 3. si obiciatur de hiis qui corruerunt

[1] I am indebted to Dr. Moore for one or two passages which had escaped me.

O.	**R.**
I. ii. 24. cum de his	I. ii. § 3. cum de hiis
27. Secundo et melius,	Vel secundo et melius,
48. moverent organa sua, sic et vox	§ 5. moverunt organa sua, sic ut vox
62. si expresse dicenti resonaret etiam pica,	§ 6. si expresse dicenti " Pica " resonaret etiam " Pica," [1]
I. iii. 16. quia cum aliquid a ratione accipere	I. iii. § 2. quia, cum de ratione accipere
21. quia si tantum	quare, si tantum
26. natura *sensuale* quidem, in quantum sonus est ;	§ 3. nam sensuale quid est, in quantum sonus est ; [2]
I. iv. 21. nec inconvenienter	I. iv. § 3. et inconvenienter
23. prius a viro quam a foemina profluisse. Rationabiliter	vel prius quam a viro, a femina profluisse. Rationabiliter [3]
26. Quod autem	§ 4. Quid autem
34. per ipsum factus	in ipsum factus
45. si responsio fuit, fuit ad Deum ; et si ad Deum fuit,	§ 5. si responsio fuit ad Deum : nam, si ad Deum fuit,
55. quo etiam gubernata sunt omnia.	quo etiam gubernata sunt omnia ?
59. ut tonitrua personeat, ignem fulgoreat,	ut tonitrua personet, ignem fulgoret, [4]
I. v. 3. ad ipsum Deum	I. v. § 1. ad ipsum Dominum
12. primum hominem	§ 1. primum nostrum
29. nostrorum effectuum	§ 2. nostrorum affectuum
I. vi. 3. non aliter intelliguntur	I. vi. § 1. non aliter intelligantur
13. huic etiam prae cunctis proprium vulgare licebit, idest maternam locutionem, praeponere : et per consequens	§ 2. hic etiam pre cunctis proprium vulgare licetur, idest maternam locutionem, et per consequens [5]

[1] The omission of the first *pica* here in the modern editions is due apparently to its omission by Trissino in his version.

[2] *Natura* is a substitution of Corbinelli for *nam*. It seems better by a slight modification of the MS. reading, *viz.*, *quidē* (= *quidem* for *quid ē*) (= *quid est*), to read " nam sensuale quidem " instead of " nam sensuale quid est " with R.

[3] As R. remarks, *profluisse* is curious. For *rationabiliter* the MSS. read *rationaliter*.

[4] The MSS. read *personeat, fulgoreat ;* the correction adopted by R. is due to Giuliani.

[5] The reading *licebit . . . praeponere* instead of *licetur* (which he did not understand) was introduced into the text by Corbinelli, the origin of it being Trissino's rendering *sarà licito preporre*.

	O.		R.

O.

I. vi. 21. ratione magis quam sensu scapulas
36. unde sum oriundus
47. nisi culpa
50. hac forma locuti sunt

60. id quod primi loquentis labia fabricaverunt

I. vii. 6. Oh semper nostra natura
10. per primam . . . eliminata

15. et poenas malorum quae commiseras
18. Non ante tertiam
23. per superbiam suam et stultitiam
27. sed et ipsum
29. Sennaar,
34. quis pater tot sustineret
39. Si quidem
42. pars amussibus tegulabant, pars trullis linebant, pars scindere rupes, pars mari, pars terrae intendebant vehere,
60. nunc et barbarius
62. sanctum idioma

I. viii. 1. Ex praecedenti memorata
4. tunc homines primum
6. humanae propaginis principaliter

R.

I. vi. § 3. rationi magis quam sensui spatulas
unde sumus oriundus
§ 4. in culpa
§ 5. hac forma locutionis locuti sunt[1]
illud quod . . . fabricarunt.

I. vii. § 1. O semper natura nostra
§ 2. per primam . . . eluminata[2]
et que commiseras[3]

§ 3. Non ante tertium
per superbam stultitiam[4]

§ 4. sed etiam ipsum
Sennear,
§ 5. quis patrum tot sustineret
§ 6. Siquidem
pars amysibus regulabant, pars trullis linebant, pars scindere rupes, pars mari, pars terra vehere intendebant,[5]
nunc barbariusque
§ 7. sacratum ydioma

I. viii. § 1. Ex precedenter memorata
tunc primum homines
humane propaginis principalis[6]

[1] Fraticelli and subsequent editors omit *locutionis* for no good reason.

[2] The MS. reading *eluminata* (*i.e.*, " deprived of light ") is rightly retained by R. Torri, followed by Fraticelli in his later editions, substituted *eliminata*, which was rejected at first by Giuliani in favour of *elimitata*, but restored in his final corrections.

[3] The MSS. read *et commiseras*. Corbinelli inserted *poenas malorum quae*. The *que* (= *quae*) supplied by R. meets the difficulty, while its omission in MSS. is easily accounted for, as he points out.

[4] MSS. *per superbiam stultitiam*.

[5] The reading *tegulabant* for *regulabant* is due to Torri, who misread the MSS. *Trullis* for the MS. *tuillis* is a correction of Witte's.

[6] R. reads *principalis* in obedience to the MSS.; otherwise he would have accepted *principaliter*, the reading of Corbinelli, as more suited to the context.

O.

I. viii. 10. demum ad fines occidentales protracta est, unde
primitus
14. advenae
15. repedassent,
20. partem Europae, partem
Asiae
21. Ab uno postea eodemque
idiomate, immunda con-
fusione recepto,
25. totum quod ab ostiis est
Danubii sive Meotidis
paludibus usque ad fines
occidentales (qui Angliae,
Italorum, Francorumque
finibus, et Oceano limi-
tantur) solum unum ob-
tinuit idioma;
49. *mare, terram,* et *vivit,*
moritur, amat, et alia

I. ix. 6. Et quia . . . salubrius bre-
viusque

R.

I. viii. demumque ad fines occidentales protracta, forte
primitus[1]
§ 2. avene[2]
repedissent,[3]
partim Europe, partim
Asie[4]
§ 3. Ab uno postea eodemque
ydiomate in vindice con-
fusione recepto,[5]
totum quod ab hostiis
Danubii sive meotidis
paludibus usque ad fines
occidentales Anglie, Yta-
lorum Francorumque fini-
bus et Occeano limitatur,
solum unum optinuit ydi-
oma,[6]
§ 5. *mare, terram, est, vivit,*
moritur, amat, alia

I. ix. § 1. Quia . . . salubrius brevi-
usque[7]

[1] *Est* was supplied by Fraticelli, who followed Torri in omitting *que*. *Forte*
is a correction of R.'s for the MS. *fore,* for which Corbinelli substituted *unde,*
after Trissino's *la onde.*

[2] R. thinks *avene* not a mere error for *advenae,* but regards it as a derivative
of *a* + *venire,* in the sense of *che viene da,* or *di fuori,* used purposely by way of
antithesis to *advenissent* in the same line. (See below, *Appendix,* p. 190, note 1.)

[3] In his text R. reads *repedassent,* because of *repedare* (I. xii. § 5), but in a
supplementary note (p. ccii) he reverts to the MS. reading *repedissent,* inasmuch
as both *repedere* and *repedare* are found. (See below, *Appendix,* p. 190, note 1.)

[4] The restoration of *partim . . . partim,* which had been altered into *partem
. . . partem* in *G,* whence it was adopted by Corbinelli and his successors, is
almost certainly right, it being the *difficilior lectio,* which can hardly have been
substituted for an earlier *partem . . . partem;* but the construction is a difficult
one.

[5] R.'s correction *in vindice* for *immunda* of the printed editions is happy, the
MS. readings being *imundice* (*T*), *inundice* (*G*), which are evident corruptions of
a primitive *inuindice.*

[6] The departure from the MS. reading, now rightly restored by R., was due
to Fraticelli.

[7] For *salubrius* here Giuliani arbitrarily substitutes *securius.*

O.

I. ix. 9. alia deserentes. Nam quod
in uno est rationale, videtur
in aliis esse causa.

16. quod convenimus

23. Gerardus de Borneil:

24. "Si m sentis fizels amics
Per ver encusar Amor."

26. Rex Navarriae:

28. Dom. Guido

29. "Nè fe amor"

30. "Nè cor gentil, prima
ch' amor"

41. Caietani,

43. Burgi S. Felicis

45. sermonum varietates quae
accidunt, una eademque
ratione patebunt.

61. in eo quod diximus temporum distantia locutionem
variari, sed potius

71. prospicere

75. quanto longiora

77. admiramur, si extimationes

80. sub invariabili . . . sermone,

94. nil aliud

I. x. 1. Trifario nunc exeunte

27. quod qui dulcius

29. et domestici

31. quia magis videntur

35. iudicium reliquentes

43. quod, ceu fistulae culmen,
hinc inde ad diversa stillicidia grundat, et aquae ad
alterna hinc inde litora per
umbricia longa distillant,

R.

I. ix. § 1. alia desinentes; nam, quod
in uno est, rationali videtur
in aliis esse causa.[1]

§ 2. quia convenimus

§ 3. Gerardus de Brunel:
Sim sentis fezelz amics,
Per ver encusera Amor.
Rex Navarre:
Dominus Guido
Nè fa amor
Nè gentil cor prima che
amor

§ 4. Caetani,
Burgi Sancti Felicis
sermonum varietates, quid
accidunt, una eademque
ratione patebit.

§ 6. in eo quod diximus "temporum," sed potius[2]

percipere
quam longiora
admiremur si extimationes[3]
sub immutabili . . . ser-
mone,

§ 7. nichil aliud

I. x. § 1. Triphario nunc existente

§ 4. quod dulcius qui
ac domestici
quia magis videtur

§ 5. iudicium relinquentes

§ 6. quod, ceu fictile culmen
hinc inde ad diversa stillicidia grundat, aquas ad
alterna hinc inde litora per
imbricia longa distillat,[4]

[1] Various emendations of this passage have been proposed. R.'s rationali
for the MS. rationale involves the smallest amount of change.

[2] The interpolation of distantia locutionem variari is due to Torri, who did
not recognise that the word "temporum" was a quotation from what D. had
just been saying.

[3] For extimationes Giuliani unnecessarily substitutes aestimationes.

[4] For fistule culmen, the reading of the MSS., which does not give a satisfactory sense, R. substitutes fictile culmen (i.e., the ridge of a tiled roof), a very
happy conjecture of Professor Vitelli; this necessitates the further slight alteration of the MS. grundant, distillant, into grundat, distillat.

O.	R.
I. x. 47. Dextrum quoque	Dextrum quidem
52. Marca Anconitana	I. x. § 6. Marchia Anconitana [1]
66. cum Anconitaneis	§ 7. cum Anconitanis
69. cum Aquileiensibus	cum Aquilegiensibus
72. Quare non a minus quatuordecim	§ 8. Quare ad minus. xiiij. [2]
I. xi. *title*. Ostenditur Italiae aliquos	*Ostenditur in Italia aliquos*
I. xi. 1. Tam . . . latino	I. xi. § 1. Quam . . . latio
8. existimant	§ 2. extimant
12. Dicimus ergo	Dicimus igitur
17. *Me sure, quinte dici*	*Mezzure, quinto dici ?* [3]
19. *sciate siate*	§ 3. *scate sciate ?*
28. " Una ferina va scopai da Cascoli çita çita sen gì a grande aina."	*Una fermana scopai da Cascìòli, Cita cita sen gia'n grande aina.*
30. Bergomates	§ 4. Pergameos [4]
34. " In te l' ora "	*Enti l' ora*
35. " Ziò fu "	*ciò fu*
36. Aquileienses	§ 5. Aquilegienses
37. *Çes fastù*	*Ces fastu ?*
38. eructant.	eructuant.
39. eiciamus,	eicimus,
42. Pratenses	§ 5. Fratenses [5]
42-3. Latini . . . Latinis	§ 6. Latii . . . Latiis
46. *Domus nova, et Dominus meus*	*domus nova et dominus meus* [6]

[1] R. substitutes *Marchia* for the MS. *Marca* in order to be in agreement with the *Ianuensis Marchia* and *Marchia Trivisiana* of the context ; but he elsewhere tolerates other inconsistencies, such as *locuntur* and *loquuntur*, *Ystrianos* and *Istria*, and the like.

[2] Modern editors, from Fraticelli downwards, interpolate *non*, and either omit *ad* or substitute *a*—an uncalled for interference with the text.

[3] Fraticelli, on the strength of a note of Corbinelli's, explains his reading of this phrase in the Roman dialect as " Sorella mia, che cosa dici ? " R.'s reading (that of the MSS.) *Mezzure* represents " Messere ".

[4] The *Bergomates* of modern editions is due to Fraticelli. *Pergamum*, as the Latin form of Bergamo, occurs *Epist.* vii. 6.

[5] While admitting *Fratenses* into his text R. is inclined to think he has been somewhat hasty in accepting it against the traditional *Pratenses* (see p. ccii). Assuming the former to be correct, R. would refer it to Fratta di Valle Tiberina, now Umbertide, which was well known on account of the neighbouring Camaldolese monastery of Monte Corona, of which St. Peter Damian was at one time abbot. (See below, *Appendix*, p. 190, note 3.)

[6] For *domus nova* Giuliani reads *domus mea*, without good reason.

.O.

R.

I. xii. *title*. De idiomate Siculo et
  Apulo.

*Quod in eodem loco diversi-
ficatur idioma secundum
quod variatur tempus.*

I. xii. 12. "per lo foco"
  14. "longamente m' hai"
  29. enitebantur,
  31. Sicilia, factum est ut quic-
      quid . . . Sicilianum voce-
      tur:
  44. accipere volumus, scilicet
      quod proditur a terrigenis
      . . . elicendum videtur,·

  50. "Traggemi . . . bolontate."
  51. accipere nolumus, sed quod

  55. sicut . . . ostendemus.
  65. prospicientibus
  67. "dir vi voglio"
  69. "vo' sì lietamente."
  71. neque Apulum

I. xii. § 2. *per lo focho*
      lungiamente m' ai
  § 3. nitebantur,
      Sicilia, factum est, quic-
      quid . . . sicilianum   vo-
      caretur: [1]
  § 5. accipere volumus secun-
      dum quod prodit a terri-
      genis . . . eliciendum vi-
      detur,[2]
      Tragemi . . . boluntate.
      accipere volumus secun-
      dum quod[3]
      sicut . . . ostendimus.
  § 7. perspicientibus
      dirẹ vi voglio[4]
      vo sì letamente
  § 8. nec apulum

I. xiii. *title*. De idiomate Tuscorum
  et Ianuensium.

*Quod in quolibet idiomate
sunt aliqua turpia, sed pre
ceteris tuscum est turpissimum.*[5]

I. xiii. 1. Post hos
  2. infruniti,

I. xiii. § 1. Post hoc
      infronıti,

---

[1] The interpolation of *ut* before *quicquid* is due to a suggestion of Witte.
The MSS. read *vocetur*, for which R. substitutes *vocaretur*, as being required by
the sense of the passage.

[2] It appears that *scilicet* for *secundum* is due to a misreading of the MSS.;
proditur a terrigenis, Fraticelli's reading, is based apparently on a misprint in
Torri, *viz.*, *proditur terrigenis;* Giuliani reads *proditur e terrigenis* without
remark, but *e* is perhaps a misprint (see his note).

[3] The old reading is due to Trissino, whose rendering was based apparently
on a misreading of the MSS., *viz.*, *sed* for *secundum*.

[4] R. places a dot under the *e* of *dire* to indicate that it is not sounded; he
uses this same symbol (which is not very appropriate in an edition like the
present) on several other occasions, *e.g.*, *lọ* (I. xv. § 5): *gentilẹ* (II. v. § 4); *corẹ*
(II. vi. § 5).

[5] The MSS. read *est excelens*, which is in contradiction with the contents of
the chapter. R. reads *est turpissimum*, some such expression being wanted.
The alteration was doubtless due to the outraged patriotism of a Tuscan scribe.

O.	R.
I. xiii. 4. plebeorum . . . intentio,	I. xiii. § 1. plebea . . . intentio,
10. Brunetum	Brunettum
19. "Manuchiamo introcque:	§ 2. *Manichiamo introque.—Noi*
Non facciamo altro"	*non facciano atro.*
22. "di Fioransa"	*De Fiorensa*
24. "in gassara . . . Luca."	*in gassarra . . . Lucca.*
26. "rinegeata . . . Siena."	*renegata . . . Siena!*
	Ch'ee chesto? [1]
35. sensimus,	§ 3. sentimus,
48. ammitterent [2]	§ 4. amitterent
49. reperire [3]	reparare
I. xiv. *title*. . . . Transpadanis . . .	. . . *transpadinis*. . . .
I. xiv. 2. laevam Italiam cunctam	I. xiv. § 1. levam Ytaliam contanter
venemur,	venemur, [4]
6. convenientiis	§ 2. convenientibus
9. mollitiem	mollitudinem
12. Hoc Romandioli omnes	Hoc Romandiolos omnes
habent,	habet,
25. Hoc . . . Vicentini habent,	§ 3. Hoc . . . Vigentinos ha-
nec non Paduani	bet, nec non Paduanos,
32. *v* consonantem	*u* consonantem [5]
34. *nove*,	*novem*,
37. errore compulsus	§ 4. errore confisus [6]
41. Inter quos unum	Inter quos omnes unum
I. xv. *title*. . . . Bononiensi.	*Bononiensium.*
I. xv. 1. de Italica silva . . . per-	I. xv. § 1. de ytala silva . . . per-
cunctari	contari
9. convicimus,	§ 2. conicimus,
13. quomodolibet	quomodocunque
14. Accipiunt etiam . . . mol-	§ 3. Accipiunt etenim [7] . . .
litiem,	mollitudinem,

[1] *Ch'ee chesto?* was omitted by Trissino, and hence by Fraticelli and succeeding editors.

[2] This, the reading of Fraticelli and Giuliani, is obviously wrong, though it
occurs in one MS.

[3] So Fraticelli and Giuliani, misled by Trissino's *trovare*.

[4] The MSS. read *contanti*; R.'s conjecture *contanter* (or, as an alternative,
contantes) is manifestly preferable to *cunctam*, which is due to Corbinelli.

[5] R. is certainly right in printing *u* here, as against the *v* of previous editions.

[6] MSS. *confessus*; R.'s emendation (he gives *confusus* as an alternative) is
preferable to Trissino's *compulsus*, which was accepted by Torri and succeeding
editors.

[7] This is a conjecture of Giuliani for the MS. *etiam*, which, however, he
retained in his text.

O.

I. xv. 17. quae propria
30. oppositorum, ut dictum est, ad laudabilem
33. Ita si
42. Guinicelli . . . Ghiselerius . . . Fabricius
44. nunquam a primo [2]
48. "il fermo core"
49. Fabritius
50. "Lo mio"
52. "soccorso,"
54. residibus
68. Latinum illustre

R.

I. xv. § 3. que proprie
§ 4. oppositorum ad laudabilem
§ 5. Itaque, si Guinizelli . . . Ghisilerius Fabrutius [1]
nunquam a proprio
lo [3] fermo core
Fabrutius [1]
Lo meo
secorso,
§ 6. residuis Latium illustre

I. xvi. *title.* De excellentia vulgaris eloquentiae, et quod communis est omnibus Italicis.
I. xvi. 5. redolentem ubique et ubique apparentem
7. tendiculis
8. in omni genere rerum
11. et illinc . . . accipiamus.
21. et de
22. scilicet quod unumquodque mensurabile sit in genere illo secundum id quod simplicissimum est in ipso genere.
30. illas intelligamus ;
37. idest morum et

I. xvi. *title.* Quod in quolibet ydiomate est aliquid pulcrum, et in nullo omnia pulcra.
I. xvi. § 1. redolentem ubique et necubi [4] apparentem tenticulis
§ 2. in omni rerum genere et illud . . . accipimus : [5] et etiam de scilicet, unumquodque mensurabile fit, secundum quod in genere est, illo quod simplicissimum est in ipso genere. [6]
§ 3. illam intelligamus ; et morum et

---

[1] The name of this Bolognese poet was not Fabrizio, but Fabruzzo, as R. points out.

[2] This is the MS. reading. R.'s conjecture has much in its favour. Giuliani's *ab ipso* is satisfactory as far as sense goes; but it is a mere arbitrary substitution, without any regard for palaeographical possibilities.

[3] *i.e.*, *'l;* see above, p. 174, note 4.

[4] An excellent emendation. Giuliani reads *nec usquam* after Witte, and quite unjustifiably substitutes *residentem* (in text) or *manentem* (in notes) for *apparentem.*

[5] MSS. *et illico . . . accipiamus;* Giuliani, after Boehmer, *ut illinc . . . accipiamus.* (See below, *Appendix*, p. 191, note 3.)

[6] This most acceptable restoration of the text is arrived at by the simple expedient of substituting *fit* for *sit*, and correcting the punctuation (introduced by Corbinelli).

O.	**R.**
I. xvi. 41. sunt actionum . . . sed in omnibus	I. xvi. § 4. sunt actiones . . . et in omnibus
49. Deus est, qui in homine	Deus est, in homine [1]
51. in hac, quam in igne:	in hac quam in elemento; [2]
56. in viridi	in viride
61. municipalia	§ 5. municipia
I. xvii. *title.* Quare hoc idioma illustre vocetur.	*Quod ex multis ydiomatibus fiat unum pulcrum ; et facit mentionem de Cino Pistoriensi.*
I. xvii. 5. faciemus patere.	I. xvii. § 1. facimus patere.
8. Per hoc quidquid illustre . . . praefulget.	§ 2. Per hoc quidem quod illustre . . . perfulgens.
32. Nonne domestici sui reges, . . . et magnates quoslibet	§ 5. Nonne domestici sui, reges, . . . et magnates, quoslibet
I. xviii. *title.* Quare hoc idioma vocetur cardinale, aulicum et curiale.	*De excellentia vulgaris eloquentie ; et quod comunis est omnibus italicis.*
I. xviii. 2. vulgarem illustrem decussamus	I. xviii. § 1. vulgare illustre decusamus
5. et quo cardo vertitur versatur [3]	ut, quo cardo vertitur, versetur
15. ut admoveant et removeant,	ut amoveant et admoveant,
17. decorari	decusari
32. velut accola	§ 2. velut acola [4]
I. xix. 9. sic est invenire	I. xix. § 1. est invenire [5]
II. i. *title.* . . . vulgari,	*vulgare,*
II. i. 1. Sollicitantes iterum celeritatem . . . , et ad calamum [6]	II. i. § 1. Sollicitantes iterum celeritatem . . . ad calamum

[1] R. passes over without remark the *qui* in previous editions.

[2] The history of this passage is curious; for the MS. *elemento* Corbinelli printed *caelo*, for which Torri substituted *igne*, which was adopted by Fraticelli and Giuliani. The latter, in his corrections, proposes an altogether absurd reconstruction of the passage, *viz.*, "in coelo, quam in elementis, *in igne, quam in terra, in hac, quam in igne*". The restoration of the MS. reading is due primarily to Witte.

[3] This reading originated apparently in a piece of carelessness on the part of Corbinelli, who printed *et* for *ut*, the change of mood being due to Maffei.

[4] R. preserves this form as having possibly a different meaning from *accola*.

[5] In a note on this passage R. draws attention to a serious gap in Giuliani's text, a whole phrase being omitted, evidently through an oversight.

[6] This is one of the passages where O. departs from the traditional reading,

O.

II. i. 8. permanet firmum exemplar, et non e contrario, quia quaedam videntur praebere primatum versui ; ergo secundum quod

27. non solum bene ipsi ruditati faciet, sed ipsum sic facere oportere videtur.

30. multa possunt.

49. nemo enim montaninis hoc dicet esse conveniens. Sed optimae conceptiones non possunt esse nisi ubi scientia et ingenium est ; ergo optima loquela non convenit rusticana tractantibus ; convenit ergo individui gratia :

66. optimis conceptionibus, ut dictum est,

70. nisi in illis

75. Quare . . . non omnes

80. bovem ephippiatum

86. perfectum

R.

II. i. § 1. permanere videtur exemplar et non e converso, que quendam videntur prebere primatum primo secundum quod [1]

§ 2. non solum bene facere, sed ipsum sic facere oportere videtur.[2]

multa possunt !

§ 5. nemo enim montaninis rusticana tractantibus hoc dicet esse conveniens ; convenit ergo individui gratia.[3]

§ 6. ut dictum est, optimis conceptionibus

nisi illis

§ 7. Quapropter . . . nec omnes bovem epiphyatum [4]

§ 8. profectum

---

viz., Pollicitantes. For *celeritatem* Giuliani arbitrarily reads *sedulitatem*, which, on the strength of Trissino's *diligenza*, he coolly assumes to have been the MS. reading.

[1] Here again R. restores order out of the chaos produced by the multitude of counsellors, by simply reading *quēdam* (= *quendam*) for the MS. *quedam* (= *quaedam*). Giuliani has taken all sorts of liberties with the text in this passage ; a little further on he, without a word of explanation, substitutes *polliciti sumus* for *polluximus*, which he evidently did not understand. Further on again he similarly substitutes *comprehendi* for *perpendi*.

[2] The interpolation in the previous editions is due to Corbinelli.

[3] This passage is much confused in the MSS. R. cuts out *Sed optimae conceptiones non possunt esse nisi ubi scientia et ingenium est ; ergo optima loquela non convenit,* inasmuch as these identical words recur in the text a few lines further on.

[4] This phrase, which, of course, is a reminiscence of Horace, *Epist.* I. xiv. 43 : " Optat ephippia bos, piger optat arare caballus," was no doubt derived by Dante from the *Magnae Derivationes* of Uguccione da Pisa. (See above, p. 112, note 5.)

O.	**R.**
II. ii. 8. illud quod dicimus, dignum esse quod dignitatem habet,	II. ii. §§ 1,2. illud quod dicimus dignum. Dicimus dignum esse quod dignitatem habet,[1]
10. sic cognito	si cognito
11. cognoscitur, in quantum huius : unde cognita dignitate, cognoscemus et dignum.	§ 2. cognoscitur in quantum habituatum, cognita dignitate cognoscemus et dignum.[2]
13. Est enim	Est etenim
16. perventum	profectum
22. sicut in aliis	§ 3. et in aliis etiam
29. manifestum est quod dignitates inter se comparantur	manifestum est ut dignitates inter se comparentur
32. et per consequens aliud dignum, aliud dignissimum esse constat.	et per consequens, aliquid dignum, aliquid dignius, aliquid dignissimum esse constat.[3]
48. videlicet spiritu vegetabili,	§ 4. spiritu videlicet vegetabili,
50. quod vegetabile est,	quod vegetabile quid est,
73. Venus, virtus,	§ 5. Venus et Virtus,
85. " Non puesc mudar q'un chantar non esparja "	§ 6. *Non posc mudar c'un cantar non exparja*
87. " L'aura amara fa'ls broils blancutz clarzir "	*L'aura amara — fal bruol brancuz—clairir.*
89. " Per solatz revelhar Que s' es "	*Per solaz reveillar Che s'es*
92. " Degno son io, che mora."	*Digno sono eo de morte.*
95. nullum Italum	nullum latium
II. iii. 3. Volentes ergo	II. iii. § 2. Volentes igitur
16. digna sunt	sunt digna
38. magis honoris afferunt suis	§ 5. magis afferunt suis [4]
47. Adhuc . . . comprehendit	§ 7. Ad hoc, . . . comprendit
49. cum ergo . . . comprehendatur,	cum igitur . . . comprendatur,

[1] R.'s repetition of *dicimus dignum* gives a satisfactory result, and is an ingenious way out of the difficulty of the MS. reading, without transgressing the limits of probability.

[2] The emendation *habituatum* for MS. *huius unde* (if that be the correct expansion of the MS. reading) is happy, but perhaps a little hazardous. (See below, *Appendix*, p. 192, note 1.)

[3] R. notes that *aliud dignius* was omitted by an oversight from Fraticelli's edition of 1861 ; it was omitted also in the third edition (1873), and hence also in O. The missing phrase is supplied in Giuliani's edition.

[4] The interpolation of *honoris* is due to Torri.

O.

II. iii. 55. in hoc palatur, quod quicquid artis reperitur in ipsis est, sed non convertitur. Hoc signum autem

II. iv. 1. adpotiavimus
8. Et quod huc usque casualiter est assumptum,
14. ergo
20. fictio rethorica, in musicaque posita.
22. qui magno sermone
25. istos[5]
26. doctrinae aliquid operae nostrae impendentes, . . . poeticas
31. excipere aequale,
32. gravatam virtutem
34. in principio *Poeticae* "Sumite materiam," etc. dicit.

R.

II. iii. §§ 7, 8. in hoc palatur,[1] quod quicquid artis reperitur, in ipsis reperitur; sed non convertitur hoc. Signum autem

II. iv. § 1. aporiavimus[2] et qui hucusque casualiter est assumptus,
§ 2. igitur fictio rethorica versificata in musicaque posita.[3]
quia magni sermone[4]
illos
doctrine operam impendentes, . . . poetrias[6]

§ 3. coequare,[7]
gravata virtute
in principio Poetrie, *Sumite materiam* dicit.

---

[1] For *palatur* Giuliani, without remark, substitutes *patet*.

[2] This is a most satisfactory emendation, by the simple substitution of *r* for *t*, of the MS. reading *apotiauimus*—a word which has been a great stumbling-block to the editors. Both *aporiari* and *aporiare* (act. and neut.) were in use in mediæval Latin. Ducange quotes the following lines from an old grammarian as to the distinction between the two :—

> Aporio, si sit activum, tanta notabit,
> Indicat et aperit, depauperat atque revelat.
> Cum neutrum, signat tunc anxior atque laboro.
> In sensu et tali deponens vult reperiri.

[3] R. interpolates *versificata* to complete the definition, and also because the *-que* (if that be the correct expansion of the symbol in the MSS.) indicates that a word is missing. We much prefer, however, his alternative conjecture, which necessitates no interpolation, and is quite legitimate palaeographically, *viz.*, *fictio rethorica musice composita.* (See below, *Appendix*, p. 192, note 4.)

[4] Corbinelli reads *quia magno sermone;* Fraticelli, Torri, Giuliani, *quia isti magnos;* the reading of O. is due to Prompt.

[5] This reading of Fraticelli and Giuliani is not noted by R.

[6] The interpolations in the traditional text are due to Corbinelli. R.'s emendation necessitates merely the alteration of the MS. *operi* into *operam;* but we are inclined to favour his alternative *operi intendentes.* (See below, *Appendix*, p. 192.)

[7] A satisfactory restoration of the right reading.

O.	R.
II. iv. 37. discretione potiri	II. iv. § 4. discretionem potiri
39. induimus	inducimus
44. cantionem ligare	§ 5. cantionem oportet ligare [1]
46. et eius	et huius
49. omittamus	obmittamus
55. Sed quia,	§ 6. Et quando,
66. et pure	§ 7. ac pure
67. tensis fidibus adsumat secure plectrum et cum more incipiat.	tensis fidibus, adsumptum secure plectrum tum movere incipiat.[2]
69. Sed cantionem, atque discretionem hanc, sicut decet, facere, hoc opus	Sed cautionem atque discretionem habere, sicut decet, hoc opus[3]
77. confiteatur eorum stultitia	confiteantur eorum stultitiam
80. a tanta.	et a tanta
II. v. 8. nullum adhuc invenimus carmen in syllabicando endecasyllabum transcendisse,	II. v. § 2. nullum adhuc invenimus in carmine sillabicando endecadem transcendisse,
13. pentasyllabum et eptasyllabum et	pentasillabum, eptasillabum et
20. speciositas	§ 3. specimen[4]
22. ubicumque ponderosa multiplicantur, et pondus.	ubicumque ponderosa multiplicantur, multiplicatur et pondus.[5]
25. incipientes	§ 4. principiantes[6]
26. de Bornello :	de B.,
27. "auziretz . . . chantars."	*ausirez . . . cantars.*

[1] Another excellent emendation.

[2] R. here very happily gets rid of what he justly calls " quel ridicolo *cum more* " of the MSS. and printed editions.

[3] The interpolation of *facere* is due to Corbinelli, who did not see that the abbreviated *hanc* of the MSS. was an evident corruption of abbreviated *habere*. It is surprising that *cantionem* should not have been corrected long ago.

[4] The uncalled-for substitution of *speciositas* is due to Witte.

[5] R. does well to supply *multiplicatur*, which might easily have dropped out, especially as *multiplicantur* ends a line (in *T*); the construction is very harsh without it.

[6] Obviously preferable to Fraticelli's *incipientes*, the MS. reading being *principantes*.

O.	R.
II. v. 34. rithmus[1]	II. v. § 4. rithimus
37. Navarriae	Navarre
42. " Al cor gentil ripara "	Al cor gentilę repara[2]
43. Messina	Messana
44. " longiamente m' hai "	lungiamente m' ài
46. " lietamente "	letamente
48. " giammai "	già mai
50. " muovi tua virtù dal cielo."	movi tua vertù da cielo.
51. Et licet hoc endecasyllabum celeberrimum carmen, ut dictum est, videatur	§ 5. Et licet hoc quod dictum est, celeberrimum carmen, ut dignum est, videatur[3]
61. Enneasyllabum	§ 6. Neasillabum
63. parisyllabos	parisillaba
75. quomodo ligare	§ 7. quomodo viere[4]
II. vi. title. De varia constructione, qua utendum est in cantionibus.	Quod ex cognitione diversorum auctorum perficitur scientia poetandi vulgariter.
II. vi. 6. modum cantionum	II. vi. § 1. modum cantionarium
15. hic quinque	§ 2. .v. hic
20. digressionis[5]	§ 3. discretionis
23. quia inferiorem	quia nec inferiorem[6]
36. Piget me cunctis, sed pietatem maiorem illorum habeo, quicumque	§ 4. Piget me, cunctis pietate maiorem, quicunque[7]
43. sua magnificentia praeparata cunctis illum facit esse dilectum.	sua magnificentia preparata cunctis, illum facit esse dilectum.[8]

[1] This appears to be merely a reproduction of a misprint in Fraticelli, who elsewhere prints *rithimus* (see ii. 9).

[2] See above, p. 174, note 4.

[3] R. thus satisfactorily, by the help of *T*, restores the text which had been mutilated by Corbinelli.

[4] This is one of the most satisfactory of R.'s restorations, although, as he explains in a prefatory note (p. cciii), it occurred to him too late to be inserted in his text (see above, pp. 165-166). The *ligare* of the printed editions is due simply to a gloss in *G*.

[5] Here O., following *G*, abandons the correct reading printed by Fraticelli and Giuliani.

[6] The omission of *nec* in all the printed editions appears to have been due to an oversight on the part of Corbinelli.

[7] R. restores the MS. reading, but there is evidently something wrong.

[8] It is difficult to decide what should be the punctuation of this passage. R. is inclined to think that a second *cunctis* has possibly dropped out.

O.	**R.**
II. vi. 48. *Totila serus*	II. vi. § 4. *Totila secundus* [1]
56. Navarriae	§ 5. Navarre [2]
57. " Dreit Amor qu 'en "	*Ire d' amor qui en*
59. "m'abelhis ... pensamens."	*m'abellis . . . pensamen ;*
60. Harnaldus Daniel :	Arnaldus Danielis,
61. "qui . . . sobrafan, que m sortz."	*che . . . sobraffan chem sorz ;*
62. Hamericus de Belinoi :	Namericus de Belnui,
63. "no pot . . . adreitamen."	*non pot . . . addreciamen ;*
64. Hamericus	Namericus
65. " que per sobrecarcar."	*che per sobre carcar*
67. " di folle impresa allo "	*de folle 'mpresa, a lo*
68. Cavalcanti.	§ 5. Cavalcantis
69. "di doglia cuor convien "	*de doglia core* [3] *conven*
71. " Avenga ch' io non aggia "	*Avegna che io aggia*
80. Ovidium in *Metamorphoseos,*	§ 6. Ovidium *Metamorfoseos,*
83. Tullium, Livium, Plinium,	Titum Livium, Plinium, [4]
86. Desistant ergo	Subsistant igitur
87. Guidonem	Guittonem
89. desuetos plebescere.	plebescere desuetos !
II. vii. *title.* Quae sint ponenda vocabula, et quae in metro vulgari cadere non possunt.	*Distinctio vocabulorum ; et que sint ponenda, et que in metro vulgaria cadere non possunt.*
II. vii. 12. quaedam pexa et irsuta, quaedam lubrica et reburra	II. vii. § 2. quedam pexa et lubrica, quedam irsuta et reburra
21. bona ratione . . . per alta declivia	§ 2. bone rationi, . . . per altera declivia
23. Intuearis ergo, lector, quantum	§ 3. Intuearis ergo, lector : attende, quantum
34. propter asperitatem, ut *gregia,* et caetera ;	§ 4. propter hausteritatem, ut *greggia* et cetera ; [5]
44. immediate post mutam locatam, quasi loquentem	§ 5. inmediate post mutam, dolata [6] quasi, loquentem

[1] There can be little doubt as to the correctness of this emendation.

[2] R. thinks this quotation is out of its place ; he inserts it between the Provençal and Italian quotations.

[3] See above, p. 174, note 4.

[4] So the MSS. The *Tullium* of Fraticelli, etc., is due to Trissino.

[5] In a prefatory note (p. cciii) R. expresses a doubt as to whether the correct reading should not be " ut *greggia* et *cetra* ". (See below, *Appendix,* p. 193.)

[6] The MSS. read *mutam dolatam,* for which Witte conjectured *mutam locatam ;* this was accepted by Fraticelli. Giuliani, without hesitation, reads *duplicatam.*

O.	R.
II. vii. 47. *virtute, . . . letizia, . . . difesa.*	II. vii. § 5. *vertute, . . . letitia, . . . defesa.*[1]
53. *sì, vo,*	§ 6. *sì, no,*[2]
60. *onore, . . . alleviato, impossibilitate, . . . avventuratissimamente,*	§ 6. *honore, . . . alleviato, impossibilità, impossibilitate, . . . inanimatissimamente,*[3]
69. *onorificabilitudinitate,*	*honorificabilitudinitate*[4]
II. viii. *title.* Quid sit cantio, et quod pluribus modis variatur.	*Ostendit quod pluribus modis variatur eloquentia vulgaris, set precipuum est per cantilenas, sive cantiones.*
II. viii. 6. quid sit	II. viii. § 1. qui sit
17. vel prout passio.	§ 3. vel prout est passio.
22. *Aeneidos*	§ 4. Eneidorum[5]
31. magis ideo prorsus denominari	magis — immo prorsus — denominari
53. ballatae et sonitus, et omnia cuiuscumque modi verba sint armonizata . . . dicimus.	§ 6. ballatas et sonitus, et omnia cuiuscunquemodi verba scilicet armonizata . . . dicemus.
58. liquentes,	linquentes,
64. generale videatur,	generale videtur,
67. cantio, prout nos quaerimus, in quantum per superexcellentiam dicitur, est aequalium stantiarum	§ 7. cantio, in quantum per superexcellentiam dicitur, ut et nos querimus, est equalium stantiarum
72. cum diximus :	cum dicimus :
73. " ch' avete intelletto "	*che avete intellecto*
74-9. Et sic patet quod cantio sit, . . . molimur.	§ 8. Et sic patet quid cantio sit, . . . molimur.
80-5. Quod autem dicimus . . . intendimus[6]	
II. ix. *title.* Quae sint principales in cantione partes, . . . pars est.	*Ponit que sint partes in cantione, . . . pars sit.*

<hr>

[1] R. does not note that Fraticelli and Giuliani read *difesa.*

[2] MSS. *uo,* but R. seems undoubtedly right in reading *no,* in accordance with a suggestion of Boehmer.

[3] There can be little doubt that R. is right in thus correcting the MS. *mammatissimamente.*

[4] On this word, see above, pp. 112-113.

[5] On this form, see below, pp. 249-250.

[6] R. transposes these two paragraphs, reading " Quod autem dicimus . . . intendimus. Et sic patet . . . molimur."

O.

II. ix. 12. stantia, hoc est mansio capax vel receptaculum totius artis.

22. innotescit

32. minime liceret quod dictum est.

34. quod est artis, comprehendetur ibi cum dicemus partium habitudinem.

36. hic[2] colligere possumus

II. x. *title.* Quid sit cantus stantiae, et quod

II. x. 17. sed in modo diversari videtur;

21. sine dieresi; et dieresim

28. "ed al gran"

29. dieresim . . . dieresis . . . dieresim vel post vel utrimque.[4]

33. dieresim . . . stantiam

37. dieresim

II. xi. *title.* De habitudine stantiae, de numero pedum et syllabarum,

II. xi. 3. haec enim

7. Incipientes ergo

8. frons cum versibus, et pedes cum syrmate sive cauda, et quidem pedes cum versibus

17. quilibet versus dimeter,

22. "della mente"

R.

II. ix. § 2. stantia — hoc est mansio capax, sive receptaculum— totius artis.

innotescet

§ 4. minime liceret: quod dictum est.

quod est ars, illud comprenditur ibi cum dicimus "partium habitudinem ".[1]

§ 5. sic colligere possimus

Ostendit quid sit stantia, et quod

II. x. § 2. sed in modis diversificari videntur;

sine diesi; et diesim[3]

e al gran

§ 3. diesim . . . diesis . . . diesim,[3] vel post vel undique.

diesim[3] . . . stantias

diesim[3]

De numero pedum et sillabarum,

II. xi. § 1. hec etenim

§ 2. Incipientes igitur

§ 2. frons cum versibus, pedes cum cauda vel sirmate, nec non pedes cum versibus[5]

§ 3. quilibet versus esset dimeter, *de la mente*

---

[1] As R. points out, these last two words must be regarded as a quotation, otherwise they could hardly stand.

[2] This appears to be due to a mere piece of carelessness on the part of Corbinelli.

[3] There can be no doubt as to what the MS. reading represents. The substitution of *dieresis* for *diesis* throughout this chapter, in which it occurs seven times, is due to Torri.

[4] Witte is responsible for this needless alteration.

[5] The reading of the previous editions was due to an accidental omission of Corbinelli, which was supplied by Fraticelli by means of Trissino's version.

O.

II. xi. 28. Et quemadmodum dicimus versus superare posse carminibus et syllabis frontem, sic dici potest frontem in his duobus posse superare versus: sicut quando quilibet versus esset duobus eptasyllabis metris, et frons esset pentametra duobus endecasyllabis et tribus eptasyllabis contexta.

38. "muovi tua virtù dal cielo"

43. posse superare carminibus et syllabis superari, et e contrario,

47. in stantia esse tres pedes et duos versus, et tres versus et duos pedes:

50. simul contexere.

60. quia iterum [2]

II. xii. *title.* fiant stantiae, . . . in carminibus.

II. xii. 8. endecasyllabum scilicet, et eptasyllabum, et pentasyllabum; quae ante alia sequenda astruximus.

17. "mi prega"

18. diximus:

19. "intelletto d' amore."

20. dico Hispanos qui poetati sunt in vulgari *oc.*

22. Hamericus de Belinoi:

23. "adreitamen."

R.

II. xi. § 3. Et quemadmodum dicimus de fronte, et de versibus posset dici; possent etenim versus superare frontem carminibus, et sillabis superari; ut si quilibet versus esset trimeter, et eptasillaba metra, et frons esset pentametra, duobus endecasillabis et tribus eptasillabis contexta.[1]

§ 4. *movi tua vertù da cielo* posse superare carminibus sillabis superatam, et e converso,

§ 5. esse in stantia tres pedes et duo versus, et tres versus et duo pedes; similiter contexere.

§ 7. quin iterum

fiant cantiones, . . . in carmine.

II. xii. § 2. endecasillabum scilicet, eptasillabum, et pentasillabum; que trisillabum [3] ante alia sequi astruximus.

§ 3. *me prega* dicimus, *intellecto d' amore.* dico Yspanos, qui poetati sunt in vulgari *oc.* Namericus de Belnui, *adrechamen.*[4]

---

[1] The MS. text of this passage is very corrupt. R. by an interpolation, which he more or less satisfactorily justifies, has effectively emended it.

[2] *Quia,* which is certainly wrong, was due originally to a misprint in Maffei's edition, whence it was copied by Fraticelli. The mistake was corrected by Torri and Giuliani.

[3] The omission of *trisillabum,* which R. now restores to the text, was due in the first instance to Trissino; he was followed by Corbinelli and all subsequent editors.

[4] An obvious correction, hitherto overlooked.

O.	**R.**
II. xii. 31. haec est	II. xii. § 4. hee sunt
34. uno eptasyllabo	§ 5. uno solo eptasillabo
41. Fabritium	Fabrutium [1]
42. " Di fermo "	*De fermo*
46. " Lo mio "	*Lo meo*
50. procedere	procedisse
54. dico *in pedibus,*	§ 6. dico " pedibus,"
55. pedibusque versibusque	pedibus versibusque
63. " Donna mi prega, perch' io voglio dire."	§ 7. *Donna me prega,*
65. " m' ha "	*m' à*
69. Hoc satis hinc, lector, sufficienter eligere potes qualiter tibi habituanda sit stantia: habitudo namque circa carmina consideranda videtur.	§ 10. Satis hinc, lector, sufficienter eligere potes qualiter tibi habituanda sit stantia habitudine que circa carmina consideranda videtur.[2]
72. Et hoc etiam	§ 8. Hoc etiam
77. pars trimetra	§ 8. pes trimeter [3]
80. sic pars altera, extrema endecasyllaba et medium eptasyllabum habeat :	et pes alter habeat secundum eptasillabum et extrema endecasillaba : [4]
85. quemadmodum de pedibus dicimus et de versibus;	§ 9. quemadmodum de pedibus, dicimus et de versibus;
87. illi ante, hi post dieresim	hii ante, hii post diesim [5]
92. sic de duobus, et de pluribus	sic de pluribus,
II. xiii. *title.* De relatione rithimorum, . . . in stantia.	*De varietate rithimorum ;* . . . *in cantione.*
II. xiii. 6. quaedam reseranda	II. xiii. § 2. quedam resecanda
7. stantia sive rithimus,	stantia sine rithimo [6]
12. " Si m fos Amors, de joi donar tan larga."	*Sem fos Amor de joi donar ;* [7]

[1] See above, p. 176, note 1. R., noting that here D. names only two poets, but gives three examples, thinks a name has been omitted; he would supply *Guidonem Guinizelli* in front of the other two.

[2] This passage (which he emends by substituting *habitudine que* for *habitudo namque*, and altering the punctuation) is placed by R. at the end of the chapter.

[3] This correction of the MS. reading (*pars trimeter*) had already been made by Trissino; but it was overlooked by Corbinelli and succeeding editors.

[4] The emendation of this passage is due to Boehmer.

[5] See above, p. 185, note 3.

[6] MSS. *sine rithimos.* Giuliani reads *sine rithimis.* The correction, made originally by Boehmer, was much needed.

[7] R. omits the concluding words of this line, as being wanting in the MSS.

O.

II. xiii. 13. diximus :
14. " Al poco giorno, ed al gran cerchio d' ombra."
28. ore tenus intimavit.
37. diversos rithimos faciunt esse
38. post dieresim
49. omnis apta licentia
60. in praemediato capitulo
64. omni modo
68. innovari
69. dum tamen
71. trimetrum
81. desinentium
83. videtur quae . . . huic appendere capitulo,
88. reperiri
92. nascentis militiae dux,[5]
95. visi sumus

II. xiv. *title.* De numero carminum et syllabarum in stantia.
II. xiv. 1. Ex quo quae sunt
6. videre oportet aliquid, et aliquid dividere, quod postea secundum partes
8. Nostra ergo
11. quaedam non : cum ea quae

16. quandoque contentive canere contingit. Quae circa sinistrum sunt verba . . . ad extremum.[8]

R.

II. xiii. § 2. dicimus,
Al poco giorno.[1]

§ 3. oretenus intimavit.[2]
diversos faciunt esse rithimos

§ 4. post diesim[3]
§ 5. omnis optata licentia
§ 6. in preinmediato capitulo omnimode
innovare
dumtaxat
trimetri

§ 7. desinentiarum[4]
§ 8. videtur ut, que . . . huic appendamus capitulo,
potiri
nascentis militie dies,
nisi sumus

Omitted.

II. xiv. § 1. Ex quo duo que sunt[6]
videre oportet aliquid ; deinde secundum partes[7]

§ 2. Nostra igitur quedam non. Nam cum ea que
quandoque contemptive canere contingit, que circa sinistra sunt verba . . . ad extremum . . .

---

[1] R. omits the concluding words of this line, as being wanting in the MSS.

[2] Giuliani arbitrarily reads *intonavit.*

[3] See above, p. 185, note 3. In this and the following passage Giuliani has taken unwarrantable liberties with the text.

[4] This correction is due to Giuliani.

[5] Here O. unadvisedly adopts Giuliani's substitution of *dux* for *dies.*

[6] R. interpolates *duo* as being wanted to complete the sense.

[7] The interpolations in the text of previous editions were due to Corbinelli.

[8] The full stop at the end in O. is a mistake due to the printers, the sentence being broken off in the middle.

APPENDIX.

THE foregoing collation of Professor Pio Rajna's critical text (R) of the *De Vulgari Eloquentia* with that of the Oxford Dante (O) was already in type when the *edizione minore* of Professor Rajna's text made its appearance. In this new edition (which was to some extent the outcome of a suggestion made by the present writer in a review of the larger work in *Romania*)[1] Professor Rajna has introduced several important modifications of the text. A collation of the emended passages (some two dozen in number), as they stand in the *edizione minore* (R[2]), with the text of the previous edition (R[1]) is given below, and will enable the student to see at a glance wherein the emendations consist. Some of these are comparatively insignificant, but not a few of them, on the other hand, are of real importance, and undoubtedly tend to the improvement of the text.

R[1].	R[2].
I. iv. § 3. ab eo qui statim ipsum plasmaverat.	ab eo qui statim plasmaverat[2]
§ 5. Oritur et hic ista questio, cum dicimus superius per viam responsionis hominem primum fuisse locutum, si responsio fuit ad Deum: nam, si ad Deum	Oritur et hic ista questio, cum dicimus superius per viam responsionis hominem primum fuisse locutum: si responsio, fuit ad Deum? Nam, si ad Deum[3]

---

[1] *Romania*, xxvi. 116-126. Professor Rajna says in his preface: "Mentre del trattato *De Vulgari Eloquentia* vengo preparando l' edizione già annunziata con commento dichiarativo, mi è parso opportuno di ridar fuori il testo critico in un' edizione minore, accessibile a tutti per la tenuità del costo, e di comodo uso. Che l' opportunità ci sia davvero, mi è stato confermato dall' assenso di coloro ai quali mi accadde di comunicare il mio disegno, e dal desiderio che di una edizione siffatta ebbe a manifestare spontaneamente, nel rendere conto della maggiore in un recente fascicolo della *Romania* (xxvi. 125), quel valente cultore degli studi danteschi che è il Paget Toynbee."

[2] (O. I. iv. 25) R. now rejects the interpolated *ipsum*, which is not in *T*, and is a later insertion in *G*.

[3] (O. I. iv. 43) The improvement in the punctuation of this passage is due to Professor Parodi.

<table>
<tr><td align="center">**R**[1].</td><td align="center">**R**[2].</td></tr>
</table>

I. viii. § 2. Sed, sive avene tunc primitus advenissent, sive ad Europam indigene repedassent,	Sed, sive advene tunc primitus advenissent, sive ad Europam indigene repedissent,[1]
§ 3. per diversa vulgaria derivatum,	per diversa vulgaria dirivatum,[2]
I. ix. § 6. quem exolescere non videremus.	quem exolescere non videmus.[3]
I. x. § 4. Tertia, que Latinorum est,	Tertia quoque, que Latinorum est,[4]
I. xi. § 5. Casentinenses et Fratenses.	Casentinenses et Pratenses.[5]
I. xii. *title. Quod in eodem loco diversificatur idioma secundum quod variatur tempus.*	Omitted.[6]
I. xiv. § 4. Veneti quoque nec sese investigati vulgaris honore dignantur ; et si quis eorum, errore confisus, vanitaret in hoc, recordetur si unquam	§ 4. Veneti quoque nec sese investigati vulgaris honore dignantur ; et si quis eorum, errore confisus, vanitaret in hoc, recordetur si unquam

[1] (O. I. viii. 13) R. here abandons the form *avene*, which he previously favoured (see above, p. 171, note 2), and reverts to the MS. reading *repedissent* for reasons already given in a supplementary note to the larger edition (see above, p. 171, note 3).

[2] (O. I. viii. 32) The reading *dirivatum* (*T*), as against *derivatum* (*G*), is supported by a reference to Uguccione da Pisa, who (s.v. *Ruo*) distinguishes between *derivare* and *dirivare* as follows : " *Derivare* est rivum de fonte ducere ; sed *dirivare* est fontem in diversos rivulos ducere. *Dirivatur* ergo grecismus in latinitatem, idest, quasi fons in rivulos ducitur ; sed latinitas *derivatur* a grecismo, idest, quasi de fonte ducitur." In the difference of reading between *T* and *G* here, R. sees an additional proof of their independence of each other.

[3] (O. I. ix. 72) R., in substituting *videmus* for *videremus* (which is the MS. reading), follows Corbinelli and the old editions.

[4] (O. I. x. 25) *Tertia quoque, que* had already been proposed by R., as an alternative reading, in a note in the larger edition ; his adoption of it now in the text is due to Professor Parodi.

[5] (O. I. xi. 42) Here R. abandons a reading the adoption of which in his previous edition he acknowledges to have been somewhat hasty (see above, p. 173, note 5).

[6] The title here does not correspond to the contents of the chapter ; R. has consequently done well to relegate it to the footnotes. O., following Fraticelli, substitutes *De idiomate Siculo et Apulo*, which was primarily due to Trissino.

R¹.

dixit. *Per le plage de Dio,
tu non veras.* Inter quos
omnes . . . Ildebrandinum
paduanum. § 5. Quare,
omnibus . . . vulgare il-
lustre.

R².

dixit. *Per le plage de Dio,
tu non veras.* § 5. Inter
quos omnes . . . Ildebrandinum paduanum. § 6.
Quare, omnibus . . . vul-
gare illustre.¹

I. xv. § 6.	si Latium illustre venamur,	si latinum illustre venamur,²
I. xvi. § 2.	omnia comparentur et pon-derentur; et illud aliorum omnium mensuram accipi-mus; sicut in numero	omnia comparentur et pon-derentur, et quod velut aliorum omnium mensu-ram accipiamus; sicut in numero³
§ 4.	in impari numero magis redolet quam in pari;	in impari numero redolet magis quam in pari;⁴
I. xviii. § 1.	frutices de ytalica silva?	frutices de ytala silva? ⁵
II. i. § 1.	ad calamum frugi operis redeuntes,	ad calamum frugi operis redeuntis,⁶
§ 2.	utrum versificantes vul-gariter debeant	utrum versificantes omnes vulgariter debeant⁷

¹ (O. I. xiv. 35-48) Inasmuch as *Inter quos omnes* does not refer to *Veneti* only, but to all the peoples who have been mentioned in the course of the chapter, R. alters the distribution of his paragraphs accordingly.

² (O. I. xv. 68) R. here reverts to the reading of the previous editions, which in his former text he had abandoned after a good deal of hesitation. Adopting a suggestion of Professor Parodi, he explains *latinum* in this case as standing for *latinum vulgare*.

³ (O. I. xvi. 10-12) None of the emendations of this difficult passage is altogether satisfactory. R. now restores to the text the *accipiamus* of the MSS., and for *et illud* reads *et quod velut*, which he evolves, with a certain plausibility, from the MS. *et illico.*

⁴ (O. I. xvi. 54) The inversion *magis redolet* for *redolet magis*, in the pre-vious edition, was due to a slip on the part of R. This divergence between O. and R. was overlooked in the collation.

⁵ (O. I. xviii. 12) R. reads *ytala* for *ytalica* here, as he had already done in a previous passage (in which the same phrase occurs, I. xv. § 1) in his former edition.

⁶ (O. II. i. 2) The slight improvement involved in reading *redeuntis* for *redeuntes* is due to Professor Parodi.

⁷ (O. II. i. 14) R. justifies the insertion of *omnes* (which was interpolated by Trissino, first on the margin of his MS. and then in his translation) by a reference to §§ 2, 6, 7 of this chapter and to § 1 of the next.

R [1].	**R** [2].

II. ii. § 2. et si cognito habituante habituatum cognoscitur in quantum habituatum, cognita dignitate cognoscemus et dignum.

§ 4. homo tripliciter spirituatus est, spiritu videlicet vegetabili, animali et rationali,

et si cognito habituante habituatum cognoscitur in quantum huiusmodi, cognita dignitate cognoscemus et dignum.[1]

homo tripliciter spirituatus est, videlicet vegetabili, animali et rationali,[2]

II. iii. § 7. Ad hoc, in artificiatis

Ad hec, in artificiatis [3]

II. iv. § 2. nichil aliud est quam fictio rethorica versificata in musicaque posita.

nichil aliud est quam fictio rethorica musice composita.[4]

II. iv. § 2. Unde nos, doctrine operam impendentes,

§ 4. debemus discretionem potiri,

Unde nos, doctrine operi operam impendentes,[5]

debemus discretione potiri,[6]

II. v. § 7. quomodo innectere quis debeat

quomodo viere quis debeat [7]

---

[1] (O. II. ii. 10-13) The reading *huiusmodi* for the MS. *huius unde* is happier still than the *habituatum* adopted in the previous edition (see above, p. 179, note 2). R. quotes examples of the use of the phrase *in quantum huiusmodi* from the *Summa* of Aquinas, and from a mediæval Latin version of Aristotle's *Analytica Posteriora*.

[2] (O. II. ii. 48) R. now rejects the *spiritu* (interpolated by Fraticelli after a suggestion of Witte) as unnecessary, the adjectives *vegetabili, animali, rationali* being here substantively in the neuter, a use which he parallels exactly from Albertus Magnus.

[3] (O. II. iii. 47) *Ad hec* is preferred by R. to *Ad hoc* as being more consonant with mediæval usage.

[4] (O. II. iv. 20) We had already expressed our preference for the reading now adopted by R. (see above, p. 180, note 3), and are pleased to find that the expression of our opinion was instrumental in bringing about the abandonment of the interpolated *versificata*. R. says: " ho finito per rinunziare alle aggiunte e per inalzare agli onori del testo un' altra congettura che avevo esposto in nota, la quale ha avuto frattanto l' approvazione del Paget Toynbee, secondo mi dice una sua lettera ".

[5] (O. II. iv. 26) This reading R. had already proposed as an alternative in his previous edition.

[6] (O. II. iv. 37) R. now admits himself to have been ill advised in substituting the acc. for the abl., *potiri* (like *uti*, its synonym) being constructed with either case in mediæval Latin.

[7] (O. II. v. 75) The restoration of *viere* to the text is now happily accomplished (see above, p. 182, note 4).

R[1].	**R**[2].
II. vi. § 6. tot reductis auctoribus ad memoriam;	tot reductis autoribus ad memoriam;[1]
II. vii. *title.* que in metro vulgaria cadere non possunt.	que in metro vulgari cadere non possunt.[2]
II. vii. § 4. ut *greggia* et cetera;	ut *greggia* et *cetra*;[3]

[1] (O. II. vi. 75) For the distinction between *auctor* and *autor* see *Conv.* IV. vi. 14-49, and above, pp. 101-102.

[2] R. now accepts the correction (*vulgari* for *vulgaria*) of previous editors, which he rejected in his previous edition.

[3] (O. II. vii. 34) See above, p. 183, note 5.

A BIOGRAPHICAL NOTICE OF DANTE IN THE 1494 EDITION OF THE *SPECULUM HISTORIALE* OF VINCENT OF BEAUVAIS [1]

THE *Speculum Historiale* forms, as is well known, the last division [2] of the *Majus Speculum*, the vast encyclopædic work of Vincent of Beauvais. As Vincent is generally supposed to have died about the year 1264,[3] it was naturally not to be expected that his *Speculum* should contain a notice of Dante, who was not born until 1265. Great was my surprise, therefore, on turning over the pages of the first Venice edition (1494) of the *Speculum Historiale*, to find the name of "Dantes alugerius" at the head of a paragraph consisting of a short biographical notice of the Florentine poet, and concluding with the date of his death (1321). Plainly in the edition before me the chronicle of Vincent had been continued by some later hand. Accordingly, on making a careful examination of the book, I found that ninety-two chapters had been interpolated towards the close of Vincent's own work, the interpolation beginning in the middle of cap. cv of Lib. **XXXII** (according to the division adopted in the Strassburg edition of 1473). Vincent's chapter commences as follows:—

De temporibus presentibus. Ecce tempora sexte etatis [4] usque ad presentem annum summatim perstringendo descripsi qui est annus christianissimi regis

[1] Reprinted, with modifications and additions, from the *English Historical Review*, April, 1895; and *Modern Quarterly of Language and Literature*, i. 51-52.

[2] A fourth part, entitled *Speculum Morale*, is included in all the printed editions of Vincent of Beauvais; but this has been conclusively shown to be a later compilation.

[3] According to one account he was alive as late as 1276.

[4] Vincent divides the history of the world into six ages: 1. From the Creation to the Flood. 2. From the Flood to Abraham. 3. From Abraham to David. 4. From David to the Capture of Jerusalem. 5. From the Capture of Jerusalem to the Coming of Christ. 6. From A.D. 1 to the end of the world.

nostri ludowici .XVIII. imperii vero friderici XXXIII.us Pontificatus autem inno-
cencii quarti secundus . Qui est porro ab incarnacione domini millesimus
.ccus xliiijus . A creacione mundi quintimillesimus .ccus vjus Et hoc duntaxat
iuxta minorem numerum quem in hac tota serie secuti sumus. Porro secundum
majorem numerum ex antiqua translacione sumptum, quem supra posuimus,
anuus presens existit ab inicio seculi sextus millesimus .ccccus xlijus . . . .

At this point, in the middle of the chapter, in the Venice edition
of 1494 (as well as in that of 1591, which is practically a reprint
of the former) the narrative of Vincent of Beauvais is suddenly
interrupted with the remark : " Hactenus Vincentii Historia.
Quae vero sequuntur usque in tempus currens, anni, videlicet
M.ccccxciiii. ex cronica nova sunt addita ".

Here, in the edition of 1591, follows a new heading : " Rerum
gestarum | Ex Historiis | Ac Chronicis fide dignis | collectarum,
et excerptarum | Quae ab Anno M.ccxliiij. usque ad M.ccccxciiij.
scitu digna visa sunt, | ad Speculum Historiale compendiosa ap-
pendix ". Then follow ninety-one chapters (unnumbered in the
edition of 1494) of the interpolated chronicle. At the end of
these is printed a Latin sapphic poem addressed " Ad deum
optimum maximum | de his quae mirabilia gessit pro iustissimo |
et excelso Maximiliano Rege | Romanorum ". At the close of
the ninety-first chapter is appended this notice : " Haec habui-
mus quae ex chronica nova adjiceremus ". Then follows another
interpolated chapter (the ninety-second), entitled, " De morte,
ac fine rerum ; " which again is followed by two short Latin
poems, one in hexameters, the other in elegiacs, on the same
subject. The next chapter (ninety-three) resumes the narrative
of Vincent at the commencement of his cap. cvi " De signis
futurae consummationis," and follows him to the end, the work
being concluded in twenty-three chapters (cvi-cxxviii) dealing
with the coming of Antichrist, Hell-fire, the Glorification of
Saints, etc.

I have searched in vain through the well-known bibliographies,
as well as through the various notices of Vincent of Beauvais, for
any account of this interpolation. The only mention of it I have
been able to find is in a meagre note by David Clément in
his *Bibliothèque Curieuse Historique et Critique,*[1] in which he

---

[1] Vol. iii. p. 82, note 62.

says of the Venice edition of 1494 of the *Speculum Historiale :*
" L'on y a ajouté un petit supplément au *Speculum Historiale*
que l'on a continué jusqu'à l'année 1494 ". The circumstance of
this addition having escaped notice is easily accounted for by the
fact that it is not introduced as an *appendix*, but as an *interpola-*
tion ; so that the conclusion of the work, being the same in
the Venice editions of 1494 and 1591, which contain the supplementary chapters, as in the Strassburg edition of 1473, which
does not, presents no clue to the bibliographer.

Among other interesting notices which occur in these interpolated chapters is one of Vincent of Beauvais himself, with a list
of his works. It will be noticed that the *Speculum Morale* is duly
included among Vincent's works, though it has no claim to rank as
such, being largely a compilation from St. Thomas Aquinas and
other contemporary writers : " Vincentius gallus patria burgundus
belvacensis historicus et theologus ordinis predicatorum pater,
per hoc ipsum tempus claruit.   Et innumerabiles historias
multis sub voluminibus comprehendit. Quatuor enim specula
edidit de omni scibili materia : Doctrinale, Morale, Naturale, et
historiale, quod usque ad annum domini M.ccliiij [a mistake for
Mccxliiij—see Vincent's own account quoted above] produxit.
Atque alia multa composuit videlicet Librum gratie, Librum
de Sancto Joanne evangelista, Librum de eruditione puerorum
regalium, et Consolatorium de morte amici. Et quammaxime
de laudibus dive ac gloriose virginis Marie tractatum celeberri-
mum edidit."

The biographical account of Dante, referred to at the beginning of this article, runs as follows [1] :—

Dantes alugerius [2] patria florentinus vates et poeta conspicuus ac theolo-
gorum [3] [*sic*] precipue tempestate ista claruit . Vir in cives suos egregia nobili-
tate venerandus : qui licet ex longo exilio damnatus tenues illi fuissent substantie,
semper tamen phisicis atque theologicis doctrinis imbutus vacavit studiis . unde
cum florentia a factione nigra pulsus fuisset parisiense gymnasium accessit . et

---

[1] It is placed at the end of cap. 91 in the edition of 1591, between an account
of the death of King John of Bohemia (1346) and a record of the marriage of
Azzo VIII. of Este to Beatrice, youngest daughter of Charles II. of Anjou (1305).

[2] The edition of 1591 reads *Aligerius.*

[3] Some word has evidently dropped out here.

cum circa poeticam scientiam eruditissimus esset opus inclytum atque divinum lingua vernacula sub titulo comedie edidit . in quo omnium celestium terrestri-umque ac infernorum profunda contemplatus singula queque historice allegorice tropologice ac anagogice descripsit . Aliud quoque de monarchia mundi . Hic cum ex gallicis regressus fuisset friderico arragonensi regi et domino cani grandi scaligero adhesit. Denique mortuo cane principe veronensi et ipse apud raven-nam Anno domini MCCCXXI etatis sue quinquagesimo sexto diem obiit.

This notice is chiefly remarkable on account of the very interesting statement that Dante attached himself to " the King Frederick of Aragon "—*friderico arragonensi regi adhesit.* There cannot be the least doubt as to the identity of the person intended. There was no king of Aragon of the name of Frederick, but there was a well-known prince of that name belonging to the royal house of Aragon who was the wearer of a royal crown : namely, Frederick, commonly known as Don Frederick, the third son of Peter III. of Aragon, who in 1296 assumed the crown of Sicily, and retained it until his death in 1337. On the death, in 1285, of Peter III., King of Aragon and Sicily, his eldest son, Alphonso, became King of Aragon, while James, the second son, succeeded to the crown of Sicily. When Alphonso died, in 1291, James succeeded him in Aragon, leaving the government of Sicily in the hands of his younger brother Frederick. A few years later, however, at the instigation of Pope Boniface VIII., James, ignoring the claims of his brother, agreed to cede Sicily to the Angevin claimant, Charles II. of Naples. The Sicilians, on hearing of this agreement, renounced their allegiance to James, and proclaimed his brother, Frederick, king in his stead, under the title of Frederick II. (1296). Charles and James thereupon made war upon Frederick, but in 1299 James withdrew his troops, and in 1302, on the failure of a fresh expedition against him under Charles of Valois and Robert, Duke of Calabria, Frederick was confirmed in possession of the kingdom of Sicily under the title of King of Trinacria,[1] receiving in marriage at the same time Charles II.'s third daughter, Eleanor.

---

[1] This title was doubtless chosen in order to emphasise the fact that Frederick was king of the island of Sicily only, and had no title to sovereignty over the Two Sicilies, a designation which included the kingdom of Naples as well as that of Sicily proper. *Cf. Par.* viii. 67, where Dante apparently alludes to this title. (See below, p. 275-276.)

A peculiar interest attaches to this statement of the chronicler as to Dante's relations with Frederick of Aragon, owing to the fact that, as every student of Dante knows, the poet never mentions that prince's name, nor refers to him, save with bitter reproach and condemnation,[1] and this, though his reign was most beneficial to the island of Sicily, and he himself appears to have been greatly beloved by his subjects. It is generally supposed that the explanation of Dante's bad opinion of him is to be found in Frederick's policy after the death of the Emperor, Henry of Luxemburg, to whom Dante had looked as the saviour of Italy. During the Emperor's lifetime, Frederick had acted as his ally against his most formidable opponent, Robert of Naples, and had had the command of the combined Genoese and Sicilian fleets. On Henry's death (in 1313) he went to Pisa, and was offered by the Pisans the lordship of their city, in the hope that he would carry on the campaign against King Robert and the Tuscan Guelfs. But Frederick, for whom the offer had no attractions, imposed such hard conditions that they practically amounted to a refusal. Leaving Pisa, he returned to Sicily, and thenceforth, withdrawing as much as possible from Italian affairs, he devoted himself mainly to the consolidation of his own kingdom.[2] It was doubtless this want of sympathy

---

[1] See *Purg.* vii. 119; *Par.* xix. 131; xx. 63. An apparent exception is in the passage (*Purg.* iii. 116) where he is referred to (as some think) as " l' onor di Cicilia ". But even if the commentators who understand this of Frederick are correct in their interpretation, it does not necessarily involve an inconsistency on Dante's part; for the opinion may be regarded as being rather that of the speaker—namley, Manfred, the prince's grandfather—than that of the poet himself in this case. Manfred would naturally take a more favourable view than Dante of the character of his grandson, who had offered such a stout and successful resistance to the representative of the hated house of Anjou.

[2] *Cf.* what Giovanni Villani says : " Federigo re di Cicilia il qual era in mare con suo stuolo . . . aggiuntosi già co' Genovesi, sentendo della morte dello 'mperadore, venne in Pisa, e non avendo potuto vedere lo 'mperadore vivo, sì il volle vedere morto. I Pisani per dotta de' guelfi di Toscana e del re Ruberto sì vollono il detto don Federigo fare loro signore ; non volle la signoria, ma per sua scusa domandò loro molto larghi patti fuori di misura, con tutto che per gli più si credette che, bene ch' e' Pisani gli avessono fatti, non avrebbe voluto lasciare la stanza di Cicilia per signoreggiare Pisa ; e così sanza grande dimoro si tornò in Cicilia." (ix. 54.)

with the fate of Italy which aroused the wrath and indignation of the Florentine poet.[1]

Whatever may have been the nature of Dante's relations with Frederick, it may be pretty safely assumed that they came to an end after the refusal of the latter to identify himself further with the Ghibelline cause in Tuscany.

The anonymous chronicler's laconic statement—*Friderico arragonensi regi adhesit*—opens up all sorts of curious speculations as to Dante's political position in the Ghibelline camp. He certainly regarded himself as a person of political importance : witness the tone of his several letters addressed to the Princes and Peoples of Italy (*Epist.* V), to the Florentine Guelfs (*Epist.* VI), and to the Emperor Henry himself (*Epist.* VII); and this statement, if it were possible to accept it without question, would go far to prove that he was in direct and personal contact with some of the most exalted members of the imperial party in Italy. Unfortunately, explicit as the statement is, and difficult as it is to see what motive there can have been for its invention, it is impossible to regard it without grave suspicion. Not only is it unsupported by evidence from any other quarter, but we have in the very next sentence an equally explicit statement which is demonstrably false, as it involves a serious blunder in chronology. The chronicler goes on to state that *after Can Grande's death* Dante himself died at Ravenna in 1321. As a matter of fact, Can Grande did not die until eight years after Dante, in 1329, as is correctly recorded in another part of the interpolated chronicle.[2] Under

---

[1] Dante's earlier denunciations of Frederick in the *Convivio* (iv. 6, ll. 182-183) and *De Vulgari Eloquentia* (i. 12, ll. 36-37), which were written probably between 1307 and 1310, were doubtless due to the contrast presented to his mind between Sicily as the centre of Italian letters under the Emperor Frederick II. and the kingdom distracted as it was by the wars of Frederick of Aragon and his Angevin rival.

[2] Cap. xxxiii of the additional chapters in the edition of 1591, which contains a notice of Can Grande. We here incidentally get another mention of Dante : " Canis scaliger, qui ex rebus strenuè gestis magnus cognomento appellatus est, . . . erat multe eloquentie princeps comesque perhumanus, nec non et in omnes liberalis, atque doctorum virorum tum ecclesiasticorum tumque oratorum et

these circumstances the statement as to Dante's relations with
Frederick of Aragon, though quite possibly based upon trust-
worthy information, must be received, if not with scepticism, at
any rate with reserve, until it can be substantiated from some
independent source.

The only other item of special interest in this somewhat
meagre account of Dante is the allusion to his straitened circumstances—"although," says the chronicler, "his means were
slender owing to his being in exile for such a long period, yet
he always found leisure for his favourite studies". This remark
lends some support to the theory propounded by the late Dr.
Scartazzini that Dante earned his livelihood during his exile by
teaching. We may suppose the chronicler's meaning to be that
in the intervals of the profession by which he was obliged to
support himself the poet found means to pursue his favourite
philosophical and theological studies. It can hardly have been
as a mere student that he went to the universities of Paris and
Bologna during his exile. It is much more probable that he
visited those places as being the centres of learning, where he
would find the two things he most needed—pupils and books.

We are told nothing in this account of the love affairs, the
military service, and the embassies, of which we hear so much in
the various biographies of Dante; but details of this sort could
perhaps hardly be expected in such a brief notice. It is
singular, however, that so little should be said about the
poet's writings, the only other work referred to besides the
Commedia being the *De Monarchia*. This is all the more
strange because Villani—whose chronicle, one would think,
must have been well known and easily accessible—in his chapter
on Dante (ix. 136) gives a complete list of the principal works
of his illustrious fellow-citizen together with their titles.[1]

The source of this hitherto unnoticed account of Dante

historicorum ac poetarum assidua familiaritate conjunctus . Inter quos Dantem
florentinum poetam ob eius doctrine prestantiam magnis honoribus semper
prosequi voluit."

[1] Save in the case of the *Convivio*, which he describes as "uno commento
sopra quattordici sue canzoni morali ".

remains to be discovered. It has every appearance of being derived from some version quite independent of the half-dozen well-known biographies of the poet, and it is much to be hoped that the original may some day come to light.

In addition to the biographical notice of Dante discussed above, the interpolated chapters in the Venice editions of the *Speculum Historiale* contain an interesting, and in some respects novel, account of the murder of Henry, son of Richard, Earl of Cornwall, King of the Romans, by his cousin, Guy de Montfort, in a church at Viterbo. The deed is usually represented as having been premeditated on the part of Guy [1]; but according to this version Guy committed the murder under a sudden impulse on unexpectedly finding himself in close proximity to the prince. It appeared that Guy and his cousin both happened to attend mass in the same church at the same hour, and Guy, who entered the church shortly after the prince, being struck by the noble bearing of the latter, learned who he was, and without compunction stabbed him to death on the spot.

Venerat ad pontificem Heinricus, adolescens Richardi regis cornubie olim comitis tunc defuncti [2] filius, multa paterni olim regni [3] negocia apud sedem apostolicam tractaturus . Guido montiffortis et ipse adolescens cum Philippo rege Francorum eodem se contulit. Forte accidit utrumque ad rem divinam sancti Laurentii [4] ecclesiam, que Viterbii est celebris, eadem hora petere. Sed Guido posterior ingressus conspectu [5] liberali ac regia potius facie adolescentem caterva [6]

---

[1] See, for instance, the account of the murder in the *Grandes Chroniques de France :* "Avant que le roy de France venist à Viterbe ne que il fust en la ville entré, Henry le fils au roy d'Alemaigne vint en la cité. Guy de Montfort sot bien sa venue, si se hasta moult de savoir son repaire et où il estoit. En moult grant pensée estoit coment il le pourroit occire." (*L'istoire au Roy Phelipe III.*, chap. xii.)

[2] The chronicler is mistaken in supposing Richard, King of the Romans, to have been dead at the time of the murder. His death did not occur till more than a year after that event.

[3] The edition of 1494 reads *regna,* that of 1591 reads *regia ;* the emendation adopted in the text was suggested to me by Mr. Charles Plummer.

[4] This again is a mistake. The real scene of the murder was not the famous church of San Lorenzo, the present cathedral, but that of San Silvestro, which was comparatively little known. (See Pinzi, *Storia di Viterbo*, ii. 288.)

[5] The editions read *conspectum.*   [6] The edition of 1591 reads *eatervam.*

famulatus stipatum [conspexit].[1] Quodam ex suis indicante Richardi filium esse didicit a quo Symon pater in anglia per dolum fuerat interfectus, nullaque loci tentus reverentia incautum aggressus interfecit. Equitibus inde suis et pariter Philippi regis deducentibus ad ruffum [2] etrurie prefectum incolumis pervenit.

I have not succeeded in identifying the "nova chronica" which is mentioned by the interpolator as the source of his continuation of the *Speculum Historiale*. Doubtless, as we gather from the remark inserted in the edition of 1591, his information was derived from various quarters. Ptolemy of Lucca ("Ptolemeus lucensis") is quoted as an authority more than once, but it is evident that his chronicle was not systematically made use of, since the account given by him of the murder of "Henry of Almain" is quite different from the one I have reproduced above.

Three years after the publication of the above, in which I expressed the hope that the source of the interesting biographical notice of Dante which I discovered in the 1494 Venice edition of the *Speculum Historiale* might be traced, Professor Hermann Grauert published an article on the subject in the *Historisches Jahrbuch*. After a careful examination of the possible sources of the notice, Professor Grauert establishes the following conclusion :—

> Das Ergebnis unserer Untersuchung ist also kurz folgendes: Der von Toynbee der Venezianer Vincenziusausgabe von 1494 entnommene Artikel über Dante ist aus Hartmann Schedels Weltchronik wörtlich nachgedruckt und geht mit jedem Satze auf Jakob Philipp von Bergamos *Supplementum Chronicarum* zurück. Dieser hat die *Divina Commedia* und des Imolesen Benvenuto grossen Kommentar benützt, lehnt sich aber vornehmlich an Boccaccios *Genealogiae deorum libri XV* an, welches Werk er in seiner Chronik in dem Boccaccio-Artikel als ein schönes ausdrücklich rühmt.

A comparison of the passage printed in the supplement to the *Speculum Historiale* of 1494, with the extracts from Philip of Bergamo and Boccaccio, to which Professor Grauert refers, will, I think, prove beyond question that the latter has satisfactorily traced to its source the brief notice to which I originally drew attention.

---

[1] I supply *conspexit*, as some such verb is needed to complete the sense.

[2] Conte Rosso degli Aldobrandeschi, whose daughter Guy had married.

"Speculum" fragment.	*Philip of Bergamo.*	*Boccaccio, " Geneal. Deorum "* (xv. 6).
Dantes alugerius patria florentinus vates et poeta conspicuus ac theologorum precipue tempestate ista claruit. Vir in cives suos egregia nobilitate venerandus : qui licet ex longo exilio damnatus tenues illi fuissent substantie, semper tamen phisicis atque theologicis doctrinis imbutus vacavit studiis. unde cum florentia a factione nigra pulsus fuisset parisiense gymnasium accessit. et cum circa poeticam scientiam eruditissimus esset opus inclytum atque divinum lingua vernacula sub titulo comedie edidit. in quo omnium celestium terrestriumque ac infernorum profunda contemplatus singula queque historice allegorice tropologice ac anagogice descripsit. Aliud quoque de monarchia mundi. Hic cum ex gallicis regressus fuisset friderico arragonensi regi et domino cani grandi scaligero adhesit.	Dantes Aligerius patria Florentinus vates et poeta conspicuus ac theologorum certe precipuus tempestate istac claruit. Vir certe in cives suos egregia nobilitate venerandus atque verendus, qui licet ex longo exilio damnatus tenues illi fuissent substancie semper tamen phisicis atque theologicis doctrinis imbutus vacavit ctudiis. Unde cum Florentia a factione nigra pulsus fuisset ad ejus ingenii magnitudinem declarandam Parisium accessit, in qua gymnasium intrans adversus quoscunque circa quamcumque facultatem volentes disputare responsionibus aut positionibus suis responder se obtulit disputaturum. Et cum hic circa poeticam scientiam eruditissimus esset, opus inclitum atque divinum lingua vernacula sub titulo Comedie edidit, in quo omnium celestium terrestriumque ac infernorum profunda speculabiliter contemplatus singula queque historice, alegorice, tropologice ac anagogice descripsit, ubi se certe catholicum et divinum theologum se esse ostendit. Aliud etiam eloquentissimum opus omni sapientia plenum edidit, videlicet de Monarchia mundi titulo prenotatum, in quo probare nititur (licet male), ita Monarchiam in imperio Romano esse, ut nullam a pontifice Romano habeat dependentiam, sed a solo deo, nisi in pertinentibus ad forum animarum.[1] Hic cum ex Galliis regressus fuisset Federico Aragonensi regi et domino Canigrandi Scaligero Veronensium principi adhesit, cum quo fuit multa semper amicitia junctus quorum auxilio persepe et frustra conatus fuit in patriam redire.	Dantem Aligeri Florentinum poetam conspicuum tanquam precipuum aliquando invoco virum. Fuit enim inter cives suos egregia nobilitate verendus et quantumcumque tenues essent illi substantie et a cura familiari et postremo a longo exilio angeretur, semper tamen physicis atque theologicis doctrinis imbutus vacavit studiis et adhuc Julia fatetur Parisius : in eadem saepissime adversus quoscumque circa quamcumque facultatem volentes responsionibus aut positionibus suis objicere disputans intravit gymnasium. Fuit et hic circa poeticam eruditissimus nec quicquam illi lauream abstulit praeter exilium. . . . Qualis fuerit, inclytum ejus testatur opus, quod sub titulo Comoediae rithmis Florentino idiomate mirabili artificio scripsit, in quo profecto se non mithicum sed catholicum atque divinum potius ostendit esse theologum.
		(xiv. 11.)
		Dantes noster Federico Aragonensi Sicilidum regi et Cani de la Scala magnifico Veronensium domino grandi fuit amicitia junctus.

The interesting statement, which I discussed in my former article, that Dante attached himself to Frederick of Aragon, King of Sicily, it now appears, originated with Boccaccio. What historical foundation there may have been for this statement we have yet to learn.

[1] Philip of Bergamo, as Professor Grauert points out, was indebted for his account of the *Divina Commedia* to the commentary of Benvenuto da Imola, and for his account of the *De Monarchia* to that given in the *Chronicon* of the Florentine archbishop Antoninus.

HOMER IN DANTE AND IN BENVENUTO DA IMOLA [1]

ONE of the striking features of the commentary of Benvenuto da Imola on the *Divina Commedia* is the frequency of his references to Homer. During the Middle Ages, down to about the middle of the fourteenth century, the Homeric poems were practically unknown to Western Europe. The *Iliad* was accessible—the term is hardly appropriate—only in the miserable epitome in Latin hexameters, commonly known as *Pindarus Thebanus de bello Trojano*, in which the twenty-four books of the original are condensed into a little more than a thousand lines.[2] A few passages both from the *Iliad* and the *Odyssey*

[1] Reprinted, with additions, from *Romania*, xxix. 403-15.

[2] Actually 1,069 lines, which are distributed into eight books of very unequal length, the fifth and seventh books containing respectively only twenty-six and fifty-five lines each, while the eighth book contains 331 lines. This epitome, which was also known as *Homerus Latinus* or *Homerus de bello Trojano*, was several times printed in the fifteenth century, *viz.*, at Venice, without date, but probably 1477 (*Proctor* 4,264); at Parma, in 1492 (*Proctor* 6,866); at Paris, in 1499 (*Proctor* 8,327); it was also twice printed at Fano at the beginning of the sixteenth century, *viz.*, in 1505 and 1515. There are four MSS. of the work in the British Museum, *viz.*, Egerton 2,630; Harl. 2,582; Harl. 2,560; and Add. 15,601 (which is incomplete). *Cf.* Joly, *Benoît de Sainte-More et le Roman de Troie*, pp. 151-4. Owing to an acrostic (*Italicus*) in the first seven lines of the poem, which run as follows, some have thought that the author was Silius Italicus :—

> "*I*ram pande mihi Pelidae diva superbi
> *T*ristia qui miseris injecit funera graiis
> *A*tque animos fortes heroum tradidit Orco.
> *L*atrantumque dedit rostris volucrumque trahendos
> *I*llorum exangues inhumatis ossibus artus,
> *C*onficiebat enim summi sententia regis.
> *C*ontulerant ex quo, etc.".

The acrostic is not obvious at first sight, as the last two letters (*-us*) of *Italicus* appear to be wanting. The explanation is to be found in the consideration that

were known to mediæval writers through the medium of Cicero, and of the Latin translations of Aristotle, in certain of whose works Homer is quoted pretty frequently. Thus Dante, who quotes Homer six times (the *Iliad* four times and the *Odyssey* twice), got all his quotations save one from Aristotle, *viz.*, *Iliad*, xxiv. 258-259, quoted in the *Vita Nuova* (§ 2, ll. 51-52), the *Convivio* (iv. 20, l. 37), and the *De Monarchia* (ii. 3, l. 55), from *Ethics*, vii. 1; — *Iliad*, ii. 204, quoted in the *De Monarchia* (i. 10, ll. 29-31), from *Metaphysics*, xii. 10; — and *Odyssey*, ix. 114, quoted in the *De Monarchia* (i. 5, ll. 34-36), from *Politics*, i. 2; the remaining passage, *Odyssey*, i. 1, quoted in the *Vita Nuova* (§ 25, ll. 90-93), comes from the *Ars Poëtica* of Horace (ll. 141-142).[1]

Benvenuto da Imola, whose commentary on the *Divina Commedia* was completed in the year 1380 or perhaps a little later,[2] quotes the *Iliad* and *Odyssey* no less than twenty-eight times.[3] The question as to how he obtained his knowledge of

---

in MSS. the same sign ⁹ stands both for *-us* and for *con-*, so that the *con-* of the seventh line may, for the purposes of the acrostic, be read as equivalent to *-us*. The acrostic is still further obscured by the fact that some editions of the poem, instead of " *Con*tulerant " read " *Per*tulerant," which spoils the acrostic altogether (*Cf.* F. Novati, *Epistolario di Coluccio Salutati*, iii. 274, note 3).

[1] That there was no translation of Homer in Dante's days we know from what Dante himself says in the *Convivio*, in an interesting passage in which he declares the impossibility of translating poetry from one language into another, without losing all the beauty and music of the original : " Sappia ciascuno che nulla cosa per legame musaico armonizzata si può della sua loquela in altra trasmutare, senza rompere tutta sua dolcezza e armonia. E questa è la ragione per che Omero non si mutò di Greco in Latino, come l' altre scritture che avemo da loro." (i. 7, ll. 91-8.)

[2] The date of the completion of the final draft of Benvenuto's commentary is fixed at about the year 1380 from internal evidence, the latest reference to contemporary events being, as is usually alleged, to the destruction of the Castle of Sant' Angelo at Rome in 1379, during the contest between the partisans of Pope Urban VI. and those of his rival, Cardinal Robert of Geneva, who became anti-Pope under the title of Clement VII. (vol. ii. pp. 8, 53). See the article on " Benvenuto da Imola and his Commentary on the Divina Commedia " (pp. 217, 221, below).

[3] Vol. i. pp. 26, 77, 124, 159; vol. ii. pp. 70, 72, 77, 87, 88, 280, 282, 286-7, 288, 448, 467, 482 ; vol. iii. pp. 38, 128, 259, 330, 339, 356, 460, 501 ; vol. iv. pp. 162, 364. His references to Homer altogether, including every mention of him, are seventy in number.

them—he certainly was totally ignorant of Greek,[1] so that he could not have read them in the original—is one of considerable interest. In Benvenuto's day, thanks to the untiring exertions of Petrarch and Boccaccio, a complete Latin translation of both the *Iliad* and the *Odyssey* was in existence in Italy. The story of how this translation came to be made is as follows[2] :—

In the year 1353 Petrarch had made the acquaintance at Avignon of Nicolas Sigeros, who was present at the papal Court as the envoy of the Greek Emperor, for the purpose of negotiating the projected union of the Greek and Latin Churches. In the following year Petrarch, to his great delight, received from Constantinople, through the good offices of Sigeros, who had returned thither, a MS. of the Homeric poems in the original Greek. His letter of thanks for this munificent gift, dated from Milan, has been preserved among the *Epistolae de rebus familiaribus*. "You have sent me," he writes to Sigeros, "from the confines of Europe a gift than which nothing could be more worthy of the donor, more gratifying to the recipient, or more noble in itself. Some make presents of gold and silver, others of gems and precious stones, others again of jewellery and goldsmith's work. You have given me Homer, and, what makes it the more precious, Homer pure and undefiled in his own tongue. Would, however, that the donor could have accompanied his gift! for, alas! your Homer has no voice for me, or rather I have no

---

[1] That Benvenuto knew no Greek is plainly evident from the absurd etymologies with which his commentary abounds, *e.g.*, "Acheron dicitur *sine salute*, ab *a*, quod est *sine*, et *chere*, quod est *Salve*" (vol. i. p. 123) ; "hypocrita interpretatur *desuper auratus*" (vol. ii. p. 168) ; "Calliope a *chalo*, quod est *bonum*, et *phonos*, quod est *sonus*" (vol. iii. p. 7); "pedagogus a *pedos*, quod est *puer*, et *goge*, quod est *ducere*" (vol. iii. p. 323); "geomantia dicitur a *geos*, quod est *terra*, et *mantos*, *divinatio*" (vol. iii. p. 497) ; "ambrosia, quasi *aurosia : aurosis* enim graece dicitur *cibus* vel *esca*" (vol. iv. p. 89) ; "Eunoè, sic dictum ab *eu*, quod est *bonum*, et *noys*, quod est *mens*" (vol. iv. p. 179) ; "Crisostomo interpretatur *os aureum*, nam *grisos* graece, *aurum* latine, et *stomox*, id est *os*" (vol. v. p. 89) ; and so on. These etymologies, of course, are not Benvenuto's own, but are taken for the most part from the *Vocabularium* of Papias, the *Magnae Derivationes* of Uguccione da Pisa, or the *Catholicon* of Giovanni da Genova.

[2] *Cf.* Hortis, *Studj sulle opere latine del Boccaccio*, pp. 502 ff. ; and Nolhac, *Pétrarque et l'humanisme*, pp. 322-323, 339 ff.

ears for him! Yet the mere sight of him rejoices me, and I often embrace him and sigh over him, and tell him how I long to hear him speak."[1] Petrarch's ignorance of Greek, over which he laments in the above letter to Sigeros, caused Homer to remain a sealed book to him for several years after he had come into possession of this precious MS., during which time he eagerly sought for some means of procuring a Latin translation, whereby he might become acquainted with the contents of his treasure, even if only at second hand. At last the wished-for opportunity presented itself. In the winter of 1358-9 he made the acquaintance at Padua of a Calabrian Greek,[2]

[1] This letter, of which the above is a brief abstract, is printed by Fracassetti, *Francisci Petrarcae Epistolae de rebus familiaribus et variae*, vol. ii. pp. 472-475 (Lib. XVIII. Epist. ii.). *Cf.* Nolhac, *op cit.* p. 323.

[2] Leontius, in order to pass as a pure Greek, gave himself out to be a native, not of Calabria, but of Thessaly, and Boccaccio consequently, not unwilling doubtless to enhance the value of the instruction he received from Leontius, frequently refers to him in his *Comento sopra la Divina Commedia* as " Leon Tessalo " (*Lez.* XII. vol. i. p. 319; *Lez.* XIX. vol. i. p. 467; *Lez.* XXVI. vol. ii. p. 48; *Lez.* XXIX. vol. ii. p. 83), or " Leone Tessalo " (*Lez.* XVI. vol. i. p. 394). Similarly in his *De Genealogia Deorum* he calls him " Leontius Thessalus " (Lib. VII. cap. 41) or " Leontius Pilatus Thessalonicensis " (Lib. XV. cap. 6). Boccaccio, however, must have known that Leontius was a Calabrian, for Petrarch had told him as much in a letter which is printed among the *Epistolae rerum senilium:* " Leo noster vere Calaber, sed ut ipse vult Thessalus, quasi nobilius sit graecum esse quam italum; idem tamen ut apud nos graecus sit, apud illos puto italus, quo scilicet utrobique peregrina nobilitetur origine " (Lib. III. Epist. v. Basle ed. p. 775). Salvini, misled by Boccaccio's calling Leontius " Leon Tessalo," in a note to *Lez.* XXIX. of the *Comento* (vol. ii. p. 83), says: " Quest' era uno Greco di Tessalonica ". Leontius seems to have been a repulsive personage, and it is a proof of their devotion to letters, and their ardent thirst for a knowledge of Greek, that Petrarch and Boccaccio endured his presence as they did. Petrarch, in the above-quoted letter to Boccaccio, speaks of him as " magna bellua "; and Boccaccio, under whose roof at Florence he lived for three years while the translation of Homer was being made, describes him as follows in his list of the authorities utilised in the *De Genealogia Deorum:* " Leontium Pilatum Thessalonicensem virum, et ut ipse asserit, praedicti Barlaae auditorem, persaepe deduco; qui quidem aspectu horridus homo est, turpi facie, barba prolixa, et capilitio nigro, et meditatione occupatus assidua, moribus incultus, nec satis urbanus homo . . . eum legentem Homerum, et mecum singulari amicitia conversantem ferè tribus annis audivi . . . illum in propriam domum suscepi, et diu hospitem habui. (Lib. XV. capp. 6, 7.) *Cf.* Hortis, *op. cit.* pp. 502-503.

Leontius (or Leo) Pilatus by name, whom he employed to make translations of certain passages from his MS. of Homer. Shortly after (at the beginning of 1360), Leontius, at the invitation of Boccaccio, went to Florence, where he was domiciled under Boccaccio's own roof, and here, at the instigation of Petrarch and at his charges,[1] he made a complete translation into Latin prose of the *Iliad* and the *Odyssey*, from a MS. which appears to have been purchased by Boccaccio for the purpose.[2] This translation, which was begun in 1360, at last came into Petrarch's hands in 1367, and was at once copied, under his superintendence, into two volumes, which are still extant, with marginal annotations in the poet's own handwriting.[3] Leontius,

---

[1] Hortis (*op. cit.* p. 508) says: "La prima versione completa d'Omero che, nell' Italia risorta alla classica letteratura, abbia veduto la luce, fu fatta per eccitamento di Francesco Petrarca, per opera di Leonzio Pilato, a spese di Giovanni Boccacci". Nolhac, however (*op. cit.* p. 345, note 2), contests this, and says it ought to be "per eccitamento e a spese di F. P.". He reconciles the respective statements of Petrarch (*Sen.* III. Epist. v. Basle ed. p. 776) and Boccaccio (*Geneal. Deor.* xv. 7), as to the expenses borne by each in the making of the translation, as follows: "Boccace a acquis de ses deniers le premier manuscrit d'Homère qui soit venu à Florence ; Pétrarque a donné a Léon Pilate la rémunération nécessaire pour le travail exécuté à l'aide de ce manuscrit".

[2] See Nolhac, *op. cit.* pp. 341-342, where he shows that it could not have been from Petrarch's MS. that the translation at Florence was made. It may be noted here that Boccaccio certainly possessed a MS. of Homer of his own, for he expressly mentions the fact in a passage of the *De Genealogia Deorum*, where he justifies himself for having introduced Greek quotations into his work: "Seu hos, seu alios dicturos non dubito quoniam ostentationis gratia graeca carmina operi meo immiscuerim, quod satis adverto non ex charitatis fomite emissum, quinimo uredine livoris impii impellente ex adusti cordis intrinseco haec emittatur objectio, impie factum est. Ast ego profecto non commovebor opitulante Deo, sed more solito humili gradu in responsum ibo. Dico igitur, si nesciunt carpentes immeritum, insipidum est ex rivulis quaerere quod possis ex fonte percipere. *Erant Homeri libri mihi, et adhuc sunt,* ex quibus multa operi nostro accommoda sumpta sunt " [Lib. XV. cap. 7). It is obvious from the context that the " Homeri libri " referred to were not the Latin translation of Leontius Pilatus, but the original Greek.

[3] Hortis, *op. cit.* p. 507, note 4 ; Nolhac, *op. cit.* p. 247. These two volumes are now in the Bibliothèque Nationale (*Par.* 7,880. 1, 2). Hortis (*op. cit.* pp. 543-576) has printed the first book of the *Iliad* and the first book of the *Odyssey* from these MSS. Nolhac (p. 349) gives good reasons for supposing that Petrarch was engaged upon the annotations to Homer at the time of his death, which took place in his study at Arquà on 18th July, 1374.

meanwhile, who had gone to Constantinople in search of other
Greek MSS., had met with a somewhat singular death at the
beginning of this same year, having been struck by lightning
during a storm in the Adriatic on his voyage back to Venice.[1]

This Latin translation of Homer was largely utilised by
Boccaccio, both in his Latin works[2] and in his commentary on
the *Divina Commedia*[3]; and there can be very little doubt that
this same translation was, directly or indirectly, the source of
Benvenuto da Imola's knowledge of Homer.

Benvenuto quotes the *Iliad* eight times, and the *Odyssey*
twenty times[4]; but only in two instances does he quote with
sufficient precision to make it possible to identify the version
of which he made use. By means of these two instances, however, I am able to prove conclusively that this version is identical

---

[1] The manner of his death is related by Petrarch in a letter to Boccaccio:
" O male igitur, o pessime actum de Leone dicam nostro, cogit enim pietas
atque ingens miseratio, sine stomacho jam de illo loqui, de quo pridem multa
cum stomacho, mutatus est animus semper meus, cum illius hominis fortuna,
quae cum misera fuerit, nunc horrenda est. . . . O quid dicam, miserabilem,
terrificamque rem audies. Jamque Bosphorum atque Propontidem, jamque
Hellespontum, Aegaeumque, et Ionium, maria Graeca transiverat, jam Italicae
telluris, ut auguror, aspectu laetus dicerem, ni natura respueret: at equidem
minus moestus, Adriacum sulcabat aequor, dum repente, mutata coeli facie
pelagique, saeva tempestas exoritur, caeterisque ad sua munera effusis, Leo
miser, malo affixus inhaeserat. Malo (inquam) vere, malorumque ultimo, quod
per omne aevum multa perpesso, dura in finem fortuna servaverat. Horret
calamus infelicis amici casum promere; ad summam, inter multas et horrisonas
coeli minas, iratus Juppiter telum torsit, quo disjectae antennae, incensaque
carbasa in favillas abiere, et lambentibus malis flammis aethereis, cunctis stratis
ac territis, solus ille noster periit—hic Leonis finis " (*Sen.* VI. Epist. i. Basle
ed. pp. 806-807).

[2] Chiefly in the *De Genealogia Deorum.* See the list of passages given by
Hortis (*op. cit.* pp. 371-2), which is, however, far from being complete.

[3] In the *Comento* the *Iliad* is quoted three times (*Lez.* XVIII. vol. i. p. 462;
Lez. XIX. vol. i. p. 467; *Lez.* XXII. vol. i. p. 511), and the *Odyssey* three
times (*Lez.* I. vol. i. p. 97; *Lez.* VII. vol. i. p. 201; *Lez.* XVIII. vol. i.
p. 466).

[4] See above, p. 205, note 3. The *Iliad* references are, vol. i. p. 26 (*Il.* xviii.
109-110); vol. i. p. 77 (*Il.* i. 1); vol. ii. p. 87 (*Il.* ii. 123-128); vol. ii. p. 88 (*Il.* i.
68-73); vol. ii. p. 280 (*Il.* v. 4); vol. ii. p. 282 (*Il.* iv. 358); vol. iii. p. 259 (*Il.*
xxiv. 765-766); vol. iii. p. 339 (*Il.* ii. 690-691).

with that made by Leontius Pilatus. The first of these two quotations (vol. ii. p. 88)[1] comes from *Iliad*, i. 69-72 :—

Homerus, primo Ilyados, dicit quod Calcas erat augur avium optimus, qui sciebat omnia praesentia, praeterita, et futura, . . . per divinationem quam sibi dederat Apollo.

The rendering of Leontius is as follows :—

Calcas Thestorides augur avium valde optimus,
Qui sciebat queque presentia queque futura et preterita . . .
Quam divinationem hanc enim dedit sibi
Phebus Apollo.[2]

The second quotation (vol. iii. p. 128),[3] which is from *Odyssey*, xi. 298-300, is more convincing still, as it contains a mistranslation, which occurs also in the version of Leontius. Benvenuto, *à propos* of Castor and Pollux, says :—

Homerus, XI Odysseae, introducit Ulyssem dicentem :
Et Ledam vidi Tyndari uxorem,
Quae sub Tyndaro fortissimos[4] genuit filios,
Castorem equo bellicosum,[5] pugillo bonum Pollucem.

Leontius Pilatus renders :—

Et Ledam vidi Tyndarei uxorem,
Que sub Tyndareo fortes sensibus genuit filios,
Castorem equo bellicosum[5] et pugillo bonum
Polydeuchea.[6]

---

[1] In the comment on *Inferno*, xx. 110.

[2] From Hortis, *op. cit.* pp. 545-546. See above, p. 208, note 3. The passage in the original is:—

Κάλχας Θεστορίδης, οἰωνοπόλων ὀχ᾽ ἄριστος ·
ὃς ᾔδη τά τ᾽ ἔοντα, τά τ᾽ ἐσσόμενα, πρό τ᾽ ἐόντα, . . .
ἣν διὰ μαντοσύνην, τήν οἱ προε Φοῖβος Ἀπόλλων.

[3] In the comment on *Purgatorio*, iv. 61.

[4] *Fortissimos* is no doubt a copyist's error for *fortes sensibus* (= κρατερόφρονε), for which it might easily be mistaken in MSS., where *sensibus* would appear in the abbreviated form.

[5] *Equo bellicosum* is meant to represent the Greek ἱππόδαμον, of which, of course, it is a misrendering, the Greek word meaning "tamer of steeds".

[6] I am indebted to the kindness of M. Gaston Raynaud of the Bibliothèque Nationale for the transcript of this passage from MS. lat. 7,880, 2 (fol. 83 ro), which, as has already been mentioned, is one of the two identical volumés into which the version of Leontius Pilatus was copied for Petrarch, and which

Of Benvenuto's twenty quotations from the *Odyssey* no less than sixteen are from the eleventh book. The eleventh book of the *Odyssey*, of course, is that which contains the description of Ulysses' visit to Hades; and this may perhaps be the reason why Benvenuto quotes almost exclusively from that book. But another explanation is possible. While the Latin translation of Homer by Leontius Pilatus was in progress at Florence, under Boccaccio's roof, Petrarch became impatient, and wrote to Boccaccio to send him at least that portion of the *Odyssey* which describes the adventures of Ulysses in the nether world.[1] In compliance with this request Boccaccio copied out the desired extract, and despatched it separately to Petrarch.[2] Now it is by no means improbable that, when later he became possessed of the whole of the Latin version of Homer, Petrarch may have placed this fragment from the eleventh book of the *Odyssey* at the disposal of Benvenuto, in whose commentary on the *Commedia* he took a warm interest, if we are to believe the evidence of Benvenuto himself. Writing to Petrarch in the spring of 1374, only a few weeks before the old poet was found dead among his books at Arquà—the death he had longed for,[3]—Benvenuto says: "You must know that last year I put the finishing touch to my commentary on Dante, about which you used so often to enquire. I will send you a copy of it as soon as I can find a safe messenger."[4] From this reference to the

contain his own annotations. See above, p. 208. The passage in the original is:—

Καὶ Λήδην εἶδον, τὴν Τυνδαρέου παράκοιτιν,
ἥ ῥ 'ὑπὸ Τυνδαρέῳ κρατερόφρονε γείνατο παῖδε,
Κάστορά θ' ἱππόδαμον καὶ πὺξ ἀγαθὸν Πολυδεύκεα.

[1] "Partem illam Odysseae, qua Ulixes it ad inferos . . . quam primum potes . . . utcumque tuis digitis exaratam" (*Sen.* iii. Epist. v. *ad fin.*, Basle ed. p. 776). *Cf.* Nolhac, *op. cit.* pp. 343-344.

[2] *Cf.* Nolhac, *op. cit.* p. 345.

[3] *Cf. Fam. praef.*, *ad fin.*: "Scribendi mihi vivendique unus (ut auguror) finis erit". (Fracassetti, i. 25-26); *Sen.* xvi. Epist. ii. (Basle ed., p. 968, *ad fin.*): "me . . . opto ut legentem aut scribentem . . . mors inveniat". *Cf.* Nolhac, *op. cit.* pp. 74, 332 (note 1), 349.

[4] "Scias me anno praeterito extremam manum commentariis meis, quae olim tanto opere efflagitasti, in Dantem praeceptorem meum imposuisse." Of

commentary it is obvious that Petrarch was not only acquainted with the fact that Benvenuto was engaged upon it, but that he also encouraged him in his task.   That Benvenuto da Imola was on terms of friendship, if not of intimacy, with Petrarch is well known.   One of the last letters written by Petrarch before his death, if not actually the last, was addressed to Benvenuto from Padua in February, 1374, in response to an enquiry from the latter as to whether poetry ought to be included among the liberal arts[1]; and it was in reply to this epistle, to which allusion is twice made in his commentary on the *Commedia*,[2] that Benvenuto wrote the letter in which the passage quoted above occurs.   Further, from a reference of Benvenuto's to Petrarch's personal habits,[3] it is evident that he had, on one occasion at least, lived under the same roof with him, either as his guest, or as his host, or at the house of a common friend. There is nothing, therefore, inherently improbable in the supposition that Petrarch supplied Benvenuto with his duplicate of the Latin version of the eleventh book of the *Odyssey*, by way of helping him in his *magnum opus* upon Dante.

Benvenuto's references to the *Odyssey*, other than to the eleventh book, are, as has been noted, four in number.   The opening line of the first book is quoted (vol. i. p. 77) from the

course Benvenuto can here only be referring to the completion of the first draft of his commentary, for he certainly made subsequent additions to it, as is evident from the reference, for instance, to the destruction of the Castle of Sant' Angelo at Rome in 1379 (vol. ii. pp. 8, 53).   See above, p. 205, note 2.   The authenticity of this letter of Benvenuto to Petrarch (of which only a portion has been preserved) has been questioned, but, as it appears, on insufficient grounds. (See Lacaita, *Benevenuti de Rambaldis de Imola Comentum super Dantis Aldigherii Comoediam*, vol. i. pp. xxviij-xxx; and Rossi-Casè, *Di Maestro Benvenuto da Imola, commentatore dantesco*, pp. 75 ff.; and *Ancora di Maestro Benvenuto*, p. 14.   For the other side of the question see articles by Novati in *Giornale Storico della Letteratura Italiana*, xiv. 258 ff.; xvii. 93.)

[1] *Sen.* xiv. Epist. xi. Basle ed. pp. 941-942.   A corrected text of this letter is printed by Rossi-Casè, *op. cit.* pp. 72-74.

[2] Vol. i. p. 10; vol. iv. p. 230.   It may be noted here that Benvenuto mentions Petrarch, whom he usually describes as " novissimus poëta Petrarcha," no less than thirty times in his commentary.

[3] Vol. i. p. 224.

Ars Poëtica of Horace—"Dic mihi, Musa, virum" (l. 141)—a passage which Petrarch, oddly enough, thought was a relic of a lost translation of Homer by Cicero.[1] From the tenth book are taken the accounts of Circe (vol. ii. pp. 286-287), and of the wallet of winds given to Ulysses by Aeolus (vol. iv. p. 162); and from the twelfth book the account of the shipwreck of Ulysses in the straits of Messina (vol. ii. p. 288).[2]

Of Benvenuto's quotations from the *Iliad*, one, that of the opening line of the first book (vol. i. p. 77): "Iram pande mihi Dea," appears to be cited (inaccurately, doubtless from memory) from the metrical epitome known as *Pindarus Thebanus de bello Trojano* already mentioned,[3] which begins

Iram pande mihi Pelidae diva superbi.

At any rate it does not come from the version of Leontius Pilatus, whose rendering of the first line of the *Iliad* is

Iram cane dea Pellidis Achillis.[4]

Iliad, xviii. 109-110 is quoted (vol. i. p. 26) from Aristotle[5]: "Ira est tam delectabilis quod Aristoteles refert Homerum dixisse quod ira est dulcior melle distillante. . ֻ . . Hoc autem scribit Homerus libro suae Iliados".

---

[1] "Translationem illam veterem Ciceronis opus, quantum intelligere est, cujus principium Arti Poëticae Flaccus inseruit, latinitati perditam, ut multa alia, et doleo et indignor". (*Var.* xxv. Fracassetti, iii. 369.)

[2] It is not impossible that Benvenuto may have derived these three accounts at second hand from the *De Genealogia Deorum* of Boccaccio, with which he was certainly acquainted, for on one occasion at least he refers to it by name: "Johannes Boccacius, verius bucca aurea, venerabilis praeceptor meus, . . . ibi [*sc.* Certaldo] pulcra opera edidit; praecipue edidit unum librum magnum et utilem ad intelligentiam poetarum, *de Genealogiis Deorum*". (vol. v. p. 164.) Boccaccio's account of Circe is in Lib. iv. cap. 14, and Lib. xi. cap. 40; that of the shipwreck of Ulysses in Lib. xi. cap. 40; and that of Ulysses and Aeolus in Lib. iii. cap. 20. In one instance, however (that of Circe), Benvenuto's account is somewhat fuller than that of Boccaccio.

[3] See above, p. 204.   [4] From Hortis, *op. cit.* p. 543.

[5] The passage occurs at the beginning of chap. ii. of the second book of the *De Rhetorica*. Aristotle, as a matter of fact, does not mention Homer, but merely gives the quotation with the observation καλῶς εἴρηται ("praeclare dictum est "). Benvenuto doubtless got the reference to Homer from a marginal gloss.

Benvenuto's other quotations from the *Iliad* are (vol. ii. p. 88) from *Iliad*, i. 69-72, which has already been mentioned[1]; (vol. ii. p. 87) from *Iliad*, ii. 123-128; (vol. iii. p. 339) from *Iliad*, ii. 690-691; (vol. ii. p. 282) from *Iliad*, iv. 358; (vol. ii. p. 280) from *Iliad*, v. 4; (vol. iii. p. 259) from *Iliad*, xxiv. 765-766. This last passage, as printed in Lacaita's edition of Benvenuto's commentary, refers to the *twenty-third* book of the *Iliad*, but this is doubtless due, either to a misprint, or to a mistake on the part of the copyists (xxiii instead of xxiiii), for the reference is certainly to the twenty-fourth book.[2]

In what way Benvenuto da Imola obtained access to the Latin version of Homer made by Leontius Pilatus remains a matter of conjecture. The eleventh book of the *Odyssey*, from which sixteen out of Benvenuto's twenty-eight quotations from Homer are taken, may very likely, as I have shown above, have been supplied to him by Petrarch. Complete MSS. of Leontius' version cannot have been common in Benvenuto's day—nor indeed do they appear to have been common at any time, for only two copies apparently are known at the present day, *viz.*, the *Iliad* and *Odyssey*, which formerly belonged to Petrarch,

---

[1] See above, p. 210.

[2] Benvenuto says: "Debes scire quod tempore mortis Hectoris Helena jam steteret in Troia per spatium viginti annorum, ut scribit Homerus xxiii (corr. xxiiii) Iliados".

That the passage Benvenuto had in mind comes from the twenty-fourth book is proved by the fact that Boccaccio in his *Comento* refers to the same passage, which he expressly states to be in the last book of the *Iliad*. He says (on *Inferno*, v. 64-65): "la quale lunga dimension di tempo fu per ispazio di venti anni, cioè dal dì che Elena fu rapita, al dì che a Menelao fu restituita; perciocchè tanto stette Elena in Troia, e alquanto più, siccome Omero nell' ultimo libro della sua Iliade dimostra laddove lei piangendo sopra il morto corpo di Ettore, fa dire quasi queste parole, che essendo ella stata venti anni appo Priamo e i figliuoli, mai Ettore non le avea detta una ingiuriosa parola". (*Lez.* xviii. vol. i. p. 462.) The passage referred to in the *Iliad* is the following (xxiv. 765-67):—

Ἤδη γὰρ νῦν μοι τόδ᾽ ἐεικοστὸν ἔτος ἐστίν,
ἐξ οὗ κεῖθεν ἔβην, καὶ ἐμῆς ἀπελήλυθα πάτρης·
ἀλλ᾽ οὔπω σεῦ ἄκουσα κακὸν ἔπος, οὐδ᾽ ἀσύφηλον.

It is not unlikely that Benvenuto took his reference to this passage at second hand from the *Comento* of Boccaccio.

now in the Bibliothèque Nationale (MS. lat. 7,880, 1, 2), and the *Iliad* in the Magliabechiana, and *Odyssey* in the Laurenziana at Florence.[1]   We may suppose, therefore, that for his other references, in so far as they were not taken at second hand from the *Comento*[2] or the *De Genealogia Deorum*[3] of Boccaccio, Benvenuto was indebted either to the oral instruction of " venerabilis praeceptor meus Boccaccius de Certaldo,"[4] or to friendly communications on the part of " Petrarcha noster,"[5] who alone, so far as we know, were in possession of copies of the translation by Leontius Pilatus.

[1] See Hortis, *op. cit.* pp. 508, 543, 562.   We find Coluccio Salutati in a letter to Francesco Bruni, dated 15th July, 1867 (ed. Novati, i. 267) referring to Homer for an account of the Sirens, but his description has every appearance of having been taken from the *De Genealogia Deorum* of Boccaccio (vii. 20).   From a letter of Salutati to Antonio Loschi, dated 21st July, 1392 (ed. Novati, ii. 354), it appears that the latter, who had in mind to make a metrical version of the *Iliad*, had read, and perhaps transcribed the translation of Leontius Pilatus, which Salutati refers to as " Homerice translationem Iliados, horridam et incultam ".   In another letter to the same correspondent, dated 29th September, 1392 (ed. Novati, ii. 398), Salutati refers to the *Iliad* and *Odyssey* in a way which gives the impression that he had read portions at least of both poems.   To judge, however, from the infrequency of his references to Homer, Salutati's acquaintance with the *Iliad* and *Odyssey* cannot have been very extensive. Besides the references already mentioned, I have only noted the following: ed. Novati, iii. 269, 274 (where the first line of the so-called Pindarus Thebanus is quoted), 389, 491, 545, 548; none of these is to the *Odyssey*.

[2] See above, p. 209, note 3.   [3] See above, p. 209, note 2 ; p. 213, note 2.

[4] *Benevenuti Comentum*, vol. i. p. 79; v. pp. 145, 164, 301.   Benvenuto several times in his commentary mentions that he derived information from Boccaccio (see, for instance, vol. i. pp. 34, 461; vol. v. p. 301); and we know from his own statement (vol. v. p. 145 : " dum audirem venerabilem praeceptorem meum Boccaccium de Certaldo legentem istum nobilem poetam in ecclesia sancti Stephani ") that he was present during a portion at least of Boccaccio's lectures on the *Divina Commedia* at Florence.   (See below, pp. 222-223.)

[5] *Benevenuti Comentum*, vol. iii. p. 145.

BENVENUTO DA IMOLA AND HIS COMMENTARY ON THE *DIVINA COMMEDIA* [1]

BENVENUTO RAMBALDI, the author of what is perhaps the most valuable commentary we possess on the *Divina Commedia*, was born at Imola between 1336 and 1340, less than twenty years after the death of Dante. He was thus the junior of his two famous contemporaries, Petrarch and Boccaccio, with both of whom he was on terms of friendship, if not of intimacy, by some thirty-five and twenty-six years respectively. The date of his death, which was long uncertain, has recently been established by the publication of a letter in which it is alluded to as having just taken place. This letter, which was written from Padua on 17th June, 1390, by Pier Paolo Vergerio, the biographer of Petrarch, to Ugo da Ferrara, runs as follows :—

I heard yesterday that that bright star of eloquence, Benvenuto of Imola, has suffered eclipse ; yet in such wise as to lose none of his proper light, nay, rather he must now shine with increased brilliancy, if we are to believe that merit in this life is rewarded after death. From us, however, he is hidden. On his account I rejoice, but on our own I lament, for we are deprived of a great light. There was a report that he had been busy with a work on the book of Valerius Maximus, which was like to surpass all that previous writers had attempted. It is not known how far this work was carried, but it is supposed that he did not complete it. If you have any information on this subject, write to me, and give such consolation as you can to your sorrowing friend. [2]

It is assumed from this letter that Benvenuto died at Ferrara ; but no record of his burial has been found, nor any trace of a

---

[1] Reprinted, with additions and corrections, from *An English Miscellany : presented to Dr. Furnivall in honour of his seventy-fifth birthday* (Oxford, 1901). I am indebted to the kindness of Professor Charles Eliot Norton for the correction of sundry inaccuracies in the article as originally printed.

[2] See Rossi-Casè, *Di Maestro Benvenuto da Imola* (Pergola, 1889), p. 96, note 1.

monument to him, such as we should naturally expect to have
been erected to so distinguished a citizen.

The year 1380 was formerly assigned as the date of Benvenuto's death, owing to the alleged absence of any allusion in
the Commentary (which was certainly supplemented from time
to time) to events subsequent to 1379; and to the fact that in
the *Libellus Augustalis*, which was generally held to have been
the latest of his writings, a mention of the young Emperor
Wenceslaus, who succeeded his father in 1378, is accompanied
by the parenthetical remark: "quid facturus sit ignoro". This
remark plainly points to the comparatively recent accession of
the emperor; and it was urged that if Benvenuto had survived
to know of the excesses committed by Wenceslaus, which gained
him the nicknames of the Cruel and the Toper, he would not
have neglected this opportunity of making some pointed allusion
to them. This argument can now, of course, only be used to
fix the date of the *Libellus*. As regards, however, the internal
evidence to be derived from the Commentary, it may be observed
that there is in that work what appears to be an undoubted
allusion to the Emperor Wenceslaus, which has escaped the
notice of Benvenuto's biographers. This allusion occurs in the
comment on the word *Cesare* in the first canto of the *Paradiso*,
line 29,[1] where, after speaking of the triumphs of the old Roman
emperors, Benvenuto adds, by way of contrast, that "our present
emperor devotes himself to the cult of Father Bacchus" ("Noster
vero imperator Liberum patrem colit"). The reference here to
the intemperate habits of Wenceslaus appears unmistakable;
and unless it be the fact, which seems unlikely, that the young
Wenceslaus, who at first gave promise of being an excellent
sovereign, was already notorious for wine-bibbing within two
years of his accession, it follows that the *terminus ad quem* of
the Commentary should be advanced somewhat beyond the year
1380.[2] The point of this remark of Benvenuto's was evidently

---

[1] *Benevenuti de Rambaldis de Imola Comentum super Dantis Aldigherii
Comoediam* (ed. J. F. Lacaita), vol. iv. p. 305.

[2] Since the above was written I have found that in his *Libellus Augustalis*,
which was certainly composed within a year or two of the accession of Wences-

lost upon the editor of the Commentary, for he has made non-sense of the passage by printing *liberum patrem* instead of *Liberum patrem*.

The main facts of Benvenuto's life, so far as it has been possible to trace them, appear to be as follows.[1] His boyhood was passed under his father's roof at Imola, until such time as he was of age to go to the neighbouring University of Bologna. It is probable that he made no long stay at Bologna, owing to the disturbed condition of the university, which was at that time constantly embroiled with the Papal authority, but transferred himself to Florence, where he spent the period between 1357 and 1360. It was no doubt at this time that Benvenuto made the acquaintance of Boccaccio ; and there can be little question that the latter, directly or indirectly, assisted him in his studies, for he no less than four times in his Commentary[2] refers to Boccaccio as "venerabilis praeceptor meus". It must have been during these years, too, that Benvenuto gained that intimate knowledge of Florence and Florentine ways which is displayed at every turn in his Commentary.

In 1361, or 1362 at the latest, he was again at Bologna, at that time under the governorship of the Spanish Cardinal Albornoz, at whose request he wrote a compendium of Roman history (under the title of *Rōmuleon*), as he himself tells us in the introductory chapter of that work. The next two or three years appear to have been spent partly in Imola, partly in Bologna, where in 1364 he had the opportunity of making the acquaintance of Petrarch, who has left a record in two of his letters[3] of his visit to Bologna in that year. Not long before this date Benvenuto's father, Compagno, who was a notary and

---

laus, Benvenuto uses a similar expression of the Emperor Charles IV. (the father and predecessor of Wenceslaus), whom he describes as "Baccho im-molans "—a reproach which appears to have been levelled at that emperor by Boccaccio also (see Cochin, *Études Italiennes*, p. 110). It is not so certain, therefore, as appeared at first sight, that the reference in the Commentary is to Wenceslaus.

[1] *Cf.* Rossi-Casè, *op. cit.*   [2] I. 79 ; V. 145, 164,. 301.

[3] *Fam.* v. 16 ; *Sen.* x. 5.

lecturer on law, and who is mentioned in the Commentary[1] as having been a neighbour of the notorious Cianghella della Tosa, had died at Imola. It is evident that by this time Benvenuto himself was a person of some importance in his native city, for in the spring of 1365 he was appointed one of the five orators who were dispatched to Avignon by the Anziani of Imola to bespeak the good offices of Pope Urban V.

While on this mission at the Papal Court at Avignon he met his future patron, Nicholas II. of Este, and once more found himself in the company of Boccaccio, who was present, as the representative of Florence, among the deputies sent from various parts of Italy to invite the Pope to abandon France and return to Rome. Several reminiscences of Benvenuto's stay at Avignon occur in the Commentary. For instance, in a note on the word *ponticelli*[2] in the eighteenth canto of the *Inferno*, l. 15, he takes occasion to mention the stone bridges over the Arno and Tiber at Florence and Rome, and couples with them the bridge over the Rhône at Avignon, which had already at that date been standing for nearly two hundred years, but of which only four arches now remain. In another passage[3] (on *Inferno*, iii. 55-57) he describes an immense crowd of tramps and beggars whom he once saw besieging the gates of the almonry at Avignon. It is in connection with Avignon too that he indulges in one of his fiercest outbursts against the corruption of the Papal Court. In his comment[4] on the passage in the nineteenth canto of the *Inferno* (ll. 90-114), where Dante rebukes the Bishops of Rome for their simony and avarice, and denounces the unholy traffic between the Scarlet Woman and the Kings of Christendom, Benvenuto does not hesitate to identify Avignon with Babylon, as Petrarch had done before him, to whose well-known sonnet[5] (beginning "Dell' empia Babilonia") he pointedly refers :—

"Our most recent poet Petrarch," he says, "takes that great Babylon to mean Avignon, the new Babylon in France, which may well be described as a great Babylon, not so much by reason of the circumference of her walls, as by

[1] V. 151.   [2] II. 4.   [3] I. 116.   [4] II. 59.
[5] *Cf.* also Petrarch's *Epist. sine titulo.*

reason of the presumption of her people. Verily is Avignon the mother of
fornication, and lust, and drunkenness, full of abomination and of all filthiness,
and seated upon the rushing waters of the Rhône, the Durance, and the Sorgue.
And verily are her prelates like the Scarlet Woman, arrayed with purple and
gold and silver and precious stones, and drunken with the blood of the martyrs,
and of Christ."

Benvenuto had had his own experience of the shameless corruption of the Papal officials at Avignon, as he relates in his
comment[1] on the trick played by Malacoda upon Dante and
Virgil as to their route in Malebolge :—

"God is my witness," he exclaims, "that a trick of this same sort was
played upon myself in the Papal Court at Avignon. I had a certain affair in
the hands of the chief treasurer of Urban V., who pretended that he was
convinced of the justice of my cause, and was exceedingly anxious to help me.
But nevertheless he kept putting me off from day to day, protesting all the time
that I was certain to succeed in the end. At last, however, when he found that
I did not make him the present he expected, he began to look askance at me—
and to tell the truth he did squint horribly, to say nothing of his moral obliquity
—and finally I was left in the lurch. And so he behaved like the devil Malacoda,
for he wanted to send me on a road which it was not in the nature of things I
should follow."

While at Avignon, Benvenuto appears to have availed himself of the opportunity to make a pilgrimage to Vaucluse,[2] which
had been abandoned by Petrarch some twelve years before.[3] On
the same occasion he visited the neighbouring cities of Arles
and Orange, certain details of which he describes from personal
observation.[4] He was present, he tells us,[5] at Arles when the
Emperor Charles IV. was crowned there, an event which took
place on 4th June, 1365. His stay in Provence probably lasted
till the autumn of 1367, when he is supposed to have returned
to Italy in the train of Urban V., who went first to Viterbo and
then to Rome. Benvenuto certainly visited Rome at one period
of his life, as is evident from several passages in his Commentary.
It may have been either on this occasion, or seventeen years
earlier at the time of the Second Jubilee in 1350, to which he
refers[6] in terms which seem to imply that he was present, à
propos of Dante's mention of the Jubilee[7] instituted by Boni-

[1] I. 118.   [2] IV. 488.   [3] In 1353.   [4] I. 326; V. 214.
        [5] I. 326.   [6] II. 6.   [7] Inf. xviii. 29.

face VIII. Nothing is known for certain of his whereabouts
during the next five years (1368-1373), save that he was not for
any length of time in his native city.   Upon his return to Italy
from his mission at Avignon, which we may gather was a failure,
he seems to have found that a change unfavourable to himself
had taken place in the affairs of Imola.   At any rate there is
no record of his holding any further public office there, and
such evidence as is available goes to prove that he never again
from this date made any considerable stay in that city.   Certain
expressions in his Commentary, such as his qualification of
Dante's apostrophe to the men of Romagna: "O Romagnuoli
tornati in bastardi,"[1] as by no means forcible enough—" Nimis
curialiter loquitur iste : immo debuisset dixisse, in spurios,
immo in mulos, specie permutata "[2]—and his comparison of
himself to Dante, as having like him suffered the miseries of
exile and poverty through the malignity of his fellow men,[3]
have been taken to imply that he was a victim to political
animosity.

   It is probable that during a part at least of this period
Benvenuto was occupied in teaching at Bologna, and in the
private exposition of the *Divina Commedia*.   The first draft
at any rate of his *magnum opus*, the Commentary on the *Commedia*, was completed in the year 1373, for in a letter to
Petrarch, written in the spring of the following year, a fragment of which is extant, he states the fact in so many
words.[4]

   " You must know," he writes, "that last year I put the finishing touch
to my Commentary on Dante, about which you used so often to inquire.   I will
send you a copy of it as soon as I can find a safe messenger." [5]

   This passage is interesting, not only as giving a positive
date for the completion of the first draft of the Commentary,

---

[1] *Purg*. xiv. 99.   [2] III. 389-390.   [3] III. 370.

[4] See Rossi-Casè, *op. cit.* p. 75.   The authenticity of this letter has been
contested by some critics (see above, p. 211, note 4).

[5] It is probable that Petrarch never saw the Commentary, for he died (18th
July, 1374) not many weeks after this letter was written.

but also as showing that Benvenuto received encouragement from the old poet in his task.

As a proof of Benvenuto's reverence for Petrarch it may be mentioned here that it was largely owing to his exertions that we are indebted for the preservation of Petrarch's Latin poem *Africa*, upon which the poet confidently based his hopes of immortality, but which had been left unfinished. Petrarch's son-in-law, Francescuolo da Brossano, contemplated either burning the incomplete MS., or, what might have proved an even worse fate, handing it over to be revised and corrected by other hands before publication. Benvenuto was strongly opposed to any such act of vandalism, and wrote not only to Francescuolo himself, but also to Boccaccio, Coluccio Salutati, and others, to urge the preservation of the poem as it had been left by the author. His letters have been lost, but several of those written to him on the subject are extant, among them two from Coluccio Salutati,[1] the tone of which is evidence of the high esteem in which Benvenuto was held by his brother men of letters.

Some time between the autumn of 1373 and the summer of 1374 Benvenuto was in Florence, where he attended Boccaccio's lectures upon the *Divina Commedia*, as he himself informs us in his comment[2] on *Paradiso*, xv. 97-98. Dante in this passage refers to the old Benedictine monastery, known as the Badia, from whose chimes, he says, in the days of Cacciaguida, Florence used to take her time. Benvenuto remarks :—

In the inner circle of Florence is the abbey of the Benedictine monks, whose church is called Santo Stefano; where the chimes used to tell the hour more regularly than in any other church in the city. At the present time, however, it is sadly neglected and out of repair, as I noticed while I was attending the lectures of my revered master, Boccaccio of Certaldo, upon the *Divina Commedia*, which he delivered in this same church.

Boccaccio began his course on 23rd October, 1373, and continued to lecture until the spring of 1375, when he was compelled by illness to break off abruptly and retire to Certaldo, where he died in the following December. Benvenuto cannot have at-

[1] See F. Novati, *Epistolario di Coluccio Salutati*, vol. i. pp. 198-204.
[2] V. 145.

tended the whole course, for it appears from the letters of
Coluccio Salutati that he was not in Florence from July, 1374,
to July, 1375.   In this latter year he was back in Bologna, and
was himself lecturing upon the *Divina Commedia*, as he records
in his Commentary[1]; and we know from the same source[2] that
he spent altogether ten years in that city.   Benvenuto's lectures
at Bologna, like those of Boccaccio at Florence, were delivered
in an official capacity, he having been appointed to fill the Dante
chair, which the Bolognese, following the example of the Florentines, founded in 1375.   It is certain, however, that his Commentary, unlike that of Boccaccio, was not composed in the first
instance for the purposes of this lectureship, for we have already
seen[3] that the first draft of it was completed in 1373, two years
before the Bologna chair was instituted.

   In 1377 Benvenuto retired from Bologna to Ferrara, where
he resided under the protection of the Marquis Niccolò II. of
Este[4]; and it was doubtless here that he put the last touches to
his Commentary, the final draft of which he formally dedicated
to the Marquis.   From a letter addressed to him here by Coluccio Salutati[5] under date 6th April, 1379, we learn that Benvenuto was engaged in teaching at Ferrara, and also that by
this time he had been for some years married, and had a family
of children growing up, which caused him some anxiety.   Here
too he wrote his most important other works, namely the
Commentaries on Lucan's *Pharsalia* (1378), on Seneca's tragedies,
and on Valerius Maximus (which was finished in 1388), as well
as the *Libellus Augustalis* (probably 1386), the two last, like the
Commentary on the *Commedia*, being dedicated to his patron
Niccolò; and at Ferrara, in all probability, he ended his days in
1390.   Besides the above works, and the *Romuleon* already
mentioned[6] as having been written at Bologna between 1361
and 1362, Benvenuto also wrote a Commentary on the Latin
Eclogues of Petrarch, which was completed before 1374, as we
know from the same letter in which he refers to the completion
of the first draft of his Commentary on Dante.

[1] I. 523.   [2] II. 16.   [3] See above, p. 221.
[4] d. 1388.   [5] *Epistolario*, i. 313-21.   [6] See above, p. 218.

As might be expected, we find frequent allusions to Bologna in the Commentary, and to Benvenuto's own experiences while he was resident there.   He loses no opportunity of bringing in a compliment, when he can honestly do so, to the illustrious city whose guest he was, and to its famous University.   " Dicitur Bononia," he says on one occasion,[1] with his characteristic fondness for punning etymologies, " quasi bona per omnia "; and he quotes in confirmation the old line:—

> Omnibus est linguis laudanda Bononia pinguis.

On another occasion[2] he speaks of the city as " mater studii, et nutrix omnium scientiarum "; and again,[3] " est Bononia nidus philosophorum, et mater legum, omniumque bonorum fertilis, humanitatis piissima nutrix ".   The inhabitants he describes[4] as of courteous manners and kindly temperament, and as being distinguished above the rest of Italy for their hospitality and geniality to strangers, whom they delight to honour.   " In proof of this," he adds, " I can quote my own experience, for I spent ten years among them."   He takes occasion also to pay a compliment to the women, mindful perhaps that the lady professor was a not unknown element in Bolognese traditions.   On the other hand he does not hesitate to be equally outspoken[5] with regard to their vices, which he condemns in no measured terms. He was especially shocked[6] at the hideous immorality which at one time during his residence was prevalent to a terrible extent among the students.   It is a proof of his moral courage that he did not shrink from reporting the matter to the Papal Legate in Bologna, who caused inquiries to be made, and by vigorous measures stamped out the iniquity.   By his action on this occasion[7] Benvenuto not only incurred very considerable odium, but he ran a grave personal risk, as he himself was well aware.   In fact there is little doubt that his departure from Bologna in 1377 was directly due to this cause.   He several times refers to his experiences as lecturer, one of which is utilised[8] as an illustration of Dante's description of the wrathful, who are repre-

[1] II. 15.   [2] II. 187.   [3] III. 390.   [4] II. 17.
[5] II. 15.   [6] I. 523.   [7] I. 524.   [8] I. 269.

sented as tearing and pounding and biting each other, "exactly," says Benvenuto, "as I once saw two of my students doing; for not content with using their fists and nails, they actually tore each other with their teeth into the bargain". Another illustration from his lectures, which he evidently recalls with a certain satisfaction, he makes use of in his comment[1] on *Purgatorio*, xv. 55-57, where Dante says that the greater the number of those who enjoy the same good, the greater the enjoyment of each in particular.

"That one and the same good," explains Benvenuto, "is not diminished by the participation of many is evident, for my single voice is conveyed to the ears of a multitude of students, and diffuses my teaching into the minds of a numerous audience, to different degrees, of course, according to their capacities; and yet it is not diminished in me, but is increased, as I remember I used to say when I was lecturing on Dante at Bologna."

In another passage[2] he refers to his difficulty at times in arriving at Dante's exact meaning, which was often a trouble to him, he says, during these same lectures. He now and then indulges in a sly hit at the Bolognese, as, for instance, when he relates an anecdote[3] reflecting on the reputation of their great legal luminary, Accursius,—how Benincasa of Arezzo, himself a distinguished jurist, being interrogated on a point of law by some Bolognese students, referred them contemptuously to their own Accursius, who he said had befouled the whole *corpus iuris*.

Many details of interest with regard to the old city of Bologna and its surroundings are supplied in the Commentary, and for the most part are here recorded for the first time, Jacopo della Lana, the Bolognese commentator, having omitted to mention them. Thus Benvenuto tells us[4] that the famous Carisenda tower, which is now (as probably in his day) only 163 ft. high, was in Dante's time considerably higher, but that a great part of it was thrown down between 1351 and 1360 by Giovanni di Oleggio, one of the Visconti of Milan, during his lordship of Bologna. This statement effectually disposes of the absurd theory, first, apparently, propounded by Goethe, and

---

[1] III. 411.   [2] IV. 336.   [3] III. 168.   [4] II. 485.

still repeated in modern guide-books, that the tower was built purposely with a lean, in order that it should attract more attention than the lofty Asinelli tower at its side, and that the inclination being excessive it was found impossible to carry it any higher.   The absurdity of this theory is in any case obvious to the careful observer, for a close inspection of the building reveals the fact that the courses of bricks, as well as the holes for the scaffolding (which still remain), run at right angles to the inclination of the tower, thus proving that the leaning is due, not to design, but to the accidental sinking of the foundations.

Benvenuto, too, is the first to give the real explanation of the term *salse*[1] (*Inf.* xviii. 51), which the earlier commentators took in the literal sense of sauce or pickle.

" To the proper understanding of this phrase," he says, "and that you may realise how many things are left unexplained through ignorance in this poem of Dante's, I would have you know that *Salse* is the name of a certain ravine outside the city of Bologna, close behind the Church of Santa Maria in Monte, into which the bodies of suicides, usurers, and other criminals used to be thrown. And I have heard boys at Bologna jeer at one another, and say tauntingly: ' Your father was flung into the *Salse* '.   It is wrong therefore to take the word in the sense of sauce, as the generality do, for such a metaphor would not be appropriate here."

He also mentions[2] an ancient building at Bologna called the *Corbis*, of which apparently no trace nor memory now remains; and he refers[3] to the *Carrobio*, the old Dogana, or Foro de' Mercanti, which was used partly as a market and partly as an exchange.   This building stood on the site of the present Palazzo della Mercanzía, and in it the money-changers and bankers used to have their quarters.   In his account[4] of the Andalò and Catalani families of Bologna he records that the ruins of the palace of the former were still to be seen in his day close to where the law-school then was; and that of the Catalani residence nothing was left but a single lofty tower, which was chiefly remarkable from the frequency with which it was struck by lightning.

Reminiscences of Florence naturally also abound, many of

[1] II. 11-12.   [2] I. 185.   [3] V. 162.   [4] II. 179-180.

them doubtless dating back to the days of his studentship, a part of which, as we have seen, was spent in that city. Of Florentine boys and their ways he gives us several delightful pictures, some derived from his own experience, some at second hand from Boccaccio. All of these are turned to good account in the Commentary. Thus Dante's mention of the *paleo* in *Paradiso*, xviii. 42, furnishes him with the opportunity of describing in detail their favourite game of whip-top, which he does with great solemnity.

"You must know,"[1] he says, "that the *paleo* is a certain object made of wood, which the Florentine boys use in one of their games. It is a sort of half top, full and squat in the upper part, and the lower part round and tapered to a point. And the boys have a cord or lash attached to a stick, and they hold the stick in their hands and whip the top with the lash when once they have got it to spin, and by continued whipping they keep up the spinning for any length of time."

Another boys' game, not confined to Florence, to which he refers[2] in illustration of *Paradiso*, xviii. 101-102, is that played of winter evenings, when a smouldering brand is taken from the fire, and beaten upon the hearth so as to make the sparks fly, by which they tell their luck, "crying, so many cities, so many castles, so many pigs, so many sheep; and in this way they make the time pass". On Boccaccio's authority he tells[3] the story of the two naughty boys who threw mud at the old statue of Mars on the Ponte Vecchio, both of whom came to a bad end in consequence, one being hanged, and the other drowned in the Arno. On the same authority he relates another anecdote in support of his contention that Dante's *lonza* was a leopard.

"*Lonza*," he says,[4] "is a Florentine word which apparently denotes a leopard, and not any other beast; for Boccaccio told me that once when a leopard was being carried through the streets of Florence, it was followed by a crowd of boys shouting, *ecco la lonza!*"

It appears from an old document preserved in the city archives, and quoted by Casini,[5] that it used to be a custom in Florence in Dante's day, if not later, to keep a caged leopard

[1] V. 212.   [2] V. 222-223.   [3] I. 461.
[4] I. 34.   [5] *Aneddoti e Studi Danteschi*, pp. 51-59.

outside the Palazzo del Podestà, so that doubtless the appearance
of the animal was familiar enough to the Florentines.

Of the Florentines themselves Benvenuto does not give
altogether a favourable account, for he speaks of them [1] as
being noted, among other things, for their gluttony and excessive vindictiveness. The Florentine ladies, he says,[2]

"are the greatest adepts in the world at the art of adorning their persons. Not
content with their natural beauty, they are always contriving how to add to it
artificially; and any defects they manage to conceal with the utmost skill.
Shortness of stature they correct by wearing high pattens; if their complexion
is swarthy they use powder, if too pale they rouge it; they dye their hair
yellow, and make their teeth like ivory; in fact, there's hardly a part of their
persons that they do not make up in some way or other."

One of the most interesting of his reminiscences of Florence
is the mention [3] of a marble statue of Venus he had seen in a
private house there, which from his description must have been
a replica from the same model as the so-called Venus de' Medici,
now in the Tribuna of the Uffizi. Lacaita, the editor of the
Commentary, rashly asserts [4] that the statue seen by Benvenuto,
of which nothing further appears to be known, was identical
with the Medici Venus—a manifest impossibility, since the
latter was not discovered until the sixteenth century at Rome.
Another interesting reference [5] is that to the ancient stone lions
of Florence, which Benvenuto says at that time were located
close to the Palazzo della Signoria, near the site of the ruined
palaces of the Uberti in the old Gardingo, not far apparently
from where they now stand.

Besides being well acquainted with Florence and Bologna,
Benvenuto was certainly familiar with many other parts of Italy.
Venice, for example, we may feel pretty sure he visited, from his
references to the Rialto,[6] and his accurate description of the
Doge's cap.[7] It was probably at Venice that he came across the
long-haired Greeks he speaks of [8]; and saw the bales of hides
from Barbary, bound with ropes of twisted grass, to which he
refers [9] in his note on the word *strambe* (*Inf.* xix. 27). Here

---

[1] I. 227; II. 391.   [2] IV. 62.   [3] III. 280.   [4] I. xxiv-xxv.
[5] II. 179.   [6] V. 5, 162.   [7] III. 315.   [8] II. 87.   [9] II. 36.

too no doubt he watched the manœuvring of a galley, and observed the wonderful discipline of the galley-slaves,[1] who would instantly stop rowing as one man at the sound of the captain's whistle—a sight which seems to have greatly impressed him, for he declares his belief that no ruler in all the world is so promptly obeyed as is the captain of a galley by his crew. It was perhaps on his way to Venice that he got that experience of the sea which he so feelingly describes on another occasion.

"Nature," he remarks[2] (on *Inf.* xi. 11), "abhors sudden changes, as we know by experience; for when a man goes on board ship for the first time, he feels upset and becomes sick; but after a while he gets accustomed to the motion, and then he finds his appetite sharper than ever it was before."

By means of the Commentary it might be possible to follow pretty closely Benvenuto's movements from place to place—not by a series of brilliant conjectures, such as enabled Mr. Gladstone and Dean Plumptre to picture Dante as a student at Oxford, or worshipping in the cathedral at Wells, but from his own explicit statements, such as "I saw," or "when I was there". It certainly would not be safe in Benvenuto's case to rely wholly upon *primâ facie* evidence, unsupported by some such assurance that he was personally present in any particular locality. A circumstantial account of Naples,[3] for instance, with accurate descriptions, as of an eye-witness, of Virgil's tomb, and the grottoes of Sejanus and of Pozzuoli, might lead the incautious reader to suppose that Benvenuto had himself visited these places; the whole account, however, comes from the *Itinerarium* of Petrarch, whence Benvenuto has conveyed it almost *verbatim*, without a hint that it is not a record of his own experience. He mentions Petrarch in this connection, it is true, but only to tell the story, which comes from the same source, of how King Robert asked Petrarch whether he thought there was any truth in the tradition that the Castello dell' Ovo had been built by Virgil by magical means; to which Petrarch replied, with a laugh, that he had always understood that Virgil was a poet, not a stonemason.

[1] V. 369.   [2] I. 364.   [3] III. 86-87.

But on many occasions he is undoubtedly recalling his own experiences. Thus we may trace him, journeying sometimes on horseback, sometimes on a mule, now riding a restive and timid animal through wild and unfamiliar country ; now settling himself into the saddle, ready to break into a gallop, at the sight of distant bands of marauders and of burning and desolated villages[1] ; now jogging along quietly, making plans for the night's lodging.[2] At one time we find him crossing the Alps, where, as he says, the old snow ever awaits the new,[3] doubtless on his way to or from Avignon ; at another he is caught in a mountain mist on the journey from Florence to Bologna over the Apennines, which brings to his mind[4] Dante's words, "Ricorditi, se mai nell' Alpe Ti colse nebbia " (*Purg*. xvii. 1-2) ; or yet again[5] he struggles painfully along the break-neck track overhanging the Genoese riviera in the direction of Turbia, the frontier-fortress, whose name gives occasion to another of his punning etymologies—"Turbia, quasi turbans viam volentibus intrare vel exire Italiam ". Under more favourable conditions we may accompany him along the shores of the Lago di Garda,[6] from the Castle of Riva at the head of the lake, close to where the Sarcha comes tumbling in with its milky waters, which have the effect, to Benvenuto's eyes, of a rushing stream of flour, down to Peschiera at the southern extremity, and the fishing-village of "olive-silvery" Sirmio, which is associated in his memory with ancient ruins and carps fried in oil.[7] From Peschiera he traverses the rich pastures watered by the Mincio, where he notes the immense herds of cattle and horses,[8] and brings us to Verona, whose amphitheatre recalls the configuration of Dante's Hell,[9] or, from another aspect, that of the Mountain of Purgatory[10] ; and so on to Vicenza, in one direction, with its wonderful labryinth,[11] and Padua with its ancient triple fortifications[12] ; or to Mantua and Parma, with its octagonal church, in the other.[13]

Benvenuto's references to his contemporaries and to con-

[1] I. 585-586. [2] III. 201. [3] I. 472. [4] III. 453. [5] III. 95.
[6] II. 80. [7] II. 81. [8] II. 82. [9] I. 185. [10] III. 43.
[11] I. 387. [12] I. 294. [13] II. 35.

temporary events are some of them of considerable interest. The persons he most often mentions are not unnaturally the two illustrious men of letters with whom, as has already been indicated, he was on terms of personal friendship, namely Petrarch and Boccaccio.

Petrarch he mentions by name no less than thirty times,[1] usually describing him as " novissimus poeta Petrarcha ". He twice records,[2] with some complacency, the fact that Petrarch had addressed an epistle to himself, from which he gives extracts ; and he refers to many of the poet's other writings, such as the *Apologia contra Gallum*,[3] the *Itinerarium Syriacum*,[4] his Eclogues [5] (on which he wrote a commentary), his Penitential Psalms,[6] and his famous letter to Boccaccio concerning Dante [7] ; to the *Africa*, apparently, he makes no allusion, nor to the *Canzoniere*, with the solitary exception of the sonnet " Dell' empia Babilonia," which, as has been seen above, he glances at *à propos* of Avignon.[8] He refers to Petrarch's coronation [9] in the Capitol at Rome in April, 1341, and to his residence at Avignon and Vaucluse [10] ; and he supplies from personal observation an interesting detail as to the abstemious habits of the poet, who, he says, was accustomed to satisfy his appetite with coarse food and rough wine or even water, and would reject dainties such as game.[11] On the authority of Petrarch he tells the following story [12] as an example of the scandals which disgraced the Papal Court of Avignon. One day two Cardinals, who were returning from the Papal palace, were besieged by a crowd of impatient applicants clamouring to know how their several affairs were progressing in the Pope's hands. In order to be rid of their importunities, one of the Cardinals, who was evidently an old hand at the practice, glibly gave an answer to each as to what

---

[1] For a list of Benvenuto's references to Petrarch and Boccaccio, as well as for detailed information regarding the authorities utilised by Benvenuto, see my *Index of Authors quoted by Benvenuto da Imola in his Commentary on the Divina Commedia*, in the *Twentieth Annual Report of the Cambridge (U.S.A.) Dante Society* (1901).

[2] I. 10 ; IV. 230. [3] I. 83. [4] I. 125. [5] III. 6.
[6] III. 145. [7] I. 79. [8] II. 59. [9] III. 225.
[10] II. 185 ; IV. 488. [11] I. 224. [12] II. 185-186.

the Pope had said in his particular case, lying and inventing
unblushingly without turning a hair.   When the crowd was thus
disposed of, his companion, who was not as yet utterly degraded,
said to the other, "Are you not ashamed to trifle with the
feelings of these poor dupes, and to fabricate answers from the
Pope, when you know we have not seen him at all to-day, nor
for many days past ?"   "On the contrary," retorted the other,
who was an inveterate jobber, "it is you that should be ashamed,
who are so dull as not yet to have learnt the ways of the Papal
Court."   Whereupon the bystanders burst out laughing, and
applauded the ready answer.   But Petrarch, who was present,
and had heard what passed, turned away in indignation and
disgust.

Benvenuto's references to Boccaccio are not so numerous as
those to Petrarch, but as a rule they are more interesting, owing
to the closer personal relations which subsisted between the
two.   "Venerabilis praeceptor meus," "placidissimus hominum,"
"suavissimus Boccatius de Certaldo," "humillimus hominum,"
"curiosus inquisitor omnium delectabilium historiarum," are
some of the terms by which Benvenuto refers to his former
master,[1] from whose works he has helped himself pretty liberally.
The *Decamerone* he avowedly quotes once only,[2] for the story of
Ghin di Tacco and the Abbot of Clugny (x. 2), but at least
eight others of the tales are laid under contribution without the
smallest acknowledgment,[3] in several cases the novel being
transcribed entire ; and no doubt other excerpts might be traced.
The *De Genealogia Deorum*,[4] the *De Montibus et Silvis*,[5] and the
De Casibus Virorum Illustrium,[6] which are quoted by name, are
elsewhere utilised in the same unscrupulous fashion, it being
apparently a matter of complete indifference whether the name
of the authority is mentioned or not.   Such proceedings, of
course, are common enough with mediæval writers, with whom
what we regard as plagiarism was a venial offence, if it was an

[1] III. 169, 265 ; I. 35 ; III. 341, 392.   [2] III. 169.
[3] I. 95, 167-168, 210, 284, 546 ; III. 314 ; IV. 382 ; V. 262.   [4] V. 164.
[5] I. 124, 509, 514 ; III. 376 ; IV. 488 ; V. 164.
[6] I. 289 ; III. 341 ; IV. 12-13 ; V. 164.

offence at all ; but the particular instances noted in the cases of Petrarch and Boccaccio are somewhat remarkable, seeing that the Commentary was written, and in part at least published, during Boccaccio's lifetime at any rate.

Boccaccio's *Vita di Dante*, sometimes named, more often not, is responsible for most of the information about Dante personally which is given in the Commentary. Several stories, however, occur here for the first time in connection with Dante. One of these [1]—how Dante expressed surprise at the beauty of Giotto's paintings, and at the ugliness of his children, to which Giotto made the well-known reply ("Quia pingo de die, sed fingo de nocte")—is as old as Macrobius, as Benvenuto himself points out. To this same passage in the Commentary is due the tradition that Dante was at Padua at the time when Giotto, as a young man, was painting his frescoes in the Chapel of the Madonna dell' Arena in that city. In connection with Dante's extraordinary facility in the matter of rhymes Benvenuto repeats [2] a quaint conceit, which had been imagined, he says, by an ardent admirer of the poet : When Dante first set about the composition of his poem, all the rhymes in the language presented themselves before him in the guise of so many lovely maidens, and each in turn humbly petitioned to be granted admittance into this great work of his genius. In answer to their prayers, Dante called first one and then another, and assigned to each its appropriate place in the poem, so that, when at last the work was complete, it was found that not a single one had been left out.

Several of the anecdotes supplied by Boccaccio have already been quoted in another connection. The most interesting piece of information Benvenuto derived from him is the account of his visit to the monastery of Monte Cassino, which is quoted [3] in the comment on *Paradiso*, xxii. 74 :—

" My revered master, Boccaccio, told me," he says, "that being once in the neighbourhood of Monte Cassino, he paid the monastery a visit, and asked if he might see the library. Whereupon one of the monks, pointing to a staircase,

[1] III. 313.   [2] IV. 166.   [3] V. 301.

said gruffly: 'Go up; it is open'. Boccaccio went up, and saw to his astonishment that the library, the storehouse of the monastic treasures, had neither door nor fastening; and on entering in he found grass growing on the windows, and all the books and benches buried in dust. When he came to turn over the books, some of which were very rare and of great value, he discovered that many of them had been mutilated and defaced by having leaves torn out, or the margins cut—a discovery which greatly distressed him. In answer to his inquiries as to how this damage had been caused, he was told that it was the work of some of the monks themselves. These vandals, desirous of making a little money, were in the habit of tearing out leaves from some of the manuscripts, and of cutting the margins off others, for the purpose of converting them into psalters and breviaries, which they afterwards sold. 'Now, student,' exclaims Benvenuto, 'go and weary your brains with the making of books!'"

The shameful maltreatment of the books at Monte Cassino, which Boccaccio so graphically here describes, fortunately seems to have been exceptional at that time in Italy, for Petrarch, who had a large experience of monastic libraries, never records any instance of their neglect, but on the contrary expresses his gratitude to the monks for their careful preservation of so many priceless treasures.[1]

Of the contemporary events alluded to by Benvenuto, that which seems to have impressed his imagination the most was the capture of the French king by the English at Poictiers (19th Sept., 1356). To this incident reference is made no less than four times[2] as a cruel instance of the reverses of fortune. He is especially indignant at the conduct of Clement VI. in granting subsidies to the French in aid of the war with England; and à propos of Dante's reference to the dealings between Clement V. and Philip the Fair, he breaks out:—

What would Dante have said if he had seen this other Clement, who was much more corrupt and more carnal than his predecessor, and poured out the whole of the immense treasure of the Church in aid of King John of France against the King of England, with the only result that both treasure and victory fell to the English, who captured the French king into the bargain![3]

Benvenuto had evidently a special dislike to the French, due perhaps to his experience of them at Avignon, and he misses no opportunity of ridiculing them. When Dante speaks of the vanity of the Sienese, which he says is even greater than that of the French,[4] Benvenuto comments[5]:—

---

[1] Nolhac, *Pétrarque et l'humanisme*, p. 39.   [2] I. 261; II. 55; III. 532; V. 248.
[3] II. 55.   [4] *Inf.* xxix. 121-123.   [5] II. 409.

Indeed, the French have ever been the vainest of all nations, as may be seen from what Julius Celsus[1] says of them; and so it is now, for we see them every day inventing new clothes, and new modes of dress; not a part of their persons but has its own special fashion—they wear chains round their necks, bracelets on their arms, long pointed shoes, short jackets which expose the very part of the body they ought to conceal, and hoods over their faces which hide the part they ought to show—in fact, there is no end to their vanities. And it makes my blood boil, he adds, to see Italians, and especially Italian nobles, trying to ape the French, and learning their language, which they claim to be the most elegant of all tongues. This claim I can nowise admit, for French is nothing but a bastard Italian, as any one can see. Not being able to pronounce *cavaliero* properly, for instance, they corrupt it into *chevalier;* and it is the same with *Signore*, which they turn into *Sir;* and so on. And the proof of what I maintain is this—that when they want to say "loquere vulgariter," that is, to speak in the vulgar tongue, they say "loquere romanice," that is, to speak romance; and their vernaculars they call romance. Italians, therefore, ought not gratuitously to slight their own noble speech and manners for those of the ignoble French.

On other occasions he jeers at the drunken habits of the French, and at their love of violence and robbery[2]; and when pointing out[3] that Vincent of Beauvais, in his *Speculum Historiale*, has made the ridiculous mistake of confounding Cato of Utica with the so-called Dionysius Cato, author of the *Disticha*, he slightingly refers to Vincent's great work as "opus vere Gallicum".

There are many other interesting allusions in the Commentary to contemporary events, some of which are introduced with telling effect. Thus, in his comment on *Purgatorio*, vi. 97-151, where Dante reproaches the Emperor Albert for his neglect of Italy, Benvenuto remarks[4]:—

Certainly former emperors did less harm by *not* coming into Italy than our present Emperor Charles of Luxemburg, grandson of the good Henry VII., has

---

[1] Julius Celsus was a scholar at Constantinople in the seventh century, who made a recension of the text of Caesar's Commentaries. In the Middle Ages (and by some even in modern times) he was regarded as the author of the Commentaries, which he was supposed to have compiled from material supplied to him by Caesar himself, whose companion in arms he was believed to have been. Benvenuto, in common with Vincent of Beauvais (in the *Speculum Historiale*), Petrarch (in the *De Viris Illustribus*), and Boccaccio (in the *De Genealogia Deorum*), quotes the Commentaries under the name of Julius Celsus (*cf.* I. 162, 417, 579; II. 257, 373, 391, 409, 462; III. 18, 31, 111, 272, 487; IV. 379, 435).

[2] II. 71; III. 530; V. 463.   [3] III. 38.   [4] III. 186-187.

done in his two visits[1] to our country ; especially on the second occasion, in the time of Urban V., when he came with an immense host, from which great things were expected ; but instead of flying the victorious eagles he brought with him a nest of harpies, and, to his everlasting infamy, piled up gold by selling the liberties of those he came to protect.

The coronation of this same Charles IV. at Arles, on 4th June, 1365, is also alluded to,[2] on which occasion, as we have already seen, Benvenuto was himself present, he being at that time in France on his mission to Urban V. at Avignon. The gallant resistance of the people of Pavia to the Visconti of Milan, under the leadership of the eloquent friar, Jacopo Bossolaro,[3] is brought in[4] as an example of the power of eloquence, à propos of the " messo del ciel " of Inferno, ix. 85, whom Benvenuto, with a curious lapse from his customary good sense, insists on identifying with the god Mercury. Dante's denunciation, in the twentieth canto of the Purgatorio, of the shameful marriage of Beatrice of Naples to the bloodthirsty Azzo of Este evokes a reference[5] to the marriage of Isabella, daughter of King John of France, the prisoner of the English, to the Milanese tyrant, Gian Galeazzo Visconti, which took place in June, 1360. Other events alluded to are the defeat and death of Pedro the Cruel of Castile at the hands of his natural brother Henry in 1368[6] ; the invasion and conquest of Cyprus by the Genoese in 1373[7] ; and the destruction of the Castle of Sant' Angelo at Rome in 1379, during the contest between the partisans of Pope Urban VI. and those of his rival, Cardinal Robert of Geneva, better known as the anti-pope Clement VII.[8] This last reference is taken by Benvenuto's editor as fixing the terminus ad quem of the Commentary, but, as has already been pointed out, he has overlooked a possible reference[9] to the Emperor Wenceslaus, which, if substantiated, would enable us to advance this limit by several years.

Dante's description of the devastation of Aegina by plague (Inferno, xxix. 58-64) gives occasion to the mention[10] of the

---

[1] Oct., 1354; May, 1368.   [2] I. 326.   [3] 1356-1359.   [4] I. 322-323.
[5] III. 532.   [6] I. 261.   [7] V. 252.   [8] II. 8, 53.   [9] IV. 305.
[10] II. 397-398.

great plagues in Italy in 1348 and 1362; in the former, which figures in the *Proemio* of Boccaccio's *Decamerone*, Benvenuto states that the mortality was especially heavy in Sicily and Sardinia, where it amounted to ninety per cent. of the whole population. There is one reference, and one only, to Cola di Rienzi, "the last of the tribunes," "Nicholaus tribunus Romae, vir magnae probitatis et prudentiae," as Benvenuto describes him [1]; this occurs à *propos* of the letters S. P. Q. R., which Rienzi once in his contempt for the Roman populace is said to have explained as *Sozzo Popolo Conchagato Romano*, whatever that may mean.

To the unsettled state of Italy, and the numerous bands of foreign mercenaries which infested the country, we find repeated reference. *À propos* of Guido del Duca's lament (in the fourteenth canto of the *Purgatorio*) over the condition of Romagna in those days, Benvenuto exclaims [2]:—

Well might I echo Guido's words, save that now his description would apply, not to one province only, but to the whole of Italy!

The "Stipendiarii," he says,[3] are like the Centaurs in the seventh circle of Hell—more beast than man; they are ever rushing to deal or receive death at the bidding of a master, whom they do not scruple to leave in the lurch whenever it suits them, especially when it comes to fighting in the open and they have no fortress nor city-walls to shelter them.

"Woe is me!" he concludes,[4] "that it has fallen to my lot to live in these evil days, when Italy is overrun with these foreign companies of every nation of Europe—bloody English, raving Germans, brutal Bretons, rapacious Gascons, and filthy Hungarians, who are all banded together for the undoing of Italy, laying waste her provinces, plundering her noble cities, and working desolation on all sides by fraud and treachery and violence."

[1] V. 181-182   [2] III. 397.   [3] I. 394-395.   [4] I. 401.

SHORTER DANTE NOTES

THE COINS DENOMINATED *SANTELENE* BY DANTE
(*CONVIVIO*, IV. 11)[1]

In a well-known passage in the fourth book of the *Convivio* Dante refers to the discovery by a peasant, while digging on the slopes of Falterona, of a large quantity of silver coins:—

> Veramente io vidi lo luogo, nelle coste d' un monte in Toscana, che si chiama Falterona, dove il più vile villano di tutta la contrada, zappando, più d' uno staio di Santelene d' argento finissimo vi trovò, che forse più di mille anni l' avevano aspettato (iv. 11, ll. 76-82).

The origin of the name *Santelene* given by Dante to these coins is by no means clear. Biscioni, in the course of a long note on the subject, states his opinion that this name was given originally to coins struck in the island of Therasia, which was subsequently called *Sant' Elena*, and is now known as *Santorin* ; he says :—

> Due maniere di moneta corrente si praticava intorno a' tempi di Dante : ed era questa la più comune, comecchè forse alla mercatura ed allo spendere la più usuale. Ciò erano i Bisanti e le Santelene : e tanto in oro, che in argento ed in rame si battevano comunemente. La loro denominazione viene da' luoghi, ne' quali (com' io suppongo) era la zecca, ove queste monete si coniavano. . . . La *Santalena*, o *Santelena*, vien denominata dal luogo, nel quale si batteva questa moneta. Questa è quell' isola nell' Arcipelago, situata dirimpetto a Candia, la quale da' Latini fu detta *Tiresia* o *Theresia*, ed anticamente *Therasia ;* di poi ne tempi bassi fu detta da' naviganti *Sant' Elena*, e in oggi si chiama *Santorini*.

Santorin (a corruption of the name of Saint Irene, the patron saint of the island), the ancient Thera (not Therasia, as Biscioni states, which is a smaller island on the west coast of Santorin), is a volcanic island in the Aegæan Sea, the southernmost of the Cyclades, about sixty miles north of Crete. Biscioni's derivation of the name of the coin from this island can, however, hardly be correct, for it does not appear that any coins were struck by the mediæval lords of Thera and Therasia. The real origin of the name is doubtless connected with St. Helena, the mother of the Emperor Constantine the Great, who was venerated as the discoverer of the Holy Sepulchre, and of the remains of the true Cross. That the coins referred to by Dante were coins actually bearing the name and portrait of St. Helena, is in the highest degree unlikely; for though, as Dr. Barclay Head, the Keeper of Coins at the British Museum, has kindly informed me, fourth century coins of that description are well known, those that are found in large numbers are not silver (like the coins mentioned by Dante), but bronze. Dr. Head adds that' the so-called "silver" coins of Helena are (as Cohen states in *Monnaies romaines*) not solid silver, but merely bronze, washed, or slightly coated, with silver. They are, however, rare in this state, and the usual metal of the coins of Helena is bronze. There are also a few rare medallions and coins of hers in gold.

Du Cange, in the chapter on *Nummi Helenae nomen prae-ferentes*, in his *Dissertatio de inferioris aevi numismatibus*, describes a number of coins bearing the name of Helena (of whose identity he is doubtful—"vix tamen constans est, cui debeant adscribi, matri ne Constantini Magni, vel Juliani Para-batae, vel etiam Crispi, si quaepiam fuit, conjugi"), and concludes that the frequent occurrence of these coins, most of which bear what appears to be a cross, led to the popular ascription to St. Helena of all coins of the eastern empire (and hence, by an easy transition, to the use of the term for coins of any descrip-tion). Du Cange says as follows :—

Utcumque sit de nummis istis Helenianis, quos una omnes Constantini Magni familiae subjecimus, ut cuique liceat inspicienti quod arriserit statuere, id constat ex iis inditam a vulgo *sanctarum Helenarum* appellationem omnibus ferme numismatibus augustorum Constantinopolitanorum aevi inferioris, maxi-meque iis quos ejusmodi rerum studiosi, propter male formatos characteres, aut vultus ipsos, vel quod nihil exquisitum contineant, solent aspernari. Quod inde forsan originem habuit, quod non Helenae duntaxat ut divis adscriptae imagines, sed et crucigeros omnes nummos, sacri phylacterii aut encolpii vice, ad collum quilibet appenderet: unde nummorum ejusmodi plerosque videmus perforatos.

The use of the term *Santelena* in Italy does not appear to have been very general in Dante's day, to judge by the infrequency of its occurrence in literature; but this may of course be due to the very fact that it was essentially a popular term, and as such was regarded as beneath the dignity of serious writers. Biscioni quotes two instances of it from an old Tuscan version of the Merlin romance :—

> Dissegli, che io arrecai in questa terra dugento ruote d' oro di quelle di Constantinopoli, e quattrocento di quelle di Santalena. . . . E aperte le cassette trovarono le ruote del Mercatante, e quelle di Costantinopoli, e quelle di Santa Lena, siccome egli dicea loro.

Another instance of its use occurs in a sonnet of Guido Cavalcanti (ed. P. Ercole, Livorno, 1885, p. 352), which begins :—

> Se non ti caggia la tua Santalena
> Giù per lo colto tra le dure zolle,
> E vegna a mano d' un forese folle,
> Che la stropicci, e rendalati a pena. . . .

The occurrence of the word in rhyme in this latter passage proves that the pronunciation (*Santélena*) adopted in recent editions of the *Convivio* (*e.g.*, those of Fraticelli, Giuliani, and in the Oxford Dante) is incorrect, and that the right pronunciation is *Santeléna*.

A MISREADING IN RECENT EDITIONS OF DANTE'S LETTER TO CAN GRANDE

(*EPISTOLAE*, X. 22)[1]

IN the three most recent editions of Dante's minor works, *viz.*, those of Fraticelli, Giuliani, and Moore (in the Oxford Dante), occurs a strange blunder, which shows how prone editors are to follow each other blindly, like so many sheep, to use Dante's simile : *E ciò che fa la prima, e l' altre fanno.*[2]

---

[1] *Giornale Storico della Letteratura Italiana*, xxx. 349-350.
[2] *Purg.* iii. 82.

In section twenty-two of his Epistle to Can Grande Dante quotes several passages from Scripture to prove the omnipresence of the "divinum lumen," concluding with one from *Ecclesiasticus :*—

> Et *Ecclesiastici* 42: Gloria Domini plenum est opus ejus.

This is the reading of the editions previous to that published at Livorno in 1842 under the editorship of Alessandro Torri. By some extraordinary caprice Torri in his edition altered *Ecclesiastici* into *Ecclesiastes*, drawing attention to his "emendation" in a note: "*Non* Ecclesiastici *ut in vulgatis*," and giving a reference (in another note) to *Ecclesiastes* v. 16, but printing the words *quadragesimo secundo* in the text. According to his reading, therefore, the passage runs :—

> Et *Ecclesiastes*, quadragesimo secundo[1]: Gloria Domini plenum est opus ejus.

Now, as every one knows, there are only *twelve* chapters in *Ecclesiastes* (there being, on the other hand, fifty-one in *Ecclesiasticus*), so that to make Dante quote the forty-second chapter of *Ecclesiastes*, as Torri does, is to make him talk nonsense! And yet, incredible as it may appear, this "emendation" of Torri's found favour, and, after being accepted by Fraticelli (in his later editions) and by Giuliani, has now, by an unfortunate oversight, found its way into the Oxford Dante.

Not the least remarkable part of the affair is the fact that, while the passage quoted by Dante does not occur in *Ecclesiastes* v. 16, to which Torri refers, it does occur *totidem verbis* in the forty-second chapter of *Ecclesiasticus* (*viz.*, in verse 16), thus proving conclusively that the reading of the earlier editions was correct, and that no alteration was called for. I may add that in the English translation of Dante's Letters by Latham, which

---

[1] This in itself is a mistake, for the preposition *in* is needed, according to Dante's usual practice in quotations (*e.g.*, we have "Lucanus in nono" just below) ; and, in any case, if the figures 42 are to be expanded, they ought to read *quadragesimus secundus* (in the nominative, upon which the genitive *Ecclesiastici* is dependent), the verb *dicit* being understood, as is evident from the previous constructions: "Dicit Spiritus Sanctus per Hieremiam," "Et Sapientia dicit".

was published not long ago under the auspices of the Cambridge (U.S.A.) Dante Society, the rightful reading *Ecclesiastici* is followed. In Dr. Scartazzini's *Prolegomeni della Divina Commedia*, on the other hand, in which the letter is printed *in extenso*, the blunder *Ecclesiastes* is faithfully reproduced.

A MISQUOTATION OF DANTE'S IN THE *CONVIVIO* (i. 12)[1]

SPEAKING of justice (*giustizia*) in the twelfth chapter of the first book of the *Convivio*, Dante says: "Questa è tanto amabile, che, siccome dice il Filosofo nel quinto dell' *Etica*, i suoi nemici l' amano, siccome sono ladroni e rubatori" (ll. 74-77).

The source of this quotation has not been identified. Dr. Moore says (*Studies in Dante*, i. 103): "There does not appear to be any such passage in Aristotle, either in the fifth book of the *Ethics*, or elsewhere". Mazzucchelli was equally unable to trace it; he remarks: "Non trovasi ciò in detto libro ne' precisi termini. Ma forse Dante ebbe sott' occhio una cattiva versione del passo [seguente]: Quoniam vero fieri potest, ut quis licet injuste agat, non tamen sit injustus: qualia nam injuste facta quispiam committens in unaquaque injustitia injustus continuo esse dicendus est? fur ne, an adulter, an latro?" (*Eth.* v. 6, ed. Giunt. 1550.)

If this indeed be the passage of which Dante was thinking it must be admitted that he has taken very considerable liberties with his original. For myself I find it impossible to believe that he could have brought himself so far to travesty the words of the "maestro della umana ragione,"[2] whom he reverently qualifies elsewhere as "degnissimo di fede e d' obbedienza".[3] I prefer to suppose rather that here, as in one or two other instances,[4] Dante's memory played him false; or that he attributed the passage to Aristotle by a slip, he having already referred to the *Ethics* a few sentences before in this same chapter. His selec-

[1] *Giornale Storico della Letteratura Italiana*, xxxiii. 178-179.
[2] *Conv.* iv. 2, ll. 138-139.   [3] *Conv.* iv. 6, ll. 50-51.
[4] See Moore, *Studies in Dante*, i. 36-37.

tion of the fifth book of the *Ethics* is easily explained by the fact that in the first two chapters of that book Aristotle discusses the subject of justice and injustice.

Dr. Moore refers to a somewhat similar sentiment in the first book of the *Republic* of Plato, but with this work, as he recognises, Dante can hardly have been acquainted.[1]

I think there can be little doubt that the ultimate source of the quotation is a passage in a work with which Dante was well acquainted, namely the *De Officiis* of Cicero.[2]   In the second book of this treatise, Cicero says : " Mea quidem sententia omnis ratio atque institutio vitae adjumenta hominum desiderat, in primisque ut habeat quibuscum possit familiares conferre sermones ; quod est difficile, nisi speciem prae te boni viri feras. Ergo etiam solitario homini atque in agro vitam agenti opinio justitiae necessaria est, eoque etiam magis quod, eam si non habebunt, nullis praesidiis saepti multis afficientur injuriis. Atque iis etiam qui vendunt, emunt, conducunt, locant, contrahendisque negotiis implicantur, justitia ad rem gerendam necessaria est, cujus tanta vis est, ut ne illi quidem, qui maleficio et scelere pascuntur, possint sine ulla particula justitiae vivere. Nam qui eorum cuipiam, qui una latrocinantur, furatur aliquid aut eripit, is sibi ne in latrocinio quidem relinquit locum, ille autem, qui archipirata dicitur, nisi aequabiliter praedam dispertiat, aut interficiatur a sociis aut relinquatur ; quin etiam leges latronum esse dicuntur quibus pareant, quas observent." (*Off.* ii. 11.)

This passage was to a certain extent a commonplace in mediæval literature, for it is quoted almost *in extenso* by Guillaume de Conches in the *Moralium Dogma* (§ 8, *De Justitia*), and by Vincent of Beauvais in the *Speculum Historiale* (vi. 10) ; and it is translated by Brunetto Latino (who doubtless took it direct from the *Moralium Dogma*) in his *Trésor :* " La

---

[1] Dante's knowledge of Plato was practically confined to the *Timaeus*, and to such scattered references as occur in the works of Aristotle, Albertus Magnus, Cicero, St. Augustine and St. Thomas Aquinas.

[2] Dante quotes from the *De Officiis* some dozen times ; and was otherwise indebted to it.   (See the article " *Officiis, De* " in my *Dante Dictionary*.)

force [de justise] est si grans que cil qui se paissent de felonie et de mesfait ne pueent pas vivre sanz aucune partie de justise ; car li larron qui emblent ensemble vuelent que justise soit entre eulx gardée, et se lor maistres ne depart igaument la proie, ou li sien compaignon l' ociront ou il le lairront ". (Lib. II. chap. lxxvi. § 1.)

It is noteworthy that neither in the *Moralium Dogma* nor in the *Trésor* is Cicero mentioned in connection with the passage.

This quotation occurs also in the *Fiore di filosofi,* a collection of aphorisms, etc., attributed, probably without foundation, to Brunetto Latino, but which at any rate belongs to the close of the thirteenth century : " La forza della giustizia è tanta, che quelli che stanno e vivono di ruberia e di mal fare non potrebbero durare sanza alcuna parte di giustizia ". And it is given, with a reference to the *De Officiis,* in the so-called *Ottimo Comento* upon the *Divina Commedia,* in the *proemio* to the eighteenth canto of the *Paradiso* : " Tullio dice, in libro *De Officiis :* Tanta è la forza di giustizia, che eziandio coloro che di male e di fellonia si pascono, non possono vivere senza alcuna particella di giustizia ".

ARISTOTLE'S *DE ANIMALIBUS* IN DANTE AND OTHER MEDIÆVAL WRITERS [1]

THE precise composition of the collection of Aristotelian books quoted by mediæval writers under the title *De Animalibus* has long been a matter of doubt. Dante in the *Convivio* twice employs the term *Degli Animali,* the reference in one case (*Conv.* ii. 9, l. 79) [2] being to Aristotle's *De Historia Animalium* (in ten books), in the other (*Conv.* ii. 3, l. 15) [3] to the *De Partibus Animalium* (in four books). In the former case, however, he refers to the *twelfth* book *Degli Animali,* but the passage quoted

---

[1] *Giornale Storico della Letteratura Italiana,* xxxiv. 273-274.

[2] " Aristotile dice nel duodecimo *degli Animali* che l' uomo è perfettissimo di tutti gli animali."

[3] Dante merely says here, " secondo la sentenza del Filosofo, in quello *degli Animali,*" without mentioning the particular book referred to. The passage alluded to occurs in the *De Partibus Animalium* (i. 5).

actually occurs in the eighth book of the *De Historia Animalium*.[1] Jourdain, in his *Traductions Latines d'Aristote*, states that in the Arabic versions of Aristotle, upon which the Latin translation of Michael Scot was based, the ten books of the *De Historia Animalium*, the five of the *De Generatione Animalium*, and the four of the *De Partibus Animalium*, were grouped together in a single collection of nineteen books.[2] In order that Dante's twelfth book *Degli Animali* should coincide with the eighth of the *Historia*, we must suppose the mediæval collection *De Animalibus*—at any rate the collection utilised by Dante— to have been made up of the four books of the *De Partibus*, the ten of the *Historia*, and the five of the *De Generatione Animalium*, in that order.[3]

Now Benvenuto da Imola, in his Commentary on the *Divina Commedia* (vol. iv. p. 104), quotes a passage from the *sixteenth* book *De Animalibus*[4]; and if the above supposition be correct this passage ought to occur in the second book of the *De Generatione Animalium*. This I find to be actually the case.[5] This solution of the question therefore, which was first in part put forward tentatively by Mazzucchelli,[6] may now be accepted as definitive, so far as Dante and Benvenuto are concerned. Before taking leave of these two authors I may mention that

---

[1] See Mazzucchelli's note in the Padua (1827) edition of the *Convito*, p. 378 ; and Moore, *Studies in Dante*, i. 152.   The reference is to *Hist. Animal.* viii. 1.

[2] " La version des *Histoires des Animaux* due à Michel Scot se compose de dix-neuf livres, parce que les Arabes joignent aux dix livres des *Histoires* les quatre livres des *Parties* et les cinq de la *Génération des Animaux ;* par exemple, Abd-Allatif cite un passage du onzième livre des *Animaux* d'Aristote qui se trouve dans le premier livre du traité des *Parties*." (p. 172 ; *cf.* pp. 327 ff.)

[3] See note 1.

[4] In the comment on *Purg.* xxv. 69 : " Nota quod, sicut scribitur xvi de Animalibus, cor est quod primo formatur et primo vivit, et ultimo moritur ".

[5] Aristotle says : " Fit autem primo principium, quod in sanguineo genere cor est : in ceteris proportionale, ut sepius dictum est.   Idque effici primum non modo sensu percipitur, sed etiam quod per obitum vita hic ultimo deficit, evenit namque in omnibus, ut quod ultimum sit, id primum deficiat : et quod primum, id ultimum." (*De Gen. Animal.* ii. 4, from *Aristotelis Opera Omnia Latine*, Venetiis, apud Juntas, MDL.-LII. vol. vi. fol. 224ro.)

[6] See note 1.

Aristotle's *De Generatione Animalium* is also separately quoted, under that title, both by the author of the *Quaestio de Aqua et Terra*,[1] and by Benvenuto.[2]

Although the collection *De Animalibus* used by Dante and Benvenuto consisted of Aristotle's nineteen books in the order indicated above, it is evident that the three individual treatises of which the nineteen books are composed were not always arranged in that identical order.[3] Albertus Magnus, for instance, made use of a collection (in the translation of Michael Scot)[4] in which the ten books of the *De Historia Animalium* came first, the four of the *De Partibus* coming next, and the five of the *De Generatione Animalium* last. And this same arrangement was in use among the Arabs as appears from the fact, mentioned by Jourdain,[5] that Abd-Allatif quotes a passage as from the eleventh book *De Animalibus* which actually occurs in the first book of the *De Partibus Animalium*.

"AENEIDORUM" IN THE *DE VULGARI ELOQUENTIA*[6]

DANTE twice[7] in the *De Vulgari Eloquentia* uses this barbarous genitive plural *Aeneidorum*, which at first sight is somewhat puzzling. It is evident, however, from the Commentary of Benvenuto da Imola on the *Divina Commedia* that *Aeneis* in the singular was treated as feminine (gen. *Aeneidos*,[8] acc. *Aenei-*

---

[1] *A. T.* § 13, l. 42. As to the genuineness of this treatise, see above, p. 55, note 1.

[2] Vol. iv. p. 296, in the comment on *Par.* i. 9.

[5] Since the above was written I have come across a passage in the *Epistolario* (iii. 450) of Coluccio Salutati in which he quotes from the *nineteenth* book of the *De Animalibus*. This passage, as Novati points out in his note, comes from the fifth book of the *De Generatione Animalium*, thus proving that Salutati followed the same arrangement as did Dante and Benvenuto da Imola.

[4] See Jourdain, *op. cit.* pp. 327 ff.

[5] *Op. cit.* pp. 172, 327. See above, p. 248, note 2.

[6] *Giornale Storico della Letteratura Italiana*, xxxiv. 274.

[7] Lib. II. cap. iv. l. 73; and Lib. II. cap. viii. l. 22. In the latter passage most printed editions read *Aeneidos*, but Rajna has rightly restored the plural form.

[8] *Aeneidos*, i. 45, 48, 60, 65, and *passim*.

dam,[1] abl. *Aeneida*[2]), but in the plural as neuter (nom., acc.
Aeneida,[3] gen. *Aeneidorum*,[4] abl. *Aeneidis*[5]). This anomalous
declension in the plural was due to the analogy of the neuter
plurals *Bucolica* and *Georgica*. Thus we find *Bucolica, Georgica,
Aeneida*, and *Bucolicorum, Georgicorum, Aeneidorum,* several
times mentioned together by Benvenuto.[6] On the other hand,
by a process familiar to philologists, the neuter plurals *Bucolica*
and *Georgica* are treated in the singular as feminines of the first
declension.[7] The form *Aeneidorum*, as Rajna points out,[8] is
frequently met with in mediæval MSS. of the *Aeneid*. For
instance it occurs in the headings to the books in a well-known
MS. of the eleventh century[9]; and more than thirty times in
a fourteenth century MS. which once belonged to Petrarch.[10]
Dante, therefore, in adopting this form was only following a
well-established practice.

PARIS AND TRISTAN IN THE *INFERNO*
(v. 67)[11]

Commentators on the *Divina Commedia* have doubted whether
Dante intended the Paris of this passage to be the lover of
Helen, or the hero of the mediæval story of *Le Chevalier Paris
et la belle Vienne*. The chief argument adduced in favour of the
latter is that Paris is here coupled by Dante with Tristan, the
hero of the famous mediæval romance of Tristan and Iseult.
The following passages, however, from various old French poems,
and from Chaucer, will show that the coupling of Paris of Troy
and Tristan, and of Helen and Iseult, as typical instances of

---

[1] *Aeneidam*, i. 51 (v. l. *Aeneida*).   [2] *Aeneidā*, i. 156 (v. l. *Aeneidis*).
[3] *Aeneida*, i. 51 (v. l. *Aeneidam*) ; iii. 87; iv. 17, 36; etc.
[4] *Aeneidorum*, i. 68 ; ii. 77 ; iii. 195 ; etc.
[5] *Aeneidis*, i. 156 (v. l. *Aeneidā*) ; v. 261.
[6] I. 51 ; iii. 87, 195 ; etc.   [7] I. 46, 47, 51, etc.
[8] *Il trattato De Vulgari Eloquentia*, per cura di Pio Rajna, p. 135, note 2.
[9] Cod. Laur., Pl. xxxix. 2.
[10] Cod. Ambros. A. 79 Inf. *Cf.* P. de Nolhac, *Pétrarque et l'humanisme*,
p. 120.
[11] See *Academy*, 7th Oct., 1887; 18th Feb., 1888; 23rd June, 1888 ; 13th
Sept., 1890.

lovers whose woes were wrought by love, was a poetical commonplace with mediæval writers.

From the *Roman de Renart* (twelfth century) :—

> Seigneurs, oï avez maint conte
> Que maint conterre vous raconte,
> Conment Paris ravi Elaine,
> Le mal qu'il en ot et la paine :
> De Tristan qui la chievre fist,
> Qui assez bellement en dist
> Et fabliaus et chancon de geste.
> > (*Branche*, ii. ll. 1-7 ; vol. i. p. 91, ed. Martin.)

From a thirteenth-century MS. belonging to the Ashburnham
Collection, from which extracts have been printed in the *Bulletin
de la Société des Anciens Textes Français* (1887, No. 2) :—

> Li corteis Tristam fu enginné
> De l'amor et de l'amisté
> Ke il out envers Ysolt la bloie.
> Si fu li beau Paris de Troie
> De Eleine e de Penelopé.

From a "Complainte" attributed to Oton de Granson, the
"flour of hem that make in Fraunce," as Chaucer styles him
(printed by M. Piaget in *Romania*, xix. 445). A lady laments
the absence of her *ami*, and declares that no lover in fiction ever
suffered as she suffers :—

> Amis, encor bien dire l'os,
> Qu'onques Tristan ne Lancelos,
> Paris, Genevre, Yseult, n'Elaine,
> N'ensuivirent si les esclos
> De loyauté, ne le propos,
> Comme je faiz, n'a si grief paine.

There can, of course, be no doubt about the identity of Paris
here.

From Chaucer's *Assembly of Foules* :—

> Semyramus, Candace and Ercules,
> Biblys, Dido, Tesbe and Piramus,
> Tristram, Isoude, Paris and Achilles,
> Eleyne, Cleopatre and Troylus,
> Silla, and eke the moder of Romulus :—
> Alle these were peynted on that other syde,
> And al her love, and in what plite they dide.
> > (ll. 288-294.)

In the two following passages Iseult and Helen are coupled together, just as Dante couples Paris and Tristan.

The first is from one of the *Chançons Royaulx* of Eustache Deschamps, who belongs to the second half of the fourteenth century (from Ballad 368 in vol. iii. of the edition of Deschamps published by the Société des Anciens Textes Français) :—

> Qu'est devenuz Denys, le roy felon,
> Job le courtois, Thobie et leur lignée,
> Aristote, Ypocras et Platon,
> Judich, Hester, bonne Penelopée,
> Royne Dydo, Pallas, Juno, Medée,
> Guenievre, *Yseult et la tresbelle Helaine,*
> Palamides, Tristan a tout s'espée ?
> Ilz sont tous mors, ce monde est chose vaine.

The second is from the Prologue of Chaucer's *Legende of Goode Women :*—

> Hyde, Absolon, thy gilte tresses clere ;
>   Ester, ley thou thy mekenesse al adoun ;
> Hyde, Jonathas, al thy frendly manere ;
>   Penelopee and Marcia Catoun
>   Make of youre wifehode no comparysoun ;
> Hyde ye youre beautyes, *Ysoude and Eleyne,*
> My lady cometh, that al this may disteyne.

These instances make it pretty clear that Dante's allusion is to the Paris " qui de Gresse ravi Helaine," and not to the comparatively unknown hero of the mediæval story—who, it may be observed, so far from being " parted from his life through love "[1] (as was the Paris mentioned by Dante), died happily at the ripe age of 105, the father of seven children, as appears from the conclusion of the story :—

Paris eult de Madame Vienne sept enfans, quatre filz et trois filles. . . . Et sachiez que quant Paris mourut il avoit de aage cent et cinq ans, et Madame Vienne mourut cinq moys après lui de l'aage de iiiixx xvii ans. Et ainsi Dieu les appella de cest monde à la gloire de Paradis, à laquelle puissions nous tous parvenir.

---

[1] *Inf.* v. 69 : " amor di nostra vita dipartille ".

"IL RE GIOVANE" IN THE *INFERNO*
(xxviii. 135) [1]

THE subjoined quotations are of interest in connection with the vexed question of the reading in *Inferno*, xxviii. 135. The majority of MSS. and printed editions are in favour of the reading *Giovanni* in preference to the historically correct *giovane*. There is not the slightest doubt that the young King Henry, " Henricus Rex junior, filius Regis Henrici," who was encouraged by Bertran de Born to rebel against his father, is the person intended. The question is whether Dante, though acquainted with the facts, was ignorant of the name of the prince, and really thought he was called John, thus confounding Prince Henry with his younger brother ; or, whether he actually knew that the prince in question was the young King Henry, " il re giovane ".

I give, to begin with, the striking passage from the poem in which Bertran de Born, the Provençal troubadour, of whom Dante is speaking in the line referred to above, laments the death of his friend, Prince Henry—a poem which was probably known to Dante :—

> Si tuit li dol el plor el marrimen
> E las dolors el dan el caitivier
> Que hom agues en est segle dolen
> Fosson ensems, sembleran tuit leugier
> Contra la mort del jove rei engles.

> If all the grief and bitterness and woe,
>   And all the pain and hurt and suffering
> That in this world of misery men know,
>   Were massed in one, 'twould seem but a light thing
>   Beside the death of the Young English King.

The extracts given below have not, so far as I am aware, been quoted before in this connection :—

---

[1] *Academy*, 21st April, 1888.   See also below, p. 284.

Chil rois [Henris] . . .
Ot. I. fil qui ot nom Henris;
Cou fu Henri li Jouenes Rois
Qui mult fu sages et cortois.

. . . .

Henris . . .
Avoit souvent guerre as françois
Et à son fill le Jouene Roi,
Avoit grant guerre et grant annoi.

. . . .

Li Jouenes Rois tant guerroia
Que il mourut, puis commença
Le roi de France à guerroier
Le roi Henri cel aversier.

The above passages occur in a short poem appended as a continuation to Wace's "Roman de Brut" in a thirteenth-century
MS., and printed by Le Roux de Lincy in his edition of Wace,
vol. i. pp. cxv-cxxvii.

The following are from a thirteenth-century poem on the
life of Thomas à Becket, where the coronation of the Young
King holds an important place, as being the event which led to
the murder of the archbishop :—

Le pere fist au fiz grant feste.
Ne oïmes en chançun n'en geste
Ki fust de riche home servi
Cum fu le jofne rois Henri.
Li peres li fist joie si grant
K'a ceu jur li fu sergant,
E, oïanz plusurs, geï
Ke sul fu rois jofne Henri,
Ne mie cist ki dunc servi.

. . . .

Mult en vint mal e encumbrer
Par le jofne roi coruner,
Sanc de arcevesque espanduz,
Autres evesques suspenduz
Et li autre escumengez
E cunfunduz e exillez,
E guerre entre fiz e pere
Meüe mortele e amere.
Enmi les anz de sa juvente,
Es anz poi plus u meins de trente,
Murut li jouvre rois Henris,
Dunt veuz e jovres sunt mariz.

(*Fragments d'une Vie de Saint Thomas de Cantorbéry*,
ed. Paul Meyer, Paris, 1885.)

Similarly, in the twelfth-century poem on the same subject by Garnier de Pont Sainte-Maxence, the prince, after his coronation, is always alluded to as the Young King :—

> Li homme l'arcevesque en Engleterre alèrent ;
> Les lettres al veil Rei al juefne Rei portèrent.

And so in the long harangue addressed to the Archbishop by his murderers :—

> Les custumes del règne vols abatre et oster.
> E al juefne Rei voels sa corone tolir.

It is possible, but hardly likely, that Dante, who was not unacquainted with English history, should have been so ignorant of the main facts in the famous struggle between Henry II. and his Archbishop as to confound Prince Henry, the Young King of the chroniclers and poets,[1] with Prince John, who never received the title of king, at any rate of England, during his father's lifetime.   It is much more probable that the ignorance was on the part of the commentators (one of whom speaks of John as the son of King Richard !) and of the copyists, who, not understanding the allusion, garbled the line, and altered *giovane*, without more ado, into *giovañi* = *giovanni*.

"IL VECCHIO ALARDO" IN THE *INFERNO*
(xxviii. 18)[2]

THE following brief account of " Il Vecchio Alardo " (*Inferno*, xxviii. 18), of whom somewhat scanty notices are given by the Dante commentators, is compiled chiefly from contemporary sources.

Alardo di Valleri, or, to give him his French name and style, Erard, "seigneur de Valéry, de Saint-Valérian et de Marolles, connétable de Champagne," was born towards the end of the twelfth century.   The year of his birth is uncertain, but it can hardly have been later than 1200.   Together with his brother, Jean de Valéry, " mes sires Jehans de Waleri li preudom," as we know from Joinville, he accompanied St. Louis on his first

---

[1] For other instances of the title " Young King " applied to Prince Henry, see above, p. 144, and note 3.

[2] See *Academy*, 4th and 18th August, 1888.

expedition to the East in 1248.   Previous to this date little or
nothing is known of his doings.   Joinville makes frequent mention of Jean, but only once refers to Erard (lix. 295), when he
records the fact that he rescued his brother from the hands of
the Turks, who had made him prisoner in a skirmish.

M. Achille Jubinal has shown (in his edition of Rustebuef,
vol. iii. p. 41) that Erard was in France in 1255, and that in the
same year he was a prisoner in Holland, whence he was ransomed
by Charles of Anjou, after a captivity of a few months only.
In 1265 he went a second time to the East, according to the
continuators of Guillaume de Tyr ("A.M.CCLXV. vindrent en
Acre li cuens de Nevers, et Erart de Valérie, et Erart de Nantuel,
et bien L chevaliers ").

In 1268, finding himself, on account of his advancing years,
unequal to the fatigues and hardships of Oriental warfare, he
set out from Palestine to return to France.   On his way he went
into Italy, where his opportune arrival was hailed with delight
by Charles of Anjou, who was on the eve of a battle with the
young Conradin.   The two armies met at Tagliacozzo, and
Charles, though inferior in numbers, was enabled by the superior
skill of Erard to utterly crush his foe and take him prisoner.
Dante says of Erard, " senz' arme vinse," [1] in allusion to his
having won the battle, not by sheer force of arms, but by his
skilful manipulation of Charles's forces, and by a stratagem
through which he lured the troops of Conradin to destruction.[2]

In the next year, 1269 (his brother having apparently died
meanwhile), Erard once more assumed the cross, and accompanied
St. Louis on his second voyage to the East.   In 1271, after the
return of this expedition, in which St. Louis had met his death,
Erard was again in France, where he appears to have remained, in
a position of high importance, until his death.   This took place,
as M. Jubinal has proved by references to documents, in the
year 1277.

[1] *Inf.* xxviii. 18.

[2] Accounts of the battle of Tagliacozzo are given in Villani, vii. 26;
Sismondi, ii. 6; *Grandes Chroniques de France* (ed. P. Paris, vol. iv): " La
Vie Monseigneur Saint Loys," chap. xcviii; as well as in the *Comentum* of
Benvenuto da Imola.

Erard is spoken of with high praise by the Burgundian poet Rustebuef in *La Complainte dou Roi de Navarre* (*i.e.*, Teobaldo II., who had also accompanied St. Louis in 1270, and had died on his way home):—

> Mes sire Erars de Valeri
> A cui onques ne s'aferi
> Nus chevaliers de loiauté,
> Diex par vos si l'avoit fet tel
> Que mieudres n'i est demorez,
> Et au loing fust tant honorez.
>
> (ll. 125-130.)

And also in *La Complainte dou Conte Huede de Nevers* (which was written in 1267, Count Eudes having died in August of that year, twelve months before the battle of Tagliacozzo):—

> Mes sire Erart, Diex vos maintiengne
> Et en bone vie vos tiengne,
> Qu'il est bien mestiers en la terre!
> Que s'il avient que tost vos preingne,
> Je dot li païs ne remaingne
> En grant dolor et en grant guerre.
>
> (ll. 109-114.)

Guiart also in his *Branche aus royaus lignaiges* (quoted by M. Jubinal) describes him as

> Un haut baron cortois et sage,
> Et plain de si grand vasselage,
> Que son cors et ses fais looient
> Tuit cil qui parler en ooient.

M. Paulin Paris, in a note to a poem by Charles of Anjou, gives in French an amusing extract from the *Libro di novelle et di bel parlar gentile* [1] (Nov. v., ed Biagi), relating to a deception practised by Erard upon St. Louis at the instance of Charles, whereby he obtained permission to hold a tourney, which had previously been forbidden by the king (*Le Romancero François*, p. 120).

---

[1] Otherwise known as the *Cento Novelle Antiche*.

"CENNAMELLA" IN THE *INFERNO*
(xxii. 10)[1]

THE original of this word *cennamella*, which from the context evidently signifies a musical instrument of some sort, has been a puzzle to Dante commentators, as the word itself was long ago to the copyists, to judge by the numerous forms (*cannamella, cemmamella, ceramella, cialamella, ciaramella*) under which it appears in the MSS. of the *Divina Commedia.*

Blanc (in his *Vocabolario Dantesco*) thinks it is perhaps connected with Lat. *calamus* or *canna.* Diez (*Etymologisches Wörterbuch*, s.v. "Ceramella") hazards the suggestion that it may be a corrupted form of the Old French *chalemel.* It almost undoubtedly comes from the same source. Starting from Lat. *calamellus* (dim. of *calamus*; whence Prov. *calamel, caramel;* O. Fr. *chalemel;* Mod. Fr. *chalumeau;* Germ. *Schalmei;* Eng. *shawm*), we have low Lat. *calamella* (explained by Du Cange as "fistulatorius calamus," *i.e.*, a reed pipe), which gave Prov., O. Sp. *caramela*, Fr. *chalemelle* and *canemelle* (both of which occur in Froissart—the former in vol. xiv. p. 157 of the *Chroniques;* the latter in vol. ii. p. 308 of the *Póesies*, in the sixth line of the Pastourelle beginning "Entre Eltem et Wesmoustier").

We thus arrive at a word *canemelle*, deriving from *calamus*, through low Lat. *calamella*,[2] almost identical in form with Ital. *cennamella* or *cannamella*, which we need scarcely hesitate to refer to the same origin. The doubling of the *n* in the Italian word might seem to present a difficulty, but it may be due to a confusion with another word, identical in form, meaning "sugar-cane". (It may be noted, too, that Du Cange gives *cannamella*, in the sense of "fistula," as another form of *calamella.*) That the double consonant is not an inherent character-

---

[1] See *Academy*, 24th November, 1888.

[2] For the interchange of *l* and *n*, compare Fr. *quenouille*, Burg. *quelonge*, Champ. *coloigne*, from Lat. *colucula;* and Fr. *Boulogne*, Ital. *Bologna*, from Lat. *Bononia.*

istic is shown by the forms *ceramella* and *cialamella*, the latter of
which, recalling as it does the Fr. *chalemelle*, affords additional
ground for assigning a common origin to the French and
Italian words.

The word, then, used by Dante signifies a wind instrument,
probably some form of pipe or whistle, since he speaks of its
employment in signalling troops:—

> Nè già con sì diversa cennamella
> Cavalier vidi mover, nè pedoni.

The chronicler, Dino Compagni, Dante's contemporary and
fellow-citizen, uses the same word in a similar sense in one of his
poems [1]:—

> Udivi suon di molte dolzi danze
> In chitarre, caribi [2] smisurati,
> Trombe, e cennamelle in concordanze.

"POZZA" IN THE *INFERNO*
(vii. 127) [3]

THIS word, which is applied by Dante to the filth of the "palude
che ha nome Stige," in which the Wrathful are punished in the
fifth circle of the *Inferno*, seems to have been overlooked by
Diez. There is not much doubt about its meaning, for the
"palude" is also spoken of as "pantano" (l. 110), "limo"
(l. 121), and "belletta negra" (l. 124); while those who are
immersed in it are "genti fangose" (l. 110). The etymology
of the word is not so certain. It might either come, with a
change of gender, from Latin *puteus*, whence Italian *pozzo*,
French *puits*, English *pit*, and (according to Diez) German
Pfütze; or from Latin *putidus* (*i.e.*, *putida*, sc. *aqua*), whence
Italian *putto*, *puzzo*, *puzza*, Old French *put*, Old Spanish *púdio*.
For the transformation of *d* in *pozza = putida*, *cf.* *sozzo = sucidus*.
For the disappearance of the qualified substantive, *cf.* the close

---

[1] Printed by Nannucci, *Man. Lett. Ital.* i. 519.   [2] *Cf. Purg.* xxxi. 132.
[3] *Academy*, 29th December, 1888.

parallel *fontana*, *sc. aqua*, and such well-known instances as French *ramage* for *chant ramage = cantus ramaticus*, *sanglier* for *porc sanglier = porcus singularis*, and the like.

Blanc (*Vocab. Dant. s.v.*) brings *pozza* from German *Pfütze*; but there is no apparent reason for supposing the German word to be older than the Italian, and they may not even have a common origin.

If the derivation from *putida* be correct, *pozza* may merely be a variation of *puzza* (the word occurs in rhyme; *cf. soso = suso*, *Inf.* x. 45; *lome = lume*, *Inf.* x. 69; and conversely *nui = noi*, *Inf.* ix. 20; *summo = sommo*, *Inf.* vii. 119; *sutto = sotto*, *Inf.* xi. 26; etc.). In this case "la lorda pozza" would mean rather the "foul stench" of the pool than the "foul pool" itself.

TWO REFERENCES TO DANTE IN EARLY FRENCH LITERATURE [1]

THE following two references to the *Divina Commedia* by early French authors are of interest to students of Dante.

The first occurs in a poem called *Le Livre de Mutation de Fortune* by Christine de Pisan,[2] a Frenchwoman born at Venice in 1363, rather more than forty years after Dante's death. Speaking of Italy and the deadly strife between the Guelphs and Ghibellines, she says :—

> Tuit s'entr'ocient à l'estrive,
> L'une part contre l'autre estrive . . .
> N'en scevent nule autre achoison
> D'eulx entrocire sans raison,
> Fors que l'un dit que tout son lin
> A tout temps esté Guibelin,
> Et lui aussi Guibelin est.
> Li autres dit que Gueffes rest
> D'ancienneté de lignage . . .

---

[1] See *Academy*, 29th June, 1889.

[2] I have pointed out elsewhere (*Romania*, xxi. 228 foll.) that Christine de Pisan also wrote one of her poems, *Le Livre du Chemin de Long Estude*, avowedly in imitation of the *Divina Commedia*.

> C'est grant dommaige
> Qu' entre eux court si mauvais usaige;
> Leurs aucteurs meismes en ont dit,
> En les blasmant, maint divers dit.
> Dant de Florence, le vaillant
> Pouete qui tout son vaillant
> Perdy pour cel estrif grevable,
> En son bel livre très notable
> En parla moult en les blasmant. . . .

She then mentions Cecco d'Ascoli, and quotes from the *Acerba* his opinion of the Bolognese, after which she returns to Dante :—

> Et Dant en parlant à Flourance,
> Où il avoit sa demourance,
> En manière de moquerie
> Lui dit que : " S'esjoisse et rie,
> Car sur terre et sur mur s'ebatent
> Ses elles et mesmes s'embatent
> Jusqu'en enfer, en quel maison
> A de ses citoiens foison ".

Christine has here freely translated the opening lines of the twenty-sixth canto of the *Inferno*.[1]

The second reference is by Geoffroy Tory in his *Champ Fleury*, published in 1529, some sixty years before the appearance of the Abbé Grangier's translation of the *Divina Commedia* (which, by the way, Dean Plumptre[2] is mistaken in styling the first translation of the *Divina Commedia* into any modern European tongue, for it was preceded by at least one version, *viz.*, that in "rims vulgars cathalans" of the fifteenth century by Andreu Febrer). Geoffroy, in giving a list of authors whose works he regarded as authorities in the matter of language, says :—

On porroit en oultre user des œuvres de Arnoul Graban et de Simon Graban son frère.   Dantes Aligerius, Florentin, comme dict mon susdict bon amy frère René Massé, faict honorable mention dudict Arnoul Graban. . . .   On porroit semblablement bien user des belles chroniques de France que mon Seigneur Cretin, nagueres chroniqueur du roy, a si bien faictes, que Homère, ne Virgile, ne Dantes n'eurent oncques plus d'excellence en leur stile.   (See Génin's edition of Palsgrave's *Eclaircissement de la Langue Française*, pp. 8-11.)

---

[1] For an account of Christine's poem see Paulin Paris, *Manuscrits François*, vol v. pp. 133 foll.

[2] *The Commedia and Canzoniere of Dante*, vol. ii. p. 467.

It is evident that neither René Macé nor Geoffroy Tory can have known much about the *Divina Commedia* or its author, for Arnoul Greban, who was the author of the "Mystère de la Passion," a poem in about 30,500 lines, was born just a hundred years after the death of Dante. The "Arnaldo" of whom "honourable mention" is made by the latter is, of course, Arnaut Daniel.[1]

DANTE AND ARNAUT DANIEL: A NOTE ON *PURGATORIO* (xxvi. 118-119)[2]

IN a well-known passage in the twenty-sixth canto of the *Purgatorio*, where Dante gives his estimate of Arnaut Daniel, he says of him :—

> Versi d' amore e prose di romanzi
> Soverchiò tutti
>
> (ll. 118-119.)

which the large majority of translators and commentators— English, German and Italian—render : "In verses of love and prose of romance he excelled all (*tutti*, *i.e.*, *tutti gli altri fabbri del parlar materno*)" ; thus making Dante imply that Arnaut was the author not only of "versi d'amore," but also of "prose di romanzi," which almost certainly is not what he intended to say.   In fact there is no ground (beyond this mistranslation and the inferences drawn from it) for supposing that Arnaut ever wrote a "romance" in prose or verse, or that Dante ever thought so.   Whenever he mentions Arnaut in the *De Vulgari Eloquentia* it is with reference to his *Cantiones* only, without a hint at any other species of composition.[3]

Further, if, as is implied in the above rendering, Dante intended to say that Arnaut surpassed all other writers in the composition of prose romances in his "parlar materno" (*i.e.*, in Provençal), he is involved in a strange contradiction, for he expressly states in the *De Vulgari Eloquentia* (i. 10) that every-thing in the "vernacular prose," whether translated or original, was in the "Lingua Oil," *i.e.*, French :—

---

[1] *Purg.* xxvi. 142.   [2] See *Academy*, 13th April, 1889.
[3] *V.E.* ii. 2, ll. 80, 86 ; 6, l. 60 ; 10, l. 26 ; 13, l. 10.

" Allegat pro se Lingua *Oil*, quod propter sui faciliorem ac delectabiliorem vulgaritatem, quicquid redactum, sive inventum est ad vulgare prosaicum, suum est " (ll. 12-16).

He then goes on to say :—

" Pro se vero argumentatur alia, scilicet *Oc*, quod vulgares eloquentes in ea primitus poetati sunt, tanquam in perfectiori, dulciorique loquela " (ll. 20-24).

Not content with attributing to Arnaut the authorship of "romances," Raynouard and Diez, with a numerous following, go so far as to specify what these romances were—one of them being a *Lancelot*, which they suppose to be the version alluded to in *Inf.* v. 128, and *Par.* xvi. 15.[1] This attribution is particularly unfortunate, since Dante in this same chapter of the *De Vulgari Eloquentia* (i. 10, ll. 18-19) makes special mention of the " Arturi Regis ambages pulcherrimae " as an example of the " vulgare prosaicum " in the " Lingua Oil ". There is little doubt that the correct rendering of the passage in the *Purgatorio* is that suggested by the comment of Buti and adopted by Lombardi and Br. Bianchi : " He surpassed all (authors of) verses of love and prose of romance"—that is to say, having regard to the passages from the *De Vulgari Eloquentia*, quoted above, " he was superior to all who have written either in Provençal (*versi d'amore*) or French (*prose di romanzi*)". This interpretation, which seems to have been first put forward by M. Gaston Paris some years ago in his " Etudes sur les Romans de la Table Ronde,"[2] has been entirely ignored by many recent translators and commentators of the *Divina Commedia*, in spite of the fact that it meets all the difficulties of the passage without in any way forcing the sense of the words.

The expression " prose di romanzi " itself has given rise to considerable difference of opinion. Diez, accepting without examination a dictum (unsupported by any evidence) of Biagioli that " nel provenzale e nell' italiano del secolo xiii *prosa* significa precisamente istoria o narrazione in versi," concludes that

---

[1] I have shown elsewhere that this hypothesis is altogether superfluous (see above, *Dante and the Lancelot Romance*, pp. 7-8).

[2] *Romania*, x. 484 foll.

by "versi d'amore" and "prose di romanzi" Dante intended to
describe simply two different styles of poetry, *viz.*, lyric and
narrative—"wenn nun Dante unter *prose* den niedern poetischen
Styl versteht, so bezeichnet er mit *versi* den höhern des Liedes".
(*Poesie der Troubadours*, p. 186.) This conclusion has met with
very general acceptance among Dante commentators; but seeing
that Dante himself used *prosa* in its modern sense (*cf. Vita Nuova*
§ 25, ll. 54-55, where he distinguishes between *prosaici dicitori*
and *dicitori per rima*), as did also his "master" Brunetto Latino
(in the *Tesoretto*: "Ma i' ho già trovato In prosa e in rimato,"
i. 99-100), and Boccaccio (*cf. Decam. Giorn. iv, Prohem. ad. init.:*
"le presenti novellette . . . in fiorentin volgare ed in prosa scritte
per me sono"; and *Vita di Dante:* "fece ancora questo valoroso
Poeta molte pistole prosaiche") and Petrarch (*cf. Canzone* 37:
"Amor, come si legge in prosa e in versi"); and seeing, further,
that there is no longer any need to credit Arnaut Daniel with the
authorship of verse romances, as was done by Fauriel, Diez and
others, and that the modern sense of *prosa* satisfies the context
in every respect, it seems hardly justifiable to wrest it from that
sense in order to meet the exigencies of a theory based upon a
series of misconceptions.

The exact sense of *romanzo* as here used by Dante has also
been the subject of discussion. It is generally, and probably
correctly, regarded as the equivalent of Old Fr. *romans;* but
Canello, in his critical edition of Arnaut Daniel,[1] holds, somewhat unnecessarily, that since Dante is speaking of a Provençal
poet, the word must be taken in the sense of the Provençal
romans: "cioè, di poesia didattico morale"; and he understands
"versi d' amore e prose di romanzi" to mean: "versi o canzoni
d' amore e poesie di metro meno artificioso, d' argomento morale
e didattico"—thus adopting the unnatural rendering of *prosa*
mentioned above.

Those who are interested in the question may find it instructive to compare the whole myth of Arnaut Daniel's authorship of "romances," as set forth in Hueffer's *Troubadours* (pp.

---

[1] *La Vita e le Opere del trovatore Arnaldo Daniello* (Halle, 1883).

45-48), with the critical examination and refutation by Canello (*op. cit.* pp. 29-38) of the arguments upon which that myth was founded.

"IL SEMPLICE LOMBARDO" IN THE *PURGATORIO* (xvi. 126) [1]

In speaking of the degenerate state into which Lombardy had fallen after the wars between Frederick II. and the Lombard towns, Dante (in the sixteenth canto of the *Purgatorio*) says that there yet survive three old men whose lives are a reproach to the " young generation " :—

> Ben v' en tre vecchi ancora, in cui rampogna
> L' antica età la nuova.
>
> (ll. 121-122.)

One of these he says is,

> Guido da Castel, che me' si noma
> Francescamente il semplice Lombardo.
>
> (ll. 125-126.)

The usual explanation of this is that the term " Lombard " was a general name in France for an Italian; but this is not much to the point, for, as Mr. Butler remarks, if Guido was a Lombard there is nothing specially French in calling him so.

The term " Lombart," however, had a more special signification in French at that time, *viz.*, *usurer*—hence our " Lombard Street," and the " Rue des Lombards " in Paris (see Du Cange, *s.v. Langobardi*, and the instances given by Godefroy, *s.v. Lombart*).[2] Now, from a note on this passage in the *Ottimo Comento*, it appears that Guido da Castel had a great reputation for hospitality to those who passed by on their way to or from France :—

Messer Guido studio in onorare li valenti uomini, che passavano per lo cammino francesco, e molti ne rimise in cavalli ed armi, che di Francia erano

---

[1] *Academy*, 1st Nov., 1890.

[2] Compare the similar use of " Caorsin," to which Dante alludes, *Inf.* xi. 50. The " Caorsini " and " Lombardi " are constantly coupled together in the mediæval edicts against usurers. See Du Cange *s.v.* " Caorcini ".

passati di qua; onorevolmente consumate loro facultadi, tornavano meno ad arnesi, ch' a loro non si convenia, a tutti diede, senza speranza di merito, cavalli, arme, danari.

Perhaps, then, the term "il semplice Lombardo," applied to Guido by his French-speaking friends, was meant as a playful description of the "honest usurer" who supplied "horses, arms and money" and never expected any return; if this were so, there would at any rate be some point in the appellation, which there hardly is according to the ordinary interpretation.

THE ART OF ILLUMINATING AT PARIS IN THE TIME OF DANTE [1]

DANTE, in the eleventh canto of the *Purgatorio*, in speaking of Oderisi of Agubbio, whose spirit he sees among the Proud in the first circle of Purgatory, describes him as "the honour of that art which is called *illuminating* in Paris," "Quell' arte che alluminare è chiamata in Parisi" (l. 80); the word *alluminare* being used instead of the usual Italian *miniare*, in order to represent the French *alluminer, enluminer,* or *illuminer* (all three were employed). At first sight one is tempted to assume that in this passage Dante says "Paris" instead of "France" simply for the sake of the rhyme (*fisi : Oderisi : Parisi*). It appears, however, that there was a special significance in the mention of Paris in connection with the art of illuminating.

M. Samuel Berger, in his interesting book on the old French Bible (*La Bible Française au Moyen Age*, Paris, 1884), shows that in the Middle Ages Paris actually was the headquarters in France of the illuminating craft. Here the miniatures which adorned the MSS. not of Bibles only, but of other works also, were produced and continually reproduced after the same design, so exactly, says M. Berger, as to resemble each other almost as closely as printed impressions.

La Bible française était, avant tout, copiée dans les grandes librairies de Paris. . . . Paris est bien le centre du travail. C'est Paris qui, à partir de l'an 1250, prend la tête dans l'œuvre de copier la Bible française. Le texte latin sur

[1] *Academy*, 26th March, 1892.

lequel la Bible a été traduite avait été corrigé dans l'Université de Paris ; la
Bible latine, revue par l'Université, a si bien laissé sa marque à la version française qui en est sortie, que les miniatures mêmes des Vulgates parisiennes ont passé
en partie dans le texte français. Il y a en effet au moyen âge une *vulgate* pour
les peintures mêmes, une tradition qui passe des Bibles de l'Université aux Bibles
françaises. . . . La tradition dominait toute l'illustration des manuscrits. Cette
tradition n'est pas spéciale aux Bibles françaises ; elle se formait à Paris dès le
XIIᵉ siècle ; elle a pris ses premiers développements dans les Bibles latines de
l'Université, copiées au milieu du XIIIᵉ siècle. . . . La Bible française était
copiée dans l'Université, dans ces ateliers où la miniature était scrupuleusement
surveillée et mieux revue que le texte, et d'où sortaient des œuvres qui se
ressemblaient quelquefois presque autant que des livres imprimés (pp. 281 ff.).

It is evident, then, that in Dante's time Paris was the great
centre for the production of illuminated MSS. of all kinds, Bibles
especially, so that in mentioning the French term Dante naturally speaks of the art as Parisian. The importance of the
illuminating craft in Paris at that date may be gathered from
the fact that it was one of the " free crafts," which were exempt
from the obligation of keeping watch and ward.

Ce sont les mestiers frans de la ville de Paris, qui ne doivent point de guet
au roy . . . paintres, ymagiers, libraires, parcheminiers, enlumineurs. (*Livre
des métiers*, 425.)

" HELIOTROPIUM " IN DANTE'S LETTER TO THE PRINCES AND PEOPLES OF ITALY

(*EPISTOLAE*, V. 1)[1]

THERE is a difficult passage in the letter of Dante to the
Princes and Peoples of Italy (" Ecce nunc tempus acceptabile "
—*Epist.* v. in the Oxford Dante) which has not yet been satisfactorily explained. The difficulty is increased by the fact that
the reading is not certain. Dante says : " Titan exorietur
pacificus, et justitia, sine sole, quasi ad (vv. ll. *quasi ut, quasi
ac*) heliotropium hebetata, cum primum jubar ille vibraverit,
revirescet ". Mr. Latham[2] translates : " Titan shall arise
pacific, and justice, which had languished without sunshine
at the end of the winter's solstice, shall grow green once
more, when first he darts forth his splendour ". He points

[1] See *Academy*, 2nd April, 1892.
[2] *A Translation of Dante's Eleven Letters*, by C. S. Latham (pp. 133-134).

out in a note that both Torri and Fraticelli take *heliotropium* in the sense of heliotrope, the plant, "fior d' eliotropio". Witte, in his review of Torri's edition of Dante's letters,[1] questions the correctness of this rendering. He believes the correct interpretation to be that adopted in the old translation attributed to Marsilio Ficino, in which *heliotropium* is taken to mean the "winter solstice"; "la quale era senza luce al termina della retrogradazione impigrita". Latham himself favours this rendering, as does the German translator of the letters, K. L. Kannegiesser, who translates: "die Gerechtigkeit, die ohne ihre Sonne gleich Pflanzen um die Zeit der Sonnenwende erstorben war". The objection to this rendering is that no other instance is known of the use of *heliotropium* in the sense of "winter-solstice". With regard to the rendering "fior d' eliotropio," Witte objects that the plant heliotrope was hardly known in Dante's time. This however is a mistake, as the plant is frequently mentioned by mediæval writers,[2] who got their knowledge of it doubtless from Pliny, or from the familiar story of the metamorphosis of Clytie by Apollo into a heliotrope plant. (*Cf.* Ovid, *Metam.* iv. 256 ff.) If Torri and Fraticelli are correct it would seem necessary for "quasi ad heliotropium" to read either "quasi ut" with Giuliani and the Oxford Dante, or "quasi ac" in accordance with a suggestion of Mr. Lowell.

It is possible, however, that Dante is here referring to one of the well-known (legendary) properties[3] of the precious stone called *heliotropium*, which, when placed in water, had the power of altering or dimming the reflection of the sun. Mention is made of this in the old French *Lapidaire de Berne*[4]:—

> Une pierre qui fait merveilles,
> Onques n'oïstes les pareilles,
> Hat nom *elyotropia* :
> Vertu et force trop i hat.

[1] *Dante-Forschungen*, i. 496-497.

[2] Uguccione da Pisa, for instance (see above, p. 112); and Giovanni da Genova, who in his *Catholicon* says: "*Helyotropium, -pii*, quaedam herba, quia solis motibus folia circumacta convertat."

[3] Dante refers to its supposed property of rendering the wearer invisible, in the *Inferno* (xxiv. 93).

[4] See Pannier, *Lapidaires français du Moyen âge* (p. 137).

Qui le met en l'aigue, si change
Le solel en color estrange,
Puis après fait l'aigue bolir,
Et movoir et en haut saillir.
(ll. 941 ff.)

A similar account is given in the *Catholicon* of Giovanni da Genova, no doubt derived from the *Origines* (xvi. 7) of Isidorus Hispalensis; and Mr. R. R. Steele quotes[1] another from Glanville:—

Heliotrope is a precious stone, and is green, and sprinkled with red drops and veins of the colour of blood. . . . If it be put in water before the sun beams, it maketh the water seeth in the vessel that it is in, and resolveth it as it were into mist, and soon after it is resolved into rain-drops. Also it seemeth that this same stone may do wonders, for if it be put in a basin with clear water, it changeth the sun beams by rebounding of the air, and seemeth to shadow them, and breedeth in the air red and sanguine colour, and as though the sun were in eclipse and darked . . . And in *Lapidario* the same meaning is said in this manner:—

> " Ex re nomen habens est heliotropia gemma,
> Quae solis radiis in aqua subjecta vacillo,
> Sanguineum reddit mutato lumine solem,
> Eclipsemque novam terris effundere cogit," etc.[2]

If Dante's reference were actually to this property of the precious stone, the meaning of the phrase " quasi ad heliotropium hebetata" would be " as it were dimmed by the heliotrope".

DID DANTE KNOW HEBREW?[3]

HAD Dante access to Hebrew literature, either of his own knowledge or through the medium of his Jewish friend, Immanuel Ben Salomo of Rome? This question has often been discussed (see T. Paur, *Jahrbuch der deutschen Gesellschaft*, iii. 423-462; iv. 667-672; K. Witte, *Dante-Forschungen*, ii. 43-47; Plumptre,

[1] See *Academy*, 9th April, 1892.

[2] The original of this passage occurs in Lib. xvi. cap. 41 of the *De Proprietatibus Rerum*, the author of which is more commonly known as Bartholomaeus Anglicus. The work was written about 1260, a few years before Dante was born. (See Jourdain, *Recherches sur les traductions latines d'Aristote*, pp. 33, 358-360.) For a similar account by Uguccione da Pisa, see above, p. 112.

[3] *Academy*, 15th October, 1892.

Commedia and Canzoniere of Dante, I. lxxv-lxxvii ; and F. Delitzsch, *Zwei Kleine Dante - Studien* in the *Zeitschrift für Kirchliche Wissenschaft* for 1888, i. 41-50). There is, however, one small point of some interest in this connection which, so far as I am aware, has hitherto been left unnoticed.

In the Targum on the Book of Esther Mordecai the Jew is continually designated by the appellation of "the Just"[1] (see Smith, *Dict. of Bible*, *s.v.* "Mordecai"), an expression which is not used of him in the biblical text. It is worthy of note, though it may be a mere coincidence, that in the passage of the *Purgatorio* (xvii. 29) where Dante sees Haman *crocifisso* (an expression, by the way, justified by the Vulgate, "Domum Aman concessi Esther, et ipsum jussi affigi cruci," *Lib. Est.* viii. 7),[2] with Ahasuerus, Esther and Mordecai grouped around him, he speaks of the last as "il giusto Mardocheo".

DANTE'S "GUIZZANTE" (*Inferno* xv. 4)—THE MEDIÆVAL PORT OF WISSANT[3]

In describing the embankment on the borders of the river Phlegethon in Hell, Dante compares it (in the fifteenth canto of the *Inferno*) to the dykes built by the Flemings along the sea coast between " Guizzante" and Bruges :—

> Quale i Fiamminghi tra Guizzante e Bruggia,
> Temendo il fiotto che ver lor s'avventa,
> Fanno lo schermo, perchè il mar si fuggia.
> (ll. 4-6.)

Most modern commentators assume that Dante is here speaking of Cadsand—a place in the Netherlands, in the province of Zeeland, about fifteen miles N.E. of Bruges—on the authority

---

[1] *Cf.* the Prologue to the Wycliffite versions of the Book of Esther : " This book of Hester, the qween, makith mynde of the riȝtful Mardochee, and of the wickidde man Aman ".

[2] So also in the Wycliffite versions : " The hous of Aman I haue grauntid to Ester, the quen, and hym I haue comaundid to be ficchid (*var.* hangid) on the cros ".

[3] See *Academy*, 10th December, 1892.

apparently of Lodovico Guicciardini, who in his description of the Low Countries (written in the sixteenth century) says of that place:—

Quest' è quel medesimo luogo, del quale il nostro gran poeta Dante fa menzione nel quintodecimo capitolo dell' Inferno, chiamandolo scorettamente, forse per errore di stampa, *Guizzante*. (See Philalethes and Lubin *in loc.*)

On the strength of this statement it has been proposed to read *Cassante*, for which, however, there appears to be no MS. authority, the only variants recorded by Witte being *Guzzante* and *Guanto*—the latter an obvious error.

One chief objection to identifying "Guizzante" with Cadsand is, that where Cadsand is mentioned by contemporary Italian writers (as, for instance, Villani, Lib. xi. cap. 70) it is called *Gaggiante*. On the other hand, "Guizzante" is the undoubted Italian form of Wissant, a place between Calais and Cape Grisnez. This is proved by a reference to Villani, who, in recording the movements of Edward III. after Crecy, describes how he marched along the coast and successively attacked Montreuil, Boulogne, Wissant and Calais:—

Partito il re Adoardo dal campo di Crecì ove avea avuta la detta vittoria, ed essendo con sua oste a Mosteruolo, credendolosi avere, ch' era della contea e dote della madre, la terra era bene guernita per lo re di Francia de' molti Franceschi rifuggiti dalla sconfitta; sì si difesono, e non la potè avere: guastolla intorno, e poi n' andò a Bologna in su lo mare, e fece il somigliante. Poi ne venne a Guizzante, e perchè non era murato, il rubò tutto; e poi vi mise fuoco, e tutta la villa guastarono. E poi ne vennono a Calese, e quello era murato e afforzato, e dieronvi battaglia più volte e nol poterono avere. (xii. 68.)

All this district at that period formed part of Flanders, as there is abundant evidence to show. The identification of the Italian "Guizzante" with Wissant is further assured by the Provençal form *Guissan*, which occurs in one of the "Complaints" of Bertran de Born for the death of the "Young King" (son of Henry II. of England). After saying that England, Normandy, Brittany, Ireland, Aquitaine, Gascony, Anjou, Maine, and Touraine, are all affected by his loss, he continues: "Let France not refrain from weeping even as far as Compiègne; nor Flanders from Ghent to the port of Wissant; let even Germany weep!"

> Engles e Norman
> Breto e Irlan,
> Guian e Gasco
> E Angeus pren dan
> E Maines e Tors ;
> Fransa tro Compenha
> De plorar nos tenha,
> E Flandres de Gan
> Trol port de *Guissan ;*
> Ploren neis li Aleman.

Again, we have in Old French the almost identical form, *Guit-sand*, which occurs in the *Chanson de Roland*, in the description of the great earthquake just before the death of Roland—"from Besançon to the port of Wissant, not a building but had its walls cracked" :—

> De Besençun tresqu'as porz de *Guitsand* (*var.* Wissant),
> Nen ad recet dunt li murs ne cravent.
>
> (ll. 1429-30.)

Wissant was a place of great importance in the Middle Ages, as being the port *par excellence* through which passed the traffic between England and the Continent. It has been identified with the *Portus Itius*, whence Cæsar crossed over into Britain ; and it appears, from the constant references to it in the Chronicles and in Old French poems, to have been used continuously as the most convenient port of departure for England down to the beginning of the fourteenth century, when the destruction of the town (which Froissart calls "une grosse ville") by Edward III. caused the adjacent port of Boulogne to be used in its stead, the English themselves after the taking of Calais in 1347, making use of the latter port.[1]

In illustration of what has been said above, I subjoin a few passages which I have come across in various Anglo-Norman poems.

---

[1] Wissant is frequently mentioned before its destruction, both by Jehan le Bel and Froissart, as the port of departure for England. For instance, the former records how, when John of Hainault was sent for by the English king to help him against the Scots, he gave orders for his force to rendezvous at Wissant. "Et quant il et toute sa compaignie furent venus à Wissant, ilz trouvèrent les naves toutes aprestées, et y mirent au plus tost qu'ilz poeurent chevaulx et harnas, et passèrent oultre, et vinrent à Douvres" (chap. vii.).

King Arthur embarks at Wissant on his way home to chastise the traitor Mordred :—

> Artus oï, et bien savoit
> Que Mordret foi ne li portoit . . .
> En Bretaigne retorneroit . . .
> Et de Mordret se vengeroit . . .
> Ensi vint Artus à *Wissant* (*var.* Guingant)
> Del parjure Mordret plaignant.
> > (Wace, *Roman de Brut*, ll. 13,437 ff.)

While at Wissant, waiting to embark for England in 1170, Becket is warned that danger awaits him on the other side of the Channel :—

> Milun s'en vient ki ert serjant
> Au passagëur de *Withsant :*
> "Sire volez ke voirs vus cunte
> De part mun seignur le cunte
> De Buloine ?   Armée gent
> De la mer par mal vus atent."
> > (*Fragments d'une Vie de Saint Thomas de Cantorbéry*, ed.
> > Paul Meyer, p. 23.)

Becket crosses in 1170 from Wissant to Sandwich, avoiding Dover for fear of his foes :—

> De sun païs veeir aveit gran desirrier . . .
> A *Huitsand* est venuz, ala par le graver,
> Pur esgarder l'oré et pur esbaneier. . . .
> Sainz Thomas l'endemain en une nef entra ;
> Deus li dona boen vent ; à Sanwiz ariva.
> Kar l'arriver de Dovre, pur la gueit, eschiva.
> > (Garnier de Pont-Sainte-Maxence, *Vie de Saint Thomas
> > de Canterbury*, ll. 4,561 ff.)

The "Young King" and William the Marshal cross from Dover to Wissant on their return to the Continent in 1175 :—

> Tot dreit à Dovre s'aveierent ;
> A mer entrerent maintenant,
> Si ariverent à *Wizant*.
> > (*Guillaume le Maréchal*, ll. 2436-38.)

Also in the fourteenth-century Anglo-Norman romance of *Fulk Fitz-Warenne* we read how the outlaw Fulk and his companions, fleeing from the wrath of King John, made for Dover, and crossed over to Wissant on their way to Paris :—

Fouke tant erra nuyt et jour qu'il vynt à Dovre; e yleqe encontra Baudwyn
. . . E se minstrent en meer, e aryverent à *Whytsond.*

For the following, which are extracted from various chronicles
and other sources, I am indebted to the dissertation of Du Cange
on the Portus Itius (*Glossarium*, vol. x. pp. 96-100). About
569, St. Wlgan, a companion of St. Columban, crossing from
England "appulit ad portum *Witsan* appellatum, qui videlicet
locus ex albentis sabuli interpretatione tale sortitur vocabulum".
Here we get a suggestion as to the origin of the name, *viz.*,
White-sand, which is repeated by another author: "Ab albedine
arenae vulgari nomine appellatur *Vintsand*".

In 933 Aethelstan's brother, being banished, crosses over
"angusto scilicet a Doeria in *Withsand* mari".

About 1069 the Abbot of Saint Riquier, being minded to
visit the English property of the monastery, "ad maris ingressum
properavit quem nominant plebeiales *Guizant*" (here again we
have a form almost identical with the Italian *Guizzante*).

In 1097 St. Anselm on his way to Rome "*Withsandum*
appulit".

In 1110 Henry I. sends his daughter Matilda on her way to
wed the Emperor Henry V., "a Dovere usque ad *Witsand*".

In 1179 Henry II., on his return from France, "navem
ascendens apud *Witsand*, in Angliam rediit".

In 1187 Henry II., crossing back to France just before his
death, "applicuit apud *Witsand in Flandria*" (here we have the
express statement that Wissant was in Flanders, as again below).

During the reign of Richard Cœur-de-Lion, John, crossing
over to France, "Applicuit *in Flandria apud Wissand*".

It is needless to give any further examples. The above are
sufficient to practically establish the identity of "Guizzante"
with Wissant, both as regards the form of the word and the
situation of the place itself. I need only remark in conclusion
that, since the name of the port of Wissant must have been
perfectly well known all over the Continent in Dante's time, it
is quite unnecessary, as certain commentators have done, to
assume that the poet had been there in person, in order to
account for his mention of it.

DANTE'S USE OF THE NAME "TRINACRIA" FOR SICILY

(*PARADISO*, VIII. 67)[1]

In the eighth canto of the *Paradiso*, Charles Martel, eldest son of Charles II. of Naples, is represented as saying that if he had lived he would have been Count of Provence (ll. 58-60), King of Apulia (ll. 61-63), and King of Hungary (ll. 64-66); and he adds (ll. 67-75) that his descendants would have ruled in "Trinacria," had it not been for the misgovernment of his grandfather, Charles of Anjou, which led to the massacre known as the "Sicilian Vespers" and the expulsion of the French from Sicily.

There is almost certainly a special significance in the use of the name "Trinacria" here, which has escaped the notice of the commentators.

At the time Charles Martel is supposed to be speaking (*i.e.*, in 1300, the date of the action of the poem), the King of Sicily was Frederick II. of Aragon (1296-1337), a member of the rival house (the representative, through Manfred's daughter Constance, of the hated Suabian dynasty), which had dispossessed the Angevins, and had remained masters of Sicily in spite of all the efforts of the latter to dislodge them. After the disastrous failure of Charles of Valois' expedition against Sicily in 1302, he was forced to conclude an ignominious peace with Frederick, who was confirmed in the sovereignty of Sicily by the title of "King of Trinacria" (this title having been adopted, doubtless, instead of that of "King of Sicily," because the latter would imply sovereignty over both the Sicilies, *i.e.*, over Naples and Apulia, which remained in the hands of the Angevins, as well as over the island of Sicily); and it was by the title of "King of Trinacria" that Frederick was recognised by Boniface VIII. in the treaty of Anagni in the following year

---

[1] *Academy*, 25th February, 1893.

(12th June, 1303).   (See Sismondi, vol. ii. ch. ix. pp. 340-341, ed. 1838.)

The employment, therefore, by Charles Martel of this particular name for Sicily lends an additional sting to his utterances (which, of course, are partly prophetic) in rebuke of his house; and there can hardly be a doubt that Dante introduced it here with that intention, and not as a mere synonym for Sicily [1] as the commentators take it.

The only writer apparently who saw that there was some point in Dante's use of the name was Vigo, who says (*Dante e la Sicilia*, p. 9):—

Notisi quì Dante non appellare l' isola nostra *Cicilia*, come usò sempre nelle prose e poesie volgari; ma bensì *Trinacria* . . . e ciò quest' unica volta; non già per la sua forma tricuspide, ma invece per ragion politica.

He does not seem, however, to have made clear what the political reason was; for Scartazzini, from whom this quotation is taken, puts a query after the last sentence, evidently not understanding the allusion.

"IL CIOTTO DI GERUSALEMME" IN THE *PARADISO* (xix. 127)—THE CLAIM OF CHARLES OF ANJOU TO THE TITLE OF JERUSALEM [2]

IN the nineteenth canto of the *Paradiso*, Dante alludes to Charles II. of Naples as "Il Ciotto di Gerusalemme," "The Cripple of Jerusalem" (he was lame, "fu sciancato alquanto," as Villani records). The title of Jerusalem Charles II. derived from his father, Charles of Anjou, King of Naples and Sicily, who claimed to have acquired the right to it by purchase from Mary of Antioch in 1272; he further claimed it in his own right, as one of the forfeited Hohenstaufen dignities, with which he had been invested by the Pope.

The title had come to the Hohenstaufen through the marriage of the Emperor Frederick II. to his second wife, Iolanthe of

---

[1] The name occurs as a synonym for Sicily several times in Dante's Latin works; *e.g.*, *V.E.* i. 12, l. 15; ii. 6, l. 48; *Ecl.* ii. 71.

[2] See *Academy*, 1st April, 1893.

Brienne, daughter of John of Brienne and Mary of Montferrat, eldest daughter of Isabella of Jerusalem and Conrad of Montferrat.[1] It appears that Frederick II.'s son, Conrad, was deprived of the title in 1243 by the Grand Council of Acre, by whom the regency of the kingdom of Jerusalem, and eventually (in 1268, in which year Conradin, Conrad's heir, was executed at Naples by Charles of Anjou after the battle of Tagliacozzo) the kingdom itself, was conferred upon the King of Cyprus. The Hohenstaufen right to the title, therefore, had expired with the last of that line.

Mary of Antioch claimed the title through her mother, Melesinda of Lusignan (married Bohemond IV. of Antioch), daughter of Isabella of Jerusalem by her fourth husband, Almaric II. of Lusignan (King of Jerusalem and Cyprus, 1197-1205). But the King of Cyprus (Hugh III., 1267-1284), the actual holder of the dignity, could show a better title to it than Mary of Antioch,[2] inasmuch as he was lineally descended from an elder sister of her mother; that is to say, he was eldest surviving grandson of Alice of Champagne (married Hugh I., King of Cyprus, 1205-1218), daughter of Isabella by her third husband, Henry II. of Champagne (King of Jerusalem, 1192-1197). Consequently, the pretension of Charles of Anjou to the crown of Jerusalem was invalid either way, since the Hohenstaufen title had lapsed, and that of Mary of Antioch was worthless as against the title of the King of Cyprus.

---

[1] Isabella was the youngest daughter of Almaric I. (King of Jerusalem, 1162-1173) and became heiress to the title by the successive deaths of her half-brother, Baldwin IV., her half-sister, Sibylla, and her nephew, Sibylla's son, Baldwin V.

[2] Hallam (*Middle Ages*, chap. iii. part 1, note) calls Mary " legitimate heiress of Jerusalem ". He has overlooked the superior claim of the royal house of Cyprus.

THE DATE OF CACCIAGUIDA'S BIRTH

(*PARADISO*, XVI. 34-39)[1]

AMONG the objections urged by the commentators against the acceptance of the year 1091 as the date of Cacciaguida's birth (*Paradiso*, xvi. 34-39) is the consideration that in that case he would have been fifty-six when, by his own account (*Paradiso*, xv. 139-148), he accompanied the Emperor Conrad III. on the Second Crusade (1147-1149)—it being assumed that no one was likely to join an expedition to the East at such an advanced age.

It may be pointed out that the force of this objection is considerably weakened by the fact that the famous veteran, Erard de Valéry (the "vecchio Alardo" of *Inferno*, xxviii. 18), was at least sixty-five when (in 1265) he made his second voyage to the Holy Land. It was on his way back from Palestine three years later that he played such an important part in the battle of Tagliacozzo (23rd August, 1268), which resulted in the defeat of the young Conradin by Charles of Anjou, and the final extinction of the Hohenstaufen dynasty.

Still more to the point is the fact that, in the following year, Erard again assumed the Cross, and accompanied St. Louis on the ill-fated last Crusade, at which time he was close upon seventy.[2]

There is nothing very extravagant, therefore, in the assumption that Cacciaguida did a similar thing at the age of fifty-six. Benvenuto da Imola, indeed, complacently makes the latter go crusading at the age of one hundred! which shows him to have been on this occasion hardly more wide awake than those ingenious commentators who represent Cacciaguida as having been born some twenty years after his own death.

---

[1] *Academy*, 22nd April, 1893.

[2] See above, *Il Vecchio Alardo*, p. 256.

HUGH CAPET IN THE *DIVINA COMMEDIA* AND THE *SATYRE MÉNIPPÉE* [1]

In a well-known passage in the *Purgatorio* (xx. 52) Dante describes Hugh Capet (whom he has apparently in several particulars confounded with his father, Hugh the Great) as "figliuol d' un beccaio di Parigi"—the son of a butcher of Paris.

There is an interesting allusion to this passage in the *Satyre Ménippée* (published in 1594, two years before the appearance of the Abbé Grangier's translation of the *Divina Commedia* into French verse), where the Cardinal de Pelvé, speaking with contempt of the Bourbon Henry IV., says:—

> Iste vero est infamis propter haeresim, et tota familia Borboniorum descendit de becario, sive mavultis de lanio, qui carnem vendebat in laniena Parisina, ut asserit quidam poeta valde amicus Sanctae sedis Apostolicae, et ideo qui noluisset mentiri. (*ed.* Ch. Read, p. 107.)

Villon has a reference to the same legend about Hugh Capet's origin :—

> Se fusse des hoirs Hue Capel,
> Qui fut extraict de boucherie,
> On ne m'eust, parmy ce drapel,
> Faict boyre à celle escorcherie.
> (*Ballade de l'Appel de Villon*, ll. 9-12.)

But how far he was indebted to Dante for this piece of information it is impossible to say. The tradition was well established in France as early as the first half of the fourteenth century, to which period belongs the *Chanson de Geste* entitled "Hugon Capet," wherein Hugh Capet himself is spoken of as a butcher :—

> Ce fu Huez Capez c'on appelle bouchier.
> (l. 11.)

Littré sought the origin of the legend in the etymology of the name *Capet*, which he took to be connected with Old Fr. *chapler* (L. *capulumare*), "to cut to pieces"; and he referred to

[1] *Academy*, 24th June, 1893.

the German form of the name, *Hugo Schapler*, as a confirmation of this hypothesis. M. Gaston Paris, however, regards this etymology as wholly fanciful, so that the origin of the myth is yet to seek. There is a curious parallel to it in the *Chanson des Saisnes* of Jean Bodel, who makes out Charlemagne to be the grandson of a neatherd, whereat M. Léon Gautier exclaims: "C'est dans une vacherie qu'aurait commencé la seconde race de nos rois, et dans une boucherie la troisième!" somewhat naïvely adding: "Si la chose était vraie, nons saurions en être fiers; mais inventer de telles fables!"

It may be remarked that Giovanni Villani, in his chapter on the Capetian kings of France, mentions that most people regarded Hugh Capet as descended from a butcher, but that some claimed him to be of noble birth :—

> Per alcuno si scrive, che fur sempre i suoi antichi e duchi e di grande lignaggio . . . ma per li più si dice, che 'l padre fu uno grande e ricco borgese di Parigi stratto di nazione di buccieri, ovvero mercantante di bestie. (iv. 4.)

Benvenuto da Imola is of opinion that Dante expressly placed on record Hugh Capet's humble origin, which he learned during his residence in Paris, in order to expose the fiction as to his noble birth :—

> Nota quod aliqui dicunt quod iste fuit nobilissimus miles de Normandia; alii quod fuit dux Aureliani. Sed Dantes curiosissimus investigator rerum memorandarum (*var.* modernarum), cum esset Parisius gratia studii, reperit quod iste Hugo de rei veritate fuerat filius carnificis. Ideo reputat fictum quidquid aliter dicatur, ad colorandum vilitatem originis, sicut multi faciunt.

AN ERRONEOUS READING IN THE *DE MONARCHIA* (ii. 3) [1]

In tracing the descent of Aeneas in the second book of the *De Monarchia* (cap. 3, ll. 58 ff.), Dante claims that he was noble in respect of all three continents; and to prove his connection with Africa, he refers to his ancestress Electra, the mother of Dardanus, whom he describes as the daughter of the African king,

[1] See *Academy*, 8th July, 1893.

Atlas. In support of this statement he quotes *Aeneid*, viii. 134-136.

Modern editors of the *De Monarchia* (*viz.*, Fraticelli, Torri, Witte and Giuliani) make nonsense of this passage by printing :—

> Dardanus . . .
> Electra, ut Graii perhibent, *et* Atlantide cretus,

an impossible Virgilian hexameter,[1] which involves an absurdity in any case, since Electra and Atlantis are, of course, one and the same person.

Strangely enough, this blunder [2] has been perpetuated by an English scholar, Mr. F. J. Church (in his translation of the *De Monarchia*), who has at the same time involved himself in another, by rendering the corrupt line, " Dardanus . . . whom the Greeks call the son of Atlas and Electra," thus confusing Atlantis, " the daughter of Atlas," with Atlas himself. He has unfortunately further confused the matter by calling Electra " grandmother " of Aeneas, a too literal translation of Dante's *avia*. Aeneas's descent from Electra, as given by Servius (in *Aen.* viii. 130), with whose commentary Dante was doubtless acquainted, is as follows : " Ex Electra, Atlantis filia, et Jove Dardanus nascitur ; ejus filius Erichthonius ; ex eo Assaracus ; ex illo Capys ; ex illo Anchises ; ex illo Aeneas ".

---

[1] The first syllable of *Atlas* and its compounds is invariably long in Virgil, though Ovid sometimes shortens it, *e.g.*, *Metam*. iv. 368.

[2] This blunder appears for the first time in the text of the *De Monarchia* printed by Fraticelli in 1839, together with the Italian translation of Marcilio Ficino. The mistake was apparently due in the first instance to Ficino, who translates : " Dardano . . . il quale, come i greci dicono, di Elettra e del figliuolo di Atlante fu generato ". Fraticelli, who was the first to print Ficino's translation, appears to have altered the Latin text so as to make it correspond (as he supposed) with the translation. The correct reading which stood for nearly three hundred years (*i.e.*, from 1559, the date of the *editio princeps*, down to Fraticelli's edition of 1839) has now been restored by Dr. Moore in the Oxford Dante. It is curious to note, in connexion with the *editio princeps*, that the printer, Joannes Oporinus, in his *Epistola Dedicatoria*, expressly states that the work is not by Dante, the celebrated poet, but by another Dante, a friend of Politian : " Dantis Aligherii, non vetustioris illius Florentini poetae celeberrimi, sed philosophi acutissimi atque doctissimi viri, et Angeli Politiani familiaris quondam ".

WAS DANTE ACQUAINTED WITH CLAUDIAN?[1]

In the almost certainly apocryphal letter of Dante to Guido da Polenta (Epist. viii. in Fraticelli's edition, Epist. iv. in that of Giuliani),[2] Dante is made to quote as Virgil's the hemistich: "minuit praesentia famam". As a matter of fact the quotation is from Claudian's *De Bello Gildonico* :—

> Vindictam mandasse sat est; plus nominis horror,
> Quam tuus ensis aget, minuit praesentia famam.
> (ll. 385-386.)

This attribution to Virgil of a passage from Claudian is one of several reasons for rejecting this letter as spurious; for it is hardly credible that any one so intimately acquainted with Virgil as Dante was, should have been guilty of such a blunder.

It is, however, curious—and the point does not seem to have been noticed before—that Dante apparently was familiar with the passage from Claudian quoted in the letter. After a discussion in the *Convivio* as to the origin and growth of good fame, in the course of which he quotes the Virgilian: "Fama . . . Mobilitate viget, viresque adquirit eundo," he concludes by saying it is evident that the image created by fame alone is always an exaggeration of the truth :—

> Apertamente adunque veder può chi vuole, che la immagine, per sola fama generata, sempre è più ampia, quale che essa sia, che non è la cosa immaginata nel vero stato. (*Convivio*, i. 3, ll. 77-82.)

He then proceeds in the next chapter to show how, on the other hand, presence has exactly the opposite effect, and unduly diminishes the actual worth of a person :—

> Mostrata la ragione innanzi, perchè la fama dilata lo bene e lo male oltre la vera quantità, resta in questo capitolo a mostrare quelle ragioni che fanno vedere perchè la presenza ristrigne per opposito. . . . Dico adunque, che per tre cagioni la presenza fa la persona di meno valore ch' ella non è. (i. 4, ll. 1-10.)

---

[1] *Academy*, 2nd December, 1893.

[2] The letter is excluded by Dr. Moore from the Oxford Dante as a " sciocca impostura ".

There certainly seems here to be a distinct reminiscence of Claudian's "minuit praesentia famam," though, of course, it is quite possible that the resemblance is merely accidental. The occurrence of the quotation, however, in the above-mentioned letter is in favour of the supposition that Dante had it in mind while writing this part of the *Convivio*, or at any rate that the forger of the letter (if it be a forgery, of which there can be very little doubt) thought so. For it is just the sort of coincidence that a skilful literary forger, such as Gian Mario Filelfo, for instance, would take care to introduce, in order to give the desired *colorito dantesco* to his fabrication; while the fact that Dante had just been quoting the *Aeneid* would account for the slip of attributing Claudian's words to Virgil.

Some think there is also a reminiscence of Claudian in Dante's description of the rape of Proserpine (*Purgatorio*, xxviii. 50-51); but Dante was more probably thinking of Ovid's account in the *Metamorphoses* (v. 385-401) than of any particular passage in Claudian's *De Raptu Proserpinae*, the former being his favourite authority in mythological matters.

It is further suggested that it was from Claudian (*De Bello Getico*, l. 75) that Dante got the name of Ephialtes (*Inferno*, xxxi. 94), this being, as has been asserted, the only passage in Latin literature in which the son of Alaeus is mentioned by name. It may be pointed out, however, that the name occurs also in the *Culex* of Virgil (l. 234), with which Dante was presumably well acquainted; and that, moreover, it is twice mentioned in Servius' Commentary on Virgil (*viz.*, in the notes on *Georgics*, i. 280, and *Aeneid*, vi. 776), which was, of course, almost as familiar to mediæval students as the poems themselves.

DID DANTE WRITE *RE GIOVANE* OR *RE GIOVANNI?*

(*INFERNO*, XXVIII. 135) [1]

In connexion with this much debated question, it is worthy of remark that in one of the *Cento Novelle Antiche* (which belong to the end of the thirteenth or the beginning of the fourteenth century) the name of the "Young King" is actually given as *John*. In this tale (No. cxlviii. in Biagi's critical edition) the Prince is called, first of all, "il Giovane Re d'Inghilterra," then "il nobile Re Giovanni d'Inghilterra," and then again, twice, "il Giovane Re".

There is not the least doubt as to the identity of the individual of whom Dante is speaking. It is admitted that the reference can be to no other than Prince Henry, second son of Henry II. of England (the eldest son, William, died in infancy), who, having been crowned during his father's lifetime, was commonly known as the "Young King"—a title by which he is almost invariably described in contemporary Latin documents, as well as in early French, Italian and Provençal literature.[2] That Dante knew he was called the "Young King" it is hardly reasonable to doubt; for he is repeatedly referred to by this title, both in the poems of Bertran de Born and in the old Provençal biography of the latter, with which, in one form or other, Dante was unquestionably familiar. The point is: was Dante aware that the "Young King's" name was Henry, or did he, like the author of the tale referred to above, think he was called John, and write *Giovanni* accordingly?

Considering that the weight of MS. evidence is overwhelmingly in favour of that reading as against *giovane* (see Moore, *Text. Crit.* p. 344), it seems at least possible after all that this may have been the case.

---

[1] *Academy*, 30th December, 1893.

[2] See above, *Il Re Giovane in the Inferno*, pp. 253-255.

DANTE'S INTERPRETATION OF "GALILEA" AS "BIANCHEZZA"

(*CONVIVIO*, IV. 22)[1]

In commenting on Mark xvi. 7 in the *Convivio* (iv. 22) Dante says: "Ite e dite alli discepoli suoi e a Pietro, che Ello li precederà in Galilea . . . cioè che la Beatitudine precederà loro in Galilea, cioè nella speculazione. Galilea è tanto a dire quanto bianchezza" (ll. 156-158, 184-187).

Whence did Dante, who is supposed to have known "small Greek and less Hebrew"—to paraphrase a familiar phrase of Ben Johnson's—get this interpretation of Galilee as "whiteness"?

By the Fathers the Hebrew word is variously interpreted. St. Augustine says: "Galilaea interpretatur vel *transmigratio* vel *revelatio*". St. Jerome says: "Galilaea *volubilitas* dicitur". St. Gaudentius: "Galilaea vel *volubilis*, vel *rota* nuncupatur, ex Hebraeo interpretata sermone". Bede says: "Galilaea interpretatur *transmigratio perpetrata*"; so Anselm and Hugh of St. Victor. Alcuin says: "Galilaea *transmigratio facta*, vel *revelatio* interpretatur". Rabanus Maurus says: "Mystice Galilaea *sublimis rota* interpretatur"; elsewhere: "Bene Galilaea *perpetrata transmigratio* interpretatur". St. Thomas Aquinas: "Galilaea ut interpretatur *transmigratio*, significat gentilitatem; sed ut interpretatur *revelatio*, significat patriam coelestem".

Dante's interpretation appears to have been due to some fanciful connexion of the word with the Greek γάλα, and was perhaps borrowed from Isidore of Seville, who says: Galilaea regio Palaestinae vocata, quod gignat candidiores homines quam Palaestina" (*Etym.* Lib. XIV. cap. iii. § 23). Isidore doubtless connected *Galilaea* with the Greek word γάλα, for he elsewhere directly refers *Gallia* to that source: "Gallia a candore populi nuncupata est, γάλα enim Graece lac dicitur" (*Ibid.* cap. iv.

---

[1] See *Academy*, 7th April, 1894.

§ 25).   A gloss on the former passage says : " Etymon Graecum cum vox sit Hebraea ".   It may be added that Isidore's account of Galilee is copied verbatim by Vincent of Beauvais in his *Speculum Historiale* (Lib. i. cap. 67).[1]

"LA SECONDA MORTE" IN THE *INFERNO* (i. 117)[2]

At the beginning of the *Inferno*, Virgil tells Dante that he will accompany him through hell, where he shall hear the shrieks of despair of the ancient spirits as in their agony they "proclaim (or 'cry upon') the second death " :—

> Trarrotti di quì per loco eterno,
> Ove udirai le disperate strida,
> Vedrai gli antichi spiriti dolenti,
> Che la seconda morte ciascun grida.
>
> (*Inf.* i. 114-117.)

The meaning of the last line in this passage is much disputed, one of the difficulties being the interpretation of the expression " la seconda morte".   Most commentators take it to signify total annihilation.   Some, looking to Rev. ii. 11 ; xx. 14 ; xxi. 8, understand it to refer to the state of the damned after the final end of temporal things.

It is interesting to note that Boëtius makes use of this same expression, " the second death," in the *De Consolatione Philosophiae*, in a passage which has been glossed by Chaucer. I quote from the version of the latter as given by Prof. Skeat in vol. ii. of the Oxford Chaucer :—

---

[1] The connection between γάλα and *Galilaea* is explicitly affirmed by Uguccione da Pisa in his *Magnae Derivationes* (*s.v. Gala*) ; he says : "*Gala* grece, latine dicitur lac . . . item a *gala* haec *Galilaea*, regio Palestinae, sic dicta quia gignat candidiores homines quam alia regio Palestinae ".   It was probably to Uguccione that Dante was indebted for the interpretation.   I have shown elsewhere that he made considerable use of Uguccione's work.   (See above, *Dante's Latin Dictionary*, pp. 97-114.)

[2] See *Academy*, 19th May, 1894.

Deeth despyseth alle heye glorie of fame: and deeth wrappeth to-gidere the heye heved̈es and the lowe, and maketh egal and evene the heyeste to the loweste. Wher wonen now the bones of trewe Fabricius? What is now Brutus, or stierne Catoun? The thinne fame, yit lastinge, of hir ydel names, is marked with a fewe lettres: but al-though that we han knowen the faire wordes of the fames of hem, it is not yeven to knowe hem that ben dede and consumpte. Liggeth thanne stille, al outrely unknowable; ne fame ne maketh yow nat knowe. And yif ye wene to liven the longer for winde of your mortal name, whan o cruel day shal ravisshe yow, thanne is the seconde deeth dwelling un-to yow.[1] GLOSE. *The first deeth he clepeth heer the departinge of the body and the sowle; and the seconde deeth he clepeth, as heer, the stintinge of the renoun of fame.*

(Book II. Met. vii. p. 49.)

It may be observed that Pietro di Dante gives just the opposite interpretation in his comment on the above-quoted passage of the *Inferno*. He says: "Allegorice pravi et vitiosi mortui sunt quodam-modo in fama, et haec est prima eorum mors; secunda est corporalis".

RAHAB'S PLACE IN DANTE'S PARADISE

(*PARADISO*, IX. 116)[2]

SOME surprise has been expressed at the position in Paradise assigned by Dante to the harlot Rahab, whom he places in the Heaven of Venus, and describes as having been the first soul (of those destined for that sphere) released by Christ from Limbo:—

> Da questo cielo . . . pria ch' altr' alma
> Del trionfo di Cristo fu assunta.
>
> (*Par.* ix. 118-120).

---

[1] This last passage runs as follows, in the original:—

> " Quod si putatis longius vitam trahi
> Mortalis aura nominis,
> Cum sera vobis rapiet hoc etiam dies,
> Jam vos secunda mors manet."

St. Thomas Aquinas in his comment on the *De Consolatione* says here: " Secunda mors hic accipitur, non sicut ab Augustino pro morte animae et corporis; sed pro morte famae, qua qui se vivere post naturalem mortem, in memoria hominum gloriantur morientur, postquam hic nullus fuerit honor ".

[2] *Academy*, 22nd September, 1894.

Apart, however, from the fact that through her marriage
with Salmon (Josh. vi. 25; Matt. i. 5) she became the ancestress of Christ—a fact insisted on by Petrus Comestor in his
Historia Scholastica (Liber *Josue*, cap. v.)—and that she is
especially mentioned both by St. Paul (Heb. xi. 31) and St.
James (James ii. 25), it may be noted that by the Fathers Rahab
was regarded as a type of the Church, the "line of scarlet
thread" which she bound in her window (Josh. ii. 21) being
typical of the blood of Christ shed for the remission of sins.
This view is expounded as follows by Isidore of Seville, with
whose writings Dante was certainly familiar:—

> Ex impiorum perditione unica domus Raab, tanquam unica Ecclesia,
> liberatur, munda a turpitudine fornicationis per fenestram confessionis in san-
> guine remissionis . . . . Quae ut salvari possit, per fenestram domus suae, tan-
> quam per os corporis sui, coccum mittit, quod est sanguinis Christi signum pro
> remissione peccatorum confiteri ad salutem.   (*Quaestiones in Vetus Testa-
> mentum—in Josue*, cap. vii. §§ 3, 4).

Petrus Comestor, with whose works Dante was also familiar,
alludes to this same interpretation in the passage of his *Historia
Scholastica* referred to above.

"LI TRE TARQUINII" IN THE *CONVIVIO*
(iv. 5)[1]

In the fifth chapter of the fourth book of the *Convivio*, Dante
enumerates the seven kings of Rome as follows: "Romolo,
Numa, Tullo, Anco, e li tre (*var. re*) *Tarquinii*" (ll. 89-91).
The omission of Servius Tullius and the inclusion of a third
Tarquin have led several editors to alter the MSS. reading in
this passage, and to substitute: "Romolo, Numa, Tullo, Anco
Marcio, Servio Tullio, e li re Tarquinii," a reading for which
apparently there is not the smallest MS. authority. In the
"Oxford Dante," Dr. Moore very properly has restored the
MSS. reading.[2]

---

[1] See *Academy*, 23rd February, 1895.

[2] In the first edition of the Oxford Dante, Dr. Moore read "li *tre* Tarquinii".
In the second edition he reads "li *re* Tarquinii," on the ground that the Virgilian

It is evident that while writing this chapter of the *Convivio* Dante had in mind *Aeneid,* vi. 756-853, the passage in which Anchises is represented as pointing out to Aeneas the long line of Alban and Roman kings, and the worthies of the common-wealth—a passage, it may be noted, from which Dante quotes repeatedly in the *De Monarchia,*[1] and with which he was there-fore undoubtedly familiar.

Now, it is remarkable that also in Virgil's list of kings Servius Tullius is omitted :—

> Quin et avo comitem sese Mavortius addet
> *Romulus.* . . .
> . . . Nosco crines incanaque menta
> Regis Romani, primam qui legibus urbem
> Fundabit (*i.e., Numa*). . . .
> > . . . Cui deinde subibit
> Otia qui rumpet patriae residesque movebit
> *Tullus* in arma viros et jam desueta triumphis
> Agmina.   Quem juxta sequitur jactantior *Ancus* . . .
> Vis et *Tarquinios reges* . . . videre ?
> > > (*Aen.* vi. 777-818.)

Virgil, as Conington points out, doubtless intended Servius Tullius to be included in "Tarquinios reges". Tullius, whose mother was a slave of Tanaquil, the wife of Tarquinius Priscus, was born in the royal palace and was brought up as the king's son ; he was closely connected with the Tarquin family, his wife having been the daughter of Tarquinius Priscus, while his own two daughters married the sons of Tarquinius. So that his inclusion with the Tarquin kings, if not strictly accurate, is not beyond the bounds of poetical licence ; and Dante, with Virgil's lines before him, may be excused for taking the same liberty.

In any case the passage of the *Aeneid* affords sufficient justi-fication for the retention of the MS. reading in the *Convivio* passage.

Tarquinios reges is strongly in favour of the latter as against " li tre Tarquinii," which, as he says, looks suspiciously like a copyist's correction, made for the purpose of bringing the number of kings up to the required seven. (See *Studies in Dante,* i. 195-196.)

[1] II. 5, ll. 98, 111, 119-120; II. 7, ll. 71-77.

There is another passage in this same chapter of the *Convivio* (iv. 5) in which Dr. Moore has restored the MS. reading— namely, "Chi dirà de' Decii e delli *Drusi* che posero la loro vita per la patria?" (ll. 122-124). Giuliani, remembering that the Decii are coupled with the Fabii in *Paradiso* vi. 47, does not scruple to substitute *Fabi* in his text for *Drusi*; while Witte, without going so far as actually to alter the text, says :—

> Mi sembra sospetto il nome dei *Drusi*, non potendo credere che l' autore voglia dar luogo fra gli uomini più illustri di Roma al tribuno Marco Livio Druso. Sospetterei dunque che siano da sostituirvi i *Curzii*, o qualche altra famiglia celebre.

There can be very little doubt, however, that Dante wrote *Drusi*, bearing in mind the Virgilian—

> Quin Decios Drusosque procul, saevumque securi
> Aspice Torquatum et referentem signa Camillum

from the same sixth book of the *Aeneid* (ll. 824-825), both "Torquato" and "Camillo" being also introduced in the same paragraph of the *Convivio*.[1]

DANTE'S STATEMENT IN THE *DE MONARCHIA* (ii. 9) AS TO THE RELATIONS OF ALEXANDER THE GREAT WITH THE ROMANS[2]

IN a well-known and very puzzling passage in the *De Monarchia* (ii. 9) Dante says, on the authority of Livy, that Alexander the Great sent ambassadors to Rome to demand submission, but died in Egypt before the reply of the Romans reached him :—

> Alexander rex Macedo maxime omnium ad palmam Monarchiae propinquans, dum per legatos ad deditionem Romanos praemoneret, apud Aegytum, ante Romanorum responsionem, ut Livius narrat, in medio quasi cursu collapsus est (ll. 61-67).

As a matter of fact, this circumstance is not mentioned by Livy, who, on the contrary, states his belief that the Romans never so much as heard of Alexander : "ne fama quidem illis notum arbitror fuisse" (ix. 18).   The attribution of this piece of information to Livy was consequently a slip on Dante's part.

Failing Livy, the next most likely authority for the statement would be Orosius, of whose *Historia adversus Paganos*, as I have shown elsewhere,[1] Dante made liberal use throughout his writings.   Orosius, however, in his account of the death of Alexander the Great, makes no mention of the Romans.   He says :—

> Post quasi circumacta meta de Oceano Indum flumen ingressus, Babylonam celeriter rediit.   Ubi eum exterritarum totius orbis provinciarum legati opperiebantur, hoc est Carthaginiensium totiusque Africae civitatum, sed et Hispanorum, Gallorum, Siciliae, Sardiniaeque, plurimae praeterea partis Italiae.   Tantus timor in summo Oriente constituti ducis populos ultimi Occidentis invaserat, ut inde peregrinam toto mundo cerneres legationem, quo vix crederes pervenisse rumorem.   Alexander vero apud Babylonam, cum adhuc sanguinem sitiens male castigata aviditate ministri insidiis venenum potasset, interiit.   (iii. 20, §§ 1-4.)

After a long search, I think I have now discovered the origin, so far as Dante is concerned, of the statement which he attributed to Livy.   In the Chronicle of Bishop Otto of Freising, with which there is good reason for supposing Dante to have been acquainted,[2] the death of Alexander is thus related :—

> Alexander totius Orientis potitus victoria, dum Romam quoque cum universo Occidente sibi subjugare parat, ab India revertitur in Babylonem, ubi exterarum gentium ex toto pene orbe ac ultimo Occidente, id est ab Hispanis, Gallis, Germania, Affrica, ac ferme omni Italia legati sibi occurrerunt, ut inde venisse cerneres legationem, quo vix tam parvo tempore crederes etiam rumorem pervenisse.   Et mirum dictu, tantus timor totum invaserat orbem, ut cum per 12 tantum imperasset annos, in summo Oriente constituto ultimi Occidentis populi timore conterriti legatos mitterent pacemque peterent.   Alexander ergo in Babylone positus, die, tempore ac loco sibi a simulacris solis et lunae in India praefixis, ministri insidiis veneno interiit.   (ii. 25.)

This account, which is obviously based upon that of Orosius, differs from the latter in the important particular that here we get the explicit statement that Alexander was meditating the subjugation of Rome, precisely the detail which strikes the attention in Dante's statement.

It may be objected that, though Otto and Dante are in

---

[1] See above, *Dante's Obligations to the Ormista*, pp. 121-136.

[2] See A. J. Butler's *Dante : his Times and his Work*, p. 5.

agreement in that particular, they are, on the other hand, at variance with regard to the place where Alexander died, since Otto says he died at *Babylon*, while Dante says he died in *Egypt*. This discrepancy, which at first sight certainly might seem fatal to the theory that Otto was Dante's authority, can be easily explained on the hypothesis that Dante, remembering that Alexander was buried in Egypt (he quotes Lucan to prove it in the very next paragraph [1] of this same chapter of the *De Monarchia*), here, as apparently elsewhere, confused the ancient Assyrian Babylon with Babylon (Old Cairo) in Egypt.   A confusion between the two Babylons is almost certainly responsible for the statement (*Inf.* v. 60) to the effect that Semiramis—

> Tenne la terra che il Soldan coregge,

i.e., was mistress of the land ruled over by the Sultan—*viz.*, Egypt.   *Cf.* Mandeville :—

> The Lond of Babyloyne, where the Sowdan dwellethe comonly . . . is not that great Babyloyne, where the Dyversitee of Langages was first made . . . when the grete Tour of Babel was begonnen to ben made.

Also Otto of Freising :—

> Ea quae nunc vulgo Babylonia vocatur, non super Eufraten . . . sed super Nilum circiter sex diaetas ab Alexandria posita est, ipsaque est Memphis, a Cambyse filio Cyri olim Babylonia vocata.   Et ibi rex Aegyptiorum, quamvis caput regni sui Alexandria sit, propter ortum balsami morari dicitur.   (vii. 3.)

Benvenuto da Imola notices the confusion, but tries to explain it away by suggesting that Dante meant to imply that Semiramis extended her empire so as to include Egypt as well as Assyria :—

> Istud non videtur aliquo modo posse stare, quia de rei veritate Semiramis nunquam tenuit illam Babiloniam, quam modo Soldanus corrigit . . . ad defensionem autoris dico, quod autor noster vult dicere quod Semiramis in tantum ampliavit regnum, quod non solum tenuit Babiloniam antiquam sed etiam Egiptum, ubi est modo alia Babilonia.

The supposition that Dante's statement about Alexander was derived from Otto receives some support from the fact (which may, however, be a mere coincidence) that the lines from Ennius (" Nec mi aurum posco," etc.), quoted by Dante in the next

[1] Ll. 67-74.

chapter of the *De Monarchia* (ii. 10, ll. 62 ff.), are also quoted
by Otto in a passage (ii. 32) about Pyrrhus a few pages after his
account of Alexander's death.   It may be added that the ultimate source of the quotation from Ennius in both cases is undoubtedly the *De Officiis* (i. 12) of Cicero.

A DOUBTFUL READING IN DANTE'S LETTER TO THE EMPEROR HENRY VII [1]

At the close of his letter to the Emperor Henry VII. Dante
apostrophises him (according to the reading of the Oxford
Dante, which is based upon that of Fraticelli) as "proles *alta*
Isai" (*i.e.*, exalted offspring of Jesse), and calls upon him to
come and overthrow the modern Goliath (*i.e.*, Philip the Fair),
and deliver Israel (*i.e.*, the oppressed Ghibellines) from the
hands of the Philistines (*i.e.*, the Neri).[2]   Reading *alta*, the
epithet is somewhat pointless, though its defenders would doubtless justify it by a reference to the "alto Arrigo" of the *Divina
Commedia* (*Par*. xvii. 82; xxx. 137).   If, however, we read
altera (which in MSS. might very easily be mistaken for *alta*),
we get a much more appropriate expression and one more in
Dante's manner.   Elsewhere Dante speaks of Henry VII. as
"alius Moyses" (*Epist*. v. 1), of the rebellious Florentines as
"alteri Babylonii" (*Epist*. vi. 2), and of Henry's son as "alter
Ascanius" (*Epist*. vii. 5).   It seems probable, therefore, that
Dante wrote not "proles *alta* Isai," but "proles *altera* Isai"
(*i.e.*, a second David).   Compare the similar expressions, "nuovo
Jason" (*Inf*. xix. 85), "nuovi Farisei" (*Inf*. xxvii. 85), "nuovo
Pilato" (*Purg*. xx. 91).

The only editor apparently who reads *altera* is Giuliani,
who, as is usual with him, alters the received text without
vouchsafing any comment or justification.   In this instance it
happens that his emendation is not only an improvement, but is
also unobjectionable on critical grounds.

---

[1] *Academy*, 11th January, 1896.   [2] *Epist*. vii. 8.

DANTE'S USE OF "RENDERSI" (*Inferno*, xxvii. 83) AND "RENDUTO" (*Purgatorio*, xx. 54) [1]

In these two passages Dante appears to use the verb *rendere* in a special sense. In the former passage (*Inf.* xxvii. 83) Guido da Montefeltro says that when he approached the close of his life "pentuto e confesso *mi rendei*". Blanc in his *Vocabolario Dantesco*, taking the verb and the participle together, explains the phrase "rendersi pentuto" as equivalent to "pentirsi," and Scartazzini agrees with him; so that, according to this interpretation, Dante merely means Guido to say, "I repented and confessed".

If, however, we turn to the Italian commentators we find a different interpretation. For instance, Fraticelli and Brunone Bianchi, taking the verb absolutely, explain "mi rendei" as "mi feci frate," "I became a monk". And this is the interpretation of several of the old commentators. Thus, the Ottimo comments; "si fece frate minore"; Benvenuto da Imola: "dedicavi me Deo"; and so Vellutello and others. Mr. Vernon in his *Readings on the Inferno* [2] states, on the authority of Lord Vernon, that Nannucci also (a weighty authority in a matter of this kind) was in favour of this interpretation.

The full expression would be "rendersi a Dio" or "a religione," the latter of which is used by Dante of Lancelot and Guido da Montefeltro in the *Convivio* (iv. 28, l. 64), where he says that in their old age they "a religione si rendêro," *i.e.*, entered a monastery. Another form of the expression was "rendersi monaco," or "rendersi frate". Thus, Villani, speaking of Louis, second son of Charles II. of Naples, who became a monk, says (vii. 95): "*Si rendè frate minore*, e poi fu vescovo di Tolosa"; and of Childeric, the last of the Merovingians, he says (ii. 12): "era uomo di niuno valore, e *rendési monaco*". The same phrase is used by Boccaccio in the *Decamerone* (*Giorn.* iv. *Nov.* 6 ad fin.): "in un monistero assai famoso di santità la figliuola di Messer Negro e la sua fante *monache si renderono*".

In *Purgatorio*, xx. 54 we get a parallel use of *renduto*, the term applied by Hugh Capet to the last of the "regi antichi" of France, who became a monk, *renduto* being used here in the same sense as the Old French *rendu*, and the Provençal *rendutz*. A familiar example of the Old French word occurs in the *Roman de la Rose*, where Faux-Semblant, in his description of the various disguises he assumes, says :—

> Autre ore sui religieuse,
> Or sui *rendue*, or sui prieuse
>
> (ll. 11,580-581),

which in the Old English translation is rendered :—

> Sometyme I am religious,
> Now lyk an anker in an hous.

Similarly, in the *Roman de Renart* a monastery is spoken of as "la maison *as rendus*". The word is common enough in this sense, as a reference to Godefroy's dictionary will show.

Instances of the similar use of *se rendre* and *rendutz* in Provençal are given by Raynouard in his *Lexique Roman ; e.g. :*—

> Ella *se rendet monga* per la dolor que ella ac de lui e de la soa mort.

And again :—

> Nos em fach hermitan
> Sentanta dos *rendutz*, e motz preyres y a.

In mediæval Latin *rendutus* and *redditus* were used in the same way, as may be seen in Du Cange.

The absolute use of *rendersi* in the special sense of "to become a monk" can also be paralleled in both Old French and Provençal—instances are supplied in plenty by Godefroy and Raynouard. It is probable, therefore, that what is after all the old interpretation of the above two passages of the "Divina Commedia" is the correct one, in spite of modern "commentatori forestieri".

DANTE AND THE BOOK OF TOBIT
PARADISO (iv. 48)[1]

ONE of the slips with which Dante has been credited is the confusion of Tobit with his son Tobias, inasmuch as in the fourth
canto of the *Paradiso* he refers to the archangel Raphael, who
healed the father, as " l' altro che Tobia rifece sano " (l. 48).   A
recent English commentator,[2] for instance, says in his note on the
passage : " Observe that Dante confuses Tobit with Tobias "—the
name of the father in the English version being not Tobias, but
Tobit.

In the Vulgate, however, the version followed by Dante,
both father and son are called Tobias, the book itself, which we
know as the " Book of Tobit," being entitled " Liber Tobiae ".
This identity of the names of father and son, which is derived
from the Chaldaic text translated by St. Jerome (see Smith's
Dictionary of the Bible, s.v. Tobit), is expressly affirmed in the
first chapter :—

> Tobias ex tribu et civitate Nephthali . . . cum factus esset vir, accepit
> uxorem Annam de tribu sua, genuitque ex ea filium, *nomen suum imponens ei.*
> (vv. 1, 9.)

Dante, therefore, is innocent of the charge of inaccuracy
brought against him by the English commentator.   Of course
this point has not been raised by the Italian commentators, who
habitually make use of the Vulgate version of the Scriptures ; to
them the fact that Dante should speak of the blind Jew as
" Tobia " would naturally present no difficulty.

It may be added that in the Wycliffite versions of the " Book
of Tobit," unlike that in our Apocrypha, the Vulgate is followed.
The above passage there runs :—

> Tobie of the linage and of the cite of Neptalim . . . whan he was maad a
> man, toc a wif, Anne of his linage ; and he gat of hir a sone, his own name
> puttende to hym.

---

[1] *Academy*, 3rd October, 1896.   [2] Mr. A. J. Butler.

"FONS PIETATIS" IN THE *DE MONARCHIA*
(ii. 5)[1]

In the fifth chapter of the second book of the *De Monarchia* Dante says: "Recte illud scriptum est, Romanum Imperium de fonte nascitur pietatis" (ll. 40-42).

This quotation has long been a puzzle to the commentators, none of whom has been able to identify the source whence it is taken. Witte, for instance, who points out that the same sentiment occurs in Dante's letter to the Princes and Peoples of Italy ("Immo ignoscet omnibus misericordiam implorantibus, cum sit Cæsar, et majestas ejus de fonte defluat pietatis"),[2] and who has succeeded in identifying nearly every one of the quotations in the *De Monarchia*, says of this passage: "Sententia unde hausta sit ignoro".

The source of this quotation appears to be the legend of St. Sylvester in the *Legenda Aurea* of Jacobus de Voragine (Archbishop of Genoa, 1292-1298). The Emperor Constantine, having been struck with leprosy on account of his persecution of the Christians, is ordered to wash in a bath of blood, to supply which three thousand unhappy youths are condemned to be sacrificed. On his way to the bath the Emperor, being met by a crowd of weeping women, stops his chariot and declares his intention of sparing the lives of the condemned youths, exclaiming that clemency ought to be the distinguishing characteristic of a Roman Emperor, inasmuch as "dignitas Romani Imperii de fonte nascitur pietatis".

Here we have the identical expression used by Dante, who, as I believe, was indebted to the *Legenda Aurea* for his version of this very legend (to which he twice refers, *viz.*, in *Inferno*, xxvii. 94; and *De Monarchia*, iii. 10, ll. 1-6), as well as for several others contained in the same collection.

My opinion that the legend of St. Sylvester in the version of

---

[1] See *Athenæum*, 26th March and 9th April, 1898. [2] *Epist.* v. 3.

Jacobus de Voragine was the source of Dante's quotation is to some extent confirmed by the fact that there is a striking parallel between what Dante has said just before, as to the subordination by the Romans of their own interests to those of mankind at large—" In gestis suis, omni cupiditate submota, quae rei publicae semper adversa est, et universali pace cum libertate dilecta, populus ille sanctus, pius et gloriosus, propria commoda neglexisse videtur, ut publica pro salute humani generis procuraret" (ll. 33-40)—and the concluding words of Constantine's speech as given in the *Legenda Aurea*: "Omnium enim se esse dominum comprobat qui servum se monstraverit pietatis. Melius est ergo me mori salva vita innocentium quam per eorum interitum vitam recuperare".

It is, of course, possible that both Dante and Jacobus de Voragine drew the expression from a common source, but prolonged research has so far failed to discover such a source.

Whatever the origin of the phrase,[1] there can be little doubt that Dante, in his use of it, intended to point to the individual whom he consistently regarded as the founder of the Roman empire, namely "pius Aeneas" (see, for instance, *Convivio*, ii. 11, ll. 38-39; and *De Monarchia*, ii. 3, ll. 46-47).

THE CHRONOLOGY OF *PARADISO*
vi. 1-6, 37-39 [2]

In the summary of Roman history put into the mouth of the Emperor Justinian by Dante in the sixth canto of the *Paradiso* occur two passages which have been somewhat of a puzzle to commentators.

In the first of these (ll. 1-6) Justinian says that when he became Emperor the Roman eagle had been at Constantinople for more than two hundred years ("cento e cent' anni e più"). According to the chronology accepted at the present day this

---

[1] The phrase occurs in the well-known hymn, "Dies irae"; but in a totally different connexion from that in which Dante uses it.

[2] *Athenæum*, 6th August, 1898.

statement presents no difficulty, the period from the foundation of
Constantinople in 324 (as distinguished from the dedication in 330)
to the accession of Justinian in 527 being just over two hundred years.   This, however, was not the chronology of Dante's
day.   Brunetto Latino, for instance, in his *Trésor* (p. 82, ed.
Chabaille) assigns the transference of the seat of empire from
Rome to Constantinople to the year 333, and the accession of
Justinian to the year 539.   This gives an interval of 206
years between the two dates, and I have little doubt that the
Trésor, with which, of course, Dante was well acquainted, was
his authority for the reckoning of "cento e cent' anni e più".

In the second passage (ll. 37-39) Justinian puts the period
from the foundation of Alba Longa to the fight between the
Horatii and Curiatii and the end of the Alban sovereignty at
300 years and more ("trecenti anni ed oltre").   The traditional
date of the fall of Troy, some thirty years after which Alba was
founded (Livy, i. 3), is B.C. 1184.   This gives 431 years (Orosius
says 414, *Hist.* ii. 4, § 1) to the foundation of Rome in 753, and
consequently considerably more than four hundred years to the
destruction of Alba by Tullus Hostilius, the third King of Rome.
If Dante were following this reckoning (as is commonly assumed
by the commentators) his "three hundred years and more"
would be a very loose way of putting it, and very unlike his
usual preciseness.   Here again, however, I think there can be
little doubt that he is following Brunetto, who, in his chapter
on Romulus and Remus in the *Trésor*, puts the foundation of
Rome at only 313 years after the fall of Troy.[1]   Benvenuto da
Imola, in his commentary, refers to a passage in the *Aeneid*
(i. 267-274) in which Virgil computes the period between the
foundation of Alba by Ascanius and the birth of Romulus and
Remus at 300 years.

---

[1] "Ainsi fu Rome commencée . . . .ccc.xiij. anz après la destruction de
Troie" (p. 44, ed. Chabaille).

"ILDEBRANDINUS PADUANUS" IN THE *DE VULGARI ELOQUENTIA* (i. 14)[1]

THE identity of the obscure poet Ildebrandinus Paduanus, of whom Dante says that he alone of the writers of Venetia attempted to write in the "curial vulgar tongue" instead of in his own local dialect,[2] and who has hitherto been little more than a mere "nominis umbra," has now at length been satisfactorily established.

Professor Michele Barbi, of Florence, recently (in 1898) printed for private circulation ("per nozze Rostagno-Cavazza") a brief but important note upon one of Dante's sonnets, to which, he points out, a reply (preserved in two MSS.) was written by one "Dominus Aldobrandino Mezabote" (read Mezabate), *i.e.*, Messer Aldobrandino de' Mezzabati of Padua. This Aldobrandino is proved by documentary evidence to have been "Capitano del Popolo" in Florence from May, 1291, to May, 1292; and Professor Pio Rajna, who is engaged upon the illustrative commentary to his critical edition of the *De Vulgari Eloquentia*, states[3] that he has no hesitation in identifying this individual with the Ildebrandinus Paduanus mentioned by Dante.

Professor Barbi's note is of interest further as establishing beyond question the fact that among the ladies of whom Dante was (or pretended to be) enamoured, at one time or other, was a certain Lisetta. A lady of this name is mentioned in connexion with Dante by the author of the *Ottimo Comento* (on *Purg.* xxxi. 58-60): "E dice Beatrice, che nè quella giovane, la quale elli nelle sue Rime chiamò pargoletta, nè quella Lisetta, nè quell' altra montanina, nè quella, nè quell' altra li dovevano gravare le penne delle ale in giù, tanto ch' elli fosse ferito da

---

[1] See *Athenæum*, 29th October, 1898.

[2] "Inter Venetos unum vidimus nitentem divertere a materno, et ad curiale vulgare intendere, videlicet Ildebrandinum Paduanum" (i. 14, ll. 41-44).

[3] In a private letter to the Author.

uno simile, o quasi simile strale "); but little attention has been paid to the circumstance, owing to the absence of any confirmatory evidence.

Evidence of Lisetta's existence, however, is in fact, as Professor Barbi shows, supplied by Dante himself. The third line of the sonnet " Per quella via che la Bellezza corre" (sonnet xliv in the Oxford Dante), instead of " Passa *una donna* baldanzosamente," as it reads in all the printed editions, ought to be " Passa Lisetta baldanzosamente," which is the reading of eight out of twelve MSS. in which the poem has been preserved. The substitution of "una donna" for "Lisetta" is due to the fact that the editors of the Giunta edition of 1527, in which Dante's sonnets were printed for the first time, made use of a MS. with the reading *licençia*—this is found in four MSS., but three of these have practically no independent value—in the place where evidently a lady's name was wanted; not knowing how to supply the required name, they, instead of printing nonsense, boldly printed "una donna," in which they have been followed by every succeeding editor down to the present day. It may be added that in three MSS. the name Lisetta reappears in the eleventh line of Dante's sonnet ("Quando Lisetta accomiatar si vede" for " E quando quella . . ."); and, which is more significant still, the sonnet of Aldobrandino in reply begins with this same name, " Lisetta voi della vergogna sciorre".

Professor Barbi, who has been entrusted by the Società Dantesca Italiana with the task of preparing critical editions of the *Vita Nuova* and *Canzoniere* of Dante, hazards the conjecture that this Lisetta may have been the "donna gentile" of the *Vita Nuova*.

A DISPUTED READING IN THE *DE MONARCHIA*
(ii. 1)[1]

In the impressive passage at the beginning of the second book of
the *De Monarchia*, in which Dante with wrath and scorn rebukes
the opposition offered to the Emperor, the Oxford Dante, following Witte, reads : "Reges et principes in hoc vitio concordantes,
ut adversentur Domino suo et unico suo Romano Principi
(ii. 1. ll. 25-27).

This is an alteration of the old reading adopted in the early
editions[2] of the treatise, which for "in hoc vitio" read "in hoc
unico," and for "unico suo" read "uncto suo"; according to
which the sense would be "kings and princes agreeing in this one
thing only, opposition to their Lord and to His anointed
Emperor". Manuscript authority exists for both readings, but
it should be noted that the important Vatican MS. (Cod. Pal.,
1729) supports the reading "uncto suo" against "unico suo".

I have very little doubt that the reading of the old editions
(which, with the substitution of *uno* for *unico* in the first place,
is accepted by Giuliani) is the correct one. Manuscript evidence
in a case of this kind is necessarily indeterminate, since in MSS.
uicio (= *vitio*) and *uīco* (= *unico*) on the one hand, and *uīco*
and *uncto* on the other, might very easily be mistaken one for the
other by careless coypists, to say nothing of the possibility of
unico for *uncto* in the second place being caught from the *unico*
in the line above. But there are several considerations, independent of the MSS., in favour of the old reading. By reading
"in hoc vitio" instead of "in hoc unico" the force of the sentence is weakened, and, as it seems to me, Dante's point is
missed; while the phrase "adversentur Domino suo et uncto
suo Romano Principi" seems obviously intended as a reference to,
and echo of, the words "Adversus Dominum et adversus Chris-

---

[1] See *Athenæum*, 21st October, 1899.

[2] That is, the *editio princeps* (1559), and the reprints of it, as well as the
editions of 1740 and 1758.

tum ejus" ("Against the Lord and against His anointed") in the verses (1-3) from the second Psalm with which this book of the *De Monarchia* opens, and which are quoted again just below.[1]

There is something more, however, than a mere question of appropriateness involved in the reading *uncto*. It has an important bearing on the vexed question as to the date of the composition of the *De Monarchia*. If *uncto* be read, the reference can only be to the Emperor Henry VII. To no other of the successors of Frederick II. contemporary with himself would Dante have dreamed of applying the term "the Lord's anointed". In a characteristic passage in the *Convivio*, where he speaks of Frederick as "the last Emperor of the Romans," he emphatically declines to recognise Rudolf and Adolf and Albert as emperors at all :—

> Federigo di Soave, ultimo Imperadore de' Romani, ultimo dico per rispetto al tempo presente, non ostante che Ridolfo e Adolfo e Alberto poi eletti sieno appresso la sua morte e de' suoi discendenti. (iv. 3, ll. 39-43.)

Now Henry VII. was crowned at Aix on 6th January, 1309 ; consequently, if *uncto* be the true reading, the *De Monarchia*, or, at any rate, the second book, must have been composed later than that date.

Boccaccio's statement (in his *Vita di Dante*) that the treàtise was written at the time of Henry VII.'s descent into Italy, which is in accordance with the most commonly received opinion, would thus be confirmed by an important piece of internal evidence.

It may be added that Witte had a strong motive for rejecting the reading *uncto*, inasmuch as he was pledged to the position that the *De Monarchia* was written before Dante's exile from Florence,[2] a position, of course, which an admitted reference to Henry VII. in the treatise would have destroyed at once.

---

[1] Ll. 33-35.

[2] In the *Prolegomena* to his edition of the treatise Witte says : "Jam plus quam viginti abhinc annos probare studui, Dantem adhuc juvenem, et ante exilium Florentiae degentem, opus nostrum scripsisse" (p. xxxvii) ; and he holds that it is to his *De Monarchia* that Dante refers in his apostrophe to Virgil in the first canto of the *Inferno* (ll. 85-87): "Dicamus igitur libros de Monarchia ante tempus Paschale anni 1300 non solum esse compositos, sed ita jam a coævis fuisse lectitatos, ut auctor non immerito de honore inde consequuto gloriari potuerit" (p. xliii).

DANTE, ARNAUT DANIEL, AND THE *TERZA RIMA* [1]

In a discussion—in an essay upon the genesis and growth of the *Divina Commedia*—as to the reasons for Dante's choice of the *terza rima*, it was incidentally suggested by Dean Plumptre that this form of verse was borrowed from the Provençal poet, Arnaut Daniel, " who had originated the yet more complicated and unmanageable *sestina* ".[2] That Arnaut did invent a particular form of *sestina*, of which he has left a specimen, appears to be unquestioned ; but there seems no ground for supposing that he ever made use of the *terza rima*, even if it existed in his time.

We have no reason to believe that Dante was acquainted with any poems of Arnaut Daniel other than the eighteen which have come down to us ; all of those from which he quotes in the *De Vulgari Eloquentia* are comprised in that number.   As may be gathered from the subjoined analysis of the rhyme-system of these eighteen poems, there is no trace in them of the sustained *terza rima* used by Dante.

The poems are here numbered according to the order in which they are given by Canello in his critical edition (in *La Vita e le Opere del Trovatore Arnaldo Daniello*) published at Halle in 1883.

If the formula ABABCBCDCDED be taken to represent the *terza rima*, the rhyme-sequence of Arnaut's poems will appear as follows—the comma being employed to denote the division into stanzas :—

1. AAAAAAAAA, BBBBBBBBB, CCCCCCCCC, DDDDDDDDD, EEEEEEEEE, EEEE (five singled-rhymed stanzas of nine lines each, with *envoi* of four lines).

2. (AAABBCDDC),[2] (BBBDDCAAC),[2] (DDDAACBBC),[2] CBBC (three pairs of stanzas of nine lines each, with *envoi* of four lines).

---

[1] See *Academy*, 31st March, 1888.

[2] See Plumptre's *Commedia and Canzoniere of Dante*, vol. ii. p. 355.

3. ABABBABA, CDCDDCDC, EFEFFEFE, GHGHHGHG, IKIKKIKI, LMLMMLML, NONOONON, ONON (seven stanzas of eight lines each, with *envoi* of four lines).

The rhyme-system in 4-17 is one of which Arnaut was the originator. Its peculiar feature is that a certain number of lines in each stanza do not rhyme within the stanza, but find their rhymes in the corresponding lines of the succeeding stanzas. This system is gradually developed in 4-9, until in 10-17 the rhyme within the stanza disappears altogether. In each poem of this series (4-17) the individual rhymes are repeated in the same sequence throughout the poem.

4. (ABCDEFFE),[6] EFFE (six eight-line stanzas with identical rhymes and same sequence, and four-line *envoi*).

5. (ABABCDE),[6] CDE (six seven-line stanzas, and three-line *envoi*).

6. (ABBACDE),[5] (five seven-line stanzas, without *envoi*).

7. (ABCDEFFGGHH),[6] GGHH (six eleven-line stanzas, and four-line *envoi*).

8. (ABCDEEFGH),[6] FGH (six nine-line stanzas, and three-line *envoi*).

9. (ABCDEFGBHHICKLMCN),[6] ICKLMCN (six seventeen-line stanzas, and seven-line *envoi*).[1]

In 10-17, as has already been observed, the rhyme within the stanza is discarded altogether.

10. (ABCDEFG),[6] EFG (six seven-line stanzas, and three-line *envoi*).

11. (ABCDEFGH),[6] GH (six eight-line stanzas, and two-line *envoi*).

12. (ABCDEFGH),[7] (GH)[2] (seven eight-line stanzas, and double two-line *envoi*).

13. (ABCDEFG),[6] EFG (six seven-line stanzas, and three-line *envoi*).

14. (ABCDEFGH),[6] GH (six eight-line stanzas, and two-line *envoi*).

---

[1] The first three lines of this poem are quoted by Dante in the *De Vulgari Eloquentia* (ii. 2, 1. 87).

15. (ABCDEFG),[6] EFG (six seven-line stanzas, and three-line *envoi*).[1]

16. (ABCDEFG),[6] EFG (six seven-line stanzas, and three-line *envoi*.).

17. (ABCDEFGH),[6] GH (six eight-line stanzas, and two-line *envoi*).[2]

In these eight poems (10-17) there are practically only two rhyme-schemes, *viz.*, seven-line stanzas and three-line *envoi* (four), and eight-line stanzas and two-line *envoi* (four).

The remaining poem is the *sestina*, in which the rhyme-system is the same as in the preceding eight, while the sequence is varied according to a fixed law, the key to which is the repetition of the last word of each stanza at the end of the first line of the succeeding stanza, thus—

18. ABCDEF, FAEBDC, CFDABE, ECBFAD, DEACFB, BDFECA, ECA (six six-line stanzas, and three-line *envoi*).

There is the further peculiarity in the *sestina* that the end words of each line in the stanza not only *rhyme* with, but are (almost invariably) *identical with*, those in each of the succeeding stanzas. This *sestina*, for instance, is built up on the words (*intra, ongla, arma, verga, oncle, cambra*), (*cambra, intra, oncle, ongla, verga, arma*), and so on, according to the scheme given above.

It will be observed that of all these rhyme-schemes the only one which at all approaches the *terza rima* in structure is that of number 3, and in this the chief characteristic of the former, namely, its continuity (as distinguished from the stanza-system), is entirely wanting. It is evident, therefore, that the origin of the *terza rima* must be sought elsewhere than in the poems of Arnaut Daniel.

---

[1] Dante quotes the first line of this poem (*Vulg. Eloq.* ii. 6, l. 61).

[2] Dante quotes the first line of this poem, and discusses its structure (*Vulg. Eloq.* ii. 13, ll. 7-12).

THE COLOUR *PERSE* IN DANTE AND OTHER MEDIÆVAL WRITERS [1]

WHAT colour Dante meant to indicate by the word *perso* we know from the very precise definition of it which he gives in the twentieth chapter of the fourth book of the *Convivio*. Commenting on lines 109-110 of the third *Canzone* [2]:—

> Dunque verrà, come dal nero il perso,
> Ciascheduna virtute da costei [3]

he says :—

> Quando appresso seguita: *Dunque verrà come dal nero il perso*, procede il testo alla difinizione di Nobiltà, la quale si cerca. . . . E rende esempio nei colori, dicendo: Siccome il *perso* dal *nero* discende; così questa, cioè Virtù, discende da Nobiltà. Il perso è un colore misto di purpureo e di nero, ma vince il nero, e da lui si denomina (ll. 1-4, 11-16).

The word is used by Dante four times in the *Divina Commedia*; viz., twice in the *Inferno*, once in the *Purgatorio*, and once in the *Paradiso*. In the first of these passages it is applied to the murky atmosphere of the second circle of Hell, "l'aer perso" (*Inf.* v. 89); in the second, Dante uses it to describe the colour of the water of the infernal stream, which he says was many shades darker than *perse* (*i.e.*, practically black): "L'acqua era buia assai vie più che persa" (*Inf.* vii. 103). In the third passage it is employed to indicate the colour of the second of the three steps by which the gate of Purgatory is approached, a colour which in this case again must be almost black, the rock of which the step is composed being described as "tinto più che perso" (*Purg.* ix. 97). In the passage in the *Paradiso* (iii. 11-12) Dante speaks of limpid still water of a certain depth,

---

[1] See *Academy*, 22nd September and 20th October, 1888; and 12th October, 1889.

[2] *Canzone* viii. in the Oxford Dante.

[3] Lyell renders:—
> " Hence must proceed, as violet from black,
> Each several virtue from nobility."

but not so deep that the bottom seems *perse :* "Acque nitide e tranquille, Non sì profonde che i fondi sien persi".[1]

Though Dante leaves us in no doubt as to the meaning of *perse*, as far as he is concerned, it is by no means so easy to determine what was the generally accepted signification of the word in other mediæval writers. This will be apparent from the subjoined examples of its use in English, Old French and Provençal, which I have collected from various sources.

The word occurs in the well-known passage of the *Prologue to the Canterbury Tales*, where Chaucer describes the dress of the Doctour of Phisik :—

> In sangwin and in pers he clad was al,
> Lyned with taffata and with sendal.
> (ll. 439-440.)

It is usually explained here as "sky blue" or "bluish grey" (Morris), apparently after the definition given by Du Cange, who describes it (*s.v. Persus*) as : "color ad caeruleum vel ad floris *persicae mali* colorem accedens," *i.e.*, sky blue or peach blossom.

It seems more probable, however, that the word indicates the colour, not of the blossom, but of the fruit—the deep purple of a ripe peach—for both Old French *pers* and Italian *perso* (as we have seen) certainly represent a colour which closely approaches to what we call a "blue black".[2]

Further on in the *Prologue* Chaucer tells us of the Reve that

> A long surcote of pers up-on he hade.
> (l. 617.)

The word occurs again in the *Romaunt of the Rose* (the English translation, in part at least, attributed to Chaucer, of the *Roman*

---

[1] It should be mentioned that many, perhaps the majority of the commentators, take *persi* here as another form of, and equivalent to, *perduti ;* in which case the meaning would be: "Not so deep that the bottom is lost to view". (See Mr. Vernon's note in his *Readings on the Paradiso*, vol. i. p. 91).

[2] It may be remarked that Diez, Littré, Scheler and others give Du Cange's definition as: "Ad *persei mali* colorem accedens," *i.e.*, resembling the colour of a peach. The latest edition of the *Glossarium* reads, as given above: "Ad *floris persicae mali* colorem," the colour of peach blossom.

de la Rose of Guillaume de Lorris and Jean de Meun), where it
is said, speaking of the month of May :—

> And then bicometh the ground so proud
> That it wol have a newe shroud,
> And maketh so queynt his robe and fayr
> That it hath hewes an hundred payr
> Of gras and floures, inde and pers,
> And many hewes ful dyvers.[1]
>   (ll. 63-68.)

In Old French *pers* is applied to a great variety of objects.
For instance, to the shades of an onyx :—

> Cestes pierres [onyches] . . . sont diverses,
> Blanches, noires, rousses et perses.
>   (L. Pannier, *Lapidaires Français*, p. 256.)

To the livid complexion of a dying man ; for example, in the
Chanson de Roland it is said of the dying Oliver :—

> Teinz fut e pers, desculurez e pales.
>   (l. 1,979.)

Du Cange quotes a similar use in Latin : "Faciem habebat
persam et credebatur mortuus".

It is used, again, of the "black and blue" of a bruise :—

> Les espaules aveit enflées
> Del grant fereiz des espées,
> La char ad perse en plusurs leus.
>   (Benoît de Sainte-More, *Roman de Troie*,
>   ll. 11,575-11,577.)

> Li mals maris enoït la déplainte,
> Entre el vergier, sa corroie a deçainte ;
> Tant la bati qu'ele en fu perse-tainte.
>   (*Cuens Guis*, ll. 15-18 ; in Paulin Paris'
>   *Romancero Français*, p. 37.)

So, in the *Roman de Renart,* we are told that Renart, after his
exploit of robbing the kites' nest, and after the vengeance taken
upon him by the kites, was found :—

---

[1] The last four lines run as follows in the original :—

> " Si scet si cointe robe faire,
> Que de colors i a cent paire,
> D'erbes, de flors indes et perses,
> Et de maintes colors diverses."

> Enmi le chemin tot envers.
> Tot out le vis et pale et pers,
> Si con il out esté blecie,
> Tout le cuir avoit detrencie.
>
> (*Branche* xi. ll. 625-629, éd. Martin.)

Wace uses it in the *Brut* of the face of a man "purple with rage" (*viz.*, of Lear when he hears Cordelia's reply):—

> Li pere fu de si grant ire,
> De maltalant devint tuz pers.
>
> (ll. 1,792-1,793.)

In the Provençal *Roman de Flamenca* it is applied to dark hair, as opposed to blonde:—

> Li Comtessa de Nivers
> . . . non ac ges los cabels pers
> An son plus blon que non es aurs.
>
> ₁(ll. 838-840.)

It was a sober colour, for Joinville (chap. cxxxv.) relates that after the return of St. Louis from the East: "Il se maintint si devotement que onques puis ne porta ne vair ne gris, ne escarlatte, ne estriers ne esperons dorez. Ses robes estoient de camelin ou de pers." N. de Wailly explains *pers* here as "drap bleu teint en guède," cloth dyed in woad.

And further, it was considered dark enough for mourning, for in a police ordinance of 1533, quoted by L. de Laborde in his *Glossaire* (p. 438), we read of "draps pers et autres accoustumés estre tendus es mortuaires".

The expressions *pers azuré, pers clair, pers noir,* mentioned by Du Cange and Laborde, are perhaps to be explained in the same way as *écarlate verte* (Marot), *escarlate vermeille* and *escarlate blance* (Froissart), *pourpre grise, pourpre rousse,* etc., where *écarlate* and *pourpre* indicate not a colour but a material.[1]

---

[1] Legrand d'Aussy (*Fabliaux*, vol. i. p. 180) suggests the following explanation of this transference of meaning:—

"Je proposerai une conjecture ; c'est que, pendant longtemps, l'écarlate et la pourpre ne s'étant employées, à cause de leur cherté, que pour la teinture des draps les plus fins, on donna, par la suite, le nom de pourpre et d'écarlate, non à la couleur, mais à l'étoffe elle-même, quelle que fût sa couleur."

The conjecture that, in the expressions *pers azuré, pers noir,* etc., the word *pers* has, like *écarlate* and *pourpre* in similar expressions, lost its meaning of

In Méon's *Blasons des XV et XVImes Siècles, pers* is applied, as distinct from blue, to the gilly-flower :—

> Girofflées sont fleurs communes,
> Mais en leur couleur différentes,
> Les unes sont blanches, aulcunes
> Sont bleues, mais plus apparentes
> Sont les perces et plus fréquentes
> En médecine.
>
> (*Blason des Fleurs*, p. 295.)

colour, and indicates simply a material, seems to be confirmed by the Provençal *perset vermeill, presset vermel* (*i.e.*, *pers vermeil*), given by Raynouard in his *Lexique Roman* (iv. 522) ; as well as by a passage in the *Paston Letters* (No. 99, vol i. p. 134 ; ed. Gairdner), where mention is made of "j. gowne of fyn perse blewe furryd with martens ". *Cf.* also the *Fabliau de la Bourse pleine de Sens*, in which a "riche borgois" is described as going to the fair at Troies, where

> " I ot assez de draperie,
> Qu'il n'ot cure de friperie,
> Mais d'escarlate tainte en graine,
> De bons pers et de bonne laine,"

and whence he brings home for his "amie,"

> " Bone robe de bons pers d'Ypre ".
>
> (Barbazan et Méon, *Fabliaux et Contes*, vol. iii.
> pp. 41-44.)

In the *Farce de Pathelin* (p. 12, ed. Jacob) the draper says to Pathelin : "Voulez-vous de ce pers cler cy ? " the "pers cler " being apparently a light-blue material.

That *écarlate* came to indicate a material without reference to colour (a point upon which Littré is somewhat doubtful) is evident, not only from the passage quoted above, but from another in *La Manière de Langage*—the dialogue is between a draper's apprentice and a customer:—

"Ore regardez, biau sire, comment vous plaist il. Veicy de bon escarlet violet, sangwytannes, et de tous autres colours que n'en peut nommer : ore esliez de tel que vous plest.—Doncques, dit un merchant : que me costera tout cest renc d'escarlat ?—Et l'autre dit ainsi : Biau sire, vous me dounrez deux miles francs."

"Scarlet " was used in English in the same way. Chaucer's "Wif of Bathe " has "hosen of fyn scarlet reed," and in the *Anatomy of Abuses* (pp. 70, 72, quoted by Morris) we read of :—

" Petticoates of the beste clothe that can be made. And sometimes they are not of clothe neither, for that is thought too base, but of scarlet, grograine, taffatie, silke and such like . . . they have kirtles either of silke, velvett, grograine, taffatie, satten, or scarlet, bordered with gardes, lace, fringes, etc."

And again in *Iohn Russells Boke of Nurture*, where the "office off a Chamburlayne " is described :—

Assuming, as seems most probable, that the flower intended is the clove gilly-flower (Lat. *Caryophyllus*), not the stock gilly-flower, *pers* here would be a shade of red, in fact, pink or carnation. This appears to be its meaning in the following passage also, where it is mentioned along with several other shades of red—a gentleman is giving orders to his "garderober" as to what purchases he is to make :—

> Je vuil que vous en irez a mon draper, et vous achaterez de lui dousze verges de fin escarlet, sis verges de rouge, huit verges de pearce, noef verges de sanguin et atant de violet et bronnet, et quinsze verges de blanket.—(*La Manière de Langage qui enseigne à Parler et à Ecrire le Français.*) [1]

In the subjoined extracts from the *Blason de la Marguerite*, *pers* obviously indicates various shades of blue, for it is applied successively to the sapphire, the turquoise and the agate :—

> Entre les pierres merveilleuses,
> On en tient sept plus précieuses,
> Le diamant, le saphyr pers,
> La ronde et blanche marguerite, etc.
>
> .   .   .   .
>
> Mais l'escarboucle en taint diverse,
> L'agathe, la torquoyse perse . . .
> Si précieuses ne sont certe.
>
> .   .   .   .

> "Or youre mastir depart his place, afore that this be seyn,
> To brusche besily about hym; loke all be pur and playn
> Whethur he were saten, sendell, vellewet, scarlet, or greyn."
>   (Ed. Furnivall, E.E.T.S., p. 178.)

Similarly "purple," like *pourpre*, denoted a material. Sir John Harrington, in his *Dyet for Every Day*, says : "I doe iudge it not to bee much amisse to vse garments of Silke or Bombace, or of purple". (Ed. Furnivall, p. 255.)

[1] The recurrence in the above quotation (which is from a work by an Englishman contemporary with Chaucer) of "sangwin and pers" together is a coincidence which may be noted. It is remarkable, too, that Dante, in a wholly different connection, couples *perso* and *sanguigno* together :—

> "Visitando vai per l'aer perso
> Noi che tignemmo il mondo di sanguigno.
>   (*Inf.* v. 89-90.)

It would be absurd, however, to suppose that it is more than the merest coincidence that Chaucer also couples together the two words (see above, p. 308), though it is well known, of course, that he was familiar with the *Divina Commedia*.

> L'agathe d'espece diverse
> Blanche ou jaune ou roug'astre ou perse . . .
> (Méon, *Blasons*, pp. 339, 340, 342.)

The following passage from Machault's *Remède de Fortune* shows that, at any rate in heraldry, the word had a well-defined meaning :—

> Saches de vray qu'en tout endroit
> Qu'on descript armes à droit
> La couleur de pers est clamée
> Azur, s'elle est à droit nommée,
> Le rouge gueules, le noir sable,
> Et le blanc argent. . . .
> (Ed. Tarbé, p. 84.)

It was used, too, in the sense of our "true-blue," for Machault says in another place :—

> Sachez que le pers signefie
> Loyaute qui hait tricherie.[1]

In the description of William the Conqueror in his *Chronique Rimée* Philippe Mousket says :—

> Ses cevaus fu de fier couviers,
> Par deseure et un cendal piers
> A flour d'or des armes le roi
> De France, et s'ot tout le conroi.
> (ll. 17,406-17,409.)

Reiffenberg explains *cendal piers* as "étoffe de soie bleu foncé chargée de fleurs de lys". But *piers* here would be rather "azure," as in the passage from Machault given above; for we learn from Robert Gaguin's *Croniques de France* that the royal blue of the arms of France was "la couleur du ciel serain" (this passage is also interesting as throwing light on the origin of the term "Jean Crapaud" for a Frenchman) :—

En ce lieu ne omettray a adjouxter ce que par nul certain aucteur ay trouvé, mais ay ouy reciter et affermer notoirement par la commune renommée, que les roys françoys avoient en leur armoyrie pour le signe de leur noblesse troys crapos, mais après ce que Clouys eut receu les sauemens chrestiens, luy fut envoyé du ciel ce que de present portent les roys, c'est assavoir troys fleurs de lys d'or soulz lesquelles est la couleur du ciel serain que les Françoys appellent azur.

---

[1] *Cf.* Chaucer's *Anelida and Arcite*, l. 330, and Skeat's note on the passage.

From the variety of examples given above, it will be seen that the colour *perse* ranges through nearly every shade of blue, from the blue-black of hair to the greenish blue of the turquoise; and it also apparently includes shades of crimson. Most frequently, however, it indicates a dark or livid blue; but in the absence of a determining object it is difficult to establish exactly what precise colour is intended. Dante's definition of it as "a mixture of purple and black, but more black than purple," will certainly not hold good in every instance, as we have seen, any more than will the later one of Cotgrave, who defines it as "skie-coloured".[1]

"SIGIERI" IN THE *PARADISO*
(x. 136)[2]

THE formerly much disputed question as to the identity of the "Sigieri" placed by Dante among the great doctors of the Church, in the Heaven of the Sun, has now been satisfactorily settled once and for all. Victor Le Clerc, in his article on Siger in the *Histoire littéraire de la France*, advanced a theory that the two mediæval Sigers (*viz.*, Siger of Brabant and Siger of Courtrai) were one and the same person. Siger of Brabant, as is well known, being a professor of the University of Paris, took a prominent part in the violent disputes which arose between the lay members of the University and the friars of the Mendicant Orders respecting the liberty of teaching; and he was, together with Guillaume of Saint-Amour, publicly refuted by Thomas Aquinas, who had been appointed by the Pope to champion the cause of the Dominican Order.

Finding it difficult to reconcile the facts of Siger's having

---

[1] Compare with this the definition of an (undated) authority given by Godefroy in his Dictionary: "Pers est aultre couleur qui approche fort du bleu, mais il est de plus clere matiere, et n'est pas sy obscur". (Sicille, *Blason des couleurs en armes.*)

[2] See *Academy*, 13th March, and 8th May, 1886; and *Athenæum*, 29th July, 1899, and 9th June, 1900.

been accused of heresy, and of his known hostility to the Dominicans, with the place assigned to him by Dante in the *Paradiso* at St. Thomas' side, Le Clerc suggested that Siger of Brabant was identical with the other Siger, who was Procureur de Sorbonne and Dean of Saint-Marie at Courtrai, and who left a bequest of books to the Sorbonne. The acceptance of his bequest, as well as the tone of certain of his writings, led Le Clerc to conclude that before his death Siger was converted from his heretical opinions, and became reconciled to the Dominicans, and that Dante gave effect, as it were, to this reconciliation by placing him side by side with St. Thomas Aquinas in Paradise among the doctors of the Church.

M. Gaston Paris, however, in a paper upon the subject read at the Institut de France,[1] pointed out that this bequest, as had been shown by M. Léopold Delisle,[2] was made, not in 1277, as had been previously supposed, but in 1341, the year in which Siger of Courtrai died. This at once disposes of Le Clerc's theory, inasmuch as the Siger mentioned in the *Paradiso* must have been already dead in 1300, the date assigned by Dante to his Vision.

It has been concluded, on the strength of Dante's mention of the fact that Siger lectured in Paris in the Rue du Fouarre:—

> Essa è la luce eterna di Sigieri[3]
> Che, leggendo nel Vico degli Strami,[4]
> Sillogizzò invidiosi veri—

[1] 25th October, 1881. See the article by M. Paris on *Siger de Brabant* in *La Poésie du Moyen Age* (pp. 165-183). Paris, 1895.

[2] In his *Cabinet des MSS. de la Bibliothèque Nationale.*

[3] M. Gaston Paris, in an article in *Romania* (xxix. 107-112) on *La Mort de Siger de Brabant*, states that Siger is referred to by Dante's son (*i.e.*, Pietro Alighieri, in his commentary on the *Commedia*) as *Sigerus Magnus*. This seems to be a mistake. What Pietro says is as follows: " Sigerius magnus philosophus fuit et theologus, natione de Brabantia, qui legit diu in vico straminum Parisiis, ubi philosophia legitur ". Surely this means no more than that Sigerius was a great philosopher and theologian.

[4] The Rue du Fouarre (*Vicus Straminis* or *Vicus Stramineus*) at Paris was so called from the straw-strewn floors of the schools. It was close to the river, in the region which is still known as the Quartier Latin, and was the centre of the Arts Schools at Paris. In the Middle Ages its name was doubtless as widely

that Dante himself attended Siger's lectures in Paris; in which case Dante must have been in Paris previous to the year 1300, since Siger was certainly dead before that date.   In order, however, to account for Dante's acquaintance with Siger and his teaching it is no longer necessary to assume that he visited Paris. In an Italian poem, called *Il Fiore*, written towards the end of the 13th century, by one Durante,[1] in imitation of the *Roman de la Rose*, it is stated that Siger "died a painful death" in Italy, "at the Court of Rome at Orvieto".[2]   This being the case, it is evident that Dante might very well have learned all he knew about Siger without going so far as Paris, or even crossing the Alps.

The exact interpretation of the lines in *Il Fiore* in which mention is made of Siger (and in which his fellow disputant, Guillaume of Saint-Amour, is also named) has been warmly disputed.   In   the   passage   in   question   "Falsenbiante"   (*i.e.*, Hypocrisy,   the   "Faux-Semblant" of the *Roman de la Rose*) is made to say :—

> Mastro Sighier non andò guari lieto :
> A ghiado il fe' morire a gran dolore,
> Nella corte di Roma, ad Orbivieto.
>   Mastro Guillelmo, il buon di Sant-Amore,
> Feci di Francia metter in divieto,
> E sbandir del reame a gran romore.
>   (*Sonetto* xcii. 9-14.)

The editor of the poem, M. F. Castets, renders "morire a ghiado" in the second line by "mourir en grande misère," thus

known as is that of the Quartier Latin at the present day.   Petrarch, who probably became familiar with the locality during his visit to Paris in 1333, refers to it in his *De Ignorantia* as "strepidulus straminum vicus".

[1] This Durante is supposed by some to be no other than Dante himself.   So far, however, no convincing arguments have been adduced in support of this theory.

[2] The Court of Rome was at Orvieto several times between 1277 (the date of the last historical mention of Siger) and 1300 (the date of the action of the Commedia).   Martin IV. was there in December, 1282 ; from 5th January to 23rd December, 1283 ; and from 6th January to 27th June, 1284.   Nicholas IV. was there from 13th June, 1290, to 19th October, 1291 ; and Boniface VIII. was there from 6th June to 31st October, 1297.

giving *ghiado* a sense which *glaive* certainly had in Old French.[1]
M. Gaston Paris, on the contrary, holds that "morire a ghiado"
signifies "to die by the sword," and he, in the first instance,
took the meaning to be that Siger was executed at the Court of
Rome at Orvieto—put to death, that is, by order of the Papal
Court—but for political reasons, not as a heretic, in which case
he would have been burnt.

New light, however, has since been thrown on the question
by the publication in my *Dante Dictionary* of an extract from
the Brabantine continuation of the chronicle of Martin of
Troppau, which is printed in vol. xxiv. of Pertz's *Monumenta
Germaniae*.[2] This extract, which occurs in the paragraph of the
chronicle devoted to the reign of the Emperor Rudolf (1272-
1292), runs as follows :—

> Hujus[3] tempore floruit Albertus, de Ordine Praedicatorum, qui multa
> scripsit praeclare de theologia, qui magistrum Sygerum in scriptis suis multum
> redarguit.[4] Qui Sygerus, natione Brabantinus, eo quod quasdam opiniones
> contra fidem tenuerat, Parisius subsistere non valens, Romanam curiam adiit,
> ibique post parvum tempus a clerico suo quasi dementi perfossus periit.

According to this statement, which appears to have escaped
the notice of previous writers upon Siger, the latter was stabbed
at the Papal Court by a mad or fanatic clerk—a manner of

---

[1] This opinion of Castets is shared by Dr. Clemens Baeumker, who recently
published a critical text of Siger's *Impossibilia* (Münster, 1898); and by M. P.
Mandonnet, in his *Siger de Brabant et l'Averroïsme Latin* (Fribourg, 1899);
as well as by several Italian authorities. (For an informing review of Dr.
Baeumker's book by Felice Tocco, see *Bullettino della Società Dantesca Italiana*,
N.S. vi. 161-168; see also the article by C. Cipolla in the *Giornale Storico della
Letteratura Italiana*, xxxiii. 149-152.)

[2] Attention was first drawn to this extract, I believe, by Mr. Charles
Plummer. As printed in my *Dictionary* it contains one or two minor inaccuracies, which were pointed out by M. Paris.

[3] In my *Dante Dictionary* I referred this to Pope Nicholas IV. As Albertus
Magnus died in 1280, and Nicholas did not become Pope till 1288, this is a
manifest impossibility. The reference, as both M. Paris and Dr. Baeumker
observe, must be to the Emperor Rudolf.

[4] M. Paris points out that nothing is known of any writing of Albertus
Magnus against Siger; and suggests that the chronicler may have confounded
Albertus with his illustrious disciple, Thomas Aquinas. (See *Romania*,
xxix. 111, note 2.)

death which may very well be described as "morire a ghiado
a gran dolore". If Siger was executed, as M. Paris originally
supposed to have been the case, the words "a gran dolore" would
have no particular point—as is recognised by Sig. C. Cipolla,[1]
who takes "a ghiado" to be equivalent to "di coltello";
whereas, on the other hand, they would be appropriate enough
of the agonies of a man who has been stabbed.

After becoming acquainted with the above extract M.
Gaston Paris at once modified his opinion as to Siger's having
been "executed," and accepted the expression in the Italian
poem :—

A ghiado il fe' morire a gran dolore,

as referring to Siger's having been stabbed, according to the
statement in the chronicle.[2]   There can be very little doubt that
this is the correct interpretation, and the controversy regarding
the manner of the death of Siger of Brabant may now be
regarded as definitely concluded.

As regards the date of Siger's death, M. P. Mandonnet, in
his work on *Siger de Brabant et l'Averroïsme Latin au XIIIme
Siècle*,[3] draws attention to a passage in a letter of John Peckham,
Archbishop of Canterbury,[4] written on 10th November, 1284,
in which, speaking of an opinion of Thomas Aquinas, which he
cannot accept, he says :—

Nec eam [opinionem] credimus a religiosis personis, sed saecularis
quibusdam duxisse originem, cujus duo praecipui defensores vel forsitan inventores miserabiliter dicuntur conclusisse dies suos in partibus transalpinis, cum
tamen non essent de illis partibus oriundi.

There cannot be the least doubt that the two persons here
referred to by the Archbishop are Siger of Brabant and Boëtius

---

[1] In the *Giornale Storico della Letteratura Italiana*, xxxiii. 151.

[2] He says (*Romania* xxix. 110 note): "M. Paget Toynbee, dans une note
envoyée à l'*Athenæum*, a montré avec toute raison que ce passage prouve que
Siger est mort par le glaíve, mais non par une exécution judiciaire". Sig.
Cipolla, as M. Paris points out, had previously conjectured that the passage in
Il Fiore referred to a murder rather than to an execution.

[3] Pp. cclxix-cclxxi.

[4] *Registrum Epistolarum Joannis Peckham*, ed. Martin, vol. iii. p. 842.
Peckham died in 1292.

of Denmark, who had been, with Siger, one of the principal authors of certain propositions which had been condemned by the Bishop of Paris in 1277.[1] It follows, therefore, from this interesting reference that Siger must have died between 7th March, 1277, the date of this condemnation, and 10th November, 1284, the date of the Archbishop's letter.

[1] See Mandonnet, *op. cit.*, pp. ccxxvi-ccxxvii, cclxiii ff.

ADDENDA

P. 129, l. 9.   Prof. Nicola Zingarelli [1] points out that Dante no doubt, in placing Semiramis among those "che amor di nostra vita dipartille" (*Inf.* v. 69), had also in mind the account of Justinus, who, in recording the death of Semiramis, says: "Ad postremum cum concubitum filii petisset, ab eodem interfecta est" (i. 2, § 10).   This detail is omitted by Orosius.

P. 140, l. 10.   To the examples of references to Peleus and his spear may be added the following, also from Chiaro Davanzati,[2] which was pointed out by Prof. Nicola Zingarelli [3] :—

> Ben è la mia gran dolglia
> Ch' io nom posso guerire,
> Se quei che m' à feruto
> Non mi sana, com Pelleus sua lanza.

[1] See *Rassegna Critica della Letteratura Italiana*, iv. 79.
[2] See D'Ancona e Comparetti, *op. cit.* iii. 63.
[3] See *Rassegna Critica della Letteratura Italiana*, iv. 78.

TABLE OF PASSAGES IN DANTE'S WORKS
QUOTED OR REFERRED TO

DIVINA COMMEDIA

INFERNO

Canto I				Page
ll. 114-117 .	.	.	.	286

Canto III				
ll. 55-57	.	.	.	219

Canto IV				
ll. 123	.	.	.	145 *n.* 2
129	.	.	.	145 *n.* 1
141	.	.	.	150
144	.	.	46 *n.* 3, 84 *n.* 1	

Canto V				
ll. 54-60	.	.	.	128
60 .	.	.	.	292
64-65	.	.	.	214 *n.* 2
67 .	.	.	.	250
69 .	.	.	.	252 *n.*
89 .	.	.	.	307
89-90	.	.	.	312 *n.* 1
127-138 .	.	.	2, 9 *n.* 1	
128	.	.	.	263
133-134 .	.	20 *n.*, 35 *n.* 1		
137	.	.	.	8

Canto VII				
ll. 1 .	.	.	.	112
103	.	.	.	307
106-107 .	.	.	.	105
110	.	.	.	259
119	.	.	.	260
121, 124 .	.	.	.	259
127	.	.	.	259

Canto IX				
ll. 20 .	.	.	.	260
85 .	.	.	.	236
97 .	.	.	.	151

Canto X				Page
ll. 45 .	.	.	.	260
69 .	.	.	.	260

Canto XI				
ll. 11 .	.	.	.	229
23-26	.	.	.	94 *n.*
26 .	.	.	.	260
97 .	.	.	.	102 *n.* 4

Canto XII			
l. 107	.	129 *n.* 2, 145 *n.* 1	

Canto XIV				
ll. 31-36	.	.	.	40-42
131	.	.	.	104
134-135 .	.	.	.	104

Canto XV				
ll. 4-6	.	.	.	270
83 .	.	.	.	161

Canto XVII				
ll. 7 .	.	.	.	120
14-17	.	.	.	115
107	.	.	.	43 *n.* 1

Canto XVIII				
ll. 15 .	.	.	.	219
29 .	.	.	.	220 *n.* 7
51 .	.	.	.	226

Canto XIX				
ll. 27 .	.	.	.	228
85 .	.	.	.	293
90-114 .	.	.	.	219

INFERNO

PURGATORIO

PURGATORIO

PARADISO

PARADISO

VITA NUOVA

CONVIVIO

TRATTATO I

TRATTATO II

CONVIVIO

Trattato III

DE MONARCHIA

Liber II

Liber III

DE VULGARI ELOQUENTIA[1]

LIBER I

LIBER II

[1] For list of passages in which Rajna's text of the *De Vulgari Eloquentia* differs from that of the Oxford Dante, see pp. 168-193.

DE VULGARI ELOQUENTIA

Liber II

EPISTOLAE

QUAESTIO DE AQUA ET TERRA

INDEX

Abd-Allatif; his quotations from the *De Animalibus*, 248 *n.* 2, 249.

Academy, v, 9 *n.* 1, 43 *n.* 4, 61 *n.* 4, 94 *n.*, 112 *n.* 3, 250 *n.* 11, 253 *n.* 1, 255 *n.* 2, 258 *n.* 1, 259 *n.* 3, 260 *n.* 1, 262 *n.* 1, 265 *n.* 1, 266 *n.* 1, 267 *n.* 1, 269 *nn.* 1, 3, 270 *n.* 3, 275 *n.* 1, 276 *n.* 1, 278 *n.* 1, 279 *n.* 1, 280 *n.* 1, 282 *n.* 1, 284 *n.* 1, 285 *n.* 1, 286 *n.* 2, 287 *n.* 2, 288 *n.* 1, 290 *n.* 1, 293 *n.* 1, 294 *n.* 1, 296 *n.* 1, 304 *n.* 1, 307 *n.* 1, 314 *n.* 2.

Accursius; Benvenuto's remark upon, 225.

Achilles; Dante's reference to his spear, 137.

Adolescenza, 110.

Adolf, Emperor; Dante's reference to, 303.

Aegidius Romanus; his account of Sardanapalus, 131 *n.* 3.

Aegina, plague of; Dante's reference to, 236.

Aeneas; Dante's estimate of, 145 *n.* 2, 280; descent of, traced by Dante, 280-281; Servius' account of, 281; list of kings of Alba and Rome seen by, 289; regarded by Dante as founder of the Roman Empire, 298.

Aeneidorum, 249, 250.

Africa; connexion of Aeneas with, 280, 281.

Aggregazione delle Stelle, Libro dell'; Dante's reference to, 58, 65.

Ahasuerus; Dante's reference to, 270.

Aimeric de Pegulhan; the Provençal life of, 147 *n.* 3; his patrons, 148; Dante's reference to, 148 *n.* 3.

Aix; coronation of Emperor Henry VII. at, 303.

Alaeus, 283.

Alardo, Il Vecchio, in the *Inferno*, 255-257, 278.

Alba; kings of, 289; dates of foundation and destruction of, 299.

Albert, Emperor; Dante's references to, 235, 303.

Albertus de Saxonia; his *Quaestiones super libros Aristotelis de Coelo et Mundo* quoted, 83-86.

Albertus Magnus; some obligations of Dante to, 38-55; his *De Intellectu*, 38, 52-53; his *De Meteoris*, 38, 40, 42, 43 *n.* 5, 44, 47, 48, 88, 156; his *De Natura Locorum*, 38; his *De Proprietatibus Elementorum*, 38, 89 *n.* 1; his *De Juventute et Senectute*, 48, 78; his *De Coelo et Mundo*, 50-52, 82, 85 *n.* 1; his *De Sensu et Sensato*, 53-54; his *De Natura et Origine Animae*, 55; his use of neuter adjectives as substantives, 192 *n.* 2; his quotations from Plato, 246 *n.* 1; the collection of the *De Animalibus* used by, 249; relations of, with Siger of Brabant, 317 *n.* 4.

Albornoz, Cardinal, 218.

Albumazar, 39, 40.

Alcuin; his interpretation of *Galilaea*, 285.

Aldobrandeschi, Conte Rosso degli, 202 *n.* 2.

Alexander Aphrodisiensis, 46 *n.* 3.

Alexander the Great; Dante's references to, 40-42, 129, 130, 142-145; his apocryphal letter to Aristotle, 41 - 42; Dante's